A VIEW
FROM THE
STANDS

BOOKS BY
JOHN KENNETH GALBRAITH
❖

American Capitalism:
The Concept of Countervailing Power

A Theory of Price Control

Economics and the Art of Controversy

The Great Crash, 1929

The Affluent Society

The Liberal Hour

Economic Development

The Scotch

The New Industrial State

The Triumph

Indian Painting
(with Mohinder Singh Randhawa)

Ambassador's Journal

Economics, Peace and Laughter

A China Passage

Economics and the Public Purpose

Money: Whence It Came, Where It Went

The Age of Uncertainty

Almost Everyone's Guide to Economics

The Nature of Mass Poverty

Annals of an Abiding Liberal

A Life in Our Times

The Voice of the Poor

The Anatomy of Power

A View from the Stands

John Kenneth Galbraith

A VIEW
FROM THE
STANDS

OF PEOPLE, POLITICS, MILITARY POWER AND THE ARTS

WITH NOTES BY THE AUTHOR

❖

Arranged and Edited by
ANDREA D. WILLIAMS

1986
HOUGHTON MIFFLIN COMPANY
▫ BOSTON ▫

Copyright © 1986 by John Kenneth Galbraith

Library of Congress Cataloging-in-Publication Data

Galbraith, John Kenneth, date.
   A view from the stands.

   Includes index.
      1. Galbraith, John Kenneth, 1908–   .   2. Economists — United
States — Biography.   3. Statesmen — United States — Biography.
   I. Williams, Andrea D.   II. Title.
   HB119.G33A3   1986   330'.092'4 [B]   86–10443
   ISBN 0-395-35319-X

PRINTED IN THE UNITED STATES OF AMERICA

P 10 9 8 7 6 5 4 3 2 1

The following essays were previously published in somewhat different form in the magazines or journals indicated:

"Two Pleas for Our Age," *The New York Review of Books*, July 17, 1980; "The Compleat Politics of Arms Control: The American Context," *Proceedings of the Groupe de Bellerive*, 1985; "The Starvation of the Cities," *The Progressive*, December 1966; "A Pioneer Approach to Affirmative Action," *The New York Times*, August 22, 1971, copyright © 1971, The New York Times Company — reprinted by permission; "Corporate Man," *The New York Times*, January 22, 1984; "The Concept of Work as a Species of Fraud," *Parade*, February 10, 1985; "The St. Pierre Syndrome," *The New York Times*, January 1, 1982; "The Script Is the Reality," *The New York Times*, September 27, 1985; "The Year of the Spy," *The New York Times*, January 5, 1986.

"H. L. Mencken," *Book World, The Washington Post*, September 14, 1980; "Ernest Hemingway," *Book Week, The New York Herald Tribune*, April 10, 1966; "Money in American Fiction," *The New York Times*, October 21, 1984; "Evelyn Waugh: Two Occupations," *Book World, The Washington Post*, November 20, 1977, and *Book World, The Washington Post*, October 5, 1980; "Malcolm Muggeridge: Two Modes," *The New York Times*, July 14, 1974, copyright © 1974, The New York Times Company — reprinted by permission, and *Book World, The Washington Post*, March 14, 1982; "William F. Buckley, Jr.: Two Moods," *World Journal Tribune*, November 3, 1966, and *New York* magazine, October 21, 1974; "Barbara Ward: Two Tributes," *Book World, The Washington Post*, September 2, 1979, and *The Economist*, June 6, 1981; "Robertson Davies," *The New York Times*, February 14, 1982; "A. J. P. Taylor," *Book World, The Washington Post*, September 4, 1983.

"The Case for Constitutional Reform at Harvard," *Harvard Alumni Magazine*, December 23, 1968, and *Harvard Alumni Magazine*, February 24, 1969; "Solemnity, Gloom and the Academic Style: A Reflection," *The New York Times*, April 30, 1976, copyright © 1976, The New York Times Company — reprinted by permission; "The Harvard Parietal Rules," *The Harvard Crimson*, November 2, 1963; "On Academic Tenure," *Harvard Magazine*, May/June 1980; "Recessional," excerpts in *The Harvard Gazette*, June 12, 1975.

"Further on Economics and the Arts," *Ethos*, Autumn 1983, and *American Theatre Magazine*, July/August 1985; "Ananda Coomaraswamy," *The New York Times*, March 12, 1978; "W. G. Archer and the Paintings of India," *The New York Times*, January 20, 1974, copyright © 1974, The New York Times Company — reprinted by permission; "Artists of the Raj," *Books and Bookmen*, November 1979; "The Paintings of Husain," *The Boston Globe*, December 1, 1974, copyright © 1974, *The Boston Globe*.

"The Beautification of America," *The Washington Post,* June 3, 1967; "Liberals and the Corporate Prose," *The New York Review of Books,* August 17, 1978; "Bailout II," *The Wall Street Journal,* August 13, 1979; "Bailout III," *The Washington Post,* October 3, 1979; "Inflation and the Conservatives," *The New York Times,* December 17, 1981; "The Budget Deficit Initiative: Some Avarice as Usual?" *The New York Times,* May 20, 1984; "Are the Rich a Dirty Secret?" *The New York Times,* November 28, 1985; "Mayhem at Harvard Stadium," *Esquire,* December 1977; "Department of Amplification," *The New Yorker,* January 14, 1967; "U.S. Embassy Geese," *The New York Times,* June 14, 1965, copyright © 1965, The New York Times Company — reprinted by permission.

"James Mill: *The History of British India,*" Introduction to the Chelsea House edition, 1968; "Anthony Trollope: *Barchester Towers,*" Introduction to the Penguin English Library edition, 1983; "Gloria Steinem: *The Beach Book,*" Introduction to the Viking Press edition, 1963; "R. A. Butler: *The Art of the Possible,*" Introduction to the Gambit edition, 1972; "Shigeto Tsuru: *The Collected Works,*" Introduction to the Kodansha edition, 1976.

"The United States," *New York* magazine, November 15, 1971; "A Very Specific Guide to the Economic Folkways of American Business and Businessmen," *Fortune,* August 1977; "Argentina," *The New Yorker,* April 21, 1986; "Introducing India," Introduction to *John Kenneth Galbraith Introduces India,* edited by Frank Moraes and Edward Howe, André Deutsch edition, 1974; "Russia," *The New Yorker,* September 3, 1984; "The Scotch: An Excursion Backward in Time," *Reader's Digest,* February 1986; "A Different Journey . . . into Television and the Economic Past," *The New York Times,* May 15, 1977, copyright © 1977, The New York Times Company — reprinted by permission.

"Winston Churchill and Franklin D. Roosevelt," *The Times Literary Supplement,* February 8, 1985, "Further on Churchill and the Churchill Style," *Esquire,* October 24, 1978; "Charles de Gaulle," *Book Week, The New York Herald Tribune,* January 23, 1966; "John Maynard Keynes," *The New York Review of Books,* November 22, 1984; "Schlesinger, Sorensen, John F. Kennedy," *The Observer,* December 1965; "Robert Kennedy on the Missile Crisis," *Book World, The Chicago Tribune,* January 19, 1969; "Chester Bowles," *The New York Times,* April 25, 1971, copyright © 1971, The New York Times Company — reprinted by permission; "Lyndon Johnson," *The Saturday Review,* November 6, 1971, copyright © 1971, *Saturday Review* magazine — reprinted by permission; "Averell Harriman," *Life* magazine, January 18, 1971; "Senator Paul Douglas," *The Progressive,* July 1972; "The Dulles Brothers — and Sister," *The New Republic,* March 18, 1978; "George Kennan," *The New York Times,* October 8, 1972, copyright © 1972, The New York Times Company — reprinted by permission; "Chairman Khrushchev," *Book World, The Washington Post,* March 14, 1971; "Henry Kissinger — and Companion," *Book World, The Washington Post,* May 6, 1979; "Mohandas (Mahatma) Gandhi," *Film Comment,* February 1983; "Muhammad Ali Jinnah," *Book World, The Washington Post,* May 27, 1984; "Lord Louis Mountbatten," *Book World, The Washington Post,* May 5, 1985.

"John F. Kennedy," *The Washington Post,* November 25, 1963; "Eleanor Roosevelt," *Esquire,* December 1983; "Richard Nixon," *The Boston Globe,* August 18, 1974, copyright © 1974, *The Boston Globe;* "Seymour Edwin Harris," *Review of Economics and Statistics,* February 1975, copyright © 1975 by The President and Fellows of Harvard College; "David Niven," *The Boston Globe,* August 3, 1983; "Henry Robinson Luce — and *Fortune* Magazine," in *Writing for Fortune* (New York: Time Inc., 1980).

The author is grateful for permission to use the following material:

Professor Henry Rosovsky's letter of May 23, 1983, to JKG, reprinted in the essay "Sexual Harassment at Harvard."

Mr. James Wade's letter to *The New Republic* of March 20, 1978, reprinted in the essay "The Dulles Brothers — and Sister."

"Poem in Prose," quoted in the essay "Archibald MacLeish," from *New and Collected Poems, 1917–1976,* copyright © 1976, Archibald MacLeish — reprinted by permission of Houghton Mifflin Company.

For Janey Siepmann
Beloved friend for forty years

· CONTENTS ·

Introduction · xiii

I Some Serious — and Not So Serious — Concerns

1.   Two Pleas for Our Age (1980)   3
2.   The Compleat Politics of Arms Control (1985)   8
3.   The Starvation of the Cities (1966)   19
4.   A Pioneer Approach to Affirmative Action (1971)   26
5.   The Convenient Reverse Logic of Our Time (1984)   34
6.   Corporate Man (1984)   39
7.   The Concept of Work as a Species of Fraud (1985)   42
8.   The St. Pierre Syndrome (1982)   46
9.   The Script Is the Reality (1985)   49
10.   The Year of the Spy (1986)   51

II Writers and Writing

1.   H. L. Mencken (1980)   57
2.   Ernest Hemingway (1966)   61
3.   John O'Hara (1978)   64
4.   Money in American Fiction (1984)   67
5.   Evelyn Waugh: Two Occupations (1977 and 1980)   75
6.   Malcolm Muggeridge: Two Modes (1974 and 1982)   80
7.   William F. Buckley, Jr.: Two Moods (1966 and 1974)   87
8.   Barbara Ward: Two Tributes (1979 and 1981)   94
9.   Robertson Davies (1982)   98
10.   A. J. P. Taylor (1983)   104

III Harvard: Fair and Sometimes Overcast

1.   The Case for Constitutional Reform at Harvard (1968)   109
2.   Innocence as Exculpation (1968)   117
3.   Solemnity, Gloom and the Academic Style:
     A Reflection (1976)   119
4.   The Harvard Parietal Rules (1963)   122

5.   Sexual Harassment at Harvard: Three Letters (1983)   124

6.   On Academic Tenure (1980)   127

7.   Recessional (1975)   129

IV   From Economics to Art

1.   The Economics of Beauty (1970)   139

2.   Further on Economics and the Arts (1983)   144

3.   Ananda Coomaraswamy (1978)   152

4.   W. G. Archer and the Paintings of India (1974)   155

5.   Artists of the Raj (1979)   159

6.   The Paintings of Husain (1974)   162

V   A Small Clutch of Letters

1.   The Beautification of America (1967)   167

2.   Liberals and the Corporate Prose (1978)   168

3.   Bailout I (1971)   170

4.   Bailout II (1979)   171

5.   Bailout III (1979)   172

6.   Inflation and the Conservatives (1981)   173

7.   The Budget Deficit Initiative: Some Avarice
           as Usual? (1984)   174

8.   Election Reportage: From the Vacuous
           to the Vulnerable (1984)   176

9.   Are the Rich a Dirty Secret? (1985)   179

10.   Mayhem at Harvard Stadium (1977)   182

11.   Department of Amplification (1966)   184

12.   U.S. Embassy Geese (1965)   186

VI   A Book of Prefaces

1.   James Mill: *The History of British India* (1968)   189

2.   Anthony Trollope: *Barchester Towers* (1983)   198

3.   Gloria Steinem: *The Beach Book* (1963)   204

4.   R. A. Butler: *The Art of the Possible* (1971)   207

5.   Shigeto Tsuru: *The Collected Works* (1976)   210

VII   A Traveler's Guide

1.   The United States (1971)   215

2.   A Very Specific Guide to the Economic Folkways
of American Business and Businessmen (1977)   230

3.   Brazil (1980)   234

4.   Argentina (1986)   247

5.   Introducing India (1974)   258

6.   Russia (1984)   264

7.   The Scotch: An Excursion Backward in Time (1984)   276

8.   A Different Journey . . . into Television and the
Economic Past (1977)   285

VIII   A Procession of Heroes — and Some Bystanders

1.   Winston Churchill and Franklin D. Roosevelt (1985)   299

2.   Further on Churchill and the Churchill Style (1978)   306

3.   Charles de Gaulle (1966)   310

4.   John Maynard Keynes (1984)   314

5.   Schlesinger, Sorensen, John F. Kennedy (1965)   322

6.   Robert Kennedy on the Missile Crisis (1969)   326

7.   Chester Bowles (1971)   329

8.   Lyndon Johnson (1971)   334

9.   Averell Harriman (1971)   341

10.   Senator Paul Douglas (1972)   344

11.   The Dulles Brothers — and Sister (1978)   348

12.   George Kennan (1972)   358

13.   Chairman Khrushchev (1971)   362

14.   Henry Kissinger — and Companion (1979)   366

15.   Mohandas (Mahatma) Gandhi (1983)   369

16.   Muhammad Ali Jinnah (1984)   374

17.   Lord Louis Mountbatten (1985)   377

IX   Portraits and Remembrances

1.   John F. Kennedy (1963)   385

2.   Eleanor Roosevelt (1983)   389

3.   Richard Nixon (1974)   393

4. Seymour Edwin Harris (1975)   397

5. George Kistiakowsky (1983)   400

6. Gunnar and Alva Myrdal (1975)   403

7. David Niven (1983)   406

8. Henry Robinson Luce — and *Fortune* Magazine (1980)   409

9. Hamish Hamilton: An Appreciation on His Eightieth Birthday (1980)   415

10. Archibald MacLeish (1982)   417

Acknowledgments · 423

Index · 425

· INTRODUCTION ·

THIS MORE THAN SLIGHTLY retrospective volume reflects the diligent efforts of two admirable friends, Andrea Williams and Janey Siepmann. Janey searched files and libraries for the items here retrieved. Andrea, for long my friend, colleague and conscience in writing (and many other matters), then made the final selection and arranged and edited them.

To choose from what I have written in the last three decades was, I judge, a demanding task. If, happily, some of the material seemed worth including, there was much that was evanescent, fugitive, wrong and deserving of, if not a decent, at least a permanent, interment. There were also some pieces that reflected conclusions and beliefs, mine and those of others, that have since changed, and some of these Andrea was, rightly and with my encouragement, inclined to keep. On various occasions in the past I have been asked, once by a former President, to tender advice on memoirs and autobiography. I have always strongly urged mention of an occasional mistaken belief or manifestation of official absurdity, the sort of thing that the memoirist tends so efficiently to siphon off. Nothing lends more credibility than tales of a few grave lapses into error.

The editing of these pieces was no slight undertaking. As I've often told, whenever some phrase I have written strikes me as having a special grace and force, I can be reasonably certain that I have said it before. There was, in consequence, the need for much intelligent deletion here, too. There was also sometimes a discriminating judgment that allowed repetition to remain for reasons of emphasis or continuity.

When the collation was completed, I read it through, sometimes changing or adding a word or two, perhaps even a sentence here and there; an author is allowed such liberties with his own work. And, after some pressure from Andrea, I wrote the headnotes that are at the beginning of various of the articles, essays and reviews. This, rather to my surprise, I enjoyed doing. The context of the pieces brought interesting matters from memory, and I found it not without amusement to recall the response of my audience when a given piece first appeared.

As this enterprise started to take form, it became evident that the available and (one hopes) worthy material far exceeded what could be contained in one volume. A View from the Stands is a selection, generally, from the less solemn offering; one day there will be another collection primarily concerned with economics. But not all here is without serious purpose. There are some items — I think especially of those on arms control and international affairs — to which I attach no slight importance.

I have said enough; this, to repeat, is the work of friends. For the words I take all responsibility. For their selection, or perhaps one should say their rescue, I yield whatever approval may accrue and add my own.

· I ·

SOME SERIOUS
— AND NOT SO SERIOUS —
CONCERNS

OF ALL THE ISSUES I've encountered over a lifetime, arms control seems to me the most urgent; success or failure here is coordinate with life or death on the planet. It is, appropriately, a theme that recurs in the essays in this first chapter. But they are also concerned in a somewhat less solemn way with other questions — foreign policy, life in the modern corporate enterprise and notably, in this age of social recidivism, with the protection of our social services and public estate.

TWO PLEAS
FOR OUR AGE

(1980)

This article, first published in The New York Review of Books, *was originally a Charter Day speech at the University of California, given on a spring day in 1980. Thus the early reference to Berkeley.*

Charter Day, next only to Commencement and the Stanford-California football game, was for long the most compelling event of the university's academic year. One spoke to a vast congregation in the Greek Theatre on the hillside above the campus. It also provided a favorable opportunity for student expression and protest, and on the day of my appearance I was warned of the likelihood of some disruption. The university laboratory at Livermore, concerned as ever with the most gruesome forms of extinction, was the subject. As my speech got under way, a group of undergraduates rose to display their highly adverse banners and placards. As I proceeded, they listened to what I was saying and resumed their seats. I recommend a similar design to anyone who must face students and their reaction on an issue such as this. Let them be disarmed by intelligent support. In 1986, Charter Day was abolished.

Berkeley, more than Paris, more than either of the two Cambridges — more certainly than any other college town — has for long been known as a place where things begin. I do not exaggerate; on matters as diverse as the Vietnam war, the civil rights of minorities, the protection of politically significant open space, down to the styles of life and personal hygiene of scholars, the Berkeley leadership has been consistent, impressive and on occasion, perhaps, unduly innovative. I am here to plead that this tradition of leadership be even more strongly assumed in the days ahead. One of the two matters for which I ask it is vital to life itself.

My first plea is for a strong revival of what anciently has been called the social ethic, what more simply is a good sense of community. This is not a subtle or sophisticated thing; it is the will, in an increasingly interdependent world, to be as concerned with what one must do jointly with others, to have as much pride in this achievement, as one has in what one does for oneself.

In the last few years we have witnessed the growth of a contrary mood, and nowhere more manifestly than here in California. That is the celebration, even the sanctification, of self-concern. A person's highest duty, it is held, is to his own income, his own personal enjoyment; freedom is the freedom to get money with the minimum of constraint and to spend it with the smallest possible contribution to public purposes.

So defined, freedom is purely a first-person affair. No attention may be given to public action that enhances the freedom of someone else. In accordance with the first-person ethic, deduction from private income for public schools, hospitals, playgrounds, libraries or public assistance to the disadvantaged or the poor means a net loss of liberty; it is not recognized that there is compensation in the enlarged well-being of those who need or enjoy these services. It is believed that the fewer the public services, the fewer the restraints on the individual. Not even the provision of income to the deprived is thought to add to freedom — although to be without income, all must agree, is a rather confining thing.

There are, of course, some exceptions to this inimical role of public services. A large and expanding military budget is not thought to be in conflict with liberty. Nor is the payment of interest on government bonds. And there can be a quiet preference even among powerful partisans of freedom for adequate public measures on behalf of air safety.

Partly because it is unwise to be too specific, the new concern for self regularly takes the form of an attack on government in the abstract. Government and the associated bureaucracy are proclaimed the great and faceless enemies of personal freedom. This avoids mention of the many good things that government does for all, including the self-concerned. And there is a further advantage in so disguising things: those involved do not wish it thought that this new preoccupation with self is a revolt of the rich against the poor. When so identified, it loses some of its appeal. For some crusades there must be a decent camouflage.

We should not be misled. The services of modern government — national, state and local — are paid for by all our citizens. In principle and to a lesser extent in practice, they are paid for in largest amount by the affluent. The everyday public services, in contrast, are most used by the poor. The affluent can, if necessary, have private education; the poor must have public schools. The very affluent, if they are, indeed, very affluent, can buy books; poorer children need a public library. It is the poor who frequent the public playgrounds and the public hospitals. Police and fire protection are especially important in the inner city. Welfare payments have a particular beneficence for the man or woman or family who has no other income; they are not needed by those of us with regular salaries or wages. Messrs. Howard Jarvis and Milton Friedman, if I may single out the most notable Californians in this new crusade for self, do not, of course, present themselves as enemies of the poor; they are friends of freedom, enemies of government. But no one should be in doubt about the object of their crusade: it is against the least fortunate of our citizens.

There are consequences of this revolt against the poor that should, I urge, be of special concern to conservatives. Capitalism did not survive in the United States or in the other industrial countries because of a rigid adherence to individualist precept — the sacrifice of those who could not make it in a stern, competitive struggle. It survived because of a continuing and generally successful effort to soften its harsh edges — to minimize the suffering and discontent of those who fail in face of competition, economic power, ethnic disadvantage or moral, mental or physical incapacity. It was this ability of modern industrial society to develop and, on occasion, to enforce a sense of community that Marx failed to foresee. The new paladins of individualism would, if thoughtlessly, seek to retrieve Marx by consigning the least fortunate of our people to the neglect and despair that a purely individualist society prescribes. This is not, I submit, a sound conservative strategy. Perhaps the disadvantaged are now too few to make a revolution. But they could make life uncomfortable for all.

More is involved, however, than compassion — or caution. At risk in this revolt is our pride. Of what do we speak when we wish to remind people of our achievements? Of what, specifically, do Californians speak? Admittedly, there is mention of swimming pools and hot tubs. And, while they lasted, there was much talk of sunshine and nonlethal air. But none of these has its origins in community effort. The greater pride of Californians has always been in the public elegance of their cities — of San Francisco and Berkeley and even Los Angeles. And in Yosemite and the other publicly protected parks. And in the great bridges, the schools and colleges and, above all, in this university. It is of these that Californians proudly speak and have always spoken, sometimes to the despair of their audiences. And it is this pride in community that the archons of self now assault.

Thus my first plea — to all here and beyond. Let word go out from Berkeley that, in a complex and interdependent world, the sense of community must be strong and ever stronger. We all agree that government, the first expression of that sense, can always be improved.

Public bureaucracies are not perfect; neither are private bureaucracies. There were shortcomings in the past, so we are told, even in the great Chrysler Corporation. But let us see the current attack on community for what it is — an attack on our sense of compassion, a revolt against the poor, a design for alienating the least fortunate, an assault on the greatest sources of our pride. Let all in this university, the inevitable and valued eccentrics apart, be evangelists for a revived sense of community against the new cult of self. There is, after all, no other community with so much to defend.

I have a second and yet more important matter for the Berkeley agenda. That is survival, a far too simple word. Its specifics do not come easily to our tongue; the mind turns almost willfully to more pleasant matters.

I would like to plead that members of what I still consider my university — faculty, graduates and students alike — unite now in a crusade to get nuclear energy under control. My concern does not embrace Rancho Seco* alone, important as that may be. It involves the more devastating, indeed the final, threat of worldwide nuclear confrontation and conflict.

The mind, as I have said, moves away from this horror. And thus it delegates decision on these matters to those who are professionally acclimated to horror. It accords power to those who do not see as reality the inevitable and final death of civilization if nuclear weapons are not controlled. It gives power to those who have made Communism in its Soviet incarnation the ultimate and lasting preoccupation of mankind. But all must come to understand that after the first nuclear exchange this university, along with all else that man has accomplished in the last five thousand years — and both capitalism and Communism — will be gone forever.

We must no longer exempt ourselves on any excuse from concern about this threat. We have been too confident and too casual for too long. We must resolve now to work to dissipate this danger; we must have a powerful citizen force to this end. Nothing in our time or in all history is or has been so important.

The Soviet leaders are not, I believe, less aware of this threat than are we; because of their close and recent association with the devastation of war, they are, I judge, deeply concerned. It is inevitable that the United States will have differences with the Soviet Union — as we have had in the past and as we have now. It is less inevitable but probable that, out of economic interest or for political advantage, some people in both countries will exploit these differences. Let us be relentlessly wary of those who find pleasure in how we differ — and in the asso-

*A controversial nuclear power plant in Sacramento County.

ciated improvement in the prospects for the weapons industries. Whatever our disagreements with the Soviets, they must not be allowed to escalate into uncontrollable confrontation. That, in the nuclear age, neither side can any longer risk. There must be a firm veto on all politicians who would accept or exploit such an escalation.

In the past there has been nothing more salutary in our governmental process than the speed with which we have discarded those public figures who have seemed to be casual about nuclear weapons and war. All who would risk uncontrolled hostility, with its ultimate threat, must now be placed under the same ban. We may disagree, as ever, on all less important matters, but let us be sure that no one is now elected, Republican or Democrat, conservative or liberal, who thinks nuclear war an option. We must make sure that all who are elected have a continuing and serious commitment, whatever the intermediate diversions, to getting the nuclear horror under control.

The University of California, more than any other institution in the world, was present at the creation — the ushering in of the age of the atom. I plead that we all now join in a new effort to get this age in hand. Let us leave our representatives in government in no doubt about our concern. This should be the newest Berkeley initiative and crusade.

There are more pleasant topics on which I could end. But even on occasions such as this, pleasure must give way to need. Our present need is for a greater surge of the common sense and concern by which alone, whatever the provocation or digression, we can rise above national and ideological differences and survive.

2

THE COMPLEAT POLITICS OF ARMS CONTROL: THE AMERICAN CONTEXT

(1985)

This paper was first published in the Proceedings *of the Colloquium of the Groupe de Bellerive, which was organized by Prince Sadruddin Aga Khan and held in Geneva in June 1985. The subject of the meeting was arms control and the control of nuclear proliferation. It was a prestigious gathering, including American legislators, European parliamentarians and representatives of numerous peace groups. I shared the platform that day with Vice President George Bush, Senator Ted Stevens of Alaska, Assistant Secretary of Defense Richard Perle and Mr. Georgy Arbatov of the Soviet Union. My task was to assess the current political position of the peace movement in the United States. I began with a mild rebuke of Arbatov, who had said that the atomic bombs were dropped on Japan largely in order to frighten the Russians, and of Secretary Perle, who had denied that on any matter having to do with weaponry and arms control the United States had ever been wrong. Such was his insouciant righteousness that I was able to congratulate the vice president and Senator Stevens on their relative moderation and reasonable tone.*

Some comments here included I omitted that day. I do not entirely subscribe to the Churchill rule that you should never criticize your government when out of the country and never cease to do so when at home. But I did, in that diverse gathering, temper my words a bit. Readers will be relieved to know that I do not do so here.

In the otherwise pleasant summer of 1976, while working on a television series for the BBC on the past and future of economics, I persuaded its producer, Adrian Malone, to go to Death Valley in California with his crew. There we sought to give a picture of how the terrain between New Haven and Philadelphia would look after the explosion of a mere four 20-megaton bombs. Such destruction is, we must agree, a wholly plausible part of the economic prospect; the filming in the valley seemed a useful way of advancing awareness of the dangers to which we are all now subject and the need for making progress toward effective arms control.

I am not sure how much our exercise accomplished; the postnuclear landscape of Death Valley did make a strong impression on me. In the years since, I have concerned myself with the threat of nuclear war and its economic consequences and the extraordinary belief that such a war could serviceably defend an economic and social system. Both capitalism and Communism are sophisticated products of a long process of economic development; neither, in anything resembling its modern form, could survive a nuclear attack. Not even the most committed ideologue will be able to tell the ashes of capitalism from the ashes of Communism, although, if they survive, there are some who will certainly try.

In these years I have become aware of one of the major problems in winning understanding of the threat of nuclear devastation. That is the depression one suffers after meetings devoted to the subject, the psychological denial that causes one to put the issue aside and seek return to the comfortable norms of ordinary life. I have also come to appreciate the nature of the whole public and political task of winning escape from the nuclear horror. As it is viewed in the United States, this involves four major steps, each of them now attracting a greater or lesser measure of attention and effort. To some degree, however, each is seen as separate from the others, and each has its own adherents and advocates. All of the required steps, I am deeply persuaded, must now be seen as closely related elements of a single larger task. And anyone who is concerned with this issue must be sensitively aware of that task as a whole.

These four requirements consist, first, of winning a full appreciation of the effects of nuclear war, as just described. Second, there is the need for an arms control design that is within the realm of popular understanding — that removes the issue at least partly from the people who have made such policy and negotiation their highly personal possession. Third, there is the need to have the civility and confidence in our relations with the Soviet Union that allow of negotiations — negotiations that proceed in the belief that both sides are serious, that neither hopes to emerge with some major advantage in weaponry and that the resulting agreements will be observed. We must hope, needless to say, for similar civility and restraint on the Russian side. Finally, there must be recognition that there are powerful forces in both the United States and the Soviet Union that are economically, professionally and bureaucratically averse, even hostile, to an effective arms agreement. There is, among other things, the very obvious need of the military power for a plausible enemy, the absence of which would have a strongly adverse effect on public support and appropriations.

All of these steps, as I have noted, are essential for ultimate success against the arms race, and it is my thought here to assess our present progress on each.

Public appreciation of the consequences of nuclear war, including the now widely accepted prospect of the nuclear winter, has been greatly enhanced in recent times. Few Americans now believe that a nuclear war is survivable or that surviving it would be worthwhile. Influential organizations — Physicians for Social Responsibility, the Council for a Livable World, the Union of Concerned Scientists, SANE, Business Executives for National Security and many others — all share credit for this achievement. Also the writings of Jonathan Schell, Carl Sagan, Theodore Draper, Harold Willens and, again, many others. The first instinct of an American on encountering some evident threat has traditionally been to form an organization to combat it; the next, for many, has been to write a book about it. A democracy, it is assumed, will always be responsive to enlightening information.

This may be too optimistic. As the present case of the Star Wars initiative indicates, the government and the military power can be resistant to almost anything except the unanimously adverse judgment of the public. An organization, a book or a speech is not a substitute, we are coming to see, for solid political influence. Nor can we accord to organizations, books and meetings all the credit for such progress as has now been made in realizing the horrors of nuclear war. The present administration in Washington has also contributed with great effect to public consciousness on this matter, although one cannot say that this achievement has always been fully intended.

The effort began during the 1980 campaign, when Mr. George Bush, as a presidential candidate, held, in a much quoted speech, that nuclear war was winnable. (He later retreated to the less than reassuring belief that it might leave some sort of military command in control.) Then in the early years of the Reagan administration we had a flood of statements on the acceptability of a limited nuclear war, on prevailing in a full-scale nuclear war, on preparing for a protracted nuclear war and on various civil defense strategies for surviving a nuclear war. This last included the death-defying promise from one exuberantly optimistic official that, with a thrown-down door and enough earth on top, "almost everyone could make it." Some thought that on Park Avenue in New York City there might be a shortage of both doors and earth. In my own community of Cambridge, Massachusetts, the normal academic calm was broken by a Civil Defense Advisory calling on us all, in the event of an atomic emergency, to climb into our automobiles and proceed westward a hundred miles to the small town of Greenfield. We were told to take our credit cards with us. (That our universities,

libraries and museums would have to be left behind was not emphasized.) As a consequence of this advisory the City Council of Cambridge,
not previously involved in matters more compelling than rent control,
condominium conversion, zoning-law changes and a new tax assessment, decided, in what may have been an unduly sanguine mood, to
have the city declared a nuclear-free zone.

My fellow Americans, it is reasonably certain, are now well aroused
to the danger of nuclear war. In a recent Yankelovich survey more
than 80 percent of them said that such a war could not be won, limited
or survived. However, a continuing awareness of our danger is still
required; we must not allow ourselves to relent or relapse into psychological denial.

The second needed step is to find a formula for arresting the arms
race that will bring the public at large into support of the necessary
action. Over nearly all of the last forty years, our policy on nuclear
weapons, including that on arms control, has been in the hands of a
small group of specialists. If one wished to speak with any influence
on the subject, even have a position, it was necessary to have knowledge
of the weapons and weapons systems involved; of what was technically
feasible as regards new weapons; of Soviet weaponry, possibilities and
intentions; and of the problems and possibilities of verification. Some
of the information was subject to security classification, secrecy; more
was subject to modification, interpretation or emphasis that would serve
the policies sought by those involved. In consequence, not more than
a few hundred people were thought qualified to speak on arms control.
Those who regarded themselves as so qualified regularly and indig-
nantly dismissed any public intrusion as uninformed and thus irresponsible. There was to the nuclear theologians, as they have been
called, an extraordinary delegation of power. Death and taxes have
traditionally been associated as the two most certain, least pleasant fates
of humankind. We have permitted a delegation of power over death
that we would not dream of allowing over taxes.

Further, those to whom this delegation has been accorded have been
subject to intense political, bureaucratic and personal rivalries, the one
certain consequence of which has been inaction or delays in action.
Arms control, not surprisingly, has been a subject on which bureaucratic
discussion has far outweighed affirmative initiative.

However, we have also had some success in these last years in the
effort to take arms control policy away from the so-called specialists.
This was the service of the bilateral freeze movement — of the campaign for the cessation by both the Soviets and ourselves of the production, testing and deployment of nuclear weapons. This is a step
toward arms control that is readily accessible to a larger public; it is

one that the Russians say they would accept. In association with the rather less portentous disavowal of any first use of nuclear weapons, the freeze made arms control policy for the first time a matter of massive public involvement, debate and political action. The monopoly of policy by the nuclear theologians was drastically invaded.

In the summer of 1980, if I may enter a personal note, I went to the Democratic National Convention in New York City to speak for a resolution supporting the freeze. We had won it enough backing to bring it to the convention floor. I shared the platform with Harold Brown, then the secretary of defense, who was there to speak for the MX missile, and we exchanged some mildly acerbic words on each other's enterprise. The MX, supported by a letter to each of the delegates from President Jimmy Carter, was voted in by a large margin. The freeze lost overwhelmingly. Now, as this is written, the MX still evokes strong opposition and is not fully approved, while the freeze, approved, polls show, by 70 percent or more of the population and with strong congressional backing, was accepted by the Democrats at the San Francisco convention in 1984 with little opposition. And the *Los Angeles Times* reported that it had a majority support among the delegates at the Republican Convention in Dallas the same year. So here, too, there has been progress.

The nuclear specialists, not surprisingly, have reacted strongly against this invasion of their territory; advocates of the freeze have been told they are naïve, gullible, predisposed to easy solutions and, though no doubt out of innocence, the agents of the USSR. Given the importance to the nuclear theologians of their monopoly of knowledge, their anger, even anguish, is surely understandable. Far from disturbing or discouraging advocates of the freeze, it should be taken as an indication of success.

The freeze movement, nonetheless, has weaknesses. It did challenge the monopoly of the issue by those who purported to understand its arcane intricacies. It did bring the American public into the arms control controversy in a highly practical way. However, at best, it is a first step. It would leave in place the terrifying arsenals that already exist. It is also vulnerable to the belief that the Russians will always cheat and that compliance cannot be verified. (Those who are well informed on these matters — the late Herbert Scoville, a former deputy director of the CIA, and others — have held to the contrary, saying that there is very little that goes on in the Soviet Union of which we in the United States are unaware. And — a much neglected calculation — while there are risks associated with possible noncompliance with arms control agreements, these must be set against the near certainty of disaster if the arms race continues and accelerates unchecked.)

Finally, the freeze has shown itself vulnerable to other attempts, real or simulated, to achieve arms control. As negotiations were resumed in Geneva in 1985, there was an undoubted tendency to relax — to say, in effect, that this new effort must be given a chance. This, I am forced to say, I regret. We must continue to exert strong pressure for an arms control measure that will take the issue away from the specialists. They have too long and too proudly held their exclusive grip on these matters while accomplishing too little. We must continue to see the threat of the freeze, which helped to get the Geneva talks under way, as a powerful alternative to bureaucratic inaction, deadlock or less than determined effort.

The third requirement for successful arms control is a more polite, civilized relationship between the United States and the Soviet Union. There is no prospect for success in an atmosphere of mutual insult, condemnation, recrimination and associated mistrust, and much remains to be done to improve our public expression. These last years have witnessed a great deal of highly damaging anti-Communist, anti-Soviet rhetoric from Washington; that the present administration disapproves of the Soviet system has been sufficiently established. But here, too, we are hearing countering voices. The National Conference of Catholic Bishops in their 1983 pastoral letter stressed the point: "Negotiations on arms control agreements in isolation, without persistent and parallel efforts to reduce the political tensions which motivate the buildup of armaments, will not suffice." The bishops went on to urge "maximum political engagement" to reduce areas of friction. In mid-December 1984, Arthur F. Burns, President Reagan's ambassador to West Germany, said, "It is particularly important that the United States . . . extend to the Soviet Union the constructive attitude, the civility and the consideration that are necessary for a useful dialogue," adding the reasonable hope that "the Soviet Union will behave in a similar fashion." In an academically careful study of ways to avoid nuclear war, colleagues of mine at Harvard University have said that "arms control must be accompanied by some improvement in U.S.–Soviet relations if humanity is to cope with its nuclear predicament." Averell Harriman, George Kennan, Barbara Tuchman and others have made the same point in rather more affirmative language. The American Committee on East-West Accord, with which I have long been associated, has found increasing public support for its advocacy of civil relations with the Soviets.

We cannot, as Ambassador Kennan and others have pointed out, expect that the Soviets will ever approve of the American economic, social and political system or we of theirs. But there can and must be a commitment to the common concern for survival. The alternative to coexistence is now no existence at all. We give up nothing when we

eschew allusions to Russian depravity or wickedness; most of such allusions are less to advise the Soviets of their sins than to rejoice one
wing of the American right.

We know that on these matters changes in our official mood are
possible. Twenty years ago Communist China was, in the accepted
Washington view, the world's leading international menace. All references were then to the Sino-Soviet bloc, the Chinese enjoying the
first mention. Armed with nuclear weapons, they were held to have
designs on all of Asia. Now in a matter of a mere two decades, Presidents
and secretaries of state must, as a matter of high obligation, make a
pilgrimage of friendship to Beijing. Mr. Reagan spoke recently of the
"so-called Chinese Communists," and we all now accept that China has
become an honorary exponent of free enterprise.

It is our hope that the pressure of public opinion will, sooner or
later, bring similar movement as regards Russia. Of late the hostile
rhetoric has diminished, at least slightly. Prior to the 1984 election
there was a strong competition to be agreeable to Mr. Gromyko —
something that must have surprised him a little. Now, as this is written,
a meeting has been scheduled between Mr. Reagan and Mr. Gorbachev.
And we have recently proposed a crisis control center — an important
step that could appreciably reduce the risk of war by accident. All this
is progress.

Yet there is still a long way to go. The man or woman who urges
better relations can still be stigmatized, if not as pro-Communist, then
as being unduly gullible. Life is still easier if one avoids such matters
and if the old assumptions are left unchallenged. In the last quarter
century, in China, North Africa and with the rise of the Euro-
Communist Party in Italy, Soviet influence has, in fact, been manifestly
in retreat. In Africa the Marxist governments of Ethiopia and Mozambique are hardly showpieces of achievement. (Marx was adamant
in his view that there could not be socialism before capitalism; he would
have been horrified at the idea of a socialist Ethiopia.) The standing
of the Soviet Union in Eastern Europe is not visibly high. Nevertheless,
and seemingly justified by the misguided action in Afghanistan, many
still assume relentless Soviet expansionism. Isms, our symbols of evil,
can survive a great deal of damaging evidence.

To have relations with the Russians that allow of negotiation must
remain a major point of emphasis. More than attention to the consequences of nuclear war, even more than pressure for action that by-
passes the nuclear theologians, this now calls for effort. It faces,
however, another enormous obstacle: the need of the modern military
power for an enemy. To this, as a final matter, I now turn.

In a speech to the National Academy of Science in 1984, Jerome Wiesner, the former science adviser to Presidents John F. Kennedy and

Lyndon Johnson, former president of the Massachusetts Institute of Technology and a quiet-spoken scholar, held that the United States "has been overtaken by the social cancer of a runaway militarism from which only widespread understanding and decisive action can save it." He added the thought that "even while the government has been engaged in a vast anti-Soviet campaign and a major arms buildup," attempts at understanding have gone forward. These are hard words, the expression of optimism notwithstanding. Certainly it is here — in the fourth of our steps back from Armageddon — that we have the greatest distance yet to go.

The military establishment in the United States, as in other countries, is presumed to serve the defense of the nation. Criticism of it is, by slight extension, taken to be criticism of one's country and thus unpatriotic. No one — congressman, commentator, columnist, scholar — wishes to be thought unpatriotic or so to consider himself. In consequence, the politician who essays a complaint about the Pentagon budget or an adverse comment on some proposed weapons system must always carefully explain that he is, nonetheless, in favor of a *strong* defense. In the last presidential election Walter Mondale agreed with President Reagan that the military budget would have to grow substantially after adjustment for inflation; the difference between the two candidates on this issue was all but microscopic.

The military power also derives its strength from its unequaled access to all or nearly all of the sources and instruments of power in the modern economy and polity. The sources of power in any social situation are three: personality, financial resources and organization. This is certainly not an age of charismatic military personality in the United States. Almost no one knows the names of the Joint Chiefs of Staff or even of their chairman; there is no Eisenhower, MacArthur or Bradley to command attention and respect; of the Vietnam era and after, only General Westmoreland will be remembered, and that will be mainly for his libel suit.

However, in both financial resources and the scale and effectiveness of organization, the military power is unparalleled in our time. Its budget for the fiscal year 1985 is $285 billion; that proposed for 1986 is $302 billion. As of September 30, 1984, there were 2,138,157 men and women in the services and 1,128,844 in the civilian bureaucracy in the Pentagon and elsewhere. This is an organization, military and civilian, of exceptional discipline. To substitute the goals and methods of the organization for one's own is a prime virtue; it is what military training is designed to ensure. The marked and surprised attention we accord to the occasional Pentagon whistle blower shows how great also is the civilian discipline, how general the acceptance of organization goals and behavior in the civilian bureaucracy.

Nor is this all. Extending out from the Pentagon are the great weapons firms, the recipients of a large share of the military budget — the firms that, along with their Washington agents, provide a major part of the present civilian leadership in the Department of Defense. The exercise of authority extends to recipients of political contributions from these firms and to advocacy for businessmen and politicians in communities dependent on military employment.

One branch of liberal or left-wing thought in the past has held that the financial resources of the modern great industrial corporation are the ultimate source of the military power. The Pentagon is merely the instrument of private corporate and financial interests. I am persuaded that we should, instead, see the Pentagon as a source of power in its own right; it has pecuniary resources at its disposal far larger than those of the largest industrial corporation, and these, in turn, support the internal discipline and the external influence. Nor should this occasion shock or surprise. In our economic system we take for granted that money or the prospect of getting it buys the compliance that is the substance of power.

But there is a further source of authority in the military power; this is education, indoctrination or, as some have called it, social and political conditioning. It is the persuasion that is bought by highly available money, manpower and the natural access of high officialdom to the public. It includes extensive control enforced by law over the information that reaches the public and the power to emphasize, even invent, information or prediction serviceable to the military. This management of information is not perfect; an exceptionally healthy tension exists as between the Pentagon and the news media. Distinction accrues to the reporter who identifies something particularly flagrant in news management or suppression. Yet of the overall success of this management — in making the case for new weapons; in identifying Soviet actions or intentions; in maintaining, above all, the impression of a plausible enemy — there can be no question.

Constitutional principle in the United States has always held that the military power should be subject to stern, restraining civilian control, but almost no one now believes that such control is effective. High civilian Defense Department officials are, without exception, enthusiastic spokesmen for the military power; in advocacy they regularly outdo the soldiers, sailors, even the airmen. A fair number of them come from the defense industries or from their Washington lobby. In the past, even liberals have felt it necessary, when taking top Pentagon positions, to prove their muscular commitment to military objectives, but they have never been the equal in this regard to the present civilian leadership. Presidents have, traditionally, been more resistant, President Eisenhower being a notable case, but in President Reagan, all will agree, we have a fully convinced exponent of the military power. It is hardly surprising that no informed American has lately been heard to speak seriously about civilian control of the military establishment.

As there is a major concentration of power in the military in the United States, so, we must assume, there is a counterpart concentration in the Soviet Union. I am not given to unilateral interpretation, blame or action. Arms control must be by negotiation — by addressing the common threat of nuclear devastation. But as Americans we must make the effort to understand our own case; we must be assured that our government is not so subordinate to the military power that it cannot accept and lead in effective arms limitation. And we must be sure that American initiatives in weapons development and deployment are not the propelling factor in the arms race. In the view of nearly all independent authorities, including two presidential science advisers — Dr. Wiesner, just mentioned, and the late Dr. George Kistiakowsky, who served President Eisenhower — we have been all but invariably the initiating force in weapons development since the construction of the first atomic bomb. And so we now remain with Star Wars. From this comes, inevitably, responsibility for leadership in control and restraint.

On the military power we are making progress; that power is being recognized and discussed, as is the absence of effective executive control. The military budget in these last years has been in sharp and highly publicized conflict with social programs and needs and with a responsible fiscal policy; this, too, has attracted much attention. There has been an increasingly critical view of specific weapons systems — the MX and the Strategic Defense Initiative. Finally, some highly publicized incompetence and corruption in the granting of military contracts have added to the opposition. There is still a long way to go in achieving a full restraint on the military power — in fully coming to terms with what Dr. Wiesner has called the military culture — but here there is at least reason for optimism.

During World War II, David Low, the British cartoonist, had his most famous character, Colonel Blimp, take notice of the extensive current concern with postwar planning. All of this planning, Blimp said, was leading to chaos, adding the cheerful thought that chaos did give maximum scope for free enterprise. So it is now in the response to the threat of nuclear war. In the United States, organizations, scores in all, are addressing themselves to one or more of the four steps here mentioned — pressing the horrifying dangers of nuclear war, urging the freeze, working for better relations with the Soviets and developing an appreciation of the military-industrial complex of which President Eisenhower so eloquently warned Americans a quarter of a century ago. In all this effort there has been, at a minimum, the chaos that allows of free enterprise.

Needed, however, is an understanding and acceptance by all so involved that no one of the four steps here outlined is sufficient in itself. Effective arms control — assurance that the government will take all possible measures to that end — will come only when there is a compelling pressure on all four fronts. For escaping the nuclear terror, we must see the whole task.

And there is another need. That is for political commitment. We will not be fully successful until senators, representatives and presidential candidates are both persuaded and committed to taking the lead effectively on the issue of arms control. This requires from us all not passive expressions of concern but active political effort. In this advocacy we must not be confined by traditional political or ideological views. All people, rich and poor, white and black, liberal and conservative, are equally at risk in the arms race. The affluent, we know, are more conservative in their political views than the less rich and the poor, but while there is some psychiatric argument to the contrary, it seems likely that enjoyment of life increases, *pari passu,* with increasing income. Accordingly, conservatives, having more of life's pleasures to lose than liberals, should, if anything, be more resistant to the prospect of nuclear annihilation.

A final point. It will be said that after all the effort — after full popular and political persuasion — we may well find the Soviets reluctant to negotiate. This, for what it may be worth, I do not believe. It is my strong impression that they are no more given to suicide than we are. The Russians have the history or the memory of three great invasions — those of Napoleon, World War I and Adolf Hitler. All, but especially the last two, brought death, sorrow and great deprivation for those who survived. In consequence, the Russians see themselves as victims in any war-induced disaster. We in the United States, on the other hand, are part of that small group on the earth's surface that has largely escaped the horrors of war, and we are therefore, if anything, more sanguine in our tendencies. This is a view of our two countries that is confirmed by others who are better informed on the Soviet scene than I am.

One thing, in any case, is sure: next time we will not escape. So we must be certain that the responsibility for continuing or increasing the risk of nuclear war is not ours. We have no slight distance yet to go; I hope you will not doubt the determination with which those of us who are so concerned intend to address the remaining miles and miles before we sleep.

3

THE STARVATION
OF THE CITIES

(1966)

This essay, published twenty years ago in The Progressive, *does not, as I reread it, fill me with hope and optimism as to our social progress or satisfaction as to the persuasive powers of those of us who address these problems. In Washington, attitudes on the issues here discussed are now worse: the market has become a miracle on which all can rely; the quarterly increase in the output of goods remains the one and total measure of social advance; government by and for the rich is now all but openly acceptable. A large and remunerative literature seeks to show that public effort on behalf of the poor is somehow socially regressive. Income is a great encouragement to the affluent, gravely damaging to the moral tone of the poor. It would be pleasant, indeed, were this article a benchmark against which one could now report progress, but what it shows, alas, is how slight the progress — if any. All so persuaded can safely omit it.*

The past quarter century, I venture to think, will be known to historians as the years of the economist. And I have little doubt that the continuing crisis of the cities is the consequence of the two great preoccupations of the members of my profession in this period: the preoccupation with production and the preoccupation with the market. Both have induced a myopia that has kept us from seeing some very great problems which these concerns have left untouched and which in some respects they have made more acute.

I do not need to argue the depth of the preoccupation in these last twenty-five years with the production of goods. In general reaction to man's ancient experience with poverty and in specific reaction to the miseries of the 1930s, we have made increased output the prime and, in some measure, the exclusive goal of domestic policy in the United States. No other has been deemed so important; it has come to be imagined by quite a few that no other is even possible.

Agreement that our main task is to increase production unites Democrats and Republicans, liberals, conservatives and even modern conservatives. The consensus extends from the Communists to the more thoughtful branches of the John Birch Society. There is a difference only on methods: liberals seek to increase output by public spending, deliberate government deficits and tax reduction, while conservatives have not entirely abandoned their faith in balanced budgets, stern law enforcement and measures to curb the socialist tendencies of the Supreme Court.* To believe we have done well in these last two and a half decades is to believe that we have had an adequate rate of economic growth. Saint Peter need only ask new arrivals what they have done to increase the Gross National Product.

Sadly, however, while economic growth is a condition necessary for solving most social problems, there are many it does not solve. And, ineluctably, it creates massive new ones.

Economic growth does not by itself provide the public services that mark our progress toward a more civilized existence and that are made essential by a higher level of private consumption.

Economic growth does not help those who, because of a careless choice of birthplace or parents, poor early environment, absence of educational opportunity, poor health, mental retardation, racial discrimination or old age, are unable to participate fully in the economy and its gains. On the contrary, it makes these disadvantages more visible and obscene.

And economic growth, we have learned, does not solve the problems of our environment and especially of our urban environment. On the contrary, it makes them infinitely more urgent.

In seeking solutions, it is imperative, first, that we maintain a sound balance between the private and public sectors of the economy. In the years following World War II, we were afflicted by the atavistic doctrine that government services are wasteful, wicked, a manifestation of individual weakness and a menace to liberty. Perhaps we are recovering from this lapse. I am specifically encouraged by a recent appeal from Senator Barry Goldwater asking for the public purchase of some undeveloped land in Arizona. Private development is threatening a beautiful mountain — and also, I gather, his view. He wants the mountain to be a public park.

Some public services — transportation, manpower training, the delivery of the mail, research and the collection of statistics — must grow if private growth is to continue. Other public services — control of water and air pollution, removal of litter — must keep pace if private growth is to be tolerable. And yet others — health services, welfare

*Coming back to this in 1985, I note, as will the reader, how liberal and conservative moods and concerns have changed here, at least, in these last twenty years.

services, help to the dependent — must expand if there is not to be an appalling contrast between the two, between what I have denoted in earlier writing as private affluence and public squalor.

Public services, we need also to bear in mind, are progressive in their effects. Colleges and universities, public parks, good and well-paid police, good health care, good public transportation, even clean streets, render their greatest benefit to the poor and especially to the urban poor. Those who regularly call for curtailment of public services should never suppose they are being neutral as between the affluent and the less so. Those who are presently calling so righteously for shelving the Great Society's war on poverty because of the Vietnam war are asking that the well-to-do taxpayer whose income is at an all-time high be protected at the expense of aid to schools in depressed areas, the Job Corps, low-income housing and youth employment. This is outrageous.

Another problem unsolved by economic expansion is that of the people who are left behind. Increasing national income benefits only those who participate in the economy and who thus establish a claim on the income it produces, but a sizable minority cannot or does not so participate, and it thus has no share in the improving well-being.

Good public services and sound environmental conditions promote such participation. Good health services increase the number of people who are physically and mentally able to take part in the economy. So does good law enforcement. And good, well-located housing. And effective action against racial discrimination. And good urban transportation.

But mostly this is what a good educational system accomplishes. There is no single cure for poverty, but we should not, in our sophistication, be afraid of the obvious. President Lyndon Johnson has observed that "education will not cure all the problems of a society . . . [but] without it no cure for any problem is possible." And he is right. A community that provides really superior schools, starting with the youngest children, and that allows the pupil to go just as far at the public expense as his abilities permit will not have many citizens who are poor; there are few college graduates and not so many high school graduates who are in the poverty brackets.

So far, my approach to the problem of poverty has been strongly traditional: we should help people to participate in the economy; we should help them to help themselves. That is good, whereas merely to help them has always been considered bad. Now I venture to think the time has come to re-examine these good Calvinist tenets, which fit so well with our idea of what saves money. We need to consider the one prompt and effective solution for poverty, which is to provide everyone with a minimum income.

The arguments against this proposal are numerous, but most of them are excuses for not thinking about a solution, even one that is so exceedingly plausible. It would, it is said, destroy incentive. Yet we now have a welfare system that could not be better designed to destroy incentive if we wanted it that way. We give the needy income, and we take away that income if the recipient gets even the poorest job. Thus we tax the marginal income of the welfare recipient at rates of 100 percent or more.

A minimum income, it is said, would keep people out of the labor market. But we do not want all the people with inadequate income to work. In 1964, of the 14.8 million children classified by the Department of Health, Education and Welfare as poor, nearly a third were in families headed by a woman. And three fifths of the children in families headed by women were so classified. Most of those women should not be working.

Idleness, we agree, is demoralizing. But even here there is a question: Why is leisure so uniformly bad for the poor and so uniformly good for the exceptionally well-to-do?

We can easily afford an income floor. It would cost about $20 billion to bring everyone up to what the Department of HEW considers a reasonable minimum. This is a third less than the amount by which personal income rose last year. It is not so much more than we will spend during the next fiscal year to restore freedom, democracy and religious liberty, as these are defined by the experts, in Vietnam. And there is no antidote for poverty that is quite so certain in its effects as the provision of income.

In recent years we have come to recognize a major defect in the fiscal system of the United States. Put briefly, it is that, with economic growth and rising incomes, the federal government, through the income and corporation taxes, gets the money, and the cities, with everything from traffic to air pollution, get the problems. This is more acutely the case when the effects of population growth and urbanization are added. Various ways have been suggested for correcting this anomaly, most of them calling for subventions to the states and cities by the federal government. Undoubtedly the best way would be for the federal government to assume the cost of providing a minimum income and thus to free the cities from the present burden of welfare costs. In these years of the urban crisis we want a system that directs funds not to the country as a whole but, by some formula, to the points of greatest need, which, unquestionably, are the large cities. To transfer income maintenance to the federal government — to free big-city budgets of a large share of their welfare payments — would be an enormous step in exactly the right direction.

·   ·   ·

I turn now to the urban environment; the problem here is surprisingly simple and universal. It is that we have for too long assumed that nearly everything must be subordinate to economic growth and that the largest possible number of problems must be left to solution by the market. Accordingly, questions of beauty, livability, even health, have been of secondary importance. Cities must grow; that is economic progress. If they are ugly, that is the price of progress. If the streets are a jungle of telephone poles, it is because people want telephones and should have them as cheaply as possible. A factory is not a pleasant or attractive neighbor; it smells of scorched rubber and is dirty. But people must have jobs and the community needs the payroll, so production should be wherever the entrepreneur thinks it will be most efficient. Highways and roadsides are made hideous by outdoor advertising and vendors of remarkably unattractive merchandise. But such incursions are held to bring money into the community.

In each case economic goals have been accorded an implicit priority. To make matters worse, quite a few people have convinced themselves that out of the chaos of economic motivation will come some tolerable result — some manifestation of unplanned but functional beauty.

Such a system of priorities and such wishful thinking can no longer be afforded. When people were insufficiently fed and clothed and sheltered, economics rightly enjoyed a high priority in social calculation. But as we move on to lower orders of need — the wants that can be stimulated only by singing commercials — economics loses any natural claim to precedence. Other goals are rightly advanced. And there is no reason to believe that an unplanned metropolis will have any better chance of beauty than an unmade bed.

It has been our common assumption that, generally speaking, the response to market incentives will take care of our needs. But in some exceptional cases, and the modern metropolis is one, we find that market incentives are inadequate. Here we must have planning. We must settle on goals — an overall architectural framework, a plan for streets and parks, a strategy for land use, specification of needed utilities — that are part of a predetermined design. We note with some surprise that we must engage in planning.

In fact, the modern city is one of the least planned parts of our economy. Our space voyages are planned. So are our weapons systems. So is our telephone service. So is our automobile production. So are most of the other requisites of an industrial civilization. We have corporations large enough to embrace the tasks of planning. They assume control of the prices at which they buy and sell, and they exercise a measurable influence over suppliers and customers. They do not leave things to the market; they would regard that as leaving them to chance.

The problem of the modern city is partly that the age of economics, with its preoccupation with private production, has denied the city the public services it needs. And it is partly that the same age, with its mistaken assumption of the rule of the market, has denied it the planning that is commonplace elsewhere in the economy.

What should we do? The successful defense and development of our urban and related living space require progress on three broad fronts.

First, we must explicitly assert the claims of the community against those of economics — its aesthetic claims especially. If a structure, facility or design is simply cheaper, more convenient or more efficient, that should no longer be decisively in its favor. If it is ugly or otherwise offensive, it should be rejected. Industry should not be in the most efficient locations but in those that impinge least on the community. Highways and streets should not be thought primarily a business opportunity; they should be places for tranquil and, if possible, agreeable travel. Air, water and landscape must, of course, be protected from pollution.

And the justification of all this should not be that the eventual cost will be less — that aesthetic considerations will pay in the long run. The justification should be that communities and people will be happier as a result.

Second, effective management of the environment will require far more effective planning and control of land use. The city cannot remain among the unplanned *lacunae* of our society. One reason is that we cannot, as at present, go on wasting space, a scarce and important asset. Even if planning and control lead to deliberation and thus to delay, we should welcome them. Once again the priority of economic considerations cannot be assumed.

We should not imagine that our traditional arrangements for guiding or directing land use will be sufficient for the purposes I have mentioned. Private land ownership is a natural and accepted way of granting economic priority; generally speaking, it accords the largest private return. And it was also right for the stage in social development when economic considerations were pre-eminent. It is not so certain that it can be accommodated to social and aesthetic goals. The record of public planners and zoning authorities when they have come in conflict with the profit motive of the private sector is not encouraging. I incline to the belief that for good urban, suburban and adjacent land use we will need to resort increasingly to public ownership of strategic land areas. Nor does it take a political genius to see the prospect here for some bloodletting.

Third and finally, it must be evident from this discussion that the city or metropolis is the key unit in the management of the environment. This means that city government must be far stronger than in the past. Cities must be run by intelligent and totally honest men who are imaginative and well motivated. They must have better and much better-paid employees. And they will need to have much, much more money. They already have the most important tasks and the least revenues. This starvation of the cities cannot continue.

⸪ 4 ⸪

A PIONEER APPROACH
TO AFFIRMATIVE ACTION

(1971)

One day nearly fifteen years ago two of my friends, Edwin Kuh (sadly and too young dead, as this goes to press) and Lester Thurow, both professors at MIT, called me to propose lunch at the Harvard Faculty Club. Their purpose was to discuss what could be done to give economic as distinct from purely legal content to the civil rights movement and the movement on behalf of women, then near its peak of strength and concern. This article, published in The New York Times Magazine, *was the result of our deliberations then and in later days. The Minorities Advancement Plan — the MAP as it is here called — was not, I judge, the first call for what was to be known as affirmative action, but it was certainly one of the more specific. I share all credit with my fellow authors.*

Though it is rewarding to my vanity to reflect on having started one of the most lengthy and intense controversies of our time — one that continues with the Reagan-Meese attack on these efforts — it is less satisfying to look at the progress that has been made. (The same, as I've said, was true when I reread the preceding essay on the cities.) Women and blacks have, as individuals, made some advances. But the upper levels of the large corporation, as also in lesser measure the upper reaches of public service, academic life and the professions, remain essentially a white male monopoly. It would be pleasant to report that, after all the discussion, more had been accomplished.

One of the plain lessons of the last twenty years is that where equality for blacks, other minorities and those so treated is concerned, good intentions are not enough. Nor is a serious commitment to reform that fails to specify the exact change to be achieved. Nor is any measure that does not have the force of law. Twenty years ago, most Americans, including many white Southerners, accepted the principle of equality in educational opportunity and believed school segregation should someday be brought to an end. And most affirmed the right of all citizens (all literate citizens, in any case) to vote — someday. And they believed that discrimination in access to restaurants, hotels and other public facilities should be stopped — someday. There was no lack of speeches affirming these goals. Nothing happened, however, until exact requirements were specified, timetables for compliance were drawn up, and those who did not comply were made subject to the force of law. Had such action not been taken, Southern schools and public facilities would still be wholly segregated, and black voters south of the Mason-Dixon Line would still be few and courageous.

The lesson on schools, voting and public facilities is one that should be applied to the most egregious discrimination still remaining in American society, which is the virtually complete monopoly by white males (literally, white non-Spanish-speaking males) of the good jobs in commerce, industry and government and the virtually complete denial of those jobs to blacks, Spanish-speaking citizens and women. The remedy here offered, including, as it does, all these groups, involves a wide-spectrum use of the word *minority,* and it will be called the Minorities Advancement Plan (or the MAP). It is flexible in design and nonarbitrary in its application. But it is clear as to the ultimate requirement — and it would have the force of law. It will occur to quite a few people to plead that what is here proposed is excellent but that it should be left to the voluntary efforts of those involved. This, however well meant, holds forth little more promise than did voluntary desegregation in the South. But first a word on the problem.

In the last ten years, concern for equality in employment has been all but exclusively confined to what may be called entry-level jobs — jobs, good or bad, that a man or woman gets coming in off the street or upon leaving school as an alternative to unemployment. That blacks, Puerto Ricans, Mexican-Americans and (where they are not disbarred for clear reasons of physical strength) women should be equally prepared for such jobs and have an equal chance to obtain them is now widely agreed in principle and extensively affirmed by law. Much, of course, still remains to be done about equality in entry-level hiring, as the current statistics on black and female unemployment graphically affirm, but it is no longer the worst area of discrimination. The worst discrimination is not in the jobs at which the many enter but in the better jobs beyond.

In the higher-salary brackets of the business corporation and the government bureaucracy, women, blacks, Spanish-speaking citizens and American Indians still have only token representation. For all practical purposes, jobs here are monopolized by white males. The figures are uncompromising. In 1969, white males accounted for only 52 percent of all wage and salary earners in private and public employment, but they had 96 percent of the jobs paying more than $15,000 a year.

Women made up about 30 percent of the full-time labor force, but only 2 percent of the women so employed were paid over $15,000.

The individual occupational classifications show an equally striking discrimination. Of the male labor force in 1969, 8 percent had jobs as salaried managers and officials, but only 2 percent of the female labor force were employed in jobs so classified. Of the male managers and officials, 30 percent — not far short of one in three — earned more than $15,000. Of the women managers and officials, only 4 percent — one in twenty-five — earned that much.

The various levels of government, though no model of equality, give women and minorities a better break than private corporations do. In the public sector in 1969, white males had 89 percent of the good jobs, that is, those paying more than $15,000. Women had 6 percent and nonwhite males 5 percent. In the private economy, by contrast, white males had 98 percent of the good jobs, while nonwhite males and women divided the remaining 2 percent. (In the federal government in late 1970, blacks, Indians, Spanish-speaking and Oriental Americans held 53.4 percent of the jobs in the GS-1, or lowest Civil Service category, and 2 percent of those in the GS-18, or highest category.)

There is no reason why anyone should try to suppress indignation over these figures; they are appalling. They show that the American economy is run by — and extensively for the benefit of — a white male elite. It is accepted only because, as was once true of segregated lunch counters and Jim Crow hotels, it has existed for so long. But the practical consequences are obvious and should be recognized. The people subject to this inequality are no longer mute or helpless; one can hardly imagine that they will permanently and peacefully accept their subordinate status. There is, accordingly, a choice before us between eliminating this discrimination or leaving it to later and much more angry remedy.

We cannot be altogether sanguine that those who are now in favored positions will see the wisdom of such pre-emptive reform. Most elites in the past have considered their supremacy part of the natural order of things, when not a matter of divine right. So it may well be with this privileged class. But there is a practical way of ending the present discrimination, and perhaps, on this occasion, foresight and common sense will rule. Perhaps for once, reform will come, at least in part, from the privileged instead of from the abused.

The proposal is that the Congress now enact legislation declaring it to be national policy that throughout the various salary brackets in both industry and government the employment of women, blacks, American Indians and Spanish-speaking minorities be in accord with their numbers in the working force. It is proposed that, to enforce this, there be created a competently staffed body, fully representative of the minority groups being assisted, which would be called the Minorities Advancement Commission.

The law would empower the commission to require any firm that has employed an average of more than five thousand people during the previous five years to submit a plan for bringing the distribution of women, blacks and Spanish-speaking workers in its salary hierarchy into conformity with the representation of these groups in the working force of the community or communities in which it operates. The time allowed for full compliance would be ten years. Firms with fewer employees and, in consequence, somewhat less flexibility in promotion and employment would be given more time, perhaps an extra year for each thousand fewer employees, so that a firm with four thousand workers would have eleven years, one with three thousand, twelve years and one with two thousand, thirteen years. Firms with fewer than two thousand employees would be exempt from the application of the law.

A similar requirement would be made binding by law on the federal government. State and local governments would be invited to bind themselves in the same way and would be encouraged to this end by the educational assistance to be mentioned presently. Educational institutions in the above employment categories — in practice, the very large ones — would be subject to similar inducement. In the case of private corporations, a maximum of the three top positions would be exempt from the operations of this legislation on the theory that in the very senior jobs selection of talent should be subject to a minimum of constraint.

In the case of corporations, this legislation would apply from just under the top positions down to a salary level set at 150 percent of the national average earnings of fully employed male workers. (In 1969, this was $10,000, so $15,000 would now be the lower limit.) This part of the corporate hierarchy would be divided into five layers, or quintiles, each with one fifth of the total salary payments. Compliance would be achieved when the appropriate share of salary in each quintile was paid to female, black or Spanish-speaking executives or other salaried workers.

Geographically, women are distributed fairly evenly over the population and also over the working population. For compliance here, the expected proportion of women in the full-time labor force would be used. This, as noted, is now approximately 30 percent. In the last ten years [roughly from 1960 to 1970] this proportion rose by 4 percentage points, so, assuming a similar increase in the next ten years, this requirement would be satisfied by the payment of 34 percent of the salary income in each quintile to women.

Blacks and Spanish-speaking minorities are not uniformly distributed throughout the country. Here the proposal is that executive and other salary payments should conform to the proportion of minority-group members in the working force (both those employed and those seeking employment) in the principal areas of operation of the firm in question. These figures, based on the Standard Metropolitan Statistical Areas as defined by the United States Bureau of the Census, would be supplied by the commission.

The reaction to this proposal from business executives, including some who are not hostile to the objective, is predictable. Surely this puts a straitjacket on the hiring of executives, specialists and other salaried personnel, for not merit but sex, color and ethnic origins become the overriding considerations. Accordingly, it is important to point out the elements of flexibility in the MAP that are thought to meet any such legitimate objection.

A firm, it has already been noted, is given ten years to comply, with added time for smaller (although by no means small) businesses. (Truly small firms are, as indicated, exempt.) But we further propose that each firm be allowed to file with the commission its preferred "track" for meeting this objective in the time suggested to it. Subject to a minimum level of progress — after two years, not less than 5 percent of the eventual goal in each of the quintiles — the corporation would be permitted to follow any route to ultimate compliance it deemed desirable. The early years could thus be devoted to recruiting, training and promoting the women and minority-group members whose advancement at the end of the period would put the firm in full compliance.

Having filed its track, the firm would be subject to penalties for failing to meets its requirements. The fine should be something more than the difference between what it is actually paying the women and minority-group members and what is required under its plan. However, a hearing procedure would be created that would allow a corporation, after notice and for good reason, to petition for an alteration in its track, providing always that it reached its required goal in the specified time and did not fall below its minimum annual rate of improvement.

American Indians, in many respects the most disadvantaged of minorities, are too few in most areas to be dealt with as a special category. It is suggested, as a partial solution, that any salary paid to American Indians might count double for compliance in any of the three categories — women, blacks or Spanish-speaking — that are established. Black or Spanish-speaking women could count for compliance as women or as members of the relevant minority — whichever category a firm prefers. Overcompliance in a higher quintile would always be a credit for the same amount (measured by salary) of undercompliance in the next lower quintile. For employers with fewer than five thousand employees the number of salary categories, that is, the quintiles, might well be reduced. Without damaging the ultimate outcome, these provisions would almost certainly eliminate any legitimate complaint based on the rigidity of the procedures here employed. What remains is the need for aggressive planning and effort to develop executive and other talent among women and the minorities. But that, precisely, is the purpose of the plan.

The MAP would, as noted, be binding on all departments and agencies of the federal government, subject to special regulations for women in the armed forces and a declaration of intent as to minority representation instead of compelled procedures in the case of the judiciary. As with corporations, each department or agency, in conjunction with the Civil Service Commission, would file a track designed to bring it into compliance in the ten-year period.

A word need now be said about the development of the requisite talent. More may be available than is commonly imagined. As long as it is assumed that the better jobs belong to white males, the search for talent will be extensively confined to white males. But certainly there will be need for an increase in executive and specialized training to fill the demand for women, blacks and Spanish-speaking personnel that the MAP would create. To this need, business, engineering and law schools would be expected to respond. But we also propose a system of grants by the federal government to the states for the support of such training by public and private institutions and for the special recruitment and preparation that the black and Spanish-speaking students would require. These grants should be seen as a device for overcoming constitutional difficulties in compelling compliance by state governments and educational institutions. Such aid would be contingent on legislation by the state governments applying the MAP to their own employment policies and to the localities with employment large enough to bring them within the range of the MAP. States forgoing such assistance and the resulting training would be subjecting corporations and other employers within their boundaries to a possible shortage of executive and specialized personnel and would prejudice their own development. Acceptance of the MAP by state and local governments and the filing of a track could also be a condition for the receipt of other federal aid.

Enacted now or in the near future, the MAP will mean that ten years hence the most glaring and indefensible form of discrimination remaining in American society will have been largely, though not yet completely, erased. The purpose of the plan is not to do the impossible but to ensure the possible.

What of the objections? There will be many. There is none that cannot be answered.

It will be claimed that, to meet the requirements of the MAP, American corporations (and public bodies) will be forced to hire a great deal of inferior talent. There is, however, no clear evidence that women, blacks or Spanish-speaking people are, in fact, intellectually inferior to white males. There will have to be accelerated development of executive and specialist talent in these groups. But that is an important purpose of the MAP, and it is for this that time is provided.

It will be asked why the MAP is confined to firms (and governmental units) employing more than two thousand people. That is because larger firms and institutions have more flexibility in their employment policies than smaller firms, and they have more highly organized procedures for executive development. Also, in these firms owners and members of owning families have given way to professional executives. And there is the inevitable political resistance encountered by a measure that seems to interfere with the prerogatives of the small businessman. As proposed here, the MAP would apply to somewhat fewer than two thousand corporations, but those two thousand currently account for roughly half of all the production of goods and services in the private sector of the economy.

It will be suggested that ten years for the compliance of the big firms is too long. If equality is right, why not now? It is important here to differentiate between appealing rhetoric and solid progress based on careful planning. Ten years to equality is far better than never, which is the present prospect.

It will be said that the plan will engender hostility on the part of deserving white males, who will see female, black, Puerto Rican or Mexican employees promoted in order to meet the requirements of the law. This seems inevitable. But it should be pointed out that anger on the part of women and the minorities is already engendered by the present discrimination, and this anger is certain to grow. Equality would seem to be the optimal situation for minimizing hostility.

It will be wondered why other recently arrived ethnic groups — Italians, Poles, Jews — are not given similar preference. Although these ethnic groups think of themselves as minorities and, on occasion, believe themselves subject to discrimination, United States Census studies show that they have higher incomes on average than fully rooted Americans. Such is specifically the case with Russians, Poles, Italians, Germans, Irish *and* English. White males of such ethnic origins are already welcomed into the club.

It will be thought that the MAP may weaken the competitive position of the business firm. This is a variant of the argument that women, blacks and Spanish-speaking personnel are either inherently inferior or suffer from inferior educational opportunity. The first supposition cannot be defended; the second is something the MAP is meant to correct. But it may also be remarked that the MAP will apply to *all* sizable firms. If there are costs, all firms will be more or less equally affected.

It will be asked why the MAP is confined simply to the higher-income jobs; why not make it applicable to the shop floor? The answer is that no reform can accomplish everything. Existing government legislation and union rules are all but exclusively focused on the production worker, and the Minorities Advancement Plan seeks to avoid conflict with these regulations, including any tangle with the unions. It is also important that our present willingness to act at the bottom be matched by a similar willingness to act at the top. As things now stand, a white construction worker can be kept out of a job by regulations that require the contractor to employ blacks. He must wonder, if he stops to think about it, why the white executive has no similar worry about his own job. Also, if women and members of the minority groups are properly represented at the top, it seems reasonably certain that they will suffer less discrimination at the bottom.

Finally, it will be said (and said and said and said) that the MAP is an unjustified interference with private business, an improper abridgment of the first rule of free enterprise, which holds that everyone should be tested by his or her ability to contribute to earnings and nothing else. The answer is that the present monopoly of good jobs by white males is indefensible and if it continues will one day result in much more drastic and disagreeable interference with private enterprise. That outcome the MAP seeks to forestall. Also, no one is now disturbed by an order requiring construction and other firms to hire black workers roughly in accordance with their representation in the community. It would be unfortunate were there to be worry about free enterprise only when the good jobs became involved.

Promotion should continue to be by merit. But we do not have promotion by merit so long as women, blacks, Indians, Puerto Ricans and Mexican-Americans are excluded from the competition. After ten years of the MAP, promotion would be much more nearly equal for everyone.

In this connection, all critics should keep one final point in mind. The choice is not between the MAP and a perfect world. The choice is between the MAP, or something very like it, and the indefensible discrimination it seeks to correct.

THE CONVENIENT
REVERSE LOGIC
OF OUR TIME

(1984)

Over a lifetime I have given not less than seventy-five, perhaps as many as a hundred, commencement addresses — forty years with an average ration of two a year but sometimes more. I look back with satisfaction and also some surprise at the restraint that has caused me never to have had them collected and published. But to the best rules there are exceptions. This speech I liked; so, I was told, did the students and parents at American University in 1984. And as to publication, The Washington Post *did reproduce nearly all of it.*

I must add a confession. Feeling that among the different audiences involved there would assuredly be a minimum of duplication, I went on that spring to use the same ideas and quite a bit of the same text at Tufts University and the University of California at Davis, to which I returned to a celebration of the fiftieth anniversary of my departure from teaching there. Anniversaries can have their own ambiguous meaning.

The commencement address is not, I think, a wholly satisfactory manifestation of our culture. There is, first, the problem of the audience: on this important day its members' thoughts are inevitably divided between nostalgic reflection on the joyful years just past and a justifiable sense of trepidation over the tasks, the travail, even the terrors, of the years to come. The speaker invariably adds to this unease by telling his or her reluctant listeners of the need to rise briskly to the challenges of the world ahead. The challenges are always unspecified; were they stated, they would almost certainly include some that the speaker has personally shown no slight talent in evading.

There are also the stern constraints on commencement oratory. It must eschew anything that smacks of partisan politics, political or sexual preference, religion or unduly firm opinion. As so often in our time, truth, as asserted, must be in a careful balance between right and wrong. No student has ever been known to confess in later life to any influence from the address that graced his or her graduation or, indeed, to any recollection of what was said. Nonetheless, there must be a speech; speeches in our culture are the vacuum that fills a vacuum.

I shall not ask you today to rise to any challenges; I intend only to give a friendly warning. I wish to tell you, at no excessive length, of the radical transformation in accustomed intellectual process that you now face as you depart from these university precincts into the larger political world. In warning you of this dramatic, even oppressive, change, I will express the hope that you will not accommodate yourselves too easily to what is the fashion in present-day political and social thought.

In these last college years you have been taught that the properly qualified mind moves from cause to effect, from diagnosis to remedy. This you take for granted. On seeing some social ill — poverty, civil disorder, international tension or danger — you identify the cause, and you move from that cause to the fitting remedial action. Not so, alas, in the world you are about to enter. In that world you will encounter a different sequence. Increasingly in recent times we have come first to identify the remedy that is most agreeable, most convenient, most in accord with major pecuniary or political interest, the one that reflects our available faculty for action; then we move from the remedy so available or desired back to a cause to which that remedy is relevant. We move back to the cause that seems most consistent with the remedy we have at hand and would therefore like to use. If this sounds rather abstruse even for your now certified capacity for abstraction, let me illustrate from recent experience.

The process of thought of which I speak I will call the Convenient Reverse Logic. The first case in point is poverty. Poverty is our most devastating social failure in this greatly affluent age and land; it is, one hopes, the heaviest burden on our social conscience. And we know from distressingly accurate measurement that it is not decreasing; the number of Americans living below the poverty level has, in these last years, gone up in a deeply depressing way.

You have been taught in college to look for the causes of poverty in ethnic disadvantage, in inadequate education, in poor health care, in larger economic policy that relies on recession and unemployment to restrain wages and prices, in the simple fact that for some people — mothers with dependent children, the handicapped, the young and the old — our economic system does not, by its nature, return the income that would provide a minimum of decency and happiness.

From these causes ordinary logical process would lead you on to the related remedies — affirmative action on behalf of minorities, better schools, better health care for the needy, an economic policy that does not use unemployment to counter inflation, income for those who, from

physical or mental handicap or family situation or obligation, are excluded from effective and rewarding participation in the economic
system.

This is not, however, the logical process of the modern world. That
is because the common feature of virtually all these remedies for poverty is that they cost money, which is an unwelcome thought to those
who must pay. The most desirable remedy is the one that comes free.
But if that is not available, it must be one that does not involve a painful
transfer of resources from the affluent to the poor. Here enters the
Convenient Reverse Logic.

From this need as to remedy we move back to the new cause of
poverty. It is that the poor lack motivation — and they lack motivation
because they are already unduly rewarded. That cause, once agreed
upon, then calls for reduced expenditure on public services and less
aid to the disadvantaged. So, in the recent past we have had, as an
antipoverty measure, a broad curtailment of income and services to
the poor.

Nor is this quite all. The Convenient Reverse Logic has been carried
yet a step further. Since it is known that nothing is more agreeable to
the affluent than a reduction in taxes, unduly high taxes in the upper-
income brackets have been identified as a cause of poor economic
performance. Just as the poor have not been working because they
have too much income, so the rich have not been working because they
have too little. This cause having been established, we have reduced
taxes on the affluent to enliven the economy further, and further improve the position of the poor. This, perhaps, is the most elegant
achievement of the Convenient Reverse Logic.

But this new way of thinking is not confined to domestic affairs. As
you go out in the world, you will meet it even more mordantly in the
field of international policy. In these last years, as you have heard and
read much of the small and unhappy republics of Central America,
you will have come to identify the valid causes of their unrest: political
alienation and disaffection have led on to civil strife and disorder. And
back of that alienation and disaffection in these countries is a bitter
legacy of poverty, inequality, political and economic oppression and
ethnic discrimination — a legacy that we would not defend or tolerate
for a season in our own country, a condition that, by our personal
example, we show to be unnecessary.

These valid causes lead, however, to enormously difficult remedies,
several of which require help from outside sources. What is required
is land reform, the breaking of the political hold of ancient oligarchies
and their supporting military regimes, better education, better hospitals, direct support to the helpless poor, the protection of ethnic minorities and, above all, the establishment of effective democracy with

justice under law. These are all matters of manifest complexity and cost; they are especially inconvenient for those whose power and privileges are at risk. But a far easier remedy is at hand: that is for the United States to supply weaponry and other military aid, to send military advisers, to conduct covert operations and to lay plans, as necessary, for armed intervention.

Working back from this remedy, one finds, by way of the Convenient Reverse Logic, the cause of the Central American unrest: it is entirely the work of ill-motivated local troublemakers, who are inspired to their troublemaking not by social deprivation and pain but by outside agitators from Cuba, Nicaragua and, ultimately, the Soviet Union. President Reagan has been moved to cite this cause in a notably comprehensive way: "The Soviet Union underlies all of the unrest that is going on . . . in the world." If this is the cause, one has only to eliminate the external influences, suppress the native agitators, and all will be peaceful, happy and well. The United States has the weapons, the CIA and the Marines, and they are all now relevant. Again you will see how cause emerges out of the most readily available remedy.

I do not wish to suggest that all leading and responsible members of our military establishment have accepted the Convenient Reverse Logic as it applies to Central America. On leaving office as Army chief of staff recently, General Edward C. Meyer observed with admirable candor that guerrilla warfare in that area does not lend itself to military solutions, adding that the local disaffection "is based on the legitimate concerns of the people." And General Wallace H. Nutting, on completing a tour of duty there, was similarly resistant to the Convenient Reverse Logic: "The fundamental causes of dissatisfaction [in that region] are the existing social, political, economic inequalities." A succession of able ambassadors have expressed themselves in like fashion, frequently, alas, to deep official sorrow.

However, the Convenient Reverse Logic has played and continues to play a consistent role in the field of military affairs — in military tactics and strategy. We saw it in World War II, Korea and Vietnam as regards air power: because we had airplanes, air power was decisive. In 1945, I had an engaging personal encounter with this kind of thinking. While investigating the effects of our air attacks on Europe, I learned that the Fifteenth (or Mediterranean) Air Force had bombed the marble yards of Carrara in German-occupied Italy. The great blocks of marble still in the quarry had had the aspect from the air of a supply dump. I asked if, when the nature of the target was identified, the bombing had been stopped. Not, I was told, before a strong effort had been made to have marble declared a strategic commodity.

This was an elementary form of the Convenient Reverse Logic. Now it has a far more sophisticated manifestation in the arms race — its most ominous exercise of all. The basic cause of the arms race, you will rightly have heard, is a deep mutual distrust between ourselves and the Soviet Union. This, in turn, sustains a strong military, bureaucratic and industrial dynamic in both countries. Each justifies its weaponry — and its plans for more — by what the other is doing, is said to be doing or is expected to do. Powerful economic, bureaucratic and political interests are well rewarded by the competition. I do not, you will note, attribute primary responsibility to either side; it takes two to make a race.

An obvious remedy for this potentially lethal competition is to establish a minimum of confidence between the two countries, this as a prelude to the yet greater task of bringing the respective military powers under control, including our own far-from-disinterested military-industrial complex. The first step is to call a halt — to freeze the competition where it stands as a preliminary indication of what we intend. None of this is easy; all requires energy, determination and, needless to say, political risk. It is far easier to let things go on as they are. So once again the Convenient Reverse Logic. We make the arms race and its near certainty of death our assurance of survival. Security proceeds from strength. We will spend the Soviets into submission. If there is to be arms control, it will come only from the possession of the requisite, ever more lethal bargaining chips. Or, through yet further expenditure and technological ventures, we will develop the ultimate remedy, Star Wars — an umbrella over all. These being the politically and economically convenient remedies, it is necessary once again to go back to look for the needed cause: the Soviets are untrustworthy, inherently suicidal, recklessly adventuresome, an intrinsically evil empire. As a result, no agreement to arrest the arms race is possible or enforceable. Again, I might note, a highly responsible group of military leaders — Admirals Gene La Rocque, Noel Gayler and John Marshall Lee, General David Jones — has rejected the Convenient Reverse Logic. We should applaud.

I have said that as you pass into the real world, you will face the need to adjust yourselves to the Convenient Reverse Logic, the logic, to repeat, that proceeds not from diagnosis to remedy but from the preferred remedy back to the requisite cause. I plead with you not to do so, and especially where the arms race is concerned; your own survival turns on your resistance to this particular march of folly. But I extend my plea: the logical process you learned in your academic years is not wrong. Instead of adapting to the world as you find it, do remain steadily with the intellectual values of your college years. There is satisfaction in the proper process of thought — in movement from actual cause to relevant response. In the world as it is today, it is far, far safer, too.

6

CORPORATE MAN

(1984)

The next five essays are, I sense, somewhat less formidable in tone. This one develops a theme to which I will return in talking of the role of money in American fiction.* It was commissioned for a section of The New York Times Magazine *devoted to, as it is claimed, modern man; thus the sexist tone. But I am compelled to point out that women executives, as and to the extent they emerge, will be bound by the same chains of which I here tell.*

Any consideration of the life and larger social existence of the modern corporate man — the executive in the reasonably senior ranks of the one thousand largest American corporations — begins and also largely ends with the effect of one all-embracing force. That is organization — the highly structured assemblage of men, and now some women, of which he is a part. It is to this, at the expense of family, friends, sex, recreation and sometimes health and effective control of alcoholic intake, that he is expected to devote his energies. Every one of us is to some degree the creature of organization and its constraints. The college professor who prides himself on his utter independence of speech and manner gives careful thought in all but the most inconvenient cases to the effect of his voice and behavior on his position in the faculty and perhaps, in some exceptional instances, to their effect on the reputation of his college or university. The business executive, however, is subject to a far more severe and comprehensive discipline. On the job it may not be quite as rigorous as that of a senior army officer, but it embraces a far larger part of his life; he is never off duty.

There are, of course, some notable rewards to society from this circumstance. Principally it provides the larger community with the services of an exceptionally hard-working body of men. Among the

*See page 67.

many charges that, justly or unjustly, have been brought against the modern corporate executive, one has never been made: not even his most relentless critic suggests that he is lazy. Supply-side economists hold that lower taxes would make him *more* productive. But they never, never suggest the corollary, which is that he is now doing less than his best.

Beyond his devotion to work, however, he is also well spoken, tolerant of disagreement, disposed always to negotiate — for that is how he spends his time — and otherwise given to persuasion rather than to command. In all respects, he is a far more agreeable figure than his predecessor, the great captain of industry, the prototypical entrepreneur.

The counterpart of this disciplined commitment to the job at hand is, unfortunately, a nearly total sacrifice of the right to personal thought and expression. And also of a wide range of personal enjoyments. It is, of course, axiomatic that no responsible corporate executive expresses himself publicly in opposition to the decisions, purposes, social effects, political activities or malfeasances of his organization. He may dissent in private. But if things get really insupportable, his only choice is to resign and explain that, although all is amicable, he feels that the time has come in his career when he should seek a well-deserved early retirement or look for "new challenges" elsewhere.

The ban on unlicensed expression is not quite the same as silence. Speeches, many speeches, must be made — to stockholders, financial analysts, business organizations, service clubs, church groups and still, on occasion, to the Boy Scouts. But there is no form of spoken literature, reputable Protestant sermons possibly excepted, that evokes such a profound lack of response. The press and other media ignore entirely such executive communications or, if something is included therein about prospective corporate earnings, subject them to a truly masterly condensation.

Though often offered with no slight vehemence, publicly expressed executive views on public policy are also ignored. Nor should the aspiring corporate leader be in doubt as to the reason. What *he* says is required by the rules and ethics of organization to be both predictable and dull. He does not speak for himself; he speaks for the firm. Good policy is not what he wants but what the organization believes it needs. In the normal case, his speech has been written and vetted by his fellow organization men, and, in the process, it has dropped to the lowest common denominator of novelty. Lindbergh, as has too often been told, could never have flown the Atlantic with a committee. It is equally certain that the General Motors management team could never have written the plays of Shakespeare or a column by Art Buchwald. Executive expression is ignored because, by the nature of organization, it must be at an adequately tedious level of stereotype and caution.

This, however, is not the only constraint on the executive. There is a subjective effect that is far more comprehensive and that is also very little noticed in our time. Every year the Harvard Business School graduates some 760 students. They are an extremely bright and diverse convocation, with, as students go, exceptionally high standards of dress and personal hygiene. It has always been a pleasure whenever I have met with them over the years. All, with the rarest exceptions, will enjoy especially ample incomes for the rest of their lives. But only the most ostentatiously eccentric will ever make any personal contribution in music, painting, the theater, films, writing, serious learning or the lower art of politics. In years past a good income was thought to allow of such diversions; that was its purpose. From the modern business executive the most that can be expected is a check in support of someone else's achievements.

The pay and perquisites accorded the corporate executive in our time are a topic of much comment and some envy. Their size owes a great deal to the convenient circumstance that in the upper reaches of the modern corporation the executive has a key role in setting them both. More attention needs to be accorded, however, to what the executive gives up in return.

This, besides the personal rights and enjoyments already mentioned, now includes even personal identity. Once, we knew the names of the heads of the great corporations — Alfred P. Sloan, Jr., of General Motors, Thomas J. Watson of IBM, Henry Ford of Ford and, assuredly, John D. Rockefeller of Standard Oil of New Jersey. Today a poll asking who are the chief executive officers of these companies would elicit only an unbroken series of blanks. The organization has taken over; it has the authority and the public recognition; its chairman or president is, perhaps rightly, unknown. The point is emphasized by what happens when he leaves office. While there, he unquestionably commands a considerable measure of respect, often deference, from his fellow executives or when he shows up for high-level meetings in Washington. On the day he steps down, he passes into an oblivion that continues complete until his name finally appears, along with a few dismissing and only approximately accurate lines, in the obituary columns.

I do not suggest that, given his sacrifices, the modern business executive is underpaid. I do note, in a somewhat circumspect defense of his liberal compensation, that to give up so much of the only life one is certain (considering the present state of knowledge on the matter) to have is surely worth something.

7

THE CONCEPT OF WORK
AS A SPECIES OF FRAUD

(1985)

This article, published in Parade, *produced an exceptionally agreeable response all but exclusively from the aging or the aged. But there was also one letter from Professor George Test of the State University of New York at Oneonta, a pleasant reminder that I was far from the first to make this argument. Here is what Mark Twain said on the subject in* A Connecticut Yankee in King Arthur's Court:

There are wise people who talk ever so knowingly and complacently about "the working classes," and satisfy themselves that a day's hard intellectual work is very much harder than a day's hard manual toil, and is righteously entitled to much bigger pay. Why, they really think that, you know, because they know all about the one, but haven't tried the other. But I know all about both; and as far as I am concerned, there isn't money enough in the universe to hire me to swing a pickaxe thirty days, but I will do the hardest kind of intellectual work for just as near nothing as you can cipher it down — and I will be satisfied, too. . . . The law of work does seem utterly unfair — but there it is, and nothing can change it: the higher the pay in enjoyment the worker gets out of it, the higher shall be his pay in cash, also.*

I would note that it has been around sixty years since I read this book; I cannot think Twain's words remained with me. How thin the line between original truth and sordid plagiarism!

All societies at all times have had their seemingly amiable forms of fraud. Apart possibly from our view of the modern great bureaucratic corporation as a market-dominated entrepreneurship no different from the corner drugstore or adjacent newsstand, our best example of such fraud is in our everyday reference to work.

*Samuel L. Clemens (Mark Twain), A Connecticut Yankee in King Arthur's Court (New York: Harper and Brothers, 1889), pp. 278–279.

For some people, a very large number in fact, *work* is a hard, tedious, physically or mentally debilitating thing; it is what men or women do in a factory, when picking fruits and vegetables on a farm, cleaning streets, staffing a sweatshop. They so labor because they are paid; they wouldn't dream of doing it otherwise. If extra factory hours are required, they are paid overtime; when the toil is over, they go gratefully home. Some anciently have been called willing or cheerful workers; this conveys the impression that there is something exceptional about those who like to work. When criminals were committed to jail in past times, it was to hard labor. Hard labor was true punishment. Such is *work*.

But we also describe as *work* what artists, scientists, other scholars, business executives, politicians and professional athletes do. (The athlete *plays* the game but keeps in condition with good, hard *work*outs.) In these occupations it is taken for granted that those so engaged will enjoy what they call their work, will even love it, and will be distraught, perhaps disoriented, when, with the march of events and age, they are denied the opportunity. When facing retirement, they will be urged to seek counseling that they may make the painful transition into leisure more easily.

All my friends in the academic world, after retiring, tell me that they are "working harder than ever." This is their way of saying they are still happy. For the elections in 1984, politicians collected several hundred million dollars so that they might have the opportunity of working as senators and representatives. Once in office all, inevitably, will tell over and over again how hard their work is. While real workers work for pay, no politician — or artist, scientist, poet or professor — can possibly admit that he or she is "in it" for the money. Perish that thought. Even the corporate executive must speak on frequent occasion of his profound sense of personal fulfillment in his job.

It is clear that we use the same term for hard, unpleasant, bitter, demanding effort and for what men and women are willing to sacrifice their own and other people's money, not to mention most of the more conventional personal enjoyments, in order to do. In using the word *work* to describe such wholly contrasting, even conflicting, designs for life, we are indulging in a uniquely transparent form of deception. And this amiable fraud has some less than amiable consequences.

For one thing, it disguises a major inequity in our basic social arrangements. Those who least enjoy their work, who must be paid to show up, who do what we should call real work, get the least pay, under all normal circumstances, for what they do. Those who most enjoy their work, who greatly prefer work to idleness, who do what is only called work, normally get the most money.

They also justify their higher compensation with a depressingly righteous indignation: they say with emphasis and often with belief, "I work *very* hard." Some years ago I ran into an economist friend at the University of Michigan in Ann Arbor, who told me with concern bordering on shock that assembly-line workers at the nearby Ford plant in Dearborn were making more money than an assistant professor at the university. It occurred to me that quite a few at Ford might prefer the more leisured life of a young professor. Certainly there seemed no need to fear any major movement of academic talent from Ann Arbor to the noisome shops in Dearborn.

It is true that the perverse tendency by which we pay more for enjoyed work than for real work has undergone some correction in recent times. The trade unions, including those at Ford, have obviously helped. So has technological change; later generations have passed from real work on the shop floor to a considerably more agreeable supervision of the robots and other automated equipment by way of computer screens. Or to more interesting service in government employment, the greatly expanded corporate bureaucracy, the health and service areas, the professions, or in the design, entertainment, artistic and artistically based industries. In industry the number who do real wage work has been about constant in recent decades; in agriculture it has greatly declined. (The number successfully escaping exhaustingly real work in agriculture has, in fact, outrun the diminishing need, which is the reason for our ever greater reliance on migrant labor, legal and extensively illegal, for work Americans will not do.)

The difference between work and real work, if still unpublicized, *is* becoming a major social issue in one important area of modern life, that of retirement. People who do real work, with eccentric exceptions, still wish to retire; sensibly enough, they look forward to a much preferred leisure. For them retirement, if adequately supported, is a human right. In contrast, people who do what meritriciously is only called work don't want to retire. Not surprisingly, they want to continue to enjoy life, and it is work, so called, that provides this enjoyment. For them continued employment has become *their* human right. And this is now being recognized in law. An arbitrary retirement age has become a form of discrimination, one increasingly banned by legislation and supporting court decision. Given the difference between work and what is called work, this was entirely predictable.

It is also right. Now and for the future we should have two retirement policies — one for real work, one for what is called work. For those who do real work, the opportunity to retire with ample income should be available at a relatively early age, almost certainly by the late fifties. Those who wish to work longer should, of course, be allowed to do so, but it can be assumed that many, if not most, will prefer leisure. For real work, to repeat, the basic right should be that of retirement.

For those who do what is only called work, the ability to retire should also exist, but the basic right should be that of continued employment. There should be no arbitrary retirement age. Physical or mental disability or decline should, unquestionably, continue to be grounds for requiring either retirement or a shift to less demanding employment; that is a matter for negotiation in the individual case. But not age as such. Nothing, in fact, is more certain than that the disabilities of age come with great irregularity as between different people. Artists of all kinds are now known to be largely immune to the ravages of time; like orchestra conductors, they can continue professionally into their nineties. Journalists and writers also carry on with only modestly diminished competence, except as they succumb to the more exigent demands of alcohol. Perhaps there is an age when surgeons should cease to operate; there is none at which they cannot contribute usefully to lesser therapy or hospital routine. Professors are, on occasion, stricken with senile decay, but it has long been noticed that this is extensively unrelated to age. (Some of the most damaging manifestations have been known to appear in the years immediately after tenure has been achieved.) A set retirement age is really a design for avoiding difficult individual judgments by imposing a harsh arbitrary rule on all. It denies the old their lifelong enjoyments. And, a less important matter perhaps, it denies society the benefit of much useful effort.

For our really important jobs, including those of legislators, judges, quite a few business executives and the President of the United States, we have already rejected the idea of compulsory retirement; we should now see the advantages of extending the benefits of continued employment to all those who work in the expanding range of occupations where work is enjoyed. The vision so much celebrated in our time of an age-heavy society would fade. We would not have a diminishing number of the young supporting a growing proportion of the old. Instead, a greatly increased proportion of the old would be enjoying themselves in occupations that are at least partly indifferent to age and in which, in consequence, the concept of retirement has become quite obsolete. They would not be a burden on the young, and they would help sustain those of their own generation who, gratefully, have been relieved from real work. Diminished if not quite gone would be the colonies of the frustrated idle in Florida and the myriad of those elsewhere in the Republic who, having been expelled from the world they greatly enjoyed, are reduced to repeating that self-serving line about working harder than ever.

· 8 ·

THE ST. PIERRE SYNDROME

(1982)

Not all issues in foreign and military policy yield to total solemnity. On occasion, absurdity must be met — or anticipated — with absurdity. So here. This short piece was published in The New York Times *on New Year's Day, 1982. Less than twenty-two months later came our massive descent on the small island of Grenada. Perhaps, though many will doubt it, I saved St. Pierre.*

Those who say that our foreign policy is inconsistent and unpredictable have one thing solidly against them. That is our deep and reliable concern about political developments presumably adverse to our interests in small countries both nearby and around the world. The objects of our attention change radically with the passage of time. As surely as we grow weary of our preoccupation with one country, or as our involvement comes to seem a bit unnecessary or foolish, or as it becomes obvious that the average American doesn't know for sure where the country is, then we can count on worry and alarm shifting to another part of the world.

Our concern is never over what bizarre, incoherent or socially angry political change promises for the unfortunate citizens of the unhappy land. We now know that socialism and Communism, with their large and complex administrative apparatus, don't work well in the poor countries of the world, just as they have also encountered grave difficulties in as sophisticated a community as Poland. And we are coming gradually to realize that socialism and Communism are irrelevant as alternatives to capitalism until there has been some prior experience of capitalism. What *does* worry us are the strategic implications of the political change.

These strategic implications are usually unspecified but are always thought to be serious. And since they are said to bear on our vital interests, no one wishes to disagree. Just twenty years ago, the country involved was Laos. Weekly and sometimes daily briefings were given to the more vulnerable journalists on the strategic threat posed by the Pathet Lao to the Plain of Jars; for a press conference, President John F. Kennedy learned the full names of all the politically and militarily significant Laotians, a notable achievement. Arthur Schlesinger, whose non-Communist credentials were and have remained adequate, was driven to express the thought that Laos was not a dagger pointed at the heart of Kansas, but this was considered daring. Laos was soon afterward returned to the strategic insignificance for which, one judges, nature intended it and for which its inhabitants unquestionably yearn.

In ensuing years, we have had as objects of strategic concern Zaire; South Vietnam, alas; Somalia and Ethiopia, both at first bastions of the free world and then outposts of Communism; Cambodia; the Yemens; and, in a very small way, the Seychelles. Like Laos, none has retained its urgent hold on our attention.

It is, however, in the last twelve months that all records have been broken both for strategic anxiety and for the speed with which this has shifted from one small country to another. In rapid sequence, we have had concern for the threat from El Salvador and then Nicaragua, this combined with recurrent worry about the menace of Cuba. And there has been grave discussion of Angola also.

It is not my intention here to press the point that there is something unworthy, undignified, derogatory or, at a minimum, lacking in grandeur in a great country squandering so much public emotion on its small neighbors or more distant unfortunates. Though I like to seem courageous, I try to protect all flanks, so I don't now wish to arouse the anger or invite the scorn of the strategic theorists. And, as a practical consideration, our compulsion in these matters is too great to leave any real hope for change. Instead, what I propose for the new year is something more practical: let us in 1982 settle on one clear and comprehensible strategic threat, stay with it, and leave all the other little chaps alone.

The choice is obvious. It is an outpost of socialism on our very own continent; it is subject to the authority of a government in which Communists play an active role. It lies squarely adjacent to the greatest trade route into the North American continent, with maritime access to the St. Lawrence River, the St. Lawrence Seaway and the Great Lakes, including our own Lake Michigan.

This object for our attention is St. Pierre and Miquelon, a French possession on Cabot Strait on the main approach to the Gulf of St. Lawrence. In this most strategic of outposts there are, in fact, not one but three main islands — Miquelon, Langlade and St. Pierre. To paraphrase Professor Schlesinger, they are not a single but a three-pronged dagger, and it is pointed right across Nova Scotia and New Brunswick at the heart of Maine. It is not known how many active Communists there are on this potential point of aggression, but one can be certain that in any convocation of fifty-nine hundred Frenchmen (the estimated population in 1977), there must be some.

The islands were the first Free French territory seized by Charles de Gaulle in 1941 as he started his march to power, and that action provoked from Washington a sharply critical strategic response at the time. Older Americans may even remember how the port of St. Pierre exploited its strategic position in the yet more distant past: in Prohibition days it was a major basing point and source of logistical support for the rum fleet, as that considerable naval force was affectionately known.

Not much domestic opposition would be heard should we concentrate on St. Pierre and Miquelon — their constituency in the United States is almost certainly small. Such action would not arouse the fear and opposition of our Latin American neighbors, as does our present Caribbean policy. The French and the Canadians undoubtedly understand our compulsion in these small-country matters and would be otherwise too sophisticated to object. It might, of course, seem a bit foolish that we were expending so much rhetoric and emotion on such insignificant territory. But significance, we now know, has ceased to be a consideration in the making of our foreign policy.

9

THE SCRIPT IS
THE REALITY

(1985)

This brief item appeared on The New York Times *Op-Ed page in the autumn of 1985, and it produced the largest response of anything I have written, long or short, solemn or otherwise, in some years. Generally, with a few notably angry exceptions, the letters were approving. Quite a number of my correspondents expressed their shared indignation over the way Mr. Reagan's aides, Acting Press Secretary Larry Speakes in particular, insist on reducing the President's script to reality.*

For a country with a major theatrical tradition — films, stage, television — we are singularly deficient in our understanding of Ronald Reagan. This is evidenced in no slight degree by his own staff and spokesmen. It also keeps us from appreciating his present differences and difficulties with the Congress.

Mr. Reagan is the first President from our theatrical culture, and he is from its most impressively American manifestation, the motion picture. In this particular art form one does not ask whether the script conforms to reality; that is a denial of the art. The script has an imaginative dimension of its own; the script *is* the reality.

So it is, inevitably, for Ronald Reagan after a lifetime respecting the rules of his craft. In consequence, no one should expect that in his everyday observations over the radio, on television and in that extraordinary Washington theater, the presidential press conference, he will conform to fact. That, to repeat, would be a denial of his art.

In keeping with this theatrical tradition, it is natural and even inevitable that the President should, by way of example, call the South African government reformist in intent; or say that segregation there has disappeared; or assert that the market will solve all problems, including population control and farm distress in Iowa. Also that some sturdy independent souls do prefer to sleep on warm street grates; that food-stamp recipients are given to walking out with a bottle of vodka along with the food; that the deficit is irrelevant; that more income will cause the rich to work harder and less income will do the same for the poor; that the Strategic Defense Initiative will provide an umbrella over us all; and that the arms race isn't a race but merely a belated effort to come abreast of the evil empire. These have been the President's script; those who challenge these propositions do not understand the role of theater in our time.

But with a moment's reflection they surely will. *Gone With the Wind, It Happened One Night* and *The Life and Games of Knute Rockne* all had their imaginative departures. Shakespeare took similar liberties with Macbeth and Henry IV, as did George Bernard Shaw with Joan of Arc and Professor Higgins. This is the nature of theater; this — high art, not low fact — is the guiding light of Ronald Reagan.

What is beyond belief, as I've said, is the failure by the men around the President to understand this. Every other day they, and especially Mr. Larry Speakes, bring him down to reality. There is even White House reference to damage control. They do not realize — no one, it appears, has ever told them — that they are dealing with an art form. Attending the theater, Mr. Speakes would feel moved to get up after every act, maybe every scene, and offer a correction. It would be a major intrusion on the play, as it is on Ronald Reagan's performance. The President and all who understand the separate integrity of the script should speak sternly to the acting press secretary.

The American public, more acute in these matters than the President's acolytes, knows or senses that it is theater. And in the manner of men and women who go to plays and the cinema or who watch *Dallas,* they find the President's script more agreeable, diverting, less grim and worrisome than the actual circumstances of everyday life. Thus Mr. Reagan's high standing in the polls.

However, a warning is in order as regards other politicians and particularly members of the Congress. Ordinary, everyday senators and representatives cannot and should not suppose themselves to be accomplished in the President's art. Not Alfonse D'Amato, not Bill Bradley, not Arlen Specter, who was once, as a prosecuting attorney, thought to have similar theatrical possibilities, not even Daniel Patrick Moynihan. For them and for their pedestrian colleagues the script and reality converge; fact remains fact. On South Africa, taxes, budget deficits, Social Security, acid rain, waste sites and steps back from a nuclear exchange, they must expect to be held to hard and often harsh reality by their constituents. The President's escape and his appreciative audience are not for them. Consequently, we must, in the days ahead, expect continuing, perhaps increasing, tension between the White House and the unfortunates in Congress who, not being artists, are accorded no artistic license. This I cannot say I wholly regret.

10

THE YEAR OF THE SPY

(1986)

While writing this for The New York Times *Op-Ed page, I expected, even hoped for, a negative reaction from some of our spies, that is, and more precisely, intelligence specialists. Instead, former "specialists" and distinguished former ambassadors wrote me of their warm approval.*

Nineteen eighty-five will, perhaps fortunately, have no great claim on history. Partly in consequence it will be remembered, at least by some, as the year of the spy, more especially as the year of the recidivist spy.

As a one-time ambassador and in the even more distant past as a participant in the sharp postwar discussions about whether the wartime intelligence activities of the Office of Strategic Services should be continued (the State Department, where I was serving, being bureaucratically opposed), I have a nostalgic acquaintance with the subject and have also a considerable continuing interest in it.

My present thoughts on the matter were stimulated by a minor incident in the city of Madras in July 1961. I was there to visit our Consulate and Dr. Thomas W. Simons, our consul general, a most learned and diligent public servant. Knowing everyone in that part of India, he had gathered them all for the occasion, and the reception line stretched for some hundreds of yards into the invisible distance. The tedium was relieved, however, when a tall, well-proportioned and visibly exuberant man arrived to pump my hand in warm friendship and to say, in a notably vigorous voice, "Mr. Ambassador, I am the superintendent of police here in Madras, and I would like to tell you that I have the most satisfactory relationship with your spies."

The surrounding audience reacted with interest.

Returning to the matter next day, I found that two Central Intelligence Agency officers attached to the consular staff had made their particular assignment known to the Indian authorities, who, in any

case, could have learned of it in those days from a few minutes' knowledgeable study of past postings in the *Foreign Service Register*. I couldn't
help feeling how much better it was that they had thus identified themselves rather than being rudely, even explosively, discovered by the
Indians, but some of my colleagues were distressed. Their indignation
was over the reference to spies. "Other countries have spies," I was
told; "Americans have intelligence specialists." An interesting distinction, I thought, and, reading the papers in these last months, I see that
it is a difference on which we still insist. Foreign spies invite our grave
indignation; the work of our intelligence personnel we righteously applaud.

Exploring the question further during my term in New Delhi, I
learned that almost no information of any kind was uncovered by our
intelligence operatives that wouldn't have come to us in the ordinary
course of events. More important, in the case of Madras there was no
information whatever that we really needed to have. What was gathered
went on to Washington to be read only by those who, having no other
responsibilities, read what no one of importance had time for — an
example of what my fellow economists call disguised unemployment.

I then pursued these matters yet further to consider our intelligence
reporting on developments of which we might wish to be aware. It led
me to formulate for circulation at the time what I hoped would thereafter be called Galbraith's First Law of Intelligence. It was that you
cannot tell anything useful about the intentions of a government that
doesn't know them itself. This is the normal situation. As a broad rule,
debate and the resolution of power conflicts on all great matters continue up to the moment of final decision. This is so with our own
government as well as with others. Generally speaking, it is better to
have no firm belief about what will be done — to have what is greatly
praised as an open mind — than to be frozen to a view of what, ultimately, will not happen.

Emerging also from my study of the problem was an awareness of
the disconcerting shortage of secrets. This was certainly true in the
United States at the time. "In this government," President John F.
Kennedy once observed, "there are no secrets except a few things I
need to know." So it was in other regimes, and so, I am sure, it remains.
I do not overstate: in all my years in government I never learned from
intelligence sources anything of great importance that I didn't already
know or wouldn't have learned well before need.

The foregoing leads on to a truly remarkable feature of our intelligence operations, which is that almost alone among government activities — the Pentagon is a partial exception — those involved do not
have to answer as to cost, and certainly not in any public way.

In the autumn of 1985, our intelligence-gathering-*cum*-espionage ran into difficulty in Ghana, and our operative there had to be retrieved. No one ever asked what secrets there were in that small country of which we were in any conceivable need or what they cost. But one need not go to Ghana to find the case for a cost-benefit calculation. In these last weeks there has been greatly enjoyed indignation at Harvard over a suitably reticent CIA subsidy to a conference on the Middle East and also to a book on Saudi Arabia by one of my colleagues at the university that was published by the Harvard University Press. Dubious matters, certainly. But no one anywhere asked one of the most compelling of questions: Why in the world was the CIA dispensing public funds in this way — paying for knowledge that any competent agent could have better gotten by talking with experts or reading in a library, and all for free? Why, in particular, was there no calculation of the value of this operation against the damage from its becoming known — as in all certainty it would? It is a calculation that one is led also to recommend to the Israelis and for that heavy work in Ghana, indeed for all intelligence and covert operations. It was the small genius of those CIA men in Madras that they had made themselves known to the Indian police.

The only form of discriminatory comment, racism of a sort, that is allowed these days is against bureaucrats, but from this our intelligence operatives are wonderfully exempt. They are also the only public servants who are consistently celebrated in our lesser literature — *spy* novels as, regrettably, they are called. I have no hope, accordingly, that this profession is in for any very serious restraint.

Like others, and if for no other reason than because I support arms control, I do concede the need to know what the Russians are doing. And given our current all but theological commitment to market incentives, I also fear that we will see even more purchase and vending of intelligence knowledge and personnel, with the associated publicity and condemnation. But I would urge as a broad rule that in the case of friendly governments we make our spies known; they will usually be so recognized in any case, and a certain amount of embarrassing publicity will thus be avoided. Let us also, with whatever difficulty, develop a concept of useless information and contemplate, however casually, the cost of its collection. And, finally, let us understand that, as regards a large area of government intention, we cannot know because those involved do not know and it is better to accept ignorance than be committed to error.

· II ·

WRITERS AND WRITING

THESE ESSAYS all have to do with writers I greatly admire. Perhaps the piece by which I am most pleased is that on Robertson Davies. No one can take much credit for discovering Mencken, Hemingway or Waugh. Davies I discovered when it was still possible to drop his name and have presumptively informed friends say, "Who is that?"

H. L. MENCKEN*

(1980)

Of all modern writers, H. L. Mencken is the one, next to Evelyn Waugh, I have enjoyed the most, and in both cases my admiration, as must be true for many others, is the triumph of English expression over ideology. To accept Mencken's and Waugh's views or to reject their prose is equally impossible.

Nothing is more damaging to literary reputation — bad writing and congenital stupidity possibly apart — than a seeming tendency to attempt too much. The reason is that much literary criticism comes from people for whom extreme specialization is a cover for either grave cerebral inadequacy or terminal laziness, the latter being a much cherished aspect of academic freedom. This supposition — that width is always at the expense of depth — was for a long time very damaging for H. L. Mencken. He was a journalist, political and social commentator, essayist, editor, philologist, literary critic, self-taught philosopher and, though mostly by his own later account, a committed *Bierstube* raconteur. No one surely could be all of these things; a man, at a minimum, should show some respect for trade union rules requiring a decent measure of specialization. Also, with all else, Mencken, even when editing *The Smart Set* and *The American Mercury*, insisted on living in Baltimore. For esoteric literary gloss only Wilmington or Memphis could have been worse.

Yet the Mencken reputation survived, and in recent times it has expanded, and these two books, thoughtfully scheduled for the hundredth anniversary of his birth, will do it more good than harm. The

*This was a review, originally published in *Book World* of *The Washington Post*, of *On Mencken*, edited by John Dorsey (New York: Knopf, 1980), and of *A Choice of Days* by H. L. Mencken, selected and with an introduction by Edward L. Galligan (New York: Knopf, 1980).

first, *On Mencken,* combines items from his recklessly diverse efforts
with comments by William Manchester (who knew and wrote of Mencken
in his last years), Huntington Cairns, Alistair Cooke, Charles A. Fecher,
Malcolm Moos, Alfred A. Knopf and others. Each of the commentators
was assigned, if somewhat informally, a different side of Mencken's
life or work. In what is by some margin the most charming of the
essays, Alfred Knopf tells of the relations between publisher and author
and includes bits from their correspondence. There is one enchanting
letter in which Mencken asks Knopf if the costs of proof alteration,
payable by the author, have not been *under*stated; on no matter whatever could Mencken resist the impulse to be different.

For some of the authors the danger in having their prose side by
side with Mencken's adept, exuberant and, on occasion, outrageous
expression should have been foreseen. One or two were impelled in
odd paragraphs to try to write like him. A bad mistake. Alistair Cooke,
called in to comment on Mencken on the American language (and
other things), wisely warned against such attempts but then did worse:
"I am saying, I think, that Mencken was only a second-rate philosopher
when he came to do a set piece, but that he was a wiser and a better
writer as a journalist, and as such an original. Like all originals, he was
a bad master. By which I mean that he is a dangerous model for authors
of lesser talent." Mencken would have given Cooke a bad time on that
effort.

Charles Fecher is much better on Mencken's political and social thought
and makes a persuasive case for its substance and consistency. One
ends up disagreeing but with a residual respect for both Fecher's language and his ideas. Malcolm Moos is good on Mencken's political
writing. Mencken had an unabashed predilection for political misjudgment, which was heightened by the extreme certainty of his statements. He didn't give Franklin D. Roosevelt and Adolf Hitler at the
beginning of their careers any chance in politics. In 1924, minutes
before John W. Davis was nominated for President, Mencken sent a
dispatch to Baltimore saying the only thing certain was that Davis
wouldn't be the choice. But political error or excess commanded some
of his very best writing, as in the case of his obituary for William Jennings Bryan. It was written straight up when word came to the *Sun*
a few days after the Scopes trial that the fairly Great Commoner
was dead. (For the reprinting of this classic, Cooke, not Moos, must be
thanked.)

Wherever the flambeaux of Chautauqua smoked and guttered, and the
bilge of idealism ran in the veins, and Baptist pastors dammed the brooks
with the sanctified, and men gathered who were weary and heavy laden,
and their wives who were full of Peruna and fecund as the shad (*Alosa*

sapidissima), there the indefatigable Jennings set up his traps and spread his bait. He knew every country town in the South and West, and he could crowd the most remote of them to suffocation by simply winding his horn. The city proletariat, transiently flustered by him in 1896, quickly penetrated his buncombe and would have no more of him; the cockney gallery jeered him at every Democratic national convention for twenty-five years. But out where the grass grows high, and the horned cattle dream away the lazy afternoons, and men still fear the powers and principalities of the air — out there between the corn-rows he held his old puissance to the end. There was no need of beaters to drive in his game. The news that he was coming was enough. For miles the flivver dust would choke the roads. And when he rose at the end of the day to discharge his Message there would be such breathless attention, such a rapt and enchanted ecstasy, such a sweet rustle of amens as the world had not known since Johann fell to Herod's Ax.

Mencken's political specialty, as Moos tells (and many others have noticed), was the national conventions, occasions that accorded him not only the greatest scope for his talent but much personal pleasure as well. And here he was ahead of his time; before anyone else, he saw them as a triumph of banality over content. One weeps that Mencken was not back to report on the folk rites of the summer just past [1980]. What pleasure he would have found in the way statesmen assailed the TelePrompTers; in the inspired indifference of the audiences; and, above all, in the solemn efforts of the great television artists, singly or in interviews with each other, to pretend that something was happening. Mencken, a full sixty-five years ago, had learned what all but the television people now know: the convention is our greatest nonevent.

I would have thought Mencken to be more reliable on literary than on political judgments (conventions apart), but in the literary world he was fallible as well. With others who are better qualified to judge, I have always thought *Babbitt* a brilliantly original but also a deeply flawed novel. George Babbitt's detour into the social, political and sexual sub-culture of Zenith is contrived and wholly unconvincing. Mencken's enthusiasm for the book was transcendent and unqualified; he could not have said more for *War and Peace*. More often, however, his literary assessments were balanced, scrupulous and, in contrast with his political comment, showed an almost ostentatious effort to be kindly as well as fair.

From the depression years on, Mencken was out of favor; he could not take Roosevelt seriously, and he could not believe that the depression was real. Accepting that he was unfashionable, he turned back to his own history. The three books that resulted — *Happy Days, Newspaper Days* and *Heathen Days* — came out either as the war was approaching or in its midst. They didn't receive the attention they deserved, for they are informative, wonderfully amusing and also more than moderately inventive. It was Mencken's view that in anything as important as autobiography, one should not be confined by fact; art has its higher claims. The second of the two Mencken volumes now being reviewed consists of selections from the three autobiographical books. The choices are excellent. If anyone has doubts, here, from *Newspaper Days,* is Mencken on the Baltimore police force in his early years as a reporter:

> They were badly paid, but they carried on their dismal work with unflagging diligence, and loved a long, hard chase almost as much as they loved a quick, brisk clubbing. Their one salient failing, taking them as a class, was their belief that any person who had been arrested, even on mere suspicion, was unquestionably and *ipso facto* guilty. . . .
>
> In those days that pestilence of Service which torments the American people today was just getting under way, and many of the multifarious duties now carried out by social workers, statisticians, truant officers, visiting nurses, psychologists, and the vast rabble of inspectors, smellers, spies and bogus experts of a hundred different faculties either fell to the police or were not discharged at all. An ordinary flatfoot in a quiet residential section had his hands full. In a single day he might have to put out a couple of kitchen fires, arrange for the removal of a dead mule, guard a poor epileptic having a fit on the sidewalk, catch a runaway horse, settle a combat with table knives between husband and wife, shoot a cat for killing pigeons, rescue a dog or a baby from a sewer, bawl out a white-wings for spilling garbage, keep order on the sidewalk at two or three funerals, and flog half a dozen bad boys for throwing horse-apples at a blind man. The cops downtown, especially along the wharves and in the red-light districts, had even more curious and complicated jobs, and some of them attained to a high degree of virtuosity.

ERNEST HEMINGWAY*

(1966)

Mary Hemingway, my friend in distant years — we served together at Time Inc. under the eye of Henry Robinson Luce — would have liked a stronger rebuke than the following review of Mr. Hotchner's book. My editor's thought on reading this piece was to wonder what Hemingway would have done with the corporate man as hero.†

The Hemingway hero is perhaps the best-known fictional man of the century — he has lust for life, forthright diction, an enormous knowledge of plain people and fancy places; is a devoted sportsman, drinker, lover and friend; and is very combative. He differs from the ordinary human male as General Curtis LeMay differs from General George Marshall, and the reasons are not entirely accidental. Hemingway's men provided a pattern on which numerous writers, would-be writers and some professors of English consciously modeled themselves, and to which a whole generation of Air Force generals conformed, these last under the impression that they had invented the type.

A. E. Hotchner was a friend of Ernest Hemingway from one day in the spring of 1948, when, as a staff member of *Cosmopolitan,* he went to Cuba with the disturbing assignment of persuading Hemingway to write an article on "The Future of Literature." They drank prodigiously, but Hotchner, with admirable efficiency, went home and copied down Hemingway's words. Later, he says, he also used a "pocket tape transistor" that preserved their dialogue complete. During the next thirteen years, in Havana and in New York, Paris, Venice, Madrid, Key

---

*This was a review, originally published in *Book Week* of *The New York Herald Tribune,* of *Papa Hemingway: A Personal Memoir* by A. E. Hotchner (New York: Random House, 1966).

†See page 39.

West, Zaragoza, Ketchum, Idaho, and the Mayo Clinic in Rochester, Minnesota, where Hemingway was suffering from severe depression, the foresighted Hotchner listened or had his tape recorder do so. This book is the presumed record of these conversations and the travels and adventures appurtenant thereto. One gathers that Mr. Hotchner was also concerned with getting the television or some other rights to Hemingway's work, but these conversations either did not get on the tape or were too delicate to be included here in any detail.

The man who emerges from it all is unmistakably a Hemingway hero — he is directly out of *The Sun Also Rises*, though suffering more than a little from the hard life, as was the aging colonel in *Across the River*. And it is an absorbing portrait, a work of no small literary skill. Some of Hemingway's friends have wondered if the author's unassisted recall could have been as total, especially after alcohol, as the published dialogue implies. And others have wondered how Hemingway, who was notoriously jealous of his privacy (and once in these pages bangs up a photographer who insufficiently respected it), could have been brought to talk so freely in front of a tape recorder. Certainly no friend, let alone a close friend, would have omitted to say that the thing was running. Mr. Hotchner implies that Hemingway did know — he refers to the recorders "we carried when we traveled." One of the *we* is evidently Hemingway.

Mrs. Ernest Hemingway was among the people who took a restrained view of Mr. Hotchner's enterprise, and she brought suit in the New York courts to prevent publication of this book. Among other grounds she alleged invasion of privacy. She lost but, in losing, won for the world of letters an example of judicial grandiloquence that, in its own way, put not only Hotchner but even her late husband in the shade. Conscious that Holmes, Brandeis, Cardozo, both the Hands and Felix Frankfurter were looking searchingly on, Justice Harry B. Frank opined: "The intellectual benefits from access to the intimate articulation and experience of figures of note and achievement are emphatically demonstrated by the enduring fame and inspirational stimulus of the works of recorders [nonelectronic] such as Plutarch, Boswell and Carlyle." This is mighty powerful backing for Mr. Hotchner, considering that he also has his publisher, Bennett Cerf, on his side. Always assuming that the justice meant the same thing in ordinary working English, I have sympathy for the finding. I agree that the case for allowing the publication of almost everything not protected by copyright or excluded by a clear application of the libel laws is strong.

But Justice Frank giveth and he also taketh away. Although he protected Mr. Hotchner against the charge of invasion of privacy, he exposed him to another and, from a purely literary and scholarly viewpoint, possibly more serious charge. That is the suspicion that the dialogues here reported had their origin with Hemingway but were improved by Hotchner. In a slightly less glittering passage Justice Frank observed that before the conversations were subject to Mr. Hotchner's "literary creation," they were "merely a disoriented conglomeration of literary expressions." This seems to give legal sanction to the surmise that Mr. Hotchner's Hemingway owes much to art.

But there are more complications. For some of the book obviously owes something to Hemingway's own contrivance — as well as to Mr. Hotchner's capacity for belief. Thus Hemingway once told, and Hotchner here retells, a fascinating story of a highly affectionate encounter with a beautiful girl — "Renaissance beauty, black hair straight, eyes round at the bottoms, Botticelli skin, breasts of Venus Rising" — in the kitchen and again on a back landing of The "21" Club. It developed next day, after she had departed, leaving Hemingway's pockets gratefully stuffed with large bills, that she was a walking or anyhow reclining death sentence; she was the mistress of Legs Diamond. I frankly think that old man Hemingway was trying out a story on young Hotchner.

There is also a problem concerning the conversations that were recorded at the Mayo Clinic while Hemingway was undergoing psychiatric treatment. These could not have been done with Hemingway's permission, for his illness had made him pathologically secretive. He wouldn't talk in a room or a car for fear it was bugged — only when walking in open country. Yet Hotchner either recorded their exchanges or took them all down. One can only conclude that Hemingway didn't know. There is a difference here, I suggest, between what is legal and what is proper. I frankly doubt if Plutarch, Carlyle or even Boswell would have reproduced, against his will, the conversation of a friend who was suffering from some mental illness. These are some of the problems posed by the book.

Mr. Hotchner is, however, a very competent craftsman who has narrative power, a gift for description and, very important for present purposes, a good sense of dialogue. He also knows that Hemingway, or the Hemingway hero, is the hero of the story, and he keeps himself well in the background. Nor is Mr. Hotchner's ability as a writer in doubt. The main question, apart from that raised by the Mayo Clinic sequence, concerns how closely the quotations, which here look so exact, repeat actual conversations. Alive, Hemingway could have corrected the dialogue — or protested it. Dead, alas, he cannot.

3

JOHN O'HARA*

(1978)

Some weeks before this book went to press, I reread a number of John O'Hara's later stories. I am now less certain of their quality than I was here or that they are going to survive or, indeed, are surviving. There is a hurried and sometimes contrived quality about them — it was his boast that having sat down of a morning to his typewriter, he rarely got up until the piece was finished — and I now think it shows. But at the time he was writing, there was no one else who so delighted his readers or did more with the people he described and into whose mouths he put the rough, assertive dialogue that, as I here say, was so largely his own invention.

The oldest free-floating literary controversy in the United States is over the merit, if any, of the novels and short stories of John O'Hara. Holding for around forty years that there is none are the people of taste and sensitivity who respond well to Marcel Proust, James Joyce and, if reluctantly, to William Faulkner. Quite a few of their compatriots would deny ever having heard of O'Hara. Speaking strongly in favor while he lived was John himself, supported, though not exclusively out of affection, by the proprietors of Random House, by William Maxwell at *The New Yorker* and Charles Poore at *The New York Times* and by some hundreds of thousands of the unwashed who read avidly what he wrote.

O'Hara's personal advocacy, including his recurrent, though unseconded, selection of himself for the Nobel and Pulitzer Prizes, for sundry honorary degrees and for membership in various deeply unresponsive clubs, was not, on the whole, helpful to his case. He also believed so completely in the class system that he constructed one of his own based on spoken language, whether the man went to Yale and, of course, on

---

*This is a review, which was never published, of *Selected Letters of John O'Hara*, edited by Matthew J. Bruccoli (New York: Random House, 1978).

the make of the automobile he drove. Good Americans prefer a classless society based firmly on property, income and occupation.

Yet more damaging was the fact that O'Hara wrote a great deal. Critics, as O'Hara himself recognized, although not with any real sympathy, are often people with a problem. With such notable exceptions as Edmund Wilson, they don't write much themselves, and quite a few can't write at all. Those who are so restrained tend, naturally enough, to react protectively against those who aren't. As they see it, writers are people who don't perceive the greatness of the literary art; if they did, they wouldn't expose their own inadequacy so shamelessly in print. "He may be a great creative writer," I once heard a Harvard colleague observe, "but I certainly wouldn't trust his literary judgment." John O'Hara, as indicated, wrote, and wrote prodigiously. First *The New Yorker;* then the annual collection; then, at intervals, small novels; then, at less frequent intervals, the big ones. There was an unpublished stockpile for his heirs when he died on April 11, 1970.

Finally, before its more clinical aspects became commonplace and compulsive, there was a question over the way O'Hara used sex. In his longer novels there is little doubt that about every fifty pages O'Hara would say to himself, "This book must sell." Forthwith he would put his people into bed, even though, as Archibald MacLeish once complained, they hadn't yet shaken hands. ("I told John he must always have them do that first.") He could then imply more as to the pleasure of the transaction and in superficially cleaner language than any writer alive, and he also loved to have the woman in the case take the initiative. All this appealed to men and also to women, but to those who lacked O'Hara's skill or were too nice, he seemed to be taking a grossly unfair advantage in his resort to sex.

Professor Matthew J. Bruccoli is a man professionally on O'Hara's side. This was earlier made evident in his biography, *The O'Hara Concern,* and also in other writing. Now he has devoted himself to collecting the O'Hara correspondence, and it is surely the best thing that has ever happened to his subject.

O'Hara's letters are written with exactly the same resource and precision of language as are his short stories, the reason being that he was a master of the first draft, which is what letters usually are. But they are also affectionate, amusing, in the early years surprisingly self-deprecatory, and they show their author's all but total commitment to his craft. They are replete with anxiety — for critical approval, social acceptance and for the winning of those prizes. But much of this comes across as a rather appealing vulnerability, a terrible need for reassurance. There was, no doubt, a nasty streak in O'Hara, but it appears here only in his dealing with publishers and editors, and no one can complain about that.

O'Hara, it might be noted, handled his own contracts and other publishing arrangements in the United States without an agent. While he could be very tough, I am not certain from reading these letters that he was altogether adept. For far too long after he was a successful author, he allowed Random House a half share of paperback and other subsidiary rights. And he seems to have left large sums piling up uncollected in order to postpone paying income tax on them. This was only postponement, and it had the effect of providing the publisher with far too much interest-free money.

Getting back to writing, I am persuaded, for what it is worth, that O'Hara was, indeed, a very good and very important writer. His novels were not as good as his short stories, although I now think better of one or two that I believed poor, and so reviewed, when they were published.

Also most of the attack on O'Hara was irrelevant. It turned extensively on whether his characters, particularly his socially selected Ivy League men and their wives, really exist. I don't believe they do. Their prototypes, whom I've encountered with regrettable frequency over the years, are certainly their equal in banality, but they are much less interesting and, if anything, less intelligent. I have even more doubt as to the existence of the saloonkeepers, garage men, small-time politicians and small-town madams whom O'Hara featured rather more than the rich, especially in his short stories, and for whose language he was said, even by the opposition, to have such an excellent ear. All these characters have some tie to reality, something either in their speech or their intense self-regard, that every reader recognizes to be true. All have the brash assurance and tendency to aggression that O'Hara wished or imagined he himself possessed. But they are, after all, only characters. Certainly they don't live where I might encounter them around Boston or New York or in Newfane, Vermont. Like his rich, they are inventions — really, a complex and extremely talented fraud. O'Hara persuaded his readers that such people exist and so speak, and in doing so, he certainly persuaded himself. Though they don't, they do improve greatly on anything in real life.

4

MONEY IN
AMERICAN FICTION

(1984)

This was an essay in The New York Times Book Review, *which allowed me with a sense of high purpose to reread old novels all through a calm and beautiful summer. There are some things for which an author should not be paid, a circumstance* The New York Times *comes close to recognizing.*

In the spring of 1958, I was invited to give some lectures in Poland by arrangement of Oskar Lange, formerly of the University of Chicago and a noted figure in the economics of the last generation, who after the war had returned to a sometimes uneasy existence in his native land. It was only a couple of years after the fall of the Stalinist regime of Bolesław Beirut. Perhaps there had been relatively safe, uncontroversial people — neurologists, internists, gynecologists, maybe even psychiatrists — who had been asked to lecture there before in the postwar era; I was the first economist with no available Marxist credentials.

I was appropriately excited by the prospect of the journey. When I arrived in Warsaw that spring day, the rubble of World War II and the fierce local combat was still depressingly in evidence, and I found, as I have previously told, that I had brought nothing except my own lectures to read. Since there is a limit to what one can do with such literature, I telephoned a friend in France to mail me some books and went to the largest of the local bookstores to see what I could find.

The selection in English was meager, all but nonexistent. In the next few weeks I read *Dombey and Son,* sent from Paris, and, for occasional relief, Frank Norris's *The Octopus,* my one local find. For a socialist sojourn Norris was a more than appropriate immersion in the abuse of power by the capitalist rich. But such was Norris's talent as a novelist — digressive, wordy, improbable and sometimes ponderously naïve — that I cannot think I would ever have finished the book as a voluntary exercise. I was compelled to his prose by the alternatives, which were Dickens or nothing at all.

It was, however, an excellent reminder of a time around the turn of the century and extending into the 1920s when American novelists — Norris, Theodore Dreiser, Upton Sinclair and, though more especially in his nonfiction, Jack London — were the highly motivated assailants of the American rich. The treatment of the affluent in American fiction is a matter to which, on various idle occasions, my attention has since turned.

While all the early-twentieth-century novelists were fiercely critical of the rich, there was some difference among them as to who should be selected for attack as the aggressors and especially who were their victims. Norris's villain, the Octopus, was the Pacific and Southwestern Railroad (for which read the Southern Pacific), together with Shelgrim, its controlling financier; S. Behrman, his venomous local agent — one suspects a slightly anti-Semitic tone — and the well-kept local press. The heroes and victims were the ranchers of the San Joaquin Valley, the relatively affluent owners of tens of thousands of acres and employers of dozens and hundreds of true working stiffs. But no sympathy whatever accrues to the latter; as compared with their unhappy employers, they get only passing mention.

In seeking to respond to the corrupt power of the railroad, the great but good ranchers sink themselves into corruption; because the railroad buys into the state regulatory commission, so, they feel, must they. But they still retain all of the reader's sympathy. The railroad monster remains the ruthless exploiter of men who, a mere thirty years or so later, would emerge in John Steinbeck's *The Grapes of Wrath* as among the least benign employers in all the land and against whom, a little later still, Cesar Chavez would arouse the indignation of half the country. By that time, it might be added, the erstwhile power of the enfeebled railroads and their generally unfortunate owners would be a matter of purely archaeological interest.

Upton Sinclair's demons were the meat packers, coal mine owners and oil magnates, and they were exploiters with a much larger social reach. Consumers as well as workers were under their heel. While Norris (who published *The Octopus* in 1901) may have done something for better railroad regulation, there is no doubt as to Upton Sinclair's role, by way of *The Jungle,* published in 1906, in winning passage of the Food and Drug Act of that year and getting improved inspection of meat.

The rich are opprobrious and damaging in *An American Tragedy* (1925) in a yet different way. Theodore Dreiser is another writer who would have suffered, though perhaps also with some advantage, from today's editors — in his novel no aspect of character or personality is ever allowed to develop from the story; all is told at length in advance but with a purpose that one comes to forgive. The author doesn't much care for Samuel Griffiths, the collar-manufacturing tycoon of Lycurgus in upstate New York, and he is even less enamored of his nasty son Gilbert. But it is not the treatment of workers or consumers by the Griffiths family that interests Dreiser; each group, so far as one can tell, is content, even happy, making or wearing the collars. It is the offensive social structure of the city, one based exclusively and, in the context of the time, quite normally on wealth, that captures his attention. "The line of demarcation and stratification between the rich and the poor in Lycurgus was as sharp as though cut by a knife or divided by a high wall." When Gilbert Griffiths puts on a bit too many airs even for a friend, a young woman of the same class, she asks, "Who does he think he is anyhow? . . . You'd think he was a Rockefeller or a Morgan."

The different and greatly superior life lived by the rich and their offspring and his chance of belonging are what cause Clyde Griffiths, the poor nephew, to drown his pregnant and unforgivably proletarian sweetheart and go ineluctably on to the electric chair. Rereading Dreiser, I was reminded how deeply he involves his reader in the problems of his characters, and nowhere so compellingly as in the desperate and fruitless search of the distraught couple for a willing, risk-taking abortionist. It was, one supposes, the experience and terror of thousands of young couples or young women every year in that time. The world moves.

In the later 1920s and the years of the great flowering of American fiction there was a major change in the treatment of the rich: they ceased to be socially offensive or economically exploitative and became positively benign. Now it was their *problems* that attracted the attention. This, perhaps surprisingly, continued to be true in the depression years of the 1930s, *The Grapes of Wrath* being something of an exception, as also the earlier novels of John Dos Passos. And Hemingway was not much concerned with the rich or the resulting class distinctions, abuses and tensions.

In *Tender Is the Night,* Scott Fitzgerald's rich had already made their money. Those who flocked from all over the Long Island North Shore to Jay Gatsby's festivals were a mixed and undiscriminating crew — "Snell . . . three days before he went to the penitentiary, so drunk out on the gravel drive that Mrs. Ulysses Swett's automobile ran over his right hand. . . . G. Earl Muldoon, brother to that Muldoon who afterward strangled his wife. . . . Henry L. Palmetto, who killed himself by jumping in front of a subway train in Times Square." And there is not much to be said for Gatsby himself, with his mob connections. But Fitzgerald is unconcerned; the nearest he gets in *The Great Gatsby* to social comment is to say that "Americans, while occasionally willing to be serfs, have always been obstinate about being peasantry," an observation eloquently devoid of any conceivable meaning. It is the lives of the rich — their enjoyments, agonies and putative insanity — that attract his interest; their social and political consequences escape him as he himself escaped such matters in his own life.

In two or three of Ring Lardner's short stories the rich are also fairly sordid specimens. Thus in *The Love Nest,* a brilliant item, a young reporter accompanies a great and successful motion picture magnate up the Hudson to spend the night at his château to learn how he shoves his wealth, along with his good Prohibition-time whiskey, down the throat of a listener and to see how he has turned his lovely actress wife, imprisoned as if in neighboring Sing Sing, into a hopeless lush. However, it could be as much to show business as to money that Lardner attributed such behavior.

With Sinclair Lewis in these years a different and surprisingly enduring theme as regards the rich entered American fiction: the marked improvement in the manners and general deportment that characterizes the old as compared with the new rich. In the shadows back of George Babbitt in Zenith — Babbitt, though solvent, is not rich — is a higher caste, far more secure, civilized and prestigious. They are the old rich, age in Zenith being a matter of one or two generations. It is appropriate that some seven years after Babbitt there comes Samuel Dodsworth, the highly successful and now extremely affluent automobile manufacturer. Being of the first generation, he is still a rather raw character, especially as compared with his wife, who, in consequence of being descended from a generation older in wealth, is far superior in dress, cultural depth and general social acceptability. However, Dodsworth, having money, is far more civilized than Babbitt, and using his money around Europe, he also undergoes major cultural repair and improvement. But he never reaches the superior standing of the family into which he has married.

As was Babbitt, Dodsworth was wholly praiseworthy as a businessman. He brought people to the Revelation car as George Babbitt had filled their housing and real estate needs. Neither abused customers or employees. It also goes without saying that as Sam Dodsworth acquired something of the deeper culture of the old rich, his marriage went promptly on the rocks.

Except possibly for Louis Auchincloss, John O'Hara is the most diligent chronicler of the lives and mores of the older American rich. Like Sinclair Lewis, he is hard on the manners of the upstarts, but those who have had their money for a little time he respects and even loves. In New York they belong to the best available clubs; in Gibbsville, to their own charmed circle. They are always thoughtfully dressed and give the most discriminating attention to their consumer durables. (It is hard to believe that the Pierce-Arrow automobile ever went out of production, for O'Hara's people alone provided a market for dozens of them.) In the matter of funerals, weddings, other social observances and sex, O'Hara's rich are fiercely independent and frequently eccentric. Only after achieving secure affluence can one be a homosexual. This independence or eccentricity is what money provides. In sharp contrast with the rich of a slightly later era, O'Hara's people have relatively few psychiatric disorders. Suicide is not unknown, but, as in *Appointment in Samarra,* it occurs as a plausible, even rational, response to misfortune.

O'Hara's rich, like others of the generation, do not abuse their workers, so far as these appear, or their much more visible servants; instead, they are rather precisely generous to other people and treat the less fortunate courteously and well. Sadly, the same cannot be said of their servants, especially their chauffeurs. The latter, drawing on the wealth and prestige of their masters and the enormous distinction accorded by the cars they drive, are, without exception, status-conscious, tough of speech and generally disagreeable. But for this the rich are not themselves to be blamed.

Coming to the modern novel, one has difficulty: that is because there are so many of them. For the last few years I've been working on a history of economics. As one approaches the present, one is filled with a sense of helplessness; in a year and possibly even in a month there is now more economic comment in the supposedly serious literature than survives from the whole of the thousand years commonly denominated as the Middle Ages. So also with modern American fiction; anyone who claims to be familiar with it all is a confessing liar. Yet there are some highly visible writers for whom the rich are a special theme. And, perhaps surprisingly, there are also here some fictional opportunities that seem to be rather badly neglected.

Of those who currently concentrate on the rich there is the already-mentioned Louis Auchincloss. Although he is in danger of repeating himself (and does so, in some measure, in his recent *The Book Class,* on the lives and preoccupations of an earlier generation of affluent New York women), I've long been convinced that he rises well above even his own considerable reputation. A writer who is Jewish, black, Irish or Italian can be a master of his ethnic identity. And one of sufficient talent, like Daniel James, writing as Danny Santiago, can capture the essence of another ethnic culture, as James does of the Los Angeles Mexican community [and for which, as Santiago, he received the Rosenthal Award of the American Academy of Arts and Letters in 1984]. But not so a WASP on WASPs. His people are not supposed to have a recognizable ethnic identity, and they would be rather annoyed at the thought. The distinguishing feature of Mr. Auchincloss's men and women is only that they live in Manhattan and are rich. With exceptions, they are also happy, as, in contrast with the poor and the aspiring, most affluent people seem to be in real life. I've never thought it at all surprising that so many try so hard to get money.

Trying to get money or to avoid losing what they think they have, some of the Auchincloss nonethnics do break the law and get put in jail, to which they go with a marked nobility of mood. There are also grave conflicts between husbands and wives, with children, with and over mistresses, and especially with aging parents. And there is trouble over wills and money. But much of this fuss is a diversion and rather enjoyed. And once again the rich are socially benign, or, more precisely, they are socially neutral. Some charitable and educational preoccupations and one or two ventures into politics aside, they do neither good nor harm. As is usual in American fiction and unlike British novels, where, in the past, the income of prospective partners was revealed down to the last pound annually, Mr. Auchincloss's people rarely marry for money. They are also pleasant and unexpectedly erudite — far more so than might be imagined or, in my more limited observation, seems plausible. I'm always astonished at how much they remember of what they learned of the classics, the plays of Molière and the arts generally from their years at Groton, Harvard and Yale and the women's colleges. I've known a great many Harvard graduates but never any culturally so accomplished.

An interesting feature of the Auchincloss and other recently depicted American rich is that they seem rarely to be involved in social climbing. One is surprised at this, for such ambition surely does exist. The most proficient of all American social climbers in modern fiction, Elliott Templeton in *The Razor's Edge,* is, in fact, the creation of Somerset Maugham, the quintessential student of superior English society. Largely ignored also are the rich who seek the prestige of political eminence or voice. All of my acquaintances who are affluent yearn to be heard seriously on political matters and, at least in past times, to tell of their latest visit to the White House.

The contrast between the nice old and the self-made rich or less rich still continues as from Sinclair Lewis's day. Harry Angstrom — Rabbit — now has a comfortable if not very secure income in John Updike's *Rabbit Is Rich.* But he is unintelligently introspective, educated only by his own experience and not well by that, appalling in his family life and pathologically concerned with sex. George Babbitt is altogether a more appealing type. In Brewer, Angstrom's hometown, as in Zenith, there remains an older, more secure culture in the background, its members frequenting a golf club to which Rabbit does not even aspire. Nice, confident, agreeable self-made men seem to be rare in American fiction.

As they are quite possibly an unexploited opportunity, so, more certainly, are some of the rich outside New York. We have had the chronicles of the Hollywood rich, but I've never encountered anything on Ronald Reagan's business and legal friends — men and women who are untroubled by art and the classics, who really enjoy spending their money and think, in an articulate and untroubled way, that the poor are the architects of their own misfortune to the extent that they aren't the expensively damaged victims of the welfare state.

Neglected also is the modern corporate executive, the university-trained managerial type, wherever he lives. Thirty years ago John Marquand made a brilliant beginning on the task of depicting him with *Sincerely, Willis Wayde,* a novel that didn't receive the attention it deserved because, I think, it was too fully abreast of its time. Willis is a highly competent, soundly schooled, relentlessly ambitious, deeply offensive graduate of the Harvard Business School; he brings the best in modern management techniques to bear on the Harcourt Mill in Clyde, Massachusetts, an old and distinguished manufacturer of industrial belting. He also brings off a greatly advantageous merger, moves the headquarters to the Middle West and, eventually, as part of a very intelligent strategy — strategic planning even then — abandons the original New England operation.

Willis Wayde is, in every way, the modern management man and an early if primitive practitioner of what my colleague Robert Reich calls paper entrepreneurship. Sloan Wilson's deliberately atypical *Man in the Gray Flannel Suit* is one of the few other examples. Perhaps the wonderful recent history of William Agee and Mary Cunningham at Bendix will be an inspiration.

In any case, there is much opportunity here for the modern novelist. Unlike the old capitalist or the self-made man, today's executive surrenders his body and, so far as available, his soul to the organization, and it is the terms of this surrender that remain to be explored, perhaps along the lines already laid down by Joseph Heller in *Something Happened.* The pay, stock options, golden parachutes, retirement benefits and other perquisites, not excluding the company jet, are fine. But their price is the subordination to the purposes of the organization of all public and most private speech, a self-censorship that is made tolerable only by being habitual and unrecognized.

The cost of this surrender to organization — to the corporate bureaucracy and to money — is what needs to be investigated and described, as also its effect on wives, families, friends, subordinates, sycophants and, inevitably, sex lives. And there should be treatment of the day of the terrible first death, which comes with the announcement that the executive is "taking early retirement" and his discovery that banality unbacked by the name of General Motors or Citibank has no audience. Then eventually the second death, the two weak paragraphs in *The New York Times*.* I for one don't need anything more on the old, charming, reputable, if psychiatrically alarming, rich. I would now like to read about those who, no longer overtly exploiting others, so willingly exploit themselves.

*My earlier piece, "Corporate Man," on page 39, has more on today's businessman and, alas, also includes this observation.

5

EVELYN WAUGH:
TWO OCCUPATIONS

NOVELIST*
(1977)

George Ball, under secretary of state in the Kennedy and Johnson administrations, ambassador to the United Nations, banker, writer, aspiring poet and great friend, affirmed my attraction to Evelyn Waugh in London in 1945. Until that time I had thought I was exploiting a discovery and following a passion that perhaps, a trifle too preciously, was peculiarly my own. Then that spring amidst the wartime wreckage George somehow acquired several copies of Scoop *and* Decline and Fall, *which he distributed to his friends, saying he didn't wish to know any man, and certainly any woman, who hadn't read and rejoiced in Evelyn Waugh.*

I first encountered Evelyn Waugh's books — and fortunately, by abundant evidence, not his person — forty years ago this coming summer. As a young Harvard instructor, I had been giving thoughtful attention to the means by which my elders in academic life arranged to travel at public or foundation expense, for I was fond of travel. Their method with foundations consisted in identifying some economic or political development in some adequately remote country and endowing it with a potential significance for the United States or for scholarship that would have astonished its progenitors.

I had selected, since the subject (as distinct from the solemnity of the persuasion) seemed unimportant, a land tenure law, the *Erbhofgesetz*, recently enacted in the Third Reich to re-establish a measure of forward-looking feudalism in German agriculture. Once having chosen Germany, I then settled on East Prussia as the proper place for field observation, it being the most distant part of the country and the only

---

*This was a review, originally published in *Book World* of *The Washington Post*, of *Decline and Fall, Vile Bodies, Black Mischief, A Handful of Dust, Scoop, Put Out More Flags* and *The Loved One* by Evelyn Waugh (Boston: Little, Brown, 1977).

part my wife, who shared my urge to travel, had never seen. An agricultural official in Berlin, who was the resident professional Harvard
man, arranged our itinerary, which included a wonderful tour of the
great Junker estates.

By a happy and unusual accident of German inefficiency, we were
received in Königsberg with unimaginable warmth and ceremony; it
appeared that the telegram telling the provincial authorities to turn
out the troops had somehow in translation promoted me from "young
American economist" to "leading American agronomist." Of this we
had no knowledge until after my wife had asked our host on the first
vast estate if there was a difference between wheat and barley. Her
previous exposure to agriculture had been at the Mineola fair.

It was too late for us to go back; neither we nor the German agricultural officials (who, before the trip was over, were assuring us in
strict confidence of their innocence of any conceivable Nazi sympathy)
could by then afford the truth. So the fraud was carried through, and,
in the course of our tour, we were joined by Douglas Logan, later Sir
Douglas and until 1975 the principal of the University of London.

He had just finished *Decline and Fall* and gave it to me. Before reading
Waugh, I had had misgivings about our deception, more as regards
the Rockefeller Foundation, which, through the Social Science Research Council, was financing our travel, than as regards the Germans;
now I discovered that I was in the great tradition of Grimes, Augustus
Fagan and Philbrick, Waugh's heroic frauds, and that I was escaping,
however briefly, from the square, honest and reprehensible world of
his Arthur Potts.

The escape was, perhaps, temporary, but the gratitude has endured.
I think Waugh one of the best novelists of the century, a view that no
longer arouses amused contempt. I find it hard to isolate Waugh's
special talent; if he is as good as I assert, it is because he possessed all
of the relevant skills — a wonderfully precise and resourceful use of
words, the ability to arrest attention with stunningly apt and unexpected
characterization, a marvelous facility with dialogue and the artistry that
makes people who are extravagantly larger than life seem real and
situations that are wonderfully entertaining but deeply improbable seem
wholly plausible.

Waugh was also unsparingly honest. Anyone with even a marginal
experience of war, as was mine, knows the awfulness of having to deal
with mentally impregnable, profoundly arrogant, congenitally stupid
men suddenly elevated to high military rank, who are also drunk. When
peace comes, especially if you have won, you resolutely put this memory
aside; no one has more eloquently and usefully kept it green than
Waugh.

To accompany American publication of the Waugh diaries (which would have been improved had some of the drinking been edited out and all of the fine scurrility left in), Little, Brown is reissuing the prewar novels — *Decline and Fall, Vile Bodies, Black Mischief, A Handful of Dust, Scoop* and *Put Out More Flags* — and his postwar paean to the embalming business, *The Loved One*. These, in my view, are Waugh's best. There is an element of higher purpose in *Brideshead Revisited* and the wartime trilogy that is foreign to his nature.

Of those now newly available, the supreme achievement, for what one reader's taste may be worth, is *Scoop*. Certainly nothing better has ever been written on the zoological instincts and manifestations of newspapermen on mob assignment and the processes by which they are guided by their editors. Until I became instructed in a practical way on American presidential campaigns and their press coverage, I had never realized what a deathlessly accurate document it is.

Scoop, like *Black Mischief*, grew out of Waugh's experiences in Ethiopia. Both books are profoundly racist, in keeping with Waugh's compulsion to search for any socially unacceptable attitude and then adopt it. But all who wish to enjoy them and remain reputable should know that there *is* mitigating circumstance. Waugh was not only anti-black but also anti-Semitic, anti-French and, with the rarest of exceptions, anti-British. Once, years ago, I asked Randolph Churchill how he managed to get along with him, having in mind that not many could get along with Randolph himself. "Well," he said, "I always promise him I won't have any Americans around." To belong to some ethnic, national or religious entity that had Waugh's approval would be disreputable as well as impossible.

CORRESPONDENT*

(1980)

The fascination in Evelyn Waugh's writing, which for some can verge on addiction, begins, of course, with his mastery of the English language, something of which he was more than aware. Often in his letters, here collected and edited by Mark Amory, his friends are rebuked, and sternly, for minor errors in usage. There is also his wonderful sense of the absurd and his extraordinary capacity for a kind of plausible exaggeration. In Waugh's letters, an older man who has not performed well on some social occasion is senile; looking back on the alcohol- and drug-induced nervous disorders of which he tells in *The Ordeal of Gilbert Pinfold* (when he heard intensely disturbing voices in

*This was a review, originally published in *Book World* of *The Washington Post*, of *The Letters of Evelyn Waugh*, edited by Mark Amory (New York: Ticknor and Fields, 1980).

his shipboard cabin), Waugh describes himself as having been insane; whenever he or his friends drink, they are described as drunk, which, conceivably, could have been true; in a letter from the United States to Randolph Churchill he says: "I spent my first evening with your friends the Luces. I am afraid it was not a success. I found him ignorant and densely stupid. Her I admired. . . ." Henry Luce could overwhelm you of an evening with sometimes obtuse and often unanswerable questions, but he was never stupid.

Finally, there is pleasure in the way Waugh sets himself to offend every reputable instinct of the reader. He is against democracy, the United States, the working classes, Jews, socialists and, recurrently, his own family. You can enjoy this, for you also come to see that it is at least partly put on. His second-person address in his letters is uniformly warm, kindly and encouraging. It is only about third persons that he is disparaging or cruel, and they, at least until now, were not expected to see what he said about them. Authors who sent their books to Waugh — a dozen or more came from Graham Greene — invariably got an appreciative word. Any criticism was carefully crafted to avoid hurt feelings. Then in comment to others he would be himself.

Some will sense that as an admirer, in fact an addict, I thought this collection wonderful, and they will be right. The letters are not to a wide circle: the largest number are to Nancy Mitford, Ann Fleming (the wife of Ian Fleming) and, among others, Lady Mary and Lady Dorothy Lygon, of whom Waugh was fond and in whose letters he regularly went on from ordinary outrage to casual obscenity. While he was serving, if that is the word, as a wartime officer, there were letters to Laura Herbert, his second wife. These end with his return from the war, and she remains a shadowy figure, notable in this correspondence only for her commitment to animal husbandry. Writing to his children, he is, by turns, sternly hortatory, amusing, loving and outrageous, and frequently all four in a single letter. The most complex exchange is with Randolph Churchill, for whom he combined a relentless dislike and recurrent affection. Writing to Laura in 1944 from Yugoslavia, where he had gone with Churchill on the famous — and, I might add, considering the personnel, almost totally incredible — mission to Tito and the Partisans, he notes, "I have got to the stage of disliking Randolph which is really more convenient than thinking I liked him & constantly trying to reconcile myself to his enormities."

Churchill's enormities were not the only ones that had to be suffered during the war. In another letter of the same year Waugh tells of his brief career as an aide to a higher officer: "I have escaped from my general. He was a dull fellow & he did not enjoy my efforts to enliven his mess. The worst I did was to pour claret in his lap." (Waugh's diaries, as his editor here points out, tell also of this incident: "The primary lack of sympathy [between myself and the general] seemed to come from my being slightly drunk in his mess on the first evening. I told him I could not change the habits of a lifetime for a whim of his.")

While on most matters Waugh is not to be taken seriously or anyhow literally, there is one exception, and that concerns his church. On anything having to do with Catholic doctrine or rules he is informed, serious and unyielding, and he does not hesitate to instruct his co-religionists in the sternest terms. At the same time he can be very hard on members of the hierarchy when he thinks them in error. One of his novels, *Black Mischief,* deals, it will be recalled, with the miracles recorded at a Nestorian monastery in Azania (read Ethiopia), including a cross that had recently fallen from heaven during a Good Friday luncheon; with a birth control gala organized by Seth, the new emperor; and with Basil Seal being treated to an orgiastic tribal dinner, at which he discovers that he has just eaten the young woman named Prudence, whom, in a manner of speaking, he loved. Waugh was rebuked for this wonderful nonsense in *The Tablet,* a journal under the patronage of the Cardinal Archbishop of Westminster. His letter in reply, a cogent, eloquent and angry document running to some thousands of words, is one of the best things in this book.

Mark Amory has deleted, he says, some insupportably slanderous remarks of Waugh's, but enough such remain to satisfy most tastes. Once in a while in dealing with the United States, there are slips — the Book-of-the-Month Club becomes the Book Society, for example — and there is a gorgeous error as regards Harvard University. In the 1940s, a soon to be defrocked priest by the name of Feeney set up shop in Cambridge and attracted a certain number of vulnerable undergraduates to his highly authoritarian heresies, which held, among other things, that heaven would be rigorously restricted to his followers and a few others. This caused terrible distress for the more sensitive of our local citizenry. Amory makes Father Feeney "the chaplain at Harvard." That would, indeed, have been a joyous thing.

6

MALCOLM MUGGERIDGE:
TWO MODES

AUTOBIOGRAPHY*
(1974)

In Malcolm Muggeridge's politics, like those of Waugh and Mencken, one can find much to deplore. But he and I are both by way of being old India hands, and this is one of the more companionate and self-regarding associations of all time. (People who know India at first hand remove themselves to a corner on all social occasions to rejoice each other in reminiscence of their shared experience.) And again, as noted in these reviews, there is the redeeming quality of the writing.

Autobiography is the most abysmal of literary forms for reasons that are often evident. Anyone who writes a book should be able to write; he should have something interesting or useful to write about, and he should be able to see his subject with some clarity and deal with it with reasonable honesty and detachment. The rarest accidents apart, the autobiographer is, in the nature of things, without all these prerequisites, except occasionally the first.

In addition, if he is a politician, he is engaged in an essentially unnatural act. The glow that was thought to be an attribute of his personality when he was a Cabinet officer, senator, governor or ambassador was, in fact, a small property on temporary loan from the government, and that loan is foreclosed the day he is fired, is counted out by the ballots or — in the extremely unusual cases where it happens — resigns. The autobiography seeks to prolong the grandeur and, naturally, fails. The prudent reader will avoid anything of this genre unless there is assurance that it was completely ghostwritten by a competent professional.

It might be added that the authorized biography is also usually a

---

*This was a review, originally published in *The New York Times Book Review*, of *Chronicles of Wasted Time, Chronicle 2: The Infernal Grove* by Malcolm Muggeridge (New York: William Morrow, 1974).

waste. Here, however, there are occasional exceptions. Once I was making the case against such writing to R. A. Butler, who, after occupying all important British Cabinet posts except that of prime minister, retired to serve as master and resident iconoclast at Trinity College, Cambridge, with which in the past I have had association as a fellow. I illustrated my point with a reference to a biography of former Prime Minister Alec Douglas-Home that was then occupying the bookshop windows but not, I believe, the attention of any readers. "It is not a bad book," said Butler. "The chap who did it is a good writer, and he didn't know Alec at all well."

These warnings will strike most people as redundant at a time when Jeb Stuart Magruder has just told of his childhood, toilet training, family and the failure of William Sloane Coffin and the other character-molding influences at Williams to teach him that he should obey the law. Soon, no doubt, we will have the ghastly revelations of John Ehrlichman, Spiro Agnew and Richard Kleindienst as well as the whole story of the passage unto Jesus of Charles Colson, a blow that Christianity may survive but that will be terrible to literature.* My warning, however, is purely by way of highlighting an exception, the only one, I venture, of the season. It is the autobiography — I should say the two autobiographies — of Malcolm Muggeridge, and they are wonderful.

Muggeridge is not a tolerant man, a point on which he strongly insists. Individuals, he feels, are often tolerable, provided they are unimportant and acting alone. Acting together, they are always depraved and without hope of redemption. So are all who have enjoyed power or attracted esteem. Churchill (especially Churchill), Roosevelt, Mrs. Roosevelt, Clement Attlee, Ramsay MacDonald, Harold Macmillan, Kennedy, Nehru (though not Gandhi), Stalin (certainly Stalin), are without redeeming social virtue. So is Muggeridge himself, but on this he is less than convincing. So are all acolytes and outriders. No one since the New Testament who has urged any form of amelioration of man's fate can hope for a good word. Reading Muggeridge, one comes to yearn for the hope, the disarming optimism, the ingenuous idealism, of Ronald Reagan, William F. Buckley, Jr., or Senator Jesse Helms.

The redeeming virtues of Malcolm Muggeridge are his writing, including his eye for illuminating detail; his memory; his capacity on occasion, one suspects, for minor historical invention; and, above all,

---

*Jeb Stuart Magruder, a minor figure in the Nixon years, had recently finished his memoirs — more accurately, had them finished — when this review was written. The other Nixon names mentioned as well as their now accomplished books will, if vaguely, be remembered.

his impeccable instinct for the absurd. Nothing that has gone before has given these qualities so much scope as writing about himself.

In an earlier volume of autobiography, *The Green Stick,* Muggeridge told of his personal background — a middle-class family in the London suburbs and an enchanting father who combined the shirt business with a willingness to mount a ladder of a Saturday night in Croydon to declaim the wonders of socialism and who, in his sixties, was elected to Parliament. From these origins young Malcolm went on to Cambridge, to teaching in India and England and to an enduring (but not confining) marriage to Kitty Dobbs, a niece of Beatrice Webb. Then came journalism. He wrote for C. P. Scott and *The Manchester Guardian* in Soviet Russia, and the experience was, to use a word that seems increasingly inescapable, traumatic. Muggeridge emerged with a transcendent detestation of both Russia and *The Guardian,* although of the two he detested *The Guardian* more. There was cause. After leaving Russia, he wrote a novel with the newspaper as the scene, and in a noteworthy exercise of selective liberalism, *The Guardian* arranged to have it suppressed.

In *The Infernal Grove* Muggeridge returns to India to be the deputy editor of *The Statesman* in Calcutta and then, in principle though not seriously in practice, to become its Simla correspondent. He follows this with a stint for Beaverbrook on *The Evening Standard,* and then comes the war. After some incomprehensible activities in England he becomes a spy or general intelligence operative in Lourenço Marques in Portuguese East Africa (now Mozambique). Later he is in Paris as some kind of liaison with or within the intelligence department of the Free French. In keeping with his deep personal commitment to anarchy, Muggeridge's account of the organizations with which he served and their responsibilities is obscure.

When telling of individual intelligence operations, however, Muggeridge is superb. After E. Howard Hunt, G. Gordon Liddy or, for that matter, Allen Dulles (whose intellectual incoherence and public disasters were at a higher level), we now know the capacity of this profession for attracting men who range from the absurd to the insane. Nothing could be more apposite to the Muggeridge talent than these people or their world. It was as though some latter-day Mencken had been inadvertently hired for a year or so as an advance man by the Reverend Billy Graham.

The British Raj in its last days in Simla, the period of which he tells, also served Muggeridge well. His picture of the small hill station where men and women walked out on the mall in the evening, gathered to curtsey and otherwise make obeisance to the viceroy and where they, almost incidentally, governed the millions in the searing plains below, is right in every detail. When I was a youngster in Canada, one of the governors general of the time was named Willingdon. He had a thin, gray, deeply depressing face and a narrow, trembling frame. The inadequacy of his presence was emphasized by the uniforms, top hats, medals and carriages with which he was clothed, decorated and moved. Watching him on a state visit to the people, one wondered, or more likely was led to wonder by the remark of some ethnically adverse adult (of whom among the Canadian Scotch there were many), if, behind it all, there lurked some human intelligence. He went on to be viceroy in India. Muggeridge makes it clear that no intelligence so lurked or needed to lurk; his most pregnant thought was how easy the country was to govern.

Some will argue that Malcolm Muggeridge is a purely destructive figure; there are always people around with a genius for the obvious. But many whom he destroys are richly deserving of the fate. The rest merit no sympathy, for they can reflect with pride that they have been devastated by a true master of the craft.

Not that Muggeridge is perfect in his preferred role. His assault on the profession or, as perhaps it must be called, the cult of intelligence is marred by a certain admiration for the British code-breaking activities at Bletchley, England, and also for some operations of his own. Additionally, if a man is without power or importance or down on his luck, Muggeridge has a perverse tendency to be completely kind. A good deal of his time in Paris in 1944 was spent helping P. G. Wodehouse, then under attack by the righteous as a seeming collaborator. So with others. These are blemishes, but there they are.

DIARIES*

(1982)

When reviewing books, one yearns for those that are all good and, if less urgently, for those that are all bad. Then one is spared the need for a balanced judgment, the gnawing sense, however repressed, that one should somehow be fair. That is the problem here. From 1924 until (as he says) fairly recent times Malcolm Muggeridge kept a diary. There are long gaps, some of days, some of weeks and several extending to years, but in the aggregate there were many hundreds of thousands of words. This volume, *Like It Was*, is a selection from all those entries, and the result is both very bad and very good. Thus the problem just mentioned.

*This was a review, originally published in *Book World* of *The Washington Post*, of *Like It Was: The Diaries of Malcolm Muggeridge*, selected and edited by John Bright-Holmes (New York: William Morrow, 1982).

In this case, however, judgment is made a trifle easier by the division of the task and blame between author and editor. The author, though not without lapses, is very good, as all his admirers would expect. It is the selection and editing in this book that are appalling, in fact unforgivable. What is worse, they are intentionally so. In an introductory paragraph, John Bright-Holmes says portentously, "All of us who have read published diaries know how destructive it can sometimes be to the unfolding of a narrative if the text is constantly interrupted by explanatory interpolations or loaded with expository footnotes." This is self-serving bosh, a transparent excuse for laziness and resulting inadequacy. Anyway, why "published" diaries? Why only "sometimes" true? How can it be said that footnotes interrupt the flow of the text? If you don't need them, you don't have to read them.

Here footnotes are desperately needed. Muggeridge, though occasionally pretending the opposite, is a companionable man with a large circle of friends, and daily he encountered men and women of interest and importance in his time. In consequence, in a journal that begins in 1932 (when the author arrived in Moscow to write for *The Manchester Guardian*) and that extends on to an editorial job in India, reportorial stints, a lecture tour in the United States and an active writing life in England, there are hundreds of names and numerous events that get mention and that are now remote as to time or place. It was the absolutely indispensable task of the editor to identify people and otherwise give necessary guidance. Instead, there is the deeply fraudulent excuse.

The editing is inadequate in other respects. A diary is the day's casual jotting; no one can pause to check all the facts. But the editor should do so or warn the reader. In India, writing for *The Statesman,* Muggeridge encounters "a wealthy Parsee" named Birla. This could only have been a member of the great industrialist family of that name. The misidentification as to religious affiliation would not be important except that the Birlas make a major point of their Hindu faith and observances as well as their commitment to Indian institutions in general. (It was in the garden of G. D. Birla, the head of the clan, that Gandhi was murdered.) Under any circumstances there should have been an explanation. Stopping in Lexington, Virginia, Muggeridge marvels that Robert E. Lee, after the defeat, should have been allowed to become head of a military college, the Virginia Military Institute. The truth, more remarkable, was that he rescued and became head of the liberal arts college that now bears his name — Washington and Lee. This slip, too, a competent editor would have caught. There are numerous other such aberrations. Mr. John Bright-Holmes, editor, for shame!

Perhaps more against the author than the editor is the repetition. In the early diaries Muggeridge is often deeply, even clinically, depressed. He is much attracted by the thought of death; there is a distant reference to a suicide attempt. Of this depression we certainly need to know; we don't need to hear of it every day. In later years Muggeridge is personally more cheerful but greatly convinced of the decay and imminent death of civilization. He has seen the past in India, the present in America and the future in Britain and Russia, and he dislikes them all. But again there is far more of this despair, tediously repeated in the same words, than even the most vacuous optimist needs to hear.

All of this is on the bad side; on the good side is, as always, his writing. Muggeridge has an unerring eye for captivating detail and, as I've elsewhere said, for absurdity and pretense. He takes his reader with him into scene and conversation, as also into the prodigious number and variety of books he reads. His Russian friends are admirably described in the early diaries, along with the all but instantaneous loss of his own socialist faith. His account of Calcutta and Simla in the last days of Empire is especially compelling. No one, E. M. Forster (and possibly Paul Scott) apart, has better caught the ambiguous relationships Indians had with the ruling race. He is very interesting on the Anglo-Indians, the most neglected and, one supposes, the most unhappy legacy of Britain to India. One follows him with fascination to Washington in the postwar years, back to the literary purlieus of London and back again to the United States for various purposes and notably for lectures and the lecture tour.

In the course of his encounters and travels Muggeridge renders judgment on a huge number of people, and his judgment is uniformly unfavorable. This it is my disposition greatly to enjoy. No British politician escapes. Dean Acheson is almost the only American of whom he has anything good to say. Harry Truman gets off to a terrible start, although later on he gets somewhat better marks. Graham Greene is admired for some of his books, condemned for others. Evelyn Waugh is nothing at all. Here, selected more or less at random, is a Muggeridge encounter and assessment:

April 9–11, 1948

Lunched with Bruce Lockhart, now rather broken-down, battered-looking, but otherwise just the same. Always rather liked him, though of course, he is completely phoney. He has had, on the whole, very good run for his money, but gives a rather touching impression of not somehow being quite satisfied with it all. Full of stories of Political Warfare, of which he was head, and of the rogueries of people like Dick Crossman, who were his subordinates. Spoke of what a terrible nuisance Randolph Churchill had been to him in the war, and of how Winston, none the less, dotes on Randolph and puts up with his bad behavior.

Bruce Lockhart rather at a loose end, I thought. He is too sharp not to see that what he has got isn't, after all, worth having, but not subtle enough to understand why not, or what is the alternative — if indeed there is one.

Some will think this a trifle rough. And so it is. But no one need take these judgments at face value. (It will occur to many that Waugh, whom Muggeridge excoriates, is a master of the satire and invective at which Muggeridge himself excels.) Rather, all should agree that it is a far better thing to be treated badly by Muggeridge than less badly by a lesser artist. My only prayer is that now in his mature years Malcolm Muggeridge hasn't run out of venom. It is very much needed for the editor of these diaries.

7

WILLIAM F. BUCKLEY, JR.:
TWO MOODS

POLITICAL CANDIDATE*
(1966)

William Buckley and I have been friends and neighbors for a long time — we both repair in the winter to the same small enclave in Switzerland to write and in times past to ski together. This has not required me to approve of his views, and he, on his side, has been at least as resistant. And I've found further advantage in our association. As for all others, thought is often for me a painful thing. But I've found over the years that if Buckley takes a strong position on any issue, I can take the opposite position without any tedious cerebration and know that I won't be wrong.

At a gathering of like-minded citizens not long before he announced his candidacy for mayor of New York, the author of this thoughtful memoir was believed by some reporters covering the proceedings to have urged New Yorkers to solve the problem of garbage disposal by throwing their trash out the window. In context there was a certain plausibility about the plan: it involved the minimum of government regulation of individual behavior; it placed the solution of the garbage problem on the shoulders of the citizens immediately concerned; it required no bureaucracy. It would also appeal to a great many New Yorkers, as a casual inspection of the city would readily establish. Some will suggest that the social cost would outweigh the private convenience. But Mr. Buckley is a conservative, and men who share his beliefs have long thought, perhaps with justification, that the plea of offsetting social cost is a wide roof under which socialists and American liberals automatically shelter any and all regulation.

However, it turned out that Mr. Buckley had been misquoted, and he disavowed the whole approach. The incident is not highly important

---

*This was a review, originally published in *The World Journal Tribune*, of *The Unmaking of a Mayor* by William F. Buckley, Jr. (New York: Viking, 1966).

in itself, but it neatly embodies the twin themes of this history. The book is concerned, first, with the inability of the New York newspapers, *The Daily News* possibly excepted, to capture the subtleties of Mr. Buckley's campaign arguments and especially the distinctions he sought to make. And it documents the terrible retreat from principle that was compelled by his pursuit of votes.

The second tendency is especially distressing. Mr. Buckley was running on the Conservative Party ticket. And he was running, specifically, because the Republican Party in general and John Lindsay in particular were deeply unfaithful to principle — because, in the author's stern view, they were willing to approve any government subsidy, handout, tax raid, public extravagance or interference with sound market theorems that paid off in the votes of some minority or special-interest group. But, alas, Mr. Buckley the vote seeker ended up doing just that himself. One could weep.

One weeps especially for his stand on the five-cent public transit fare. In New York for half a century this, in one form or another, has been the supreme test that divided the politicians from the politically principled. In its modern incarnation it applies to the Staten Island ferry, which, because its fare is so low, requires a subsidy that is a levy against every taxpayer in the City of New York. It lifts from Staten Islanders the price they should pay for the splendor and isolation but admitted inconvenience of living on an island. It encourages living there and thus raises the value of their taxable property at the expense of New York's other citizens. But in order to capture votes on Staten Island, Mr. Buckley came out for keeping the five-cent ferry fare. He justified his stand by simplistic calculations that sought support for the theory that the total cost for a Staten Islander of going by bus to the ferry and then taking the subway uptown should not exceed that of a ride on the mainland. The natural cost of awkward location was thus elided; the equally good claim of anyone in the remote reaches of Brooklyn for subsidized travel to a subway station was callously ignored.

Nor was this all. In New York and elsewhere, as everyone knows, automobile and truck owners are numerous, strong and politically powerful. Mr. Buckley yielded without evident thought to their power; he accepted their unspoken contention that there should be streets, including some brand-new ones, built and maintained for them to travel on without charge. The bicyclists are far less numerous, far less articulate and, even though healthier, not nearly so well organized. Mr. Buckley, to his credit, agreed to build them streets or paths, too. But in shocking contrast to his automatic surrender to the motorists' lobby, he proposed to charge the bicyclists fifteen cents every time they went on their thoroughfares. One could go on. The pristine Buckley proposed that people go into the market, retain their own policemen and deduct the cost from their city tax bill. By election time the vote-conscious Buckley was plumping for a fully socialized and even stronger police force.

All good conservatives in moments of doubt about doctrine appeal to Professor Milton Friedman of the University of Chicago [later of the Hoover Institution on War, Revolution and Peace at Stanford University]. He is, as Mr. Buckley notes in this volume, their highest priest. Yet I shudder to think of Professor Friedman's reaction to the foregoing, especially to that five-cent fare. Only one brief election campaign and Mr. Buckley has become to conservatism what Leon Trotsky was to Soviet socialism and Nikita Khrushchev was to the Stalinist tradition.

The most interesting part of this chronicle, at least from the purely scientific point of view, is Mr. Buckley's retreat from principle. But a greater portion of the book tells of his troubles with the press. And he early on gives the reason: it's that damn market again. Nothing was ever so good in theory, so intolerable in politics. "For reasons perfectly understandable in commercial terms," writes Buckley, "the press cares about the scandal, much less about subsequent developments tending to dissipate the scandal — less, in a word, about exact history, exactly understood." This was tough. For throughout the campaign, Mr. Buckley was engaged in precise and sensitive delineations that the press simply couldn't grasp and, after explanation, wouldn't later report. On the aforementioned matter of the garbage, he never advocated throwing it out the window; he merely said that this was as justified a form of protest against Mayor Lindsay as its use against the denial of minority rights. In a famous speech to the New York socialized police under the auspices of the Holy Name Society, he didn't approve police behavior in Selma, Alabama; he was merely critical of those who, on encountering it, complained. He didn't attack any minority, but he sternly denounced the claim by minorities to special political consideration. He never opposed the integration of schools, but he did insist (as would I, in fact) that it be subordinate to sound education.

As stated, these distinctions are quite clear. But in the heat of a New York political battle, warmed further by Mr. Buckley, the reporters missed the points to a man. Now with this book members of the press have a chance to get straightened out at last, and I hope they take it. Perhaps the only thing missing is some guide to when Mr. Buckley intends — as seems occasionally the case — to imply a trifle more than his words convey; he is not at all bad at that. Still, one can only applaud Mr. Buckley's effort to hold the reporters to the highest standards of fairness and precision. And one reflects with real satisfaction that his own *National Review* will henceforth, no doubt, conform to the Justinian standards now prescribed by its editor. I wonder if it isn't just as well that Joseph R. McCarthy didn't live to see the day. Joe was not a subtle man; he could never have risen to Mr. Buckley's new standard, to his insistence on "exact history, exactly understood." In consequence, the late senator would have taken terrible punishment, poor man, at the hands of his old friend.

When Mr. Buckley announced his candidacy last year, a New York friend of mine, who is a pillar of such reform as is currently available in the city, commented that the new entry into the race ensured, at least, that the campaign would not be without amusement. One day last winter, while Bill and I were both in Switzerland skiing, he called and asked me to accompany him down a mountain of modest difficulty. He was then working on this book, and I found myself exploiting the opportunity of our mutual athletic endeavor to offer advice on his writing. I advised him to forswear all temptations to statesmanship and give rein to his genuine talent for humor, invective and malevolence. He didn't entirely reject this wise counsel; there are instances of all three in the book, and they are excellent of their kind. But serious purpose does intrude, and that, given the purpose, firm and infirm, is too bad.

DIPLOMAT*

(1974)

Let no one doubt that the United Nations, though it is one of the principal claims of New York City to civic distinction, is greatly ignored by New Yorkers and their newspapers. Almost no one knew — and there was almost no press mention — of the appointment last year of William F. Buckley, Jr., to the American delegation to the Twenty-eighth Session of the General Assembly, with special responsibility for human rights, a designation not to be compared with putting Spiro Agnew in charge of the IRS but certainly on a par with President Ford's assignment of Secretary of Agriculture Earl Butz, no friend of low food prices, to the recently retitled Cost of Living Council.

I, also, was unaware of the appointment, and my innocence is even less to be forgiven, for I know Mr. Buckley well, consider him an excellent companion and have often debated with him for pleasure and what has seemed to be adequate compensation. I also now learn that I was responsible, in a marginal way, for his elevation. In 1969, Buckley was nominated by President Nixon to the United States Advisory Commission on Information, but Senator William Fulbright held up approval by the Senate Foreign Relations Committee. I wrote to

*This was a review, originally published in *New York* magazine, of *United Nations Journal* by William F. Buckley, Jr. (New York: G. P. Putnam's, 1974).

support the candidate, pointing out that the commission was the single most functionless component of the entire federal bureaucracy, the then still extant Subversive Activities Control Board possibly excepted, and it was, thus, an ideal place for a man of Mr. Buckley's distinctive views. Senator Fulbright replied immediately that he saw much depth to my argument, and soon afterward Mr. Buckley was approved. When Buckley's UN appointment was under consideration last year, one question in the administration was whether Fulbright would agree to it. It was finally decided that, having gone along once, he would go along again. And so it developed.

This was not entirely unfortunate, for Mr. Buckley's adverse impact on human rights seems to have been wholly negligible. And he has now written an account of his tour of duty, if that is the term, that is interesting, very informative and highly amusing. It does, of course, have to be approached in the appropriate frame of mind. Charles Taft, commenting on the frequent references to his brother Robert's fine mind, once said that it was the excellent instrument Bob used to reach the wrong conclusion. The same is true of Mr. Buckley's typewriter. Buckley greatly prefers the rich to the poor, the strong to the weak, and is powerfully committed to the proposition that virtue lies with big and adequately militant, though suitably non-Communist, battalions. All this the reader must know and ignore. In the United Nations Buckley found himself ideologically committed to the South Africans and the Portuguese, not because they were white but because they were the last available exponents of colonialism and the rule of the many by the few. (The discovery by the Portuguese, not long after Mr. Buckley's service ended, that their imperialism was a costly anachronism must have been a keen disappointment to him.) All this, too, must be ignored, as it can be with surprising ease.

What remains is by far the best description presently available of day-to-day life in the United Nations and in the American delegation, of the related and supporting operations of the Department of State and of the associated protocol and ceremony. Speeches, staff meetings, dinners, committee discussions, negotiations and the principal performers are described with high professional skill. One forgets that such matters are meant to be boring. There is even advantage in having the account from someone with the Buckley *Weltanschauung*, if it can be so enhanced. Works by writers of more initial sympathy for the UN have had an inevitable gloss and are cluttered with injunctions to the reader as to what should be believed. The Buckley instinct is to make all behavior somewhat smaller, or anyhow worse, than life. This is more plausible and certainly more interesting than the views of those who improve on reality. And, as noted, Mr. Buckley doesn't seriously invite belief.

Nor do the distinguished guests of the city much suffer. I was previously, to my loss, unaware of the existence of Jamil Baroody, for many, many years deputy permanent representative of the Kingdom of Saudi Arabia to the United Nations. Despite his natural sympathy for the Saudi Arabian version of democracy, Buckley clashed with Baroody, and the book leaves one with the feeling that Baroody, though not the most succinct or logical of parliamentarians, is, in fact, one of the most shrewd, acute and interesting people around. Buckley is especially good in describing the frequently tendentious and implausible oratory at the UN. This does set one wondering what he would say were he similarly exposed to his political co-religionists in Washington. Were he to surrender to consistency even slightly, what would he say of the oratory of Strom Thurmond or Jesse Helms?

Also quite wonderful, as well as reassuring, is the way the United Nations captured Buckley. As his labors, as they might loosely be called, continued, he became quite absorbed in the work of the organization and emerged at the end, if not a devout supporter, at least with a considerable commitment to its tasks. The ability of the UN so to inspire faith has always been one of its strengths, and evidently no material is too resistant. Mr. Buckley, to be sure, makes a routine disavowal of such faith, but the disavowal is disavowed by the book itself.

Equally impressive was the way the Department of State and the United States Mission to the United Nations tamed Buckley while, at the same time, keeping him right in there as a member of the team. At a dinner for the U.S. delegation and staff given by Ambassador John Scali in the opening days of the session, Buckley proposed that the United States seek support for an invitation to Alexander Solzhenitsyn to address the General Assembly. It was the kind of fresh, original thought that all must have been expecting from him, and certainly the State Department people could not have handled it better. They reacted with real enthusiasm; got into the parliamentary details involved; worked these through to a possible solution; concluded that, with luck, the invitation could go forward within five years; decided that some other country should take the initiative; agreed that Albania and Mexico were the only possibilities; and concluded that neither would do. Of Buckley's proposal nothing more was then heard. Later, when he thought to offer a few of his own ideas on human rights, he was reminded that all American delegates were, under the legislation governing such matters, required to support the position of the President who had appointed them. And when he proposed to give a speech of less than spectacular content on freedom of international movement as a human right — for Russian scholars wanting to leave Russia as distinct, perhaps, from American subversives — John Scali praised it warmly and had it suppressed. Once, at the beginning of his tour, Mr.

Buckley got the permission of his State Department trainer to enter an objection to a highly irrelevant speech by Mr. Baroody, but he was later charged with exercising personal discretion in the matter. He was eventually forgiven when he explained that he was, indeed, acting after proper consultation. It was, one senses, a very good way for the department people to make the point about who was in control. Through all this discipline, Buckley was kept in the very best of humor. I finished the book with a marked appreciation of John Scali; he is a deft and powerful operator.

In the winter of 1961, when liberals foregathered at the White House, State Department and Pentagon in the early days of the Kennedy administration, their processing by the bureaucracy was a wonderful thing to watch. Admittedly, some of those so assembling had expressed doubts about Secretary Dulles, the eternal verities of the cold war and whether the American destiny was completely coordinate with the defeat of the Pathet Lao in Laos. The people at State and elsewhere were pleased to see scholars who were capable of thought. But they continued to stress, beyond all else, the reality of the Communist menace. Everyone knew that the Communists were omniscient, omnipotent and not given to rest. To be useful, you had to be aboard in this battle. We newcomers were greatly valued, but we had to recognize facts and cooperate or we would be in terrible trouble.

Most of those arriving in Washington came to accept that they must be realistic. The cold war had to be fought; it would now be done at a higher level of intelligence and grammar. Some of us, however, were depressed. Reading Buckley on his tour at the UN, seeing how he was brought aboard *détente,* one realizes that this bureaucratic operation works both ways. There is a lot to be said for it.

8

BARBARA WARD:
TWO TRIBUTES

IN ADMIRATION*
(1979)

Barbara Ward Jackson, as will be evident from these pieces, I greatly loved.

Barbara Ward, a one-time editor of *The Economist,* a one-time Columbia University professor, for two or three exceptionally agreeable years my colleague teaching economic development at Harvard, is a prolific writer of books on economics and politics and in recent years a member — a life peer — of the House of Lords. She has also, for a long time, been in exceptionally poor health. Instead of surrendering to tedious pain and reading Trollope, she accumulated and read every recent government and United Nations document and every current book or research publication in accessible language on energy, nuclear energy, the recycling of wastes, the environment, food, agriculture, post-Keynesian economics, the modern city and its problems, housing, the bitter tasks and prospects of the poor countries and a half-dozen other equally urgent or repellent subjects. She then wrote *Progress for a Small Planet,* selecting and summarizing from this information and giving judiciously, sometimes too cautiously, her own view.

By all accepted standards of scholarly and political discussion, it is a terrible thing she has done. No one, it is held, can speak competently over such a wide range of knowledge. Also, she writes on deeply technical matters in clear English and without jargon; this doesn't inspire confidence. Obscurity, besides covering up incomplete thought, is often meant to suggest that the thought was deep.

Worst of all, Barbara Ward retains an absolute conviction that by social and cooperative effort and by intelligent resort to government, people can solve in a reasonably prompt way most of the problems by which, through fear or in reality, they are oppressed, including those

---

*This was a review, originally published in *Book World* of *The Washington Post,* of *Progress for a Small Planet* by Barbara Ward (New York: W. W. Norton, 1979).

of dwindling energy supply, air pollution, deteriorating urban living, inadequate nutrition and lagging economic development. She has often in the past been criticized for this kind of optimism, but she hasn't learned. This book comes at an especially inauspicious moment, when so many are proclaiming so ardently the virtues of self-centered individualism for an increasingly interdependent world and when the really sophisticated politicians are joining the revolt of the rich against the poor. Certainly the author gets low marks for timing. No book could strike a more bizarre note in this year of Arthur Laffer, Milton Friedman and good old Howard Jarvis.

Accepting the risk of eccentricity, I found both her information and her faith quite wonderful. It had not previously occurred to me that solar energy (with some geothermal support) now raises the indoor temperature of our house in Cambridge, Massachusetts, from minus 240 degrees centigrade to within a few degrees of a livable level even in the middle of a New England winter and that I rely on President Carter's energy management for only the minuscule fraction that remains. While I doubt that, as she avers, it is "a nagging concern in open societies . . . [that] stock options, business expenses, the 'three-martini lunch' are added to the basically still feudal differences in levels of pay, say, between a black doorman and the head of General Motors," I do think it should produce more nagging than it does, especially in a time when efforts are being made to restrain wages and cut back on welfare.

On various other matters I also think Barbara Ward is too sanguine. She sets much store by public and community initiative and cooperation in poor countries. I am persuaded, as was Marx (coincidentally, I, of course, hasten to say), that economic development is itself an education in social cohesiveness and cooperation. In consequence, the poor lands — China, with her ancient experience in government, being a possible exception — are deeply handicapped in most forms of joint and public effort. They face with great difficulty the large administrative tasks of social and socialist experiment.

However, though I'm not as optimistic as Barbara Ward, I would be ashamed, after reading her book, to think that I am in any way disposed to be cynical. I hope that thousands of others will read it and be similarly moved and improved.

IN MEMORY*

(1981)

Barbara Ward, as mostly she was called, was my friend for thirty-five years, one of the closest anywhere in the world. As I will tell, I first

*This piece was a memorial tribute in *The Economist*, June 6, 1981.

met her in Berlin in 1946. A little later, *The New York Times* sent me, in a routine way, one of her books to review. I read it with a growing awareness that this was not, indeed, a routine volume; *The West at Bay* was a wonderfully lucid, calm and persuasive statement of the problems that the postwar industrial countries had to solve were their peacetime achievement to match their wartime success. And along with the problems were possible solutions, a more demanding thing. I called *The Times* to say that this was a much more important book than the editors imagined, and the result was a front-page review. This helped to launch our friendship; Barbara was never negligent of such attention. Nor, I hasten to say, am I. As always, like attracted like.

Then in later years she came to Harvard to join Edward Mason and me in one of the pioneer courses in economic development — in the economics of the poor lands. She may well have doubled both the interest and the attendance. I also encountered her in the political family of Adlai Stevenson and as a friend of John F. Kennedy and Lyndon Johnson. Once, when President Johnson, in an imaginative moment, mentioned in a press conference that he was taking time off for his reading, an unnecessarily intrusive reporter asked him what books. LBJ passed quickly over the Gideon Bible and, happily, remembered Barbara Ward. Barbara's last book, *Progress for a Small Planet*, was surely as informed, informing, compassionate and practical as her first, and it was written long after anyone of lesser courage and determination would have surrendered to the relentlessly spreading cancer that, for nearly two decades, she had so bravely resisted.

As were so many others, I was greatly instructed by Barbara, but that was not the basis of our friendship. Far more, it was based on her talent for wide-ranging conversation. And a shared delight in the mildly insane. This last I will greatly miss. There were elements of this in our first encounter in Berlin in 1946; I allow myself here an excerpt from my memoirs:

> Edward Mason and I were housed on Am Hirschsprungstrasse in the house of Bernhard Rust, the former Nazi education minister. Of vast scale, it featured, with much other vulgarity, lascivious beds, gilt plumbing and sunken baths of synthetic malachite. One day I traveled to the British zone to collect Barbara Ward, later Baroness Jackson, then on the staff of *The Economist,* a diverse and talented writer, a woman of rare and slender beauty with a gift for effective and often devastating expression. In the car on the way back she eloquently denounced the unaccustomed luxury in which officers of the British occupation forces were living in Hamburg and Berlin. Then she came to our house.*

---

*John Kenneth Galbraith, *A Life in Our Times* (Boston: Houghton Mifflin, 1981), p. 253.

In 1968, Harvard awarded the honorary degree of Doctor of Laws *(sic)* to the Shah of Iran. Barbara, who already had an honorary doctorate from the university, sat with me on the platform. In accordance with Harvard custom, the names of those receiving the degrees had been kept secret. When the Shah, flanked by his security guards, arrived, all rose. Barbara and I, along with Martin Peretz, now the publisher of *The New Republic,* kept visibly to our seats. It was not a protest we had agreed on, only our common response to Harvard's discovery that the Shah was an exponent of academic and political liberty.

And other such moments we shared.

I do not weep for Barbara. When I called her a few weeks ago in the hospital, I could not doubt from our brief exchange that life had become at last truly insupportable. I weep instead for myself and all who similarly rejoiced in this lovely, beloved, brilliant and accomplished companion.

9

ROBERTSON DAVIES

(1982)

Among the few prerogatives of the president of the American Academy and Institute of Arts and Letters is an influential voice in selecting who will give the Blashfield Lecture, which in the view of the academy and, one trusts, others is the most distinguished literary lectureship of the year. Without difficulty I persuaded my fellow members to invite Robertson Davies in 1985. I have, as I said on introducing him, never thought it necessary to rise entirely above patronage — in this case for a fellow native son — but rarely, if ever, has favoritism in such matters been so rewarding. The lecture was imaginative, literate and otherwise compelling, as one would expect from reading Davies's novels.

This essay was written at the request of The New York Times Book Review.

Many years ago I learned that nothing gives more pleasure than the well-perceived failure of an allegedly educated man to know what he is supposed to know. I gave such pleasure some ten years past when a friend and neighbor of marked scholarly attainment discovered that I didn't know about Robertson Davies. "And you a Canadian, too!"

I've since read nearly all of Davies's nondramatic works, and I now find occasional reward myself in encountering academic colleagues professionally well grounded in modern language and literature who don't know about Davies or who dissemble in a highly transparent way when asked if they do. They should, indeed, be ashamed; he is one of the most learned, amusing and otherwise accomplished novelists of our day and, as I shall urge, of our century.

As to my own early ignorance, I don't admit to any special guilt because of being a Canadian. Although I am fond in a normal way of the land of my birth, I have never set store by that branch of literature which seeks a special Canadian identity, psyche or scene. The country is geographically too vast and ethnically too diverse to allow of anything of the sort. Robertson Davies's novels have their setting in Canada, but they are for the world.

Davies's most notable achievement is his Deptford trilogy — *Fifth Business, The Manticore* and *World of Wonders* — all of which touch upon the life of a schoolmaster, one Dunstan Ramsay, who comes (or perhaps escapes) from a small town in southwestern Ontario. The imaginary Deptford is closely modeled on Thamesville, Ontario, a village of five hundred souls some twenty or thirty miles from the slightly larger town of Dutton (population around eight hundred in the early part of this century), near which I was born and to which I journeyed by horse and buggy for my high school instruction.

Everything about Deptford-*cum*-Thamesville has a powerful ring of truth. The social hierarchy of Thamesville was like Dutton's; similarly, the resulting social tensions among the young. Political and other civic responsibilities were entrusted to the same solemn and extensively self-selected leaders; a rewarding sense of superiority was provided by the equally available jokesmiths, drunks, idlers and idiots. The Protestant denominations were the same in both towns, and the congregations were differentiated not by doctrine or faith — matters that no one discussed, much less understood — but by accident of birth. In both towns there was a deep concern for third-person misbehavior. Sexual intercourse between consenting adults duly united in matrimony was severely suspect; any other variation was a subject for hushed but obsessive conversation, a terrible thing made worse by the frequency of occurrence. In one novel Davies tells of the prayer of the good Protestants who thus transgress: "O God, forgive me, but for God's sake keep this under Your hat."

Davies's father was the editor, publisher and owner of the weekly newspaper in Thamesville, but when his son was still young, the family departed for the more considerable town of Renfrew, northwest of Ottawa. It is, therefore, of a schoolboy's memories of a small town that Robertson Davies writes. He went on to Upper Canada College, the most unabashedly elitist of Canadian preparatory schools, and to Queen's University and Balliol College, Oxford. While in England, he became interested in the theater, and in the years just before the outbreak of World War II, he went to London, where he had small parts and a peripheral role in stage management at the Old Vic and in its theater school. In later years he has written plays with, one judges, consistently disappointing results. (His productions have had limited audiences, limited runs or both.) But his knowledge of the theater has provided him, no reader can doubt, with both material and mood for his novels. One sometimes imagines, on reading them, that he is seeing his story as on a stage.

Davies returned to Canada to become literary editor of *Saturday*

Night, the Canadian journal of the arts, politics, public affairs and good thoughts, and editor and eventually publisher of *The Peterborough Examiner,* an evening newspaper in a city of some fifty thousand people in the scenically attractive but agriculturally unpromising countryside seventy-five miles northeast of Toronto. In his twenty years at *The Examiner* he made it into one of the best newspapers in Canada or on the American continent by the simple device of insisting (as he has said) that the standards of excellence claimed by papers in New York, London or Zürich were equally applicable, if not always equally achievable, in what the untactful would call the Canadian back country. One reason that the paper was good was his own writing — sharp, amusing and rich in fantasy. His articles were later assembled into books purporting to be observations on the life, times, reflections and encounters of one Samuel Marchbanks.

Then, in 1962, Davies quit the routine of a newspaperman to become a professor of English at the University of Toronto and master of its Massey College, a relatively new institution devoted to graduate study. His example is one that all in the newspaper business should contemplate. The first of the Deptford trilogy, *Fifth Business,* came out in 1970 to a select audience; the other two came along in the five years following. The years at the university also brought a notable amount of literary criticism, casual writing and essays. And now a new novel, *The Rebel Angels,* is about to make its appearance. It is obvious that he has carried over into his literary life the work habits of a newspaperman, a disconcerting thing for his academic colleagues.

Davies is a fine writer — deft, resourceful and very funny. But his claim to distinction is his imagination, which he supports with an extraordinary range of wholly unpredictable information. *Fifth Business* is, supposedly, the autobiography of the aforementioned Dunstan Ramsay, the long-time history master and one-time headmaster of a school for privileged boys in Toronto; it is written in the form of a protest to the present headmaster against the account given of Ramsay's life and services on his retirement in 1969. (It could be the longest communication in the history of such discontents, and both the reader and author forget for long chapters that it is so intended.)

The school actually figures only marginally in the story, which sketches both Ramsay's overseas duty in World War I (when, slightly to his horror, he won a Victoria Cross and lost a leg) and his sad, affectionate association with a Mrs. Dempster (whose mental illness and confinement he traces to an accident for which he feels a grave and continuing responsibility). There is more than a suggestion here of Davies's interest in psychology, which becomes a major theme in his later novels. But Ramsay himself has a more esoteric interest in religious history and, particularly, the lives and times of the saints, a subject that creeps extensively into *Fifth Business.*

In *World of Wonders,* the last volume of the trilogy, Mrs. Dempster's son (she was married to an aggressively mean local preacher) tells the story of his life as a famous magician, a profession he entered after he was abducted at an early age by a carnival that came through the town of Deptford. Here Davies reveals what seems a truly astonishing knowledge of the principles and practice of magic and assorted sleights-of-hand — and, if less surprisingly, a great knowledge of the theater. But merely to mention these subjects is to do less than justice to the range of Davies's information.

Fitzgerald, Hemingway and even Faulkner dealt with a world with which the reader feels some connection; similarly located and circumstanced, one might see what they saw. Davies deals with matters far beyond ordinary experience; yet one finds oneself taking his word for it and according him full faith and credit. Even if he invents the way a magician practices his art, one has to believe that the invention is at least the equal of the original.

The new novel, *The Rebel Angels* — no one should try to explain Davies's titles — yields to none of the others in either diverse and arcane knowledge or complexity of theme. Its principal setting is the College of St. John and the Holy Ghost, one of the older church-related colleges of the University of Toronto and known, inevitably, to all but its rector as Spook. The action spills over into a neighboring college called Ploughwright, which bears a certain resemblance to Massey College. (I imagine that the name Ploughwright itself owes something to the once great Massey-Harris farm equipment company that provided the Massey endowment.)

The story concerns the intricately intertwined lives of Maria Magdalena Theotoky, a supremely beautiful graduate student of Hungarian, Polish and Gypsy origin who has a special interest in Rabelais; the Reverend Simon Darcourt, who teaches New Testament Greek; Brother John Parlabane, a brilliantly articulate and profoundly troublesome dropout from academic and religious life; and, although the list is far from complete, a highly offensive professor of Renaissance European culture and related matters named Urquhart McVarish.

There are alternating chapters by Maria Theotoky and Simon Darcourt, and the device allows two different accounts and perceptions of the same flow of events. It is less confusing, once one becomes accustomed to it, than might be expected; in fact, it serves exceedingly well. The action proceeds from the death of a certain Francis Cornish, who has made his businesslike nephew his executor and three professors (including McVarish and Darcourt) the advisers on the disposition of his estate, which includes a vast, uncatalogued collection of paintings and old and distinguished books and manuscripts. The story continues with almost everyone falling in love with Maria or having his life hilariously disrupted by Parlabane and goes on through college dinners and Gypsy cuisine to an extravagant homosexual liaison and a murder and suicide. The lovely Maria then, in the only commonplace development of the novel, marries the most unexpected of her suitors.

There is a convention that, in describing a novel, one shouldn't give away the plot. But the attraction here for me is in the style of the story, the fun, and in the truly massive array of information the book, like its predecessors, conveys: the lore of the Gypsies of Eastern Europe, the scientific investigation of human feces, the work and times of Philippus Aureolus Paracelsus and of Rabelais, the theory and practice of shoplifting, the manners and morals of art collectors and their dependent scholars and much, much more.

It is a fair comment that one does not ever come into close proximity with Davies's characters. Maria Theotoky is exceedingly beautiful — so one is repeatedly told. And sexually very compelling. But the reader must take the author's word for it; her beauty and sexuality do not otherwise emerge. And with the others on the stage the reader in the audience is never deeply involved. I don't offer this as a criticism; for me at least it is pleasant to read of people who are immensely attractive, knowledgeable and interesting whom I am not impelled either to love or to hate.

Not all of the events in a Davies novel, as distinct from the information, are plausible. In *World of Wonders* the young Dempster, who eventually becomes Magnus Eisengrim, the master magician, was kidnapped from Deptford by a carnival company after a homosexual rape by one of its members. But in real life the criminals would not have escaped; they would have been pursued relentlessly throughout the Dominion, as it was then called, and with a certain breathless appreciation. Crime was rare then in Canada and greatly respected.

Dunstan Ramsay's war wound and his long survival in a coma under the care of a lovely English nurse also take some believing. So, I thought, does the seduction of Maria in *The Rebel Angels,* and so also quite a bit of *The Manticore,* the second novel in the trilogy. In it, David Staunton, son of Dunstan Ramsay's friend and rival, explores through Jungian analysis his own response to the death of his father, who for unknown reasons drove his Cadillac at high speed off a dock and deep into Lake Ontario. But again, if all novels excluded the unlikely, the production of them would drop rather more severely than new housing starts.

This brings me back to economics, my own field of presumed learning and one of the few to which Robertson Davies almost never adverts. In economic prediction there is a large element of wishful thought, as all but some financial reporters and the hopelessly gullible know. This is now evident in the Reagan economists' account of the benign consequences of a large deficit. In literary matters things are quite different. Even allowing for the bias that comes from our joint provenance in the flat and generally fertile countryside of southwestern Ontario and association with the same university, I can still be completely objective about the future of Davies's novels. They will be recognized with the very best work of this century. And they will continue to sell and be read. And those who say in the years ahead that they don't know about Robertson Davies will be a source of even more amusement than was I when I so confessed.

10

A. J. P. TAYLOR*

(1983)

In my earlier review of Malcolm Muggeridge's Chronicles, *I said that auto-biography is an increasingly depraved form. In Britain it is the last futile gasp of the more forgettable of British politicians. In the United States it is a minor source of revenue for former public officials — national security advisers, pres-idential assistants, secretaries of state and defense — with special emphasis on malefactors and those who have otherwise abused the public trust. And, increas-ingly, we have the lifelong confessions of the more accomplished embezzlers and financial prestidigitators, the more spectacular rapists and criminals of the time. Publishers now wait for them outside the courtroom or consort with them im-mediately on arrest. But, as I say of Muggeridge, there are exceptions to this sordid trend, and yet another is A. J. P. — to his friends, Alan — Taylor.*

When a historian writes in a highly entertaining way for a large au-dience and when, additionally, he takes seriously his television ap-pearances and does a regular column for a medium-low-brow newspaper (*The Sunday Express* in London), there are deep and serious grounds for questioning his scholarly and academic credentials. Or, more pre-cisely, they are certain to be questioned, and this is especially likely in England, although there, perhaps, the television is slightly more to be forgiven. Such public exposure over a long, extraordinarily varied, interesting and productive life has been the problem of A. J. P. Taylor, one he has managed to surmount brilliantly. The reason is that when he has turned to his historical writing, he has been as careful, even meticulous, as the scholars of recognized competence in his field, and, in addition, he has shown a phenomenally greater capacity than they for continuous, committed labor. I couldn't possibly claim to have read

*This was a review, originally published in *Book World* of *The Washington Post*, of *A Personal History* by A. J. P. Taylor (New York:1983).

all twenty-eight of his books; I have read, among others, those on the causes and courses of the two world wars and, needless to say, many of his essays on history and the work of other historians. All have seemed to me extremely good, and so certainly is this autobiography.

It begins with his family sources in the west of England, with particular reference to his father, an affluent cotton merchant and mill manager, who, along with his mother, had an overriding commitment to Liberal politics, radical reform and the working classes. From the parents came the son's lifelong leaning to the left, including a Communist passage, a continuing but markedly unorthodox association with the Labour Party and an often eloquent identification with good or lost causes, ranging from outspoken opposition to the Suez misadventure in 1956 to support of nuclear disarmament later and now.

After an early Quaker education, of which, like his family history, he is required by his historian's conscience to tell slightly more than one needs, he went on to Oriel College, Oxford, thence to study in Vienna (from which came his later interest in the Hapsburgs), to a teaching post at Manchester University, and from there to his enduring association with Magdalen College, Oxford, an association involving a remarkable combination of love and discontent. (His American publisher describes Alan Taylor in the publicity for the book as the son of "well-to-do trade unionists," the Ford Lecturer in English History at Oxford — one year he gave the prestigious Ford Lectures there — an honorary fellow of Magdalen, something he became only after his retirement, and, perhaps thoughtfully, changes his youthful Communism to mere harmless socialism. For shame! Publishers should at least scan quickly the books they publish.)

Within the framework of his account of his academic career, Taylor tells of his books, his sometimes revised view of what he has written and of the controversy his writings aroused. The most notable of the rows was over his case that Adolf Hitler had no master plan but acted in response to opportunity or seeming opportunity and out of what was a far from atypical conception of German destiny. Taylor professes some unconvincing discontent that what was once an aberrant argument has now become the conventional view. There are other matters on which his conclusions, originally deemed exceptional or even bizarre, have gained substantial acceptance.

Taylor tells also of his on-and-off life at the BBC, which he vastly enjoyed and where he was a recurrent object of grave political concern and of protest emanating from the highest government levels. The notion that the BBC is somehow immune to political pressure is a self-serving myth of that great organization that no one should ever accept. He tells of his colleagues, friends and associates and, with a notable excision, of his family life. One of his less obscure acquaintances, who moved in for a time at Oxford to live and drink at the Taylors' expense, was Dylan Thomas. Taylor remembers him with unrelieved distaste, dislike and possibly even abhorrence.

Taylor is very interesting, perhaps without wholly intending it, on the anthropology of academic life in Britain. In the United States this can involve intricately accomplished political designs, and those who have become learned in academic political practice have long been a threat in the larger Washington struggle. (No fewer than four Harvard faculty members — Henry Kissinger, James Schlesinger, John Dunlop and Daniel Patrick Moynihan — made it to, or very near, the top in recent Republican administrations and did well with the Democrats also.) But one does not deprecate the achievement of American scholars in saying that there is a range of imaginative and durable viciousness in the British university infighting that outdoes our best efforts and makes especially nice reading. So it is with Taylor's accounts of scholarly finger twisting, backbiting, garroting and occasional knifing at Manchester and, at a much higher level of artistry, during his many years at Oxford. I enjoyed reading of this very much.

In the preface to this book Taylor tells that when the manuscript was first submitted to his British publisher, the latter's lawyer identified seventy-six possible bases for a libel suit. All had to be cleaned up, and the result, he thinks, is a temperate tone, for which he apologizes. I doubt that the reader will share his distress. A more serious problem concerns his personal life. He must be the first, or anyhow one of the first, Oxford dons ever to admit publicly to, much less describe, a heterosexual sex life. Taylor has been married three times, but his second wife, the sister of a prominent British politician and Cabinet officer, forbade any mention whatever of their association. In consequence, when they had children, to whom Taylor is devoted, these appear, as it were, out of nowhere. No conception, no pregnancy, no birth, not even a virgin birth — just a gift direct from heaven. It's all slightly implausible. Perhaps this was British libel law again; I hadn't previously realized it could exclude mention of marriage. At least until very recent times this liaison, in England as in the United States, has been thought quite respectable and also, in a general way, a matter of public record. This, however, is a minor complaint about an otherwise excellent book.

· III ·

HARVARD:
FAIR AND
SOMETIMES OVERCAST

OVER A MATTER of fifty years and more, my relations with Harvard have been generally very amiable. But occasionally I have sought improvement in this great and ancient institution. Few things are regarded with greater unease than criticism from within.

THE CASE FOR
CONSTITUTIONAL REFORM
AT HARVARD

(1968)

When this "Case" was published in the Harvard Alumni Bulletin, *soon to become* Harvard Magazine, *it provoked an unprecedented response from Harvard graduates and the university officialdom. All of it was unfavorable. The disapproving letters are not here; as my editor agreed, one cannot ask for permission to reprint that about which one intends to be mean. I venture to think, however, that the content will be evident.*

As the last of the reproving documents came in and my "Reply" was published, the student revolt of 1969, as it was called, broke out. The university administration, overly excited and sadly out of touch with the attitudes of the students, called on the Massachusetts State Police, who, not without enjoyment, hurtled the dissenters out of University Hall, the principal administration building, which they had occupied. There was some damage, if not to life, then to limb. These youngsters, wanting greatly to be at Harvard, greatly pleased, even proud, to be there, were perhaps the least dangerous rebels in all the long history of revolution. If they had simply been left alone, boredom would, as ever with students, soon have solved the problem.

In ensuing months, calm and competent faculty members were mobilized to have charge of matters, a Faculty Council was brought into being to bridge the constitutional hiatus here identified, and the president of the university moved gently and innocuously into retirement. The letters of protest, I allow myself to say, did not continue.

The book by Nobel Prize–winning James Watson to which reference is made was The Double Helix, *an exceedingly interesting and amusing account of his adventures and discoveries in biological science and a best seller when ultimately published by Atheneum. As I tell in the next piece, "Innocence as Exculpation," it was vetoed by the Harvard authorities primarily because, in speaking of his fellow scientists, he was thought to lack tact.*

I have argued in the past that the governing structure of the older and more mature American universities is obsolete. Specifically, what should have been a transitional arrangement for a particular stage of development has been allowed to become permanent. In the last century a governing board of businessmen, bankers and lawyers (along with churchmen) who were selected for their respectability and general eminence in the world of affairs made a measure of sense. The internal life of the seminary was simple; such a board could have a fair knowledge of its needs and problems. It inspired practical confidence in the minds of prospective donors and persuaded them to part with funds. And it acted as a buffer against heresy hunters while, as needed, suppressing heresy within.

In the modern and mature university this form of government is an anachronism. A lay board can, by its nature, have little comprehension of the vast and complex scientific and scholarly life of the university it presumes to govern. It is not clear that, given the strength of the university in the modern community, protection against outside witch hunters is necessary, and in any case the governing board is no longer thought of as providing it. (In state universities, in fact, it is a channel for bringing political views and obscurantist positions to bear on the faculty.) The suppression of internal heresy, to the extent that it exists, is no longer, even surreptitiously, a well-regarded function of a governing board. The latter has only a marginal relation to money raising in the older universities, for professors and deans in search of grants go directly to the government and the foundations. And for gifts and the annual accrual of funds that are available from the affluent as an alternative to being taxed, the professional money raiser is increasingly necessary. In modern times both the state and private corporations turn as a matter of course to university faculties for the discharge of complex practical tasks. Professors, rather more than members of governing boards, get called to Washington or to corporate headquarters. That businessmen, bankers or practicing lawyers have some capacity for managing things not vouchsafed to the professor no longer squares with the contemporary experience. Their eminence is associated with a period when a particular prestige came with personal economic success.

Few, I venture to think, will dispute that these changes have occurred. But we should not be surprised if their recitation has brought no passionate demand for action in a community like Harvard. On decisive matters such as appointments, curriculum and research, the faculty has long since assumed full power. The Board of Overseers and the Corporation may belong to another day, but surely, it has been said, the system works. Surely what has existed for so long is sufficiently sanctified that it should be tolerated, perhaps cherished. It may even be assumed that such is its sanctity that it should be spared discussion.

Or at least it was possible to believe all this until last spring [1968].

Then came the student explosion at Columbia University. There, a bad government had also been sanctified by time. There, it is now accepted as the conventional wisdom, the constitutional arrangements, which were designed originally for a small liberal arts college, were gravely at fault. Communication between a board chosen for personal economic eminence, an administration of limited imagination and competence and the faculty, students and surrounding community is agreed to have been seriously inadequate. There is now much talk of "restructuring." In consequence, no other institution, not even Harvard, can assume that its governing arrangements are adequate. When very specific defects arising from obsolescence can be listed, most readers of the *Harvard Alumni Bulletin* will, I believe, agree that introspection and reform are called for. Better act before rather than after there is trouble. Here are the plausible symptoms of constitutional obsolescence at Harvard:

1. The members of the principal governing board, the Corporation, are now wholly unknown to the faculty. Not a dozen faculty members could name them or recognize them on sight. This sufficiently suggests the limits on communication between the two bodies. The president is, in theory, a bridge between them, but it would surely be a miracle were he able to represent each to the other in all the innumerable aspects of university affairs. This means that the Corporation must act either on the basis of insufficient information or on none at all. Or it can, upon recognizing this to be the case, abdicate responsibility.

2. Although the foregoing problem has been partly solved by moving decisive academic power from the Corporation to the faculty, this transfer is by no means complete. Thus, the Corporation retains the power to appoint the president of the university. In the absence of communication, and given also the age of its members and their comparative lack of scientific and scholarly qualification, there is no reason to expect that in the future it will make a choice that will be approved by or will even be acceptable to the faculty. The possibilities for mischief here are obvious.

3. The Corporation is equally limited in qualification for its other appointive power. I found it interesting last year to inquire of members of the law school faculty if they agreed that they were insufficiently competent in their subject or insufficiently practiced in the arts of self-government to select their own dean. Did they agree that the decision should lie with the superior professional ability of the practicing lawyers on the Corporation? Their best answer was that they expected to be consulted on (and, in the end, to control) the appointment. In other words, the present governing procedures were tolerable only because they didn't apply.

4. The ultimate governing authority of any university is relevant to the erstwhile nonacademic concerns and aberrations of the students —

extracurricular activities of the traditional sort and unseemly and in-
discriminate resort to idleness, sex, alcohol and athletics. Here, in the
case of Harvard, the Corporation or rather its appointees have been
able to establish, by precept and instruction, acceptable standards for
student behavior. But it is hard to feel the same confidence in the
Corporation as the ultimate authority for dealing with student reaction
to the Vietnam war, to recruitment for the armed services or to weapons
manufacture, the draft or political action and protest. It would be
surprising were this body, representing as it does rather specific American political and social interests, able to speak or act in a fully mean-
ingful way on these matters. In the last year crises have been avoided
by *ad hoc* action while various window-dressing efforts at student-faculty
consultation have been contrived. The first could well fail in face of
some more serious emergency. The second, backed by no real authority
on the part of faculty participants, will not, one imagines, be taken very
seriously by students for very long.

5. There are disturbing signs that the narrow spectrum of political
and social opinion from which the membership of the Corporation has
anciently been drawn makes it unable to react sensitively to issues of
the real world. An informed and sophisticated governing body would
never have rejected James Watson's now famous book — without even
reading it, one is told. On a more important point I find myself reacting
with more acerbity. In the last three years no question has been as
important in and for the universities of the United States as the Vietnam
war. Had the academic community left the issue to be dealt with by
the students alone, their frustration, anger and sense of alienation and
rejection would have been extreme. At Harvard, as elsewhere, many
older members of the faculty and academic community have worked
hard to reverse public policy on this ghastly mistake and to develop
public understanding of the error. It cannot be said that they have had
much help or even encouragement from the university government,
either corporately or individually. On an issue of transcendent importance to the university the governing boards have been largely silent,
even by all outward signs indifferent.

6. I come now to a more difficult and less certain point. Under the
present structure, the growth of the university and related budgeting
are not subject to any overall design. The resources centrally controlled
by the Corporation are heavily committed to maintenance while growth
must depend on the availability of money from the federal government,
including the military establishment; from industry; from the energy
and connections of the relevant faculty members; or for disciplines that
are currently fashionable. Those not so favored must suffer. The remedy one imagines to be a strong budget committee, reflecting the full
scientific and scholarly competence of the faculty, to establish priorities

and to guide money raising and use in accordance with competently formulated goals. This is not in sight. Nor should nongovernance be mistaken for good governance. The fact that those in the well-nourished fields of study do not complain and the others see little hope in doing so should not persuade anyone that all is well.

Other deficiencies in the present government of the university could be cited, including, some of us have long supposed, in its fund-raising procedures. But enough has been said to suggest defects that are both real and dangerous. The experience of Columbia is there for all to read. And no one at Harvard will be persuaded by the view — permissible to J. Edgar Hoover, perhaps, but to few others — that trouble is purely the work of self-motivated agitators. Like the tip of an iceberg, agitators are always only the visible part of a larger mass.

The answer, to repeat, is to modernize the government of the university before rather than after trouble starts. The governing authority must have a range of professional and scholarly competence coordinate with the problems with which it must deal. This means vastly increased faculty participation in the government of the university or (as in guiding growth) replacing the present nongovernment. It means also a mechanism for informed, authoritative and socially sensitive communication with the students. And it calls for an informed and socially sensitive reaction, where this is required, to the world outside. It will impose responsibilities that many, perhaps most, faculty members, myself included, would happily avoid. A study looking to such modernization and the needed legislation should obviously get under way forthwith. There will be little pleasure in saying I told you so after present faults have been fully revealed by some crisis. It will be a pleasure, however, that those who urge modernization can hardly be expected to deny themselves if nothing is done.

REPLY

(1969)

In addition to a great number of letters sent to me and to the *Harvard Alumni Bulletin*, Mr. Richard R. Edmonds of *The Harvard Crimson* has published a rather telling critique of my article, and President Pusey has, along with offering one or two specific criticisms, suggested that I was wrong on "just about everything." I would like in this reply to respond to their points as well as to those in the larger correspondence, although I am a bit at a loss as to how to react to Mr. Pusey's observation beyond saying that some will think that what it offers in authority and comprehensiveness it may lack in more meticulous argument. I am also a trifle uncertain how to answer the letters of Mr. Alexander Cooper and Mr. James White, who anchor their objection not to the weaknesses of my case but to their dislike of me personally. This leaves me no remedy but to become lovable, a difficult thing to accomplish quickly after a lifetime largely devoted to cultivating the opposite traits. I rejoice in Mr. Jacobson and, to a point, in Mr. Stanley. However, I must tell Mr. Stanley that I am not an advocate of student participation in academic decision or administration. A university is a community of scholars responsibly devoted to conserving, enlarging and perpetuating knowledge. There must be certain standards of admission to this responsibility, and neither the registration nor the brief tenure of the student is enough. That a university should be sensitive to the needs of the students and allow them to govern their own lives is, of course, taken for granted. Now let me turn to my more serious critics.

On one matter I do not escape unscathed. I argued that the present line of authority running from the Corporation and the president through their appointees, the deans, is not well designed to deal with the social tensions within the modern university. Mr. Coolidge, Mr. Cabot and Mr. Edmonds have all pointed out that, as regards the students, the faculty already has decisive power — more than it uses. They are right. The problem is not a constitutional one; it is how to bring this authority more effectively to bear.

On other points I must stand firm. Mr. Coolidge's argument, made also by Mr. Pusey, that selection of the president by the faculty would lead to political division cannot be accepted for a moment. That is the case made against all democracy, all self-government. It places my distinguished friends in the dubious company of those who, on following the troops into the presidential palace, always proclaim that they are sparing the unhappy country in question the perils and obscenities of political faction. It is the case that could be made for having the President of the United States selected by the Supreme Court. It does not deal at all with my point, which, while conceding that the self-governed may select badly, argues that authority in the form of the Corporation — which is unknown to the faculty, culturally and psychologically distant therefrom and from the complexities of modern science and the diversities of modern scholarship — will most likely do worse.

As to the selection of the deans, Mr. Coolidge and also Mr. Pusey seem to be saying that, through consultation, the faculty now has the effective voice. If so, there should be no objection to giving substance to the reality and making selection by the faculty a matter of formal procedure. A great university, devoted avowedly to truth, should not need to go in for elaborate self-deception. Presumably the faculties in question will govern better if it is clearly recognized that the responsibility is theirs.

Mr. Coolidge is doubtful about foreign precedents and suggests that in England control by the faculty has periodically led to conditions "so chaotic that there had to be a general housecleaning." I cannot think of any modern experience that bears him out; I suspect that his observation would evoke considerable surprise at both Oxford and Cambridge. There would also be interest in who has done (or will do) the housecleaning.

Throughout, in fact, Mr. Coolidge seems to be saying that the Corporation and also (more imaginatively) the Board of Overseers exercise a great and useful power, aided in the case of the Corporation by a judicial estrangement from the faculty and its affairs. These bodies should be left to govern as now. But he also says that, in effect, all important power is now exercised by the faculty, so there is no need to give it more. Mr. Coolidge is a most distinguished lawyer and one of the world's most agreeable and persuasive men. But not even he can have it both ways.

I have already given in to Mr. Cabot on the power of the faculty in relation to the students. I resolutely deny him his point on the superior ability of the businessman to run things, including universities. There are always exceptions to any rule; Mr. Cabot himself could be one. But the day when a pecuniary society proclaimed the businessman the all-purpose custodian of the tasks of education, church and state is over. Businessmen, we may all agree, will generally be better at running businesses. But scientists and scholars will generally be better at running universities. If there is any rule, it is that each will do best what he knows most about.

I had expected considerable punishment on my criticism of the formal university leadership on Vietnam. I was careful to suggest that stronger concern on the part of individuals would have been a substitute for corporate action. There is opposition on this issue, including that of Mr. Edmonds, who observes that the faculty has also, as a body, ducked the problem. Nonetheless I must dig in. This has been the great moral question of the last five years, and this terrible misadventure has had a devastating effect on the universities and on their relation to the federal government. No one has been in doubt as to the overwhelming student and faculty position on the matter. The impression given by the formal Harvard leadership, president and Corporation, is one of neutrality. This continues to suggest a divorce from the moral concerns of the university community of which it is a part. That was what I meant.

Now let me mention a few of my original points to which (Mr. Pusey's omnibus protest apart) there has been no objection, although it would perhaps be rash to assume that silence means complete consent. No one has objected to my statement that the Corporation recruits itself from a narrow and highly unrepresentative spectrum of American life; or that the assumption that the Corporation is governing when, in fact, it is not (or cannot) may lead to nongovernment and the neglect of important tasks; or that one manifestation of this is the absence of any overall design for the development of the university, including the care and nurturing of those departments which are not the natural favorites of the government and the foundations; or that even if none of this is true and total perfection in Harvard government can be assumed, it might be safer to have a study just to affirm that perfection.

2

INNOCENCE AS EXCULPATION

(1968)

The preceding essay tells of the refusal of the Harvard authorities to publish James Watson's excellent book. This is a footnote to that action. Perhaps it should be noted that when The Double Helix *was published by Atheneum, it encountered none of the difficulties so greatly feared or anyhow offered as an excuse for not publishing by the Harvard University Press.*

March 11, 1968

To the Editors of *The Harvard Crimson:*

My distinguished colleague Talcott Parsons, with whom I agree on most matters, has charged the Harvard president and Corporation with suppression of academic freedom in vetoing the decision of the Syndics of the Harvard University Press to publish *The Double Helix* by Professor James Watson. I believe this is unjust, and I rise in a limited way to their defense.

The reason for this action was not, I suggest, indifference to academic freedom. Had the book defended, always with appropriate scholarship, some socially unpalatable subject — neo-Bolshevism, sodomy, the therapeutic use of hashish, hard-core pornography — the president and Corporation would have recognized that a question of principle was involved, and they would not have interfered. But Mr. Watson's book deals with an arcane problem of science, a still more difficult problem of the scientific personality, a highly subjective question of libel and an even more unassessable threat of legal action. In sidestepping a professional squabble or avoiding a lawsuit, the Corporation, one may assume, saw no question of principle. It also, unfortunately, failed to see that these were questions on which an occasional gathering of excellent but inexperienced laymen would inevitably be uninformed;

it sought advice from its lawyers. Again it did not recognize that this was to reinforce innocence with innocence. From some experience I can attest that there are few matters on which the successful lawyer, odd accidents of individual personality and aptitude apart, is so hopelessly at a loss as those he encounters in the delicate jungle of literary controversy, literary law and publishing procedure generally.

So the issue was not suppression. The action was the consequence, ultimately, of the progressive divorce of the Corporation, which operates under an ancient charter relevant to a small and simple college, from the complex realities of the modern academic world. It is wrong, accordingly, to attribute to repression what, in all fairness, must be blamed on ill-advised interference and the resulting ineptitude. On the assumption that God prefers ineptitude to wicked intent, one is right to ask for charitable judgment.

3

SOLEMNITY, GLOOM
AND THE ACADEMIC STYLE:
A REFLECTION

(1976)

In 1976, following my retirement from active teaching, The Harvard Lampoon, *a magazine of good cheer, called forth in Boston a major convocation of its editors, former editors, readers, intended readers and friends and presented me with a purple and gold Cadillac Eldorado convertible, a check for $10,000 and the offer of a free vacation in Las Vegas, which my wife and I did not accept. The car, which unhappily would not fit in our driveway, let alone our garage, we did accept and put into storage. Then, with the permission of the donors, we allowed it to be sold for the benefit of WGBH (public television station) at its auction a year later. All this largesse from* The Lampoon *was not a reward for the economic knowledge I had conveyed over the years; it was, I was told, because I had done something to lighten the tedium of college life. I was required, in turn, to describe to the audience of nostalgic* Lampoon *alumni the academic style at Harvard, as I do in this essay derived from my speech.*

In these last years I have been led to reflect on the extreme solemnity that has become the modern academic style — and not least at Harvard. I do not suppose that universities were ever joyously amusing places; certainly professors were always expected to take themselves rather seriously. Still, as I move about the university's purlieus and attend its meetings, social exercises and other rituals, I cannot but think that we have become exceptionally grave these days, given even to an ostentatious gloom. That is now the academic style. Perhaps the reasons should be examined.

Partly, of course, solemnity derives from what we are compelled to teach. This, on occasion, is so funny that to relax even for a moment would be fatal. In economics we dutifully explain that a country can have inflation or it can have recession, but it can never have both at the same time. And all this while it does. As we proceed into more advanced and theoretically more refined instruction, we cease to discuss corporations of any puissance, trade unions of any power or the existence of intercourse, in the platonic sense, between these and the government. There is no independent exercise of power; all and everyone are subordinate to market forces. Were we even to smile as we thus lectured, brighter students, if any, might catch on.

The professors of government must be equally on guard against levity. This is a democracy, and its citizens, like its consumers, are sovereign. Subsidies to politicians, whether emanating from Nelson Rockefeller, Northrop or Gulf Oil, are not meant to affect the distribution of power; they serve only to affirm the deeply philanthropic instincts of the American people. Power remains with the White House and the Congress; perish the thought that it should have passed to the Pentagon.

Even greater solemnity is required of those who teach the law. Some weeks ago the dean of the Harvard Law School is believed to have issued a ukase against laughter to all professors concerned with the subject of legal ethics. It was on the day after the former dean of the University of Chicago Law School, Mr. Edward Levi, presided over the unveiling of the portrait of former Attorney General Richard Kleindienst on the walls of the Department of Justice. There would, he said, be no chuckles, no mention of G. Gordon Liddy, Watergate or the legal inhibitions on perjury. One presumes that he reminded all students attending that John Mitchell's portrait would, sometime in the future, also be unveiled, but only by the dean of a medium-grade correspondence school.

The historians are the gloomiest case of all. Although they have no current conflict between scholarship and reality, they, too, must reflect on what they teach. In this year of bicentennial self-congratulation they must consider (as I believe Eugene McCarthy first said) that in these last two hundred years we've moved on from George Washington to Richard Nixon, from John Adams to Spiro Agnew, from John Jay to John Mitchell and from Alexander Hamilton to John B. Connally. Understandably, the more sensitive come into the Faculty Club, after a lecture, distraught with grief.

The subject matter we teach is not the only cause of our solemnity. Once, Harvard professors were judged by the president of the university and in theory, if not in fact, by the genial Harvard graduates who served on the Board of Overseers and the Visiting Committees. Those who made the evaluations were safely at a distance. One could enjoy an occasional laugh in classrooms, department meetings or in public, confident in the knowledge that no one vital to one's career was watching. Now professors are judged by their peers; that means we can never relax.

When I returned to Harvard after World War II, the chief auditor of our virtue in the economics department was Sinclair Weeks, sometime senator from Massachusetts and later President Eisenhower's secretary of commerce. Three generations of Weekses had served the Massachusetts citizenry with no trace of a generation gap; all had rigorously identified the public interest with that of the rich. Shortly after Sinclair took over at Commerce, he fired the head of the Bureau of Standards for finding, against the wishes of a West Coast entrepreneur, that Glauber's salt — sodium sulfate — was worthless as a battery additive. The scientists protested violently. Bernard DeVoto came to Weeks's defense, saying that he was the first politician so brave as to stake his career on the proposition that a battery could be improved by giving it a laxative. It was a joyous moment. But one cannot afford such fun with one's academic colleagues. They may not like your laughter and will one day hold it against you.

There are other reasons for our style. Since we are Harvard professors, we know, uniquely among American parents, that our offspring will never be as brilliant as we are. They may end up teaching at some lesser Ivy League school or, God forbid, some agriculturally oriented academy in the Farm Belt. That is a grim thing on which to reflect. Those of us who are older also observe with grief the kind of Harvard professor who now gets selected for public service. We can hardly avoid showing our sorrow as we think how much better material there used to be in our time, how much wiser the appointments that included us.

An aspect of grave harassment also suggests deep devotion to one's work; this, indeed, has long been so. A propensity to amusement, in contrast, could be thought to imply idleness. This is now especially important, because Harvard may be the only considerable community in the world, the Pentagon possibly excepted, where the effort to simulate effort can exceed the effort itself. After three months' vacation in the summer, a professor may feel obliged to take a sabbatical leave in the autumn so that he will be rested and ready for a winter committed to a course on the work ethic.

Such are the sources of the modern academic style. It has been said of sexual congress — as I was brought up to call it — that the pleasure is momentary, the position is ridiculous and the expense is damnable. Considering what laughter does to our dignity, to our reputation and thus to our academic income, our attitude must inevitably be the same toward any lapse from solemnity. In my youth I tried hard to master the Harvard academic style and often believed I had succeeded. You tell me today that, sadly, I did not. It is nice sometimes to be rewarded for failure.

4

THE HARVARD PARIETAL RULES

(1963)

For decades, at meetings of the faculty and the staffs of the Harvard Houses and at gatherings of the administrative officers of the university, the parietal rules — briefly, the rules governing the circumstances under which male undergraduates could entertain women in their rooms — were endlessly debated. They had an unrelenting attraction for the dirty faculty mind. Once, in the 1930s, after long debate at Winthrop House, the Harvard residential center with which I was then (as I am still) associated, it was agreed that women might be entertained at specific hours so long as it was the rule that the door to the room or suite remained open. The restraint was abandoned when a colleague and I drafted the version to be posted and published. It said, "All sexual intercourse in Winthrop House shall hereafter be in public."

The world does move; all efforts to regulate such matters have now for many years been abandoned. This letter, I might note, was widely reprinted at colleges across the Republic.

November 2, 1963

To the Editor of *The Harvard Crimson:*

I can't tell you how depressing it is to find Harvard having another discussion of those so-called parietal rules. For forty years, undergraduates with a special talent for banal controversy, and no doubt a secondary interest in sex, have known that this subject could be counted on to arouse a certain frustrated maternalism which lurks, however unhappily, in the interstices of any academic administration. The resulting debate has invariably combined exceptional dreariness with a crushing misinterpretation of the nature of a university.

The responsibility of the university to its students is to provide the best teaching that can be associated with the scientific, literary, artistic or other scholarly preoccupations of the faculty. Additionally, it should provide libraries, laboratories and, though less indispensably, places of residence. Once, when Harvard College was in part a privileged academy for the socially visible, it needed to assure parents that their more retarded or irresponsible offspring would have the supervision of men of the scoutmaster type, who, however ineffectually, would try to protect them from the natural penalties of indolence, alcohol or lust. All this, happily, is now over. Thousands of men and women clamor for admission for the serious purposes of the university, and it can be part of our bargain with them that they look after themselves.

Accordingly, the rules of the academic community need only reflect its special requirements — the quiet good order and opportunity for undisturbed sleep that facilitate reflection and study. No effort need be made or should be made to protect individuals from the consequences of their own errors, indiscretions or passions. Parents of Harvard and Radcliffe applicants who feel that their children need a more protective environment should be put firmly on notice so that they may send them elsewhere. It is clear that we will have all the students we can accommodate from among those who accept this bargain, and presumably they will be more mature. We will need waste no energy or money in providing the surrogates of parenthood beyond the appointed time. There will be misfortunes, but it will be recognized that these are inherent in personality and are not the result of any failure at efforts to control it. Our deans will be able to turn gratefully to the more welcome tasks of teaching and scholarship. Above all, no moral or biological question being involved, we will be spared, praise God, any further discussion of these rules. Those who (one hopes on the basis of some special competence) are fascinated by the question of whether undergraduates are improved or damaged by fornication can organize private discussion groups or, if married, talk about it with their wives.

5

SEXUAL HARASSMENT
AT HARVARD:
THREE LETTERS

(1983)

The subject of sex recurs, if with less solemnity, in the following communications. The council referred to in the first excerpt is, as indicated, the Faculty Council, the inner legislative body of the Harvard faculty, of which there has been earlier mention in this book. Henry Rosovsky was, until 1984, the greatly able and respected dean of the Faculty of Arts and Sciences, the number two post in the Harvard administration. As here shown, no Harvard dean ever answers a letter without giving some indication of need for financial support, such as the endowment of a new academic chair. Dean Rosovsky's letter is published with his more than generous permission.

EXCERPT FROM A LETTER REPORTING ON FACULTY COUNCIL
DISCUSSIONS OF SEXUAL HARASSMENT AT HARVARD ADDRESSED
TO THE HARVARD FACULTY BY DEAN HENRY ROSOVSKY.

April 1983

Dear Colleagues:

The council discussed various kinds of personal relationships between faculty members and students. Members of the council generally agreed that, in addition to the harassing behavior described below, certain other kinds of relationships are wrong whenever they take place within an instructional context.

Amorous relationships that might be appropriate in other circumstances are always wrong when they occur between any teacher or officer of the university and any student for whom he or she has a professional responsibility. Further, such relationships may have the effect of undermining the atmosphere of trust on which the educational process depends. Implicit in the idea of professionalism is the recognition by those in positions of authority that in their relationships with students there is always an element of power. It is incumbent upon those with authority not to abuse, nor to seem to abuse, the power with which they are entrusted. . . .

Other amorous relationships between members of the faculty and students, occurring outside the instructional context, may also lead to difficulties. In a personal relationship between an officer and a student for whom the officer has no current professional responsibility, the officer should be sensitive to the constant possibility that he or she may unexpectedly be placed in a position of responsibility for the student's instruction or evaluation. Relationships between officers and students are always fundamentally asymmetric in nature. . . .

LETTER TO DEAN HENRY ROSOVSKY FROM PROFESSOR JOHN KENNETH GALBRAITH.

May 9, 1983

Dear Henry:

I was, as you will presently understand, both enchanted and distressed by your recent communication on behalf of the Faculty Council, entitled "Sexual Harassment, Related Matters." My pleasure had to do with the eloquence and delicacy of the language in which, in keeping with Harvard standards in such matters, your letter is couched. The reference to "amorous relationships" in the "instructional context" is superb and reflects an acute sense of Harvard faculty and even New England sensibilities. For some years I have been an adviser to one of our well-known dictionaries — *The American Heritage Dictionary*, to be precise. I am today instructing its editors as to the usage to which henceforth they must conform if they are to have our approval here in Cambridge.

My distress is personal. Just over forty-five years ago, already a well-fledged member of the Harvard faculty on a three-year appointment, I fell in love with a young female student. It was not in an instructional context; however, noninstructional amour is a "situation" against which you also warn. A not wholly unpredictable consequence of this lapse from faculty and professional decorum, as now required, was that we were married. So, and even happily, we have remained. But now my distress. As a senior member of this community, I am acutely conscious of my need to be an example for younger and possibly more ardent members of the faculty. I must do everything possible to retrieve my error. My wife, needless to say, shares my concern. What would you advise?

LETTER FROM DEAN HENRY ROSOVSKY TO PROFESSOR JOHN
KENNETH GALBRAITH.

May 23, 1983

Dear Ken:

I am delighted that my letter on sexual harassment caused some
enchantment in your life. However, I also deeply regret having caused
distress. My warnings against noninstructional amour are not especially
severe: mainly I urge the practice of "sensitivity." Knowing you, I am
sure that was never a problem. But I do understand your *ex post* feelings
of discomfort.

Two thoughts come to mind: one humane and the other decanal.
The incident in question, by your own account, occurred over forty-
five years ago. I believe that the statute of limitations applies. As a dean
and as someone who has recently been accused by a member of the
faculty of behaving in the manner of a cardinal, I would be delighted
to sell you an indulgence. How about a chair to celebrate your happy
union and also a time when amour — instructional and noninstructional — was in fashion?

6

ON ACADEMIC TENURE

(1980)

Academic tenure is a sacred institution; so is the selection and promotion of professors by their peers. As this letter to Harvard Magazine *tells, I am not quite prepared to propose alternatives. There may not be any. But certainly in economics departments, and I suspect elsewhere in the social sciences, the consideration of candidates for tenure can be, and is, a time for weeding out those with heretical tendency or even an inconvenient inclination to independent thought.*

January 16, 1980

To the Editor of *Harvard Magazine:*

In academic life all matters, however sacred, should presumably be open for discussion, and, accordingly, we must welcome Professor Daniel F. Melia's recently expressed doubts as to the modern value of academic tenure.

His case is that tenure, which is meant to protect the scholar of unpopular or eccentric view or deportment, in fact protects the person who is intellectually absent, preternaturally senile or particularly accomplished in professional lassitude. I believe Professor Melia has a point. All in university life are acquainted with the individual who achieves a lifetime of idleness by relating academic freedom to insufficient teaching effort, discussion of the depth of his unwritten books or accounts of the brilliance of his unfinished research. But I also believe that Professor Melia has missed something even more important.

If academic tenure now protects relatively few unpopular or dissident views in the modern university, it could be because there are so few such views to protect. And that, in turn, is because consideration for tenure is extensively an occasion for weeding out those with such tendency. The real threat to academic freedom thus lies not in the firing of professors with nonconformist views but in the nonselection and nonpromotion of those with such views. This exclusion is then strengthened by another institution that is sacred to university tradition and also above discussion, and that is the judgment of the person by his academic peers and elders. In this judgment there is a natural likelihood, perhaps a near certainty, that, as in modern corporate and government bureaucracy, quality and even excellence will be perceived as whatever most resembles those making the judgment. Certainly that has always been my standard. The Harvard *ad hoc* or outside reviewing committee acknowledges this problem but, by rubber stamping departmental decisions, rarely effects much change. So this academic cloning, combined with a general instinct to peace and conformity, acts further to ensure against inconvenient nonconformity or dissent. It ensures that mediocrity, where it exists, will be perpetuated along with conformity; it is only rarely that a bad department rises much above itself in its appointments.

I am not quite prepared to urge the abandonment of tenure and the present arrangements for passing judgment. Maybe, as Churchill said of democracy, we have the worst of all systems except for the alternatives. But I would join Professor Melia in proposing a more active discussion of a system that, for too long, has been thought above debate.

7

RECESSIONAL

(1975)

This communication was also occasioned by retirement; it was the Class Day speech given when I ceased regular teaching. Some of it was first published by The Harvard Gazette, *the highly useful house organ of the university, but, as I couldn't help noticing, it carefully omitted my reference to the dubious upward progress at Winthrop House from being anti-Irish to being anti-Semitic. This is still a somewhat sensitive subject even when one is recounting now distant history.*

The Confi-Guide *is the assessment of Harvard courses and teachers put out for the benefit of the students by* The Harvard Crimson, *the undergraduate newspaper. By those who are accorded favorable comment, it is a well-regarded document; others have grave reservations.*

There are echoes here, I note, of two previous essays — one on the parietal rules and the other on the Harvard academic style. Much of what is called scholarship is, in practice, the plagiarism of oneself or other people.

You will probably expect me to tell you how pleased and honored I am to be graduating with the Class of 1975. I *am* honored but not pleased. Of late I have searched diligently to discover the advantages of age, and there is, I have concluded, only one. It is that lovely women treat your approaches with understanding rather than with disdain. And in my case that benefit came some years back. I'm now retiring a few moments ahead of statutory compulsion because I don't wish to risk similar kindness in my classes.

I've thought often of doing a treatise on aging at Harvard: "Institutional and Psychological Aspects of Academic Gerontocracy," I would call it. Were I younger, the title would get me tenure. All Harvard professors are deeply rational people; there is only one respect in which we falter. Without exception, we consider ourselves uniquely exempt from the ordinary human tendency to intellectual and physical enfeeblement. We all believe that we have been selected for that experience of immortality, that enduring vitality, so far awarded by the Almighty only to General Francisco Franco and perhaps, as I've indicated elsewhere, J. Edgar Hoover.

Your invitation suggested that I reflect on the forty-one years that I've been at Harvard — or, as some of my colleagues would prefer, the forty-one years that I have frequently *not* been at Harvard. I must confess that, on the whole, I've liked the place. On balance, also, it has improved. And my period of observation — extending to slightly over 12 percent of the total life of the institution — has not been negligible. You may trust my conclusions completely.

The biggest improvement has been in the students. When I first arrived, Winthrop House, with which I have retained a happy though somewhat exiguous association, was considered the most progressive residential enclave in the whole academic community. It had just gone on in those years from being anti-Irish to being anti-Semitic. No other part of the university was quite so advanced.

You mustn't think I am exaggerating. When I joined the Winthrop House staff in the autumn of 1935, I was made to take my turn as a member of the House admissions committee. I was told to select only students of the highest quality, although nothing in my earlier education — a degree in animal husbandry from the Ontario Agricultural College, another in agricultural economics from the University of California at Berkeley — had prepared me for the subtleties of this judgment. Help was at hand, however, in the established procedures; I was presented with the chart that was in regular use throughout the university for categorizing the students who had been admitted. This had five columns; on top of each was a cabalistic symbol — St. GX, E & A, O.P., H.S. and X. I was also given the key to this code: St. GX meant St. Paul's, St. Mark's and, as I recall, Groton and Middlesex; these, I was told, or perhaps I knew, were the supreme private schools. E & A were Exeter and Andover, also private schools but flawed by size and incipient guilt feelings about democracy; O.P. was Other Private and, frankly speaking, not good; H.S. was public High School and not really good at all; X was a Jewish student wherever and however educated.

To get quality was comparatively straightforward: one took as many as possible from the left-hand columns, most of all the St. GX's, and took as few as one dared of those on the far right. No H.S.'s. No X's. I don't recall that I had any great sense of moral outrage at these distinctions. I did, however, prove intellectually incapable of mastering the further niceties that were involved. The very first afternoon I admitted to the House Theodore White, a truly brilliant student, later the historian of presidential campaigns. I hadn't realized that anyone with that name could be of anything but impeccable Anglo-Saxon antecedents. So after only one day's service I was dropped from the committee as incompetent.

In that relaxed time a preoccupation with intellectual matters was even more damaging to one's social position than previous attendance at the wrong school. It was the age of the gentleman's C, and there flourished, or anyhow existed, around Harvard Square a scrofulous collection of academies that undertook for a fee to get even the most retarded undergraduate up to that grade. Much of their instruction was in sociology, for that was the field most favored by the delinquent. It was known to be a very difficult subject to fail, perhaps partly because the difference between what was right and what was wrong in the material covered was almost completely unclear.

Excessive study was also identified with what is now called ethnicity; bookishness was the natural flaw of those who, having no ethnic claim to quality, had been admitted on the basis of merit.

I suppose that there were then undergraduates who edited *The Crimson;* I can honestly say that I didn't know one. Nor, though I lived in a House and was normally involved in the life of the college, did it ever occur to me to read that newspaper on a daily basis. Better, even, to read *The Boston Transcript.* In recent times, there has been improvement, and few things have given me more pleasure than, subject to occasional aberration, *The Crimson's* informed, mature, skeptical and surprisingly grammatical columns.

Undergraduate esteem in the 1930s was occasionally sought in athletics. But more often it was something that some students assumed and the rest conceded. Aristocracies are often marked by such effortless assumption of superiority, enhanced by a special grace in the enjoyment of sex, alcohol and leisure. This was the case then. So greatly were these supplementary proficiencies admired, especially the consumption of alcohol, that the most distinguished of the alumni returned to the football games each autumn to show their continuing virtuosity. I went once, in 1934, to a game with Dartmouth.* Neither the athletic contest nor the general depravity of the onlookers appealed to me, and I've been to only one game since. Even though the standard of behavior on autumn Saturdays has, I am told, improved, my example is one you shouldn't feel obliged to reject. Some things in life are intrinsically without style or charm, and one is the effort to relive, however briefly, the enjoyments of your youth. Burned in my memory of these football fiestas is the boast of one celebrant, a student or returning graduate, that he could dive from the top floor of a Winthrop House entry headfirst down the stairwell onto the cement two or three floors below and survive. All cheered him on. He was wrong.

Women were confined in those days to their ghetto at Radcliffe. We

---

*See "Mayhem at Harvard Stadium," page 182.

repeated our lectures there, often perfunctorily; we went for the small extra pay involved. The audience was believed to have its thoughts mostly on marriage, which may well have been true; a woman who wasn't engaged by graduation was thought a failure and often called "a typical Radcliffe girl." Faithfully once each year the faculty debated the liberalization of the parietal rules, and in opposing change, the more daring faculty members made nasty little jokes abut sex. Had I to mention the greatest improvement at Harvard over these last forty years, it would be the conversion of its undergraduates from a slightly ludicrous aristocracy to a somewhat serious meritocracy. The next most important advance has been toward treating women as citizens.

The achievement on behalf of women was brought about not by the administration, not by the faculty, but by the students. This leads me to a word on the role of students in reform — or what goes by that name. Student preoccupation with social issues has increased wonderfully in the past forty years, and it has been, I believe, for the general good of the university and the outside world. But, though I am sensitive to the need for being nice on this occasion, I don't want to give such social involvement my unqualified endorsement. There is, first, its instability. In the last decade or so, students have gone on from civil rights (in Mississippi rather than in Roxbury or Harlem), to the Vietnam war, to Eugene McCarthy, to the inadequacies of the ROTC, to university reform, to women's rights, to the environment, and they have ended up, in many cases, with a deep concern for joining a good income with a high sense of compassion by proceeding to the practice of medicine. Social awareness in the student body is inconsistent and has a high susceptibility to changing fashion and perhaps to boredom. Most social change, by contrast, requires long, persistent effort — often the energy and devotion of a lifetime.

I am also far from enthusiastic about student participation in educational policy, academic administration or the selection of the faculty. Besides the instability of interest just mentioned, it is nearly inevitable that student concern with educational reform will end up with a proposal for the liberalization of standards, liberalization being a euphemism for the lowering of standards. There is much to be said for seeking to liberate as many people as possible from the burden of physical toil, but liberation from the burden of mental toil in one's college years is premature. Any compilation of the hundred best universities in the world would list a vast majority of American and Canadian institutions, and this is partly because we have been much more zealous on this continent in protecting our standards, in requiring students to work.

The relation of students to teaching is more complex. There is no doubt that a strong and vigorous reaction by students to the quality of their instruction is valuable. I've never known a professor who wasn't, at least surreptitiously, a reader of the *Confi-Guide,* for we all want to know how we are judged, how we should improve. Those who deplore its ratings are those who get a low score and, more especially, those who aren't mentioned.

In these last weeks I've wondered how a professor leaving Harvard might best celebrate his departure. Rightly or wrongly, there has been some complaint in recent years abut the quality of our economics instruction. Since all economists believe in competition and pecuniary incentives, I have decided to offer an award in the economics department in each of the next ten years or so to the professor whose teaching is adjudged by the graduate students to have been personally the most helpful and academically the most useful. I realize that all will not think such student judgment a valid test of professional merit. It will, accordingly, be understood that anyone holding this opinion who receives the award is at liberty to decline it. One often hears that, in appraising their teachers, students mistake popularity for substance, but it is my impression that the teaching of those who make this charge invariably lacks both.

Student judgment on instruction is valuable, as most will agree, except when it is adverse. Student participation in the selection and promotion of faculty, on the other hand, I believe and have often said, is unwise and unuseful. The selection and promotion of faculty is a matter for careful, mature, professional deliberation. It is not for students. And it is vital that those making the decisions be required to live with their mistakes. This also excludes student participation, for they are here and soon gone.

The changes in the faculty in the last four decades seem to me much less dramatic than those in the student body — although my judgment is unquestionably impaired by the lessened awe with which, with age, one views Harvard professors. Social position — an old Boston or WASP name — still counted in 1934. But even then the departments that were considered the aristocratic strongholds — English, comparative literature, history — were under assault. Here the most powerful influence, as in the pressure for merit in the student body, was that of James B. Conant. Of all the men and women I've known in academic life, he was the most committed to reform, the least committed to making a point of it. Once, in later years, President Kennedy accused me of being more interested in alarming people with my own designs for reform than in pursuing them; he thought it better to talk less and do more. President Conant was a man of the Kennedy persuasion.

In the 1930s and 1940s, the Harvard faculty, especially in the social sciences, was far more conscious of its critics — especially the alumni —

than it is now. The department of economics was then suspect for its radicalism, of all things; for this reason, and because economics then seemed a dangerous subject, the economists operated under the close and suspicious scrutiny of the businessmen on the Board of Overseers and on its Visiting Committee. It was a tendency of which I speak poignantly, for I was, I believe, the principal object of their concern. There was a high-level insurrection in the Board of Overseers in 1948 and 1949 when its members were presented with the awful prospect of my being made a professor. Their reaction was to become a major cross for me to bear, for ever since I've been conscious of the need, whenever possible, to justify their fears. If I've been tempted to lapse into a comfortable silence on some contentious issue, the thought has assailed me: Sinclair Weeks, the most primitive of our watchdogs, would be pleased.

It was President Conant who put down the revolt over my appointment. Much later he came into my office one day to talk about *The Affluent Society*, which had just been published, and I tried to thank him for giving me the opportunity to write it. He was terribly embarrassed. So was I, and I quickly dropped the subject. Later we served together briefly on the supervisory body of the Office of Economic Opportunity — the poverty program. One day a speaker was commenting on the role of alcoholism as a cause of poverty, and Conant expressed the opinion that the social group displaying the highest incidence of this disease was probably the Harvard alumni. I concluded that he, too, had attended one of those football games.

My comments on Dr. Conant are not meant to reflect pejoratively on his successor, who was president for the greater part of my time at Harvard. As a university matures, its deepest tendency is for power and associated responsibility to pass to the faculty, and Mr. Pusey was excellently cast for facilitating and expediting this transition. Men serve in many different ways.

Outside interference is no longer a problem for the faculty; no doubt that is a good thing. But it must be replaced by a consistent and careful scrutiny from within. No institution, not even a university department, should be free from continuous thoughtful inspection and comment. The reason is simple: excellence in teaching is completely subjective, and this is especially so in the social sciences and the humanities. In the absence of informed scrutiny, there is not the slightest doubt — and here I venture to repeat a point I've long emphasized — that it will be defined as whatever most closely resembles the work of those making the judgment. And it will also be whatever is least discomforting to those rendering the decision. The reference to comfort I would especially stress. Harvard has always had two kinds of professors, the inside people and the outside people. The insiders make their lives within the university community; the outsiders are only associated with it. The outside men — most of us, alas, have been men — are the best known; the insiders are the most useful. They serve on the committees, help in the administration, know the students, attend at the Houses, see the university as the embodiment of their own lives. They are the truly unselfish scholars.

But they are also subject to a temptation, which is to subside too deeply into the comforts of the academic routine — to see preoccupation with public affairs, involvement with public issues, participation in heated debate or occasional descent into acrimony, as somehow beneath their academic dignity. How much more scientific — how much more deeply in the spirit of good scholarship — to avoid such worldly hassle. How much better to commute from house to office, from wife to secretary, from children to computer, without the distractions of controversy. A friend of mine calls it the Belmont Syndrome, after the suburban haven to which so many professors retreat at night. That is unfair; the temptation operates equally with residence in Newton, Lexington or Cambridge.

In these last years the American as also the world economy has been functioning with less than complete precision. Economists are now very numerous at Harvard — far more so than in the 1930s. The level of sophistication is vastly higher. One would expect that the present economic crisis would have brought a great flow of discussion and recommendations from these scholars — recommendations that were contradictory, contentious, perhaps condemned as gratuitous, politically biased or grossly damaging to business confidence, but ones reflecting deep professional concern and involvement. Alas, however, there has been little such response. Excellent explanations are available — explanations as to why disease is not really the business of the doctor. I don't believe them. Nor should you. It is the Belmont Syndrome at work.

Perhaps we might look to the past to see how things should be. So involved were Harvard economists in the days of Professor Alvin Hansen, who died last week, that Washington officials came up to Cambridge to sit in on his seminars and discuss what should be done. Hansen was a very, very controversial figure. He lived in Belmont.

So much for now. There is a view of Harvard, heard occasionally in faculty meetings and always in speeches at alumni dinners, that this university is touched with a special divinity. In consequence, mistakes are impossible, enlightened progress inevitable. The university is, perhaps, the only product of human design that is so blessed. Not even the Supreme Court, *The New York Times* or the British House of Com-

mons is thought to prove with similar certainty the absolute perfecti-
bility of man. I would have greatly enhanced my reputation with all
who share this vision had I been able to conclude that everything forty
years ago was wonderful and improvement ever since has been unremitting. It was a temptation.

There is also a deeply intellectual current, articulated more often in
gatherings of students than of faculty, that everything without exception is getting worse. That is the nature of man; Harvard leads the
way. Even at this late stage in life, I would have deepened my reputation
for grave social perception had I sought to persuade you that this was
true. But the thought could not be put down: things, as always, are
terribly mixed. So, after careful reflection, I concluded that today I
would give no thought to my reputation and give you instead the exact
truth.

· IV ·

FROM ECONOMICS TO ART

OVER THE LAST twenty years at Harvard, earlier as a trustee
of the Twentieth Century Fund and in other roles, I've been
much devoted to the building of bridges between economics
and the arts — to showing, above all, that with economic
advance it is the arts and not technology that gain the center
of our social focus.

1

THE ECONOMICS OF BEAUTY

(1970)

This essay is based on a lecture given long in the past before the Danish Society of Industrial Design in Copenhagen. It was my first venture into a subject that now lies close to my heart. A few of the ideas here expressed reappeared many years later in the piece that follows this one.

As living standards rise — as man multiplies the goods he consumes and the artifacts with which he surrounds himself — we are entitled to believe, or at least to hope, that quantitative measurements give way to qualitative ones. The original need is for food to satisfy hunger and for enough to satisfy it completely; after that its quality becomes of concern. The original need is for enough clothes to cover and enough houseroom to shelter; thereafter the function of clothing and housing is to please. And so it goes. The problem of quantitative satisfaction is one for science and technology — and for effective economic organization. That of qualitative satisfaction is for the artist to solve. It has been a common assumption that science and engineering represent, in some subjective sense, man's last frontier. This is not so. Beyond the age of the engineer and the scientist lies the age of the artist.

Yet in the present stage of industrial development (and perhaps for quite some time to come) there is (and will be) a sharp conflict between the differing needs of science and engineering and the arts. In this conflict the artist comes off badly, is relegated to a secondary role. This, I may add, is partly because the artist doesn't understand his own problem or perceive his own function.

Specifically, engineering and science, as they are applied to everyday life, are highly organized. It is not individuals who cover the streets and highways of the developed countries with automobiles (and the vacant lots with their wrecks) but great bureaucratic organizations. And it is such organizations that send men to the moon, make modern weaponry, fly the Atlantic and make chemicals, steel, beer and an appalling number of television programs. All these products are the accomplishment not of individuals but of teams. Each member of the team is a specialist; each specialist combines his slice of specialized knowledge with those of other specialists for a result far beyond the capacity of any one person. The modern industrial corporation is large partly because it is the frame — the holding company — for the very complex organization that modern science and technology require.

Such organization is inhospitable to the artist. The notion of specialization has no real meaning in art; the artist as an individual is coordinate with a complete area of endeavor and achievement. So the artist, unlike the engineer or the scientist, fits badly into organization. This is one reason the great industrial corporations enjoy their greatest success in those areas — steel, oil, aluminum, copper, chemicals, space exploration, weapons production — where the artist is not needed. And it is not surprising that in those industries where design *is* needed — the production of automobiles, for example — the reputation of the large corporation is often far from notable, except perhaps for its banality.

There is minor confirmation of the point in the fact that a whole branch of literature — Budd Schulberg's *What Makes Sammy Run?*, Evelyn Waugh's "Excursion in Reality," and others — tells what happens when the artist encounters the once highly bureaucratic world of the movies or the still highly organized world of television. And it is further confirmation that where the artist is inescapable — dress and fabric design, Danish furniture, the theater, the modern film — the size of the firm employing him tends to be relatively small, the organization relatively simple. In the rare cases of good automobile design, there is usually identification with the name of one man, not a team. Two or three years ago a Du Pont executive commented to me on the point: "One can always hire chemists and chemical engineers and fit them into the organization. But the designers of our fabrics are another matter. There we are without confidence in ourselves. Design we contract out." He added the thought that artists wouldn't live in Wilmington, Delaware.

The lesson is that the modern large-scale organization — what I have called the technostructure — lends itself well to science and technology but badly to art. A number of other lessons seem to me to follow from this central circumstance. Let me suggest a few.

First, let us recognize that what people cannot do, they will ordinarily proclaim to be unimportant. Those who are poor in mathematics will assert the unimportance of numbers. The man who is unsuccessful in love will deplore women. The large industrial organization, since it doesn't easily use the services of art, deprecates art. Technical efficiency and scientific virtuosity, the hallmarks of industrial success, are said to be what the public wants, and the public must be served. Beauty is for the effete and not for the average man or woman, who, it is argued, will not pay for it.

To a greater extent than we realize, our values tend to be those of the great industrial bureaucracies, their truths the accepted truths. We must come to understand that their deprecation of art, their exaltation of technical and scientific excellence, are self-serving and self-protective. The artist must not be intimidated, for it is the artist, not the engineer or the scientist, who is the person of ultimate economic importance. He or she gives the quality that people ultimately seek.

Next, it is said by the exponents of bureaucratic method that they serve the taste of the majority, and that taste is intrinsically bad. It will, indeed, *be* bad if there is no alternative, but given a choice, people have, I think, a greater instinct for beauty than we often imagine. The man or woman who provides an alternative can be a disturbing influence — someone whose competition is to be feared. The makers of good low-budget films in the 1960s focused attention on the earlier tasteless extravaganzas of M-G-M. Pay television in the United States brings fear to the commercial networks because it may set in motion an uncontrollable demand for better programming. Perhaps there are furniture manufacturers in the world who feel the same way about Danes. The lesson, a harsh one, is that good design will, on occasion, be rejected not because it is commercially unprofitable but because it is commercially threatening.

We must recognize, next, that public response to good design, while more reliable than often imagined, will not always be immediate. It is a highly conditioned reaction, reflecting a judgment that is mature and educated rather than spontaneous. Yet the market test is often a spontaneous judgment: if people do not immediately respond, the design is thought to be bad and is rejected. In technical economic terms, the demand curve for art is a function of time. It moves to the right by virtue of being in existence — of the product's being on the market. The public initially rejects what, given time, it will enthusiastically accept. This means that for good design there will always — or almost always — be a noncommercial leading edge. The latter is provided by a small minority of patrons who share the artist's perception. Costs will be high, volume small. Maybe there will have to be subsidy. And there is always the possibility that, in the end, the public will not buy. But — and this is the important thing — only time will tell, for time and exposure are essential ingredients in acceptance.

It follows from the foregoing that market testing of any given design can be not only artistically disappointing but also commercially unwise. And even worse will be decisions based on what someone who is not an artist thinks the public will accept. As the public may at first reject what it will later come to love, so, even more vehemently, will those who claim to be knowledgeable about the public taste. In choosing what will eventually have universal acceptance, there is no alternative to trusting the artist. Artists have long suspected that this is the aesthetically better course; they should not doubt that it is (or can be) commercially better as well.

In a world where it is recognized that artists are commercially important, the next question concerns the standards by which they are selected. As men once asked who judged the judge, we now must ask what art qualifies a man or woman to be called a good artist. The choice, I have sufficiently established, cannot be made by the public; art, in a very real sense, is not democratic. Nor can the ultimate judgment lie with engineers, marketing experts or managers. At best they will be unreliable; at worst they will try to second-guess what the public wants.

Selection must reflect an artistic consensus. The best artist is the one who is so regarded by his fellow artists. There is nothing remarkable about this; scientists are judged by their peers, and this should be the case for painters, sculptors and designers. If the artistic community that renders the judgment is mediocre, so will be the selection; if the community's standards are good, so will be its judgment.

I come now to my final point: What is the role of the larger community, and more particularly of the state, in all this? This too, I think, follows from the preceding view of things.

Industry is not, as I've said, intrinsically hospitable to the artist; it regards with suspicion what it cannot easily assimilate. And its attitudes are deeply influential in the community and state. In consequence, and not surprisingly, the modern state associates rather more sober prestige and a great deal more economic ability with the scientist and engineer than with the artist. Its scientific institutes and engineering colleges are assumed to be far more useful than its art faculties and schools of design.

Yet this should not be; it is not a reflection of the underlying economic reality. The state has three major functions that it must perform for the arts, and these it will neglect to its very practical economic disadvantage. It must first, of course, provide for the education of artists. In the past, this has often been thought to be best accomplished by *ad hoc* arrangements between artist and teacher, arrangements encouraged, appropriately, by hunger and other forms of hardship. The viability of this I doubt. Support to the arts may require more informal educational structures than in the case of science or engineering, but the support given to talented art students and their teachers should never be more niggardly than that given to budding physicists or technicians.

It is also the responsibility of the state to encourage the arts just as it encourages the sciences. Here I have no novelties to offer. Encouragement varies with the art form; public museums, state patronage, sponsorship of exhibitions, financial awards to artists, are all important. The only radical point I would urge, as matters now stand, is that the support be generous.

Last among the functions of the state is to support the cutting edge of innovation — to sustain *ad interim* what, as we have seen, only time will make commercially rewarding. Patronage may be useful here — subsidy is perhaps more so. Any style of painting, any form of music, any design that artists know to be good, should have a source of support pending the day when the public finds it to be good. This is a difficult thing for the state to do; it will constantly find itself paying for things its citizens think (and will continue to think) eccentric. But it is of the highest importance.

Such is my fleeting view of the economics of beauty. It is perhaps shocking that one should have to speak tentatively on a subject of such merit — that only now an economist should be venturing into a matter that is of such significance in our civilized world. But better late, I trust, than never.

2

FURTHER ON ECONOMICS
AND THE ARTS

(1983)

This sequel to the essay preceding was, first, the Williams Memorial Lecture of the Arts Council of Great Britain and then in variously revised forms a lecture at the Royal Institute of British Architects, the Stratford Shakespeare Festival in Stratford, Ontario, and the National Assembly of State Art Agencies in Hartford, Connecticut. Finally, it became an article for both Ethos *and* American Theatre Magazine. *Recycling is the metaphor that comes to mind. Only my knowledge of the infinite kindness and restraint of my critics allows me thus to tempt them.*

What follows is the most complete treatment of this vital subject I have achieved.

Some fifteen years ago I inaugurated at Harvard a seminar on the economics of the arts. Except possibly by the students, the course was regarded with general disapproval. My artist friends saw it — to the extent that they saw it at all — as a rather philistine performance; nothing could so surely degrade art as an association with economics, a point to which I will return. My fellow economists saw my enterprise as essentially frivolous, possibly even eccentric. It was not the sort of thing with which the true scholar should be concerned; economics has to do with monetarism, budget deficits and the theory of rational expectations.

Both the artists and the economists were reacting in accordance with the accepted traditions of their discipline or profession. The artist's world is sufficient unto itself; as an indication of merit, economic reward is incidental, unimportant and perhaps perverse. Admiring mention is made of the starving artist, almost never of the affluent one. In modern times artists do get very rich, notably in Hollywood and New York but even in Paris. Partly as a consequence the relevant forms of artistic endeavor — films, television and popular music recordings — are considered to be on the fringe of artistic achievement. Money being involved, they are not "true art."

The attitude of professional economists toward the arts is less equivocal, which is to say they hardly ever think about them. One of the problems — and in some measure one of the pleasures — of my seminar was the nearly total absence of professionally qualified reading matter. Economists get their backs into steel, automobiles, chemicals and textiles. No economist is quite respectable who does not have a thoughtful view on the prospects of the high-technology industries — the "high-tech sector." Art, on the other hand, is outside their purview. Though things are said to be better now, *The New York Times* reported in late 1982 that the Broadway theater was suffering severely from the current recession — the worst season in many years. No economist turned his or her attention to the problem. No newspaper would have thought it an appropriate story for the business pages — or for an economic reporter. The greatest economic figure of this century, John Maynard Keynes, was deeply interested in the arts. This was thought quite remarkable — his biographers always mention it with some wonder. But even Keynes was not especially concerned to build bridges between economics and the arts. He only lived in the two worlds; he didn't try to merge them.

I am persuaded that there is, in fact, a close relationship between economics and the arts and that there are extremely practical rewards from a better understanding of this relationship and of the role of the artist in the modern economy.

We should begin with the question of how the artist is supported. Alone among all participants in economic and social life, he or she has been judged by performance without consideration for compensation. Poverty is thought consistent with great artistic achievement; it may even be good for it. From Aristotle's approval of slavery to Herbert Spencer's Social Darwinism — the improvement of the race by the economic euthanasia of the poor — social thought has been noted for the convenience of its conclusions. This is the case here; we believe we can have great artistic performance without paying for it.

There are four other aspects to the relationship between economics and the arts that are of increasing, even urgent, concern. The first is the important role of objects of art — paintings, sculptures and other artistic artifacts — in the capital stock of the modern community, with the problems of management thus implied. The second is the expanding role of all art in the standard of living and thus as a constituent factor in the economy as a whole. Third, there is the extremely important and much neglected connection between art and general industrial achievement. The artist, I shall argue, is a modern key to

business success no less than the scientist or engineer. Finally, there is
the frequent tendency for art and especially architecture to be subordinate to economics — a truly disastrous thing. I come to each of these
matters in turn.

In recent times, notably in the last ten years, art has become a major
object of investment. Competing with those who advise on the purchase
of stocks, bonds and real estate, and rivaling them in self-confidence
and frequent incompetence, are those who advise on investment in
objects of art. Once the man of wealth went to the counting house or
his bank safe-deposit box to view the results of his financial acumen;
now very often he looks at his walls.

I see no great and solemn difficulties in this development as regards
either the artist or the investor. Much of this investment goes to building
up the capital values in established works of art. The rewards do often
accrue, alas, not to the artists but to those who, fortuitously, inherit or
otherwise possess. But, in the manner of the trickle-down effect of the
supply-side economists, something accrues to the established painter
or sculptor, and some high-risk capital goes to the man or woman who
still has a reputation to make or, however recklessly, is trying something
new. This is good; the adverse effect of money on artists has been
greatly exaggerated. The cases of Raphael, Titian, Michelangelo, Leo-
nardo and of others from Rubens down to Picasso show that great art
can overcome the perils of great personal wealth. Nor is there need to
reserve much concern for the investors. While some will gain, others
will suffer loss. It is a well-established feature of the capitalist system
that fools (along with quite a few other people) and their money are
regularly separated. We should encourage investment in art and the
arts and worry not at all about the enrichment of artists or the losses
to investors.

There is, however, a much more serious problem here for those who
safeguard artistic treasures in our museums. They are now the custodians of resources of great pecuniary value in all countries; increasingly this wealth will be the object of avaricious or incompetent attention.
It must be closely watched; there must be a powerful presumption
against its dissipation for any purpose whatever. The pressures are not
slight, and they will grow.

In particular, we must not assume that there is greater safety in these
matters when we entrust administrative decisions to people outside the
artistic and professional curatorial world. In recent times large American museums, including the Metropolitan in New York, have moved
to accord major responsibility to professional administrators. The task,
it is held, is too large, too complex, the responsibility too great, for the
ordinary professional museum director from the artistic world. This is

wrong. Anyone of average aptitude can master the elements of admin-istration. Were it otherwise, modern business and government would be in a sad state of disarray. It is safer and better and wiser that we leave the policy judgments on artistic matters to those with both an understanding of and a deep moral commitment to the arts. We should not believe that there is some superior financial wisdom with which those who guard our artistic treasures must be endowed.

The next aspect of the relationship between economics and the arts has to do with the growth of the national income and product. That the arts add in a significant way to economic product is a matter little mentioned in our time, but their contribution is both important and extremely durable. Who from the sixteenth century has contributed to economic activity so consistently, year in and year out, as Shakespeare? Or from the seventeenth century as Molière? Or in modern times as Messrs. Gilbert and Sullivan or George Gershwin? Had these been businessmen or engineers or scientists, we would not question that they had added to the Gross National Product. My one-time Harvard colleague Joseph Schumpeter noted with much pleasure that each spring the American young of the most resolutely democratic instinct depart for Europe to see the monuments of past despotism. He could as well have said that they celebrate the continuing economic contribution of the arts. Can one suppose that even the Wright brothers did more for the travel industry than did Michelangelo, Raphael, Titian or Sir Christopher Wren?

Such is the lesson of the past — the past contribution of the arts to economic product — but it continues and expands in our own time. As individuals and nations increase in wealth, art in its various manifestations becomes an increasingly important part of the living standard. Good figures are not available; we are, in the best legal phrasing, absent a good definition as to what is art. But there are things we can accept that we cannot count. Affluent princes, merchants and churchly congregations turned throughout history to art; it was the affluent who purchased and conserved our present treasure. Bread, clothing, shelter, various material artifacts and possibly alcohol have the first claim on income; when these are obtained, people turn to beauty, and the visual and performing arts become, increasingly, a part of daily life. When life is meager, so is the artistic expression; with affluence, it expands. And so, more than incidentally, does the public responsibility to, and of, the artist. I speak particularly of the latter.

The artist has long been a socially acceptable figure or something more; a painter or musician adds esteem to a public occasion that even a successful and moderately articulate banker does not. But for all somber economic and political matters the artist has been considered peripheral and irrelevant. No one has imagined that the painter or musician had the same right to be heard on economic or political questions — to enter or speak in Parliament — as the person solidly associated with the production of goods. This the artist, broadly speaking, once accepted. Now, however, in the modern society of relatively high well-being — a well-being that survives even the attentions of modern governments and their ability to tax — the economic contribution of the painter, sculptor, film maker, theatrical producer or musician is increasingly great, and with this goes the right to speak and be heard on economic and related social and political concerns.

But more than a right is involved; there is the duty of the artist to participate so that the arts will be better served by the state. We have in our time a wide variety of public and social intervention on behalf of established industry. Education, scientific research, patent protection, tax incentives, public bailouts of failed enterprises, are all seen as legitimate forms of public and social support to the industrial sector. In the modern affluent community the economic justification for education in, and public support to, the arts should not be less than that for any other aspect of economic life. Science and the arts serve equally the standard of living; they serve similarly the growth in the Gross National Product. This is not recognized in our conventional fascination with the engineer and the scientist. What is required is a strong, responsible participation in national affairs by all concerned with the arts.

I come now to the third part of the relationship between art and economics: the importance of the artist in orthodox industrial development.

It is the not wholly harmless vanity of the scientist and the engineer that they are on the frontier of modern industrial achievement. It is the scientist and the engineer who open the way to new lines of economic activity; it is they who are responsible for the improvements that make possible the progress and survival of established industry. In the older industrial countries we look with some despair on the state of our older industry. And we look with hope on that which incorporates the new and higher technology, feeling that that is where our salvation lies.

I do not, of course, want to minimize the role of technological achievement. I do wish that more of it was directed to raising the excellence of our civilian products and less to making the weaponry that promises the destruction of all civilian life and, let us not doubt, our whole artistic heritage as well. But we must cease to suppose that science and the resulting technological achievement are the last step in industrial advance. Beyond science and engineering is, once again, the artist; he or she is a growing part of our national product; willingly or unwillingly, the artist is also vital to ordinary industrial progress in the modern world.

The basic point is a simple one, and it applies to the widest range of industrial products: after utility comes design; after things *work* well, people want them to *look* well. And design depends not alone on the availability of artists; it invokes the depth and quality of the whole artistic tradition. It is on this that modern industrial success has come to depend.

Proof is wonderfully evident once we learn to look for it. One of the miracles of industrial achievement in the second half of the twentieth century has been Italy. Since World War II, she has gone from one public disaster to another with one of the highest rates of economic growth of any country in the Western industrial world. No one has cited in explanation the superiority of Italian engineering or Italian science. Or her industrial management. Or the precision of her government policy and administration. Or the discipline and cooperativeness of her unions and labor force. Italy hs been economically successful over the last thirty-five years because Italian design is better — because her products appeal more deeply to the world's artistic sense. And Italian design reflects, in turn, the superb commitment of Italy to artistic excellence extending over the centuries and continuing down to the present day. Such is the role of the artist in the modern Italian economic success.

But the Italian case is only the most vivid. The industries of Paris, New York and London — textile design, interior decorating, dress manufacture, advertising, film making and theater — all survive in these otherwise economically inhospitable surroundings because of their juxtaposition to the arts. And there is ample indication that they survive better in consequence — are less vulnerable both to the competition of the new lands and the devastation of modern economic policy — than the solid industrial establishments of traditional economic achievement, the steel mills, automobile factories and coal mines. There has been little notice or discussion of the fact that in the older industrial countries the cities that best survive are those which coexist with a strong artistic tradition.

Nor is this all. The artistic tradition preserves and cultivates an important form of economic enterprise, the small nonbureaucratic firm. The artist, it has long been known, fits badly into organization; he is the obverse of the organization man. In consequence, those industries that have an artistic orientation tend to be small, more flexible, less prone to the immobility and frequent inefficiency of the modern great private or public bureaucracy. Association with the arts thus helps to preserve a smaller, more resilient form of enterprise. My friend and one-time colleague the late Fritz Schumacher made memorable the phrase "Small is beautiful." It could equally have been "Beautiful is small."

I come now to the final juxtaposition of art and economics, one that I offer with a certain unnatural diffidence. The artist tends, on occasion, to be subordinate to economics — its unduly obsequious servant. Much criticism of this has been heard; the painter, theatrical producer or composer who has his eye too obviously on the market or box office has for long been made to suffer for his sin. An imaginative range of invective has condemned the prostitution, as it is said, of his talent. The artist should have only one master, his own artistic sense and conscience.

We must also recognize, however, that compromise, even when unwelcome, is a rule of life. Compromise is especially certain in the case of one particular art form, architecture, for there is little building anywhere in the world that does not have to make concessions to economic purpose. All architecture is, and must be, in greater or lesser measure in the service of economics. No other form of art is quite so vulnerable to economic influence, management and control.

This influence should, of course, be recognized. And, I would argue, also resisted — resisted far more effectively than in the last century or so. I put the matter strongly: nothing that is built strictly and single-mindedly for economic purpose is ever very good. The good architect must always be at odds with economics, including the economic constraints of his client. There will, inevitably, be some compromises, but never must it be supposed that the architect is wholly and naturally subordinate to economic purpose.

Proof on this matter is palpable. None of the great architectural masterpieces of the past was subordinate to utility. The medieval cathedral builders were not told to provide a simple sheltering place of worship reflecting the modest economic resources of the age. Shah Jahan did not tell his unknown architectural genius to provide a plain and decent last resting place for Mumtaz Mahal, something along the lines of one of the better mausoleums at Forest Lawn. I've mentioned Professor Schumpeter's comment on the pilgrimages to see the architectural achievements of despotism. They are sought out not because of the genius of past tyranny but because their design and construction were free from economic restriction.

In the 1950s, if I may make a personal case, the United States built an Embassy Chancery in New Delhi; the architect was Edward Durell Stone. It is a building of great beauty and minimal utility. Most of the space in the center is given to a lovely water garden; the offices were a pleasant afterthought. I was in India in the years after it was completed, and I never entered it, however dreary the day's occupation, that my heart didn't lift a little in response. The Chancery was made possible because our shipment of food to the Indians had endowed us with many millions of otherwise unusable rupees. The opportunity cost was negligible. And because the building was sufficiently remote from Washington, neither the cost nor the subordination of utility to imagination and charm became a matter of critical comment.

Not since my days in New Delhi have I questioned the importance of according the architect the maximum ascendancy over the lesser art of economics. We have built more in this century than in all earlier history combined, and there is only a small fraction of it that attracts our wonder. There should be no doubt as to the reason: our modern architects have been unduly in the service of economics.

ANANDA COOMARASWAMY*

(1978)

The world of Indian painting is one in which, since I discovered it during a sojourn on the subcontinent in 1956, I have spent much time. Ananda Coomaraswamy, as I here tell, brought this world to the West.

A harmless enjoyment in life, one that has been raised to a minor art form in the academic community in which I reside, is the ability to speak knowledgeably about someone, preferably someone of importance, of whom your audience has never heard.† For all so inclined, as well as others of better scholarly tone, these three volumes are nearly ideal. Outside a narrow specialist world, Ananda K. Coomaraswamy is adequately unknown, but his contributions in the first half of this century to the history of art, to the sources of traditional crafts and to numerous other subjects were varied and, subject to some dispute, of high interest.

What is not in doubt is that Coomaraswamy largely discovered and then described one of the world's great art treasures, the paintings of the princely courts of western and northern India, especially those in the small-to-minuscule states in the valleys and on the foothills of the Himalayas above the Punjab Plain. And he rescued hundreds of the best examples, mostly for the Museum of Fine Arts in Boston or, as it was then called, the Boston Museum. I use the word *rescued* advisedly; the paintings, often offensively called miniatures, are in fragile colors on even more friable paper, and they were previously possessed by people who had no real sense of their worth. Had Ananda Coomara-

---

* This was a review, originally published in *The New York Times Book Review*, of *Coomaraswamy: His Life and Work* by Roger Lipsey, and *Coomaraswamy*, Volume 1, *Selected Papers, Traditional Art and Symbolism*, and Volume 2, *Selected Papers, Metaphysics*, edited by Roger Lipsey (Princeton: Princeton University Press, 1978).
† See my essay on Robertson Davies, page 98.

swamy not recognized and assembled them, most would have been lost to rubbish heaps, sunlight, white ants or casual purchase, as many must have been lost before and some are still being lost today.

Coomaraswamy was born in 1877 of parents whose background was a metaphor of his life. His father was a Ceylonese lawyer and political leader, the first Asian to be admitted to the practice of law in Britain. His mother was an intelligent Englishwoman with an interest in Eastern life and thought, who became a widow when her son was two years old. Ananda Coomaraswamy, like his parents, was destined to live between the two worlds — spiritually and artistically in Asia, physically, except for brief periods, in England and New England.

As an adult, he went first, however, to Ceylon, and in consequence of a brilliant academic career in science at the University of London, he was named head of the newly formed Mineralogical Survey there. His interest was soon to shift from the physical sciences to crafts and arts, and, in 1908, he published his first major work as an art historian, *Mediaeval Sinhalese Art.* He came also in these years to identify himself increasingly with India, which was a relatively easy step, for his father was of the Tamil minority in Ceylon (he had been their representative on the colonial Legislative Council), a community that had migrated from India a few hundred years earlier.*

By the time this first book was published, Coomaraswamy had returned to England and, with the aid of a substantial inheritance, established himself in a rather grand house in the Cotswolds. He quickly made himself a participant in English cultural and intellectual life and was soon involved in the rather incredible debate then in progress as to whether India had ever produced any art worthy of the name. It was the Establishment view, more or less, that it had not. Though it had hardly been so planned, the fruits of Coomaraswamy's journeys back to India from 1909 to 1913 (when he also came into close association with the Tagore family) went far to convince even the most parochial that it had. For it was then that he identified, classified, discussed and acquired the work of the anonymous seventeenth- and eighteenth-century painters (including some who lived as late as the early decades of the last century) that had been done in the *ateliers* of the courts of Rajasthan (as it now is) and the Punjab Hills.

From India Coomaraswamy also brought back nationalist and *swaraj* views, though he was never a political activist, and he developed some very serious doubts as to whether any Indian or Ceylonese was obliged to get himself killed for England in the trenches in France. Given the passions of the time, it was not a wholly comfortable position to hold in the Cotswolds, and, in 1917, he moved to Boston.

*And which in recent times has been in a state of severe tension with the Sinhalese majority.

There can be inspired works of art and equally inspired action by the people who buy, house, hang and care for them; there was such inspiration then. Though Coomaraswamy and his collection were nearly unknown at the time, the Boston Museum soon absorbed them both, and there he remained, serving first as a keeper and then as a fellow, all the while reading and writing prodigiously until he died, in 1947.

Coomaraswamy rarely encountered an artistically accomplished woman without marrying her; it was his talented fourth wife, Doña Luisa, who set about assembling and annotating his papers after his death. Then, when she died, Professor Roger Lipsey, variously of the University of Texas, Princeton and the State University of New York, took over the task and in it had the help and encouragement of Dr. Rama P. Coomaraswamy, the distinguished New York surgeon who is Ananda's son. These volumes are the result.

As his reviewer, one should obviously have the same breadth of interest and knowledge as Coomaraswamy, and to be a competent judge of the selections here made, one should have read all his published papers. I fail both tests, although there is much comfort in the thought that there is no one alive who would pass. The subject matter of the volume on metaphysics is beyond my pedestrian reach, for stating as truth what can only be imagined always worries me. But that is an old and trite complaint. The essays on traditional art, ranging from that of Buddhist Asia to that of the New York/New England Shakers, are varied, imaginative, incredibly learned and sometimes nearly incomprehensible. I found them all fascinating.

It is probably with the volume on Coomaraswamy's life and work that the decently curious general reader should begin. It is clearly and carefully written and documented — all in all, what is called a good scholarly job. Professor Lipsey has provided less than diligent admirers of both Coomaraswamy and Indian painting with far more than they had any right to hope for or expect — an excellent and comprehensive introduction to Coomaraswamy in the original.

W. G. ARCHER AND
THE PAINTINGS OF INDIA*

(1974)

W. G. Archer was a quiet, unassuming man of great charm who was loved by all who knew him. As Ananda Coomaraswamy was responsible for the collection of Indian paintings at the Boston Museum of Fine Arts, so Archer catalogued and celebrated those at the Victoria and Albert Museum in London.

To the traveler looking north from the Punjab Plain in India, the Himalayas seem to rise as a sudden, great, impermeable wall. But this is an illusion. First there are foothills with valleys behind or between. Other valleys, some wide, some mere clefts in the wall, run far into the mountains. The most famous of these, the Vale of Kashmir, lies deep behind the first Himalayan range. To this day these valleys, that of Kashmir apart, are little visited, to outsiders not much known. On those who do know them, they exert a compelling fascination. Partly this is because of their contrast with the plains; unlike the latter — Kipling's sand under a burning glass — the valleys are cool and green with fresh, fast streams. Partly it is the women, who are tall, clear-skinned, erect and, one senses, confidently aware of their India-wide reputation for beauty. Partly it is the mountains. All other mountains the eye associates with the earth; these belong to another, more remote world related to the heavens.

It is also part of the magic of these valleys that for 175 years — from, say, 1650 to 1825 — they nurtured some of the world's best painting. In Mughal times and for a bit longer, as the British extended their influence north and west from Calcutta and Madras, the valleys and adjacent hills were ruled by Rajput (Hindu) feudatories. Some of the

*This was a review, orginally published in *The New York Times Book Review*, of *Indian Paintings from the Punjab Hills: A Survey and History of Pahari Miniature Painting* by W. G. Archer (London and New York: Sotheby Parke Bernet, 1974).

states were of appreciable size — Kangra, the most notable, was around eighty miles long by thirty-five wide. More were very small — a few villages, as in the case of Kotta, in an area five miles by ten. Under the relaxed eyes of the Mughal rulers, who exacted a little rent, the princes of these states inhabited large, romantic, rather squalid forts and sallied forth for sport, love and war, the last having principally the purpose, recreation apart, of winning tribute from their less powerful neighbors. In moments of repose, the rajahs contemplated the work of their artists. Almost two thirds of the mountain kingdoms had a tradition of painting; any court with any claim to distinction supported an *atelier*. This could not have cost very much, for the artists, with rare exceptions, were anonymous and, like the carpenters with whom they ranked in caste, often badly paid.

Tens of thousands of paintings were accomplished in these courts, most of them indubitably bad. But many — many thousands, in fact — were exquisite. Of the good and bad alike the world was in ignorance until early in the twentieth century, when both, but particularly some of the good ones, began turning up in the bazaars of Amritsar and Lahore. There they caught the eye of Ananda K. Coomaraswamy,* a sensitive and eloquent Ceylonese scholar, who published the first study of this subject and who also, more than incidentally, brought some of the best of the paintings into the collection of the Museum of Fine Arts in Boston.

Coomaraswamy's description of the work has never been bettered. It creates, he said, "a magic world where all men are heroic, all women are beautiful, passionate and shy, beasts both wild and tame are the friends of man, and trees and flowers are conscious of the footsteps of the Bridegroom as he passes by. This magic world is not unreal or fanciful, but a world of imagination and eternity, visible to all who do not refuse to see with the transfiguring eyes of love." He could have added that the paintings were done with a delicacy of line and mastery of color that have not often been equaled.

Others took up the study where Coomaraswamy left off. One was Karl Khandalawala, author of the notable work *Pahari Miniature Painting;* another was a truly eclectic figure of the twentieth century — a civil servant, university administrator, natural historian, orchardist, agriculturist, soil conservationist and art historian — Mohinder Singh Randhawa. A third, W. G. Archer, was their friend and Randhawa's colleague in the truly great Indian Civil Service. In 1947, when Indian independence brought his secondary preoccupation as an imperial administrator to an end, Archer reverted to his major interest, which was Indian art and literature. He became keeper of the Indian Section of

*See the preceding essay.

the Victoria and Albert Museum in London and set about writing the definitive work on, as it is called, Pahari painting, or paintings from the Punjab Hills. This is it.

For the Christmas trade each year, as all are aware, the book publishers in the Christian world produce lovely art books, resplendent with color. Some people buy them for those of their relatives who are known to have taste. Some buy them apologetically, even clandestinely, because such volumes have a questionable reputation: they are thought by the sensitive to substitute size for erudition and cost for any conceivable artistic interest. However, no one can have any misgivings about this work. It is the ultimate in careful, literate, uncompromising scholarship.

Except for the frontispiece, Archer has eschewed all color plates; black-and-white pictures carefully selected and reproduced serve better his purpose of exemplifying the work of every court and period. Also, he can have hundreds of them without raising the cost of the book above the already adequate $84. After a general introduction, he traces the history of the state and the history of painting (if any) at each of the thirty-five courts. Very often he doesn't have much to go on. The rajahs of the hill states were not compulsive memoirists; few had archives in excess of what could be carried on horseback. Many, one suspects, were illiterate. Archer had to rely on the reports of visitors, bits and pieces of recorded history, the researches and recollections of other scholars and savants and the ample but misty accumulation of oral legend.

Visiting India in 1956, and specifically the Bharat Kala Bhavan in Benares, I fell in love with Indian painting, a susceptibility to which I had previously thought myself professionally and perhaps ethnically immune. Since then I have traveled through the valleys, studied the pictures by the hundreds of hours, read, I think, everything in English on the subject, co-authored a book on Indian art, much of it on this painting, and been allowed to converse at length more or less as an equal with the exceptionally select company of people who know the subject. Alas, none of this qualifies me to disagree with W. G. Archer. I cite two examples of my surrender.

Some of the most distinctive and beautiful painting of the Punjab Hills was done at the tiny court of Guler. (According to received but deeply improbable history, this court owed its origins to a notably amiable ruler of the neighboring state of Kangra, who, around 1405, fell into a well while hunting. When bailed out by a passing merchant twenty-seven days later, he found that his wives had immolated themselves on a pyre, as decency then required, and his younger brother had succeeded to the throne. Rather than make a nuisance of himself, he founded a new kingdom.) Some ten or eleven years ago, I learned from an old pandit down from the hills that he had recently sold two superb paintings to a tourist trap. I redeemed them, not without profit to the entrepreneur, and they are now, safely I hope, in a museum; it could have been my major service to this art. For a decade I've ascribed them with much assurance to Guler, the style of painting they most resemble, and they have been so catalogued and displayed. Archer says of one, "Its stiff pallor . . . decisively separates it from Guler painting, and the arrow-shaped floral patterns on the cushions . . . also connect[s] it with a centre [Basohli] further to the West." He is equally firm on the other.

Similarly on the origins of Pahari painting itself. Many believe it began in these valleys in the mid-seventeenth century as the Mughal power in Delhi under Aurangzeb was becoming antagonistic to artists and generally falling into confusion and disrepute. (The Mughals never tidied up the problem of succession. The kingdom went to the son who with the most foresight slaughtered his siblings. This led to mistrust, ill will, a lack of family solidarity and much fighting. Additionally, an ambitious son occasionally found it advantageous to have his father assassinated in order to be able to dispatch his brothers at the most propitious time.) It seems reasonable to suppose that, devoid of patrons and patronage, the artists took rather literally to the hills, where they established a new tradition. The sophistication of their work in these highly unsophisticated courts would seem to affirm that hypothesis, but Archer, alas, does not agree. He thinks it only a nice theory for which, unfortunately, there is no supporting evidence. Again I must yield on what I have always believed, for in this book one knows oneself to be truly in the hands of the master.

⁌ 5 ⁌

ARTISTS OF THE RAJ*

(1979)

*This short item is to serve two purposes: to show the breadth and depth of the
artistic interests of the Archer family and to recall a nearly forgotten circumstance, the movement of British artists to India, who went there to capture
something of the Indian scene and to do portraits and earn income that could
not be had in England.*

As the British Raj moved north and west in India from Bengal, it came
upon one of the most prolific and enchanting artistic traditions the
world has known flourishing in the *ateliers* of the princes in the capitals
of the princely states. Sadly, the talent of these artists was less than
fully appreciated by the servants and soldiers of the East India Company, and, indeed, it was not fully discovered and valued until the
present century. But most people at most times have sought the tenuous
association with immortality that comes from portraits or photographs.
And, when far away, all, without known exception, wish for pictures
with which to inform and impress the less fortunate or the less adventuresome back home. The men of the Company retained the Indian
artists to depict themselves, their houses, servants, daily routine, camp
life and, extensively, the odd flora and fauna of India. In time, this art
created by the Indians for their rulers achieved a name — the Company
School. Many of its portraits of Englishmen have a vaguely Oriental
aspect.
    What is far less known, even to those who have lived in the enchanted
world of Indian painting, is that there was also a companion flow of
talent out from England to take advantage of the Indian patronage

*This was a review, originally published in *Books and Bookmen* in England, of *India and
British Portraiture, 1770–1825* by Mildred Archer (London and New York: Sotheby Parke
Bernet, 1979).

and scene. It is of this that Mildred Archer, a fully certified member of the society of old India hands, tells in this most elegant (and expensive) of books. Mrs. Archer is perhaps the most admirably qualified person for her task in the world. For around a quarter of a century she has been in charge of the prints and drawings collection of the India Office in London. At work and at home she has been a diligent student of both Indian and British painting, and, with all else, she had the incomparable good fortune of being married to the late W. G. Archer.*

It was money, a greatly underestimated thing in the history of art, that drew British painters out to Calcutta and Madras. In the late eighteenth century the market for portraiture was thin in Britain, except for the work of such great figures as Reynolds and Gainsborough. And it was made worse by the feeling that anything that seemed good could be done better by a French artist or an Italian. But in India, because of the remunerative conjunction of government and commerce that still, in many cases, returned revenue to the same person, fortunes were being made. And this was by people who saw themselves, perhaps rightly, as doing strange and even heroic tasks in a strange land, all, needless to say, while wearing the brilliant official and military accouterments of the time. Commissions were also available from the Indian princes, who viewed themselves with at least as much admiration as the Europeans and to whom, as to Indian women, the English artists regularly gave a decent English look.

To this market — getting the permission of the East India Company and accepting the time-consuming journey around the Cape — the artists, including miniaturists, came. Some, like Thomas Hickey and Robert Home, adopted the country and remained for life. Others, such as Tilly Kettle, one of the pioneers, stayed a few years, accumulated a stock of rupees and went home. One or two, such as John Alefounder, succumbed to the climate and gave up. Alefounder, a minor figure, went home and killed himself with a penknife. Several were of little talent, although none so insignificant, one judges, that he didn't get invited to paint Warren Hastings if the governor general and the painter were there at the same time. Of portraits of Hastings there is a plethora.

Mrs. Archer deals thoroughly with all of these artists; I am persuaded that no one will ever learn a great deal more about any of them. Were the book concerned only with their art, however, one might complain; there is surely more here, including more about lesser figures, than one needs. Fortunately there is also much else. In telling of the work and lives of the painters, Mrs. Archer speaks in lucid and effective language of the social and cultural life of Calcutta and Madras at the

*See the preceding essay.

time, and with excursions to Oudh and into Mysore. And complementing her writing are hundreds of paintings and drawings, mostly in black and white but with a few vivid color plates, all selected and arranged with thought and taste to add a wide dimension of their own. Until someone can conduct a tour back to the early days of the extraordinary encounter of these two cultures, this book is, maybe, the next best thing.

THE PAINTINGS OF HUSAIN

(1974)

I here celebrate the work and personality of an artist whose paintings are known to a modest circle in India, Switzerland and New York. I do not set great store by my judgment in these matters; I do believe he deserves to be better appreciated.

I first met Maqbool Fida Husain, perhaps the most distinguished of modern Indian artists, in the intense light of an Indian morning sometime in 1963. He had come to the Embassy Residence to paint a portrait of my wife, and we chatted as he set up his easel. I yearn to think that I am on easy terms with artists; with Husain that was no problem. Then I went off to the Chancery and returned two or three hours later to find him packing up; the painting was finished. Once in a gallery in Delhi I had seen a Husain exhibition, and for the new portrait I had, literally, a rush of recognition. Deft drawing and high color, with the marvelous random touch of eccentricity, mark his works, and all were there.

Since that morning I've had occasional personal encounters with Husain. I remember them all — meetings in India, the opening of an exhibition in New York, a wonderful visit in Switzerland. He is a quiet man with an inner light and humor, piercing eyes and the face of a slightly bemused Biblical prophet. The reference to the Bible should not be thought inappropriate; Husain is a Muslim, but Islam is presumed to be tolerant; Christians are people of the Book.

He was born in Sholapur, Maharashtra State, in India in 1915, the only son of a middle-class family. His father, a man evidently of some inner tension, was an accountant. That Husain had a marked gift for drawing was early observed; he showed also, and retains, a special talent for verse. So, with the logic that often applies in such matters, he was apprenticed to a tailor. It was thought, his biographers have said, that anyone so endowed could cut cloth with grace and precision.

Fortunately it was not a durable commitment, and he continued to paint in every spare moment. He had some limited instruction while still in high school and a year of further study under N. S. Bendre, a teacher of quality, at the Indore School of Art. Thence he went on to Bombay to devote himself fully to painting.

The early years in Bombay involved all of the hardships that are assumed by those not experiencing them to be so salutary for the artistic soul. Husain's first earnings as a painter came from doing billboards, but gradually in the years of World War II and after, his work began to reach a widening circle of admirers, first in India and then beyond, in Europe and the United States.

However, Husain's roots remained strongly in his native land. Many have sensed in his paintings, and I would like to think that I do also, the tensions, anxiety and, on occasion, pessimism that Muslim India has experienced in consequence of partition and the recurring outbreaks of communal conflict on the subcontinent.

Husain is a prodigious worker. I suppose for most great painters, as was said so often of Picasso, painting is not something they do but something they live. Brush and palette are as his instrument to the musician — without them the artist does not exist. Certainly this is so of Husain. Visitors to any exhibition of his work will see a representative showing; if they turn to a book on Husain, they will find, I suspect, a nearly new fare; and if they are so fortunate as to go to another, different exhibition, the paintings there, in all probability, will also be new.

Husain's work is prodigious not only in quantity but also in variety. His painting has had many themes and moods and also been of many styles. I have often thought that it would be a test of one's knowledge of art over the last forty years if one could detect the influences bearing at various times on Husain. He is a man deeply conscious of the world around him and totally aware of what artists in the world around are doing. Perhaps, however, it would not be such a good test after all, for if Husain is eclectic, he is also *sui generis*. Far more in his work, one senses, has come from within than from without.

He is, as well, an amused and bemused man. The amusement carries over into his painting. Indians are presumed to be a solemn people, but one will miss something of Husain if one doesn't allow for an occasional quiet spoof. This is true in particular of his pen-and-ink drawings; no one has made people or elephants more hilariously funny.

I sometimes wonder if others are as embarrassed as I am in writing about painting. I have in the past found pleasure in telling of the work of the seventeenth- and eighteenth-century artists of India; there are legends to be recounted, symbols to be interpreted, things not readily available to the casual eye to be pointed out. The writer here has some advantage over the viewer. But many descriptions of modern painting say in condescending tones what the person who reads them can see for himself or herself. And in work such as that of Husain I am never certain that what I see is what comes to the eyes of others. One's interchange with art is an exclusive thing. Who can tell others what they should or will see? I therefore here content myself with inviting, even urging, all who read this to enjoy their own personal and richly rewarding interchange with Husain.

· V ·

A SMALL CLUTCH OF LETTERS

I WRITE LETTERS to the newspapers not to persuade people, for which such communications are largely worthless, but to please myself, to celebrate absurdity and because the truth on many matters is a most agreeable weapon, and I rejoice to think that it causes embarrassment, even some slight pain.

THE BEAUTIFICATION OF AMERICA

(1967)

The cleaning up of our roadsides is an old interest of mine, one to which I might claim to have made at least a marginal contribution, for I addressed the need for it in The Affluent Society. *More perhaps to the point, as a member of an advisory committee to Governor Philip Hoff in Vermont, I joined in urging the action that made that state among the first to give precedence to unspoiled meadows and fields.*

May 31, 1967

To the Editor of *The Washington Post:*

As the battle over the billboards reopens in Washington, I trust that all will be aware of the high moral ground the enemies of the grass and trees now plan to occupy. Speaking in mid-April to a House Public Works Subcommittee, Mr. Paul Spooner, Jr., general counsel of the Roadside Business Association, said: "Let the ambition and initiative of the sign companies and the advertisers determine where signs should go. It is not fair to beautify America at the expense of outdoor advertising."

2

LIBERALS
AND THE CORPORATE PROSE

(1978)

A greatly merited rebuke to Mobil. As to the remedial effect, I am less sure.

July 24, 1978

To the Editor of *The New York Review of Books:*

In your issue of June 15, an advertisement for Mobil Oil Corporation tells of the utter inability of the firm to "understand why so many liberals in this country are so hostile to private business." I would like to give those concerned an answer to their question: it is not so much hostility as suspicion, and this is extensively because the people who write such ads are manifestly so incompetent. Theirs, sadly, is an occupation in which substantial pay seems never to compensate for low professional ability. But blame must also be accepted by the executives who pass on the resulting prose. They are hopelessly inept, intellectually negligent or, possibly to their credit, they don't read this awful tripe.

Thus the advertisement in question notes that liberals have been among the prime movers in the enactment of the nation's social legislation — Social Security, public housing, school lunches and the like. It goes on to say:

> . . . All of these programs have to be financed by revenues derived mainly from taxes on individual and corporate income.
>
> The greater these incomes — which is to say, the more prosperous American business is — the greater the tax revenues. When incomes drop, as in a recession, so do tax revenues. Social programs then have to be reduced accordingly or supported by deficit financing, which over any extended period means inflation. For the poor and for people living on fixed incomes, inflation is the cruelest tyranny of all.

The inescapable meaning of the above is that inflation is caused by recessions. This, all, including all liberals, are expected to believe. Many who come up against such reasoning or nonreasoning will suppose that something is being hidden. The less suspicious but less charitable will adopt that slightly snobbish attitude toward business that the writers for Mobil identify and deplore. It's hard not to feel superior when faced with such logic as theirs.

But their incompetence could be even more damaging; it could also inspire concern. Most liberals would agree that if we are to get oil from the North Slope or the North Sea and automobiles by the millions to use it, we must have sizable corporations. But they may be led to wonder if those who manage the engineering, quality control, cost control, auditing and marketing in those firms are as retarded, as error-prone, as those who handle the advertising.

BAILOUT I

(1971)

That great corporate executives, when in trouble, will turn to Washington, we now take for granted. So they do in the three letters that follow. What is enchanting is the feeling that just before boarding the corporate jet for the journey of supplication, they must make a speech on the eternal verities of unfettered free enterprise.

July 27, 1971

To the Editor of *The New York Times:*

Mr. William H. Moore, chairman of the board of Bankers Trust, appears in your pages today on behalf of the loan guarantee for Lockheed. He begins by telling of his deep faith in free enterprise; he ends by asking for fast action from Washington — "Let's get on with the job." He neglects to mention that if Lockheed suffers the normal consequences of its own mismanagement, his bank will take a substantial bath. He should, in truth, disclose interest. But he should also confess that he is the kind of free enterpriser who is steadfast in his faith up to the very point where money may be made or lost. Then, like most others, he rushes hell-for-breakfast to the government. Wouldn't you prefer an honest socialist?

BAILOUT II

(1979)

August 6, 1979

To the Editor of *The Wall Street Journal:*

As a conscientious student of the free enterprise system, I note with no slight interest the request of the Chrysler Corporation for a billion-dollar bailout by the United States government, this being presented by some as an advanced tax rebate on as yet unearned profits. This request, one cannot doubt, will be granted. Even the finest and firmest free enterprise principles, we know, can be bent, as required, to pecuniary and corporate need. And government handouts, however debilitating to the poor, have never been thought inimical to the affluent.

However, it does seem fair, especially as one reflects on the impressive sum involved, that those providing this largesse should seek some small concessions. Thus if, as taxpayers, we are to invest $1 billion in Chrysler, could we not be accorded an appropriate equity or ownership position? This is usually thought a reasonable claim by people who are putting up capital. [After some fervent, even tearful, resistance, this was eventually accorded.] Also, as Chrysler becomes a publicly funded business, may we not properly ask that its executives confine their compensation to, say, the general range of pay thought acceptable for the President of the United States? Their present compensation is now rather higher, although not, it is evident, as a reward for good profit performance. And most important of all, could we not ask that all corporations and all corporate executives who approve or acquiesce by their silence in this expansive new public activity refrain most scrupulously from any more of their criticism of big government?

BAILOUT III

(1979)

September 25, 1979

To the Editor of *The Washington Post:*

It is now amply established in all of the industrial countries that if a corporation is large enough, it can no longer be allowed to fail and go out of business. So it was with Lockheed and the Eastern railroads in this country, with Leyland and Rolls-Royce in Britain and with dozens of large French and Italian firms. Socialism in our time comes not from socialists but from the heads of large corporations when they learn from their bankers that resort must be had to the government and fast.

This being the tendency, and because hardship for hard-working people is too readily prescribed for others, I now urge the government to underwrite Chrysler's new debts. I hope that my fellow liberals, after extracting moderate amusement from the revised attitudes toward government intervention so demonstrated, will do likewise. But taking cognizance of the full-page advertisements recently run by Chrysler, could we not ask that the company in its plea forgo its ritualistic free enterprise rhetoric about wanting to be saved by the market? And also its curious thought that it is not asking for a bailout? Chrysler is asking to be saved by the government, not the market; if the government assumes responsibility for the corporation's new debts, Chrysler is, indeed, being bailed out. If, as citizens and taxpayers, we are to come to its rescue, surely we can be given credit for our generosity.

An added thought: Were a man drowning in heavy seas, Chrysler copywriters would have him say, "I'm a strong swimmer; I can save myself. But do quickly throw me a life preserver to keep me from drowning, and please call it a minor flotation device."

INFLATION
AND THE CONSERVATIVES

(1981)

Another small effort to afflict the economically righteous with their forsaken principles — in this case the modern conservative commitment to the budget heresies of John Maynard Keynes.

December 11, 1981

To the Editor of *The New York Times:*

In today's columns you tell of a large convocation of presumptively conservative economists under the auspices of the avowedly conservative American Enterprise Institute in Washington. The subject of their discussion was inflation. All so assembled, with the exception of Mr. Herbert Stein, a member and chairman of the Council of Economic Advisers in earlier Republican times, are reported as approving of or, at a minimum, acquiescing in the impressive budget deficits now in prospect, given the fiscal designs of President Reagan.

There was a time when conservative economists were thought to be principled, even dogmatic, in their commitment to fiscal austerity. And a liberal can join in hoping that this may still be the case when, as now, a recurrence of inflation remains a serious threat, an incomes and prices policy is eschewed and an absence of fiscal restraint thus means an even greater reliance on murderous interest rates and tight money. Or more inflation.

It is not my instinct, God forbid, to instruct my conservative friends on matters of public virtue. But one can hardly avoid the thought that partisan loyalty has here replaced professional conviction — that an administration that calls itself conservative can do no wrong. In proof, one has only to contemplate what would have been the response at that distinguished symposium were a similar budget deficit being similarly defended by a liberal President and administration.

THE BUDGET DEFICIT INITIATIVE:
SOME AVARICE AS USUAL?

(1984)

The Establishment — economists, former public officials, a huge procession of corporate executives — mobilized its energies in 1984 against the Reagan deficits. At first glance this seemed a worthy enterprise, which I was asked to join. I did not; there was an unduly obvious intrusion of self-interest on the vital question of taxes and who was to pay them.

May 9, 1984

To the Editor of *The New York Times:*

With others I am impressed by the initiative that has led the past secretaries of the treasury and commerce to urge steps to reduce the budget deficit. And I am impressed by the number of former high public officials, academic figures and, notably, leading businessmen who joined in this effort, as indicated in the double-page appeal published in recent days in your newspaper. The issue, as the statement avows, is, indeed, too serious to be left to politics as usual. But, alas, as I had occasion to make known to leaders of this movement when approached on the matter, it is also too important to be left to Establishment myopia and executive self-concern, these also as usual.

This shortsightedness or worse emerges on the matter of taxation. Rightly it is held that effective action on the deficit will require tax increases. And there is merit in the contention that in a country of general well-being there is a place for consumption taxes. The old liberal case against such taxes diminishes when, for a largely affluent population, they curtail consumption of no great urgency and provide income for welfare, education and other services of high importance to the poor. Properly levied with proper use of the resulting revenues, these taxes can be progressive in effect. What is unforgivable in the statement under consideration is the transparent avoidance of any suggestion that personal or corporate income taxes might be increased, this in the aftermath of the Reagan reductions, with their high absolute reward in the top tax brackets — brackets in which, one hopes only incidentally, many of the signers of this statement are happily situated. It was, all the signatories know, the ill-considered reductions in personal and corporate income taxes that, along with the increases in the military budget, led to the deficit in the first place.

The statement attempts to give gloss to embarrassingly suspect self-interest by reference to the need "to avoid weakening incentives to work, save and invest." Are the corporation executives who signed this statement thus confessing that they were idling away their time before the Reagan tax reduction, that they needed its stimulus to get them back to work? Do they really believe that tax reductions for individuals have much to do with the willingness of corporations to invest, a point to which attention was drawn many years ago by John Maynard Keynes? And, most of all, can it really be supposed that Americans are politically so retarded that they don't know that the word *incentive* as here employed is, in normal use, an exceptionally unpersuasive cover for justifying more income for oneself?

To repeat, the plea against politics as usual is, indeed, appropriate. But equally appropriate and far more necessary is a plea against what can only appear, justly or unjustly, as smug protection of personal pecuniary interest.

8

ELECTION REPORTAGE:
FROM THE VACUOUS
TO THE VULNERABLE

(1984)

On occasion, reflecting my enjoyment in the exercise, I've written letters that never got sent. This one, as indicated, was to The New York Times. *It was much too long, and, alas, I didn't think it could be shortened.*

October 29, 1984

To the Editor of *The New York Times:*

It is reasonably well accepted that the media — newspapers, television, the radio — should inform the public on a wide range of subjects extending from politics to personal hygiene. The time has now come for the public to inform the media that their coverage of electoral campaigns is, not to put too fine a point on the matter, a national disgrace. The disgrace is not lessened by the evident fact that those involved have a high sense of professional accomplishment in their error. The matters I here address reflect some past personal experience in political campaigns, but I am principally impressed with how rapidly in recent elections things have become worse.

The first of the two major faults is the concentration on political strategy and tactics as opposed to issues in nearly, if not quite all, reporting. In the Democratic primaries of 1984, only the most diligent or accidentally fortunate reader could have learned where the various candidates stood on economic policy, arms control, the military budget or, for that matter, abortion. Senator Gary Hart was thought solidly associated with new ideas, which, however, almost no one paused to identify; there was only brief mention of the position of the other candidates against the B-1 bomber, the MX or high interest rates. What the reader was given, instead, was enduring comment on the strategic details of each candidate's campaign: his reliance on personality as opposed to organization, his supply of money and what access that allowed him to buy more television commercials and, above all, his plans for the various primaries — where he would make a major or only a token effort; where he would stand or stand aside; what he expected the other candidates to do; how he would contend with their more pedestrian strategies. One had wonderful information on the candidate's itineraries and his reception at meetings, nothing or next to nothing on what he said there.

The reasons for this emphasis (or misemphasis) are not, I think, seriously in doubt. As compared with comment on issues, it is enormously economical of intellectual effort. Reporting a presidential campaign is hard enough work without having to resort to thought. Additionally, a huge supply of untaxing material is available from the campaign manager, a political figure who, out of greatly misplaced self-confidence, claims a penetrating knowledge of how campaigns are conducted and won and who manages thus to impress reporters until the day of final defeat, after which he or she is never heard from again. Of the near infinity of such political geniuses in the last fifty years only James A. Farley is remembered, and his achievement belonged, in fact, to Franklin D. Roosevelt; had he managed a Reubin Askew, Farley would also have been forgotten. The myth of strategic genius is, however, an appealing thing while it lasts; all reporters have an enhanced sense of their own perception in telling of it; and, as I have noted, the manager in question has a compelling, sometimes pathological, desire to communicate his own strategic wisdom to the people covering his candidate. This is not a case of the blind leading the blind; it is a powerful manifestation of the vacuous leading the vulnerable.

There is a deeper reason for this emphasis on alleged strategy as opposed to issues. It is a requirement of the modern, highly institutionalized press, television and radio that political reporting must be objective — which is to say it must be neutral. One cannot have a reporter passing judgment or seeming to pass judgment on a candidate's position on deficit spending, survival in a nuclear-armed world or silent prayer in the schools. But it is very difficult to report a candidate's views on these matters without allowing common sense or, more especially, absurdity to shine through. This is perhaps especially true of Ronald Reagan on the budget deficit and school prayer, but it is a general problem. So the reporter, when he gets to issues, runs the risk that editors will suddenly come alert, that questions will be asked in the sacred name of so-called objectivity. Far better and certainly far safer to stick with the candidate's thinking on by-passing Maine, ignoring the nonbinding preference vote in Vermont, coming down hard on downstate Illinois as the very heart of the American political scene.

The second electoral aberration of the modern media is, of course, the devotion to polling. This, also, is wholly undemanding intellectually.

It is far, far easier to tell who is numerically ahead and who behind than to get into the tedious business of telling what is being said and how, in consequence, people are reacting. Polls have also a persuasive if spurious aspect of neutrality — spurious because they favor the front-runner right up until the day when, in the frequent manner of such phenomena, they are proved to have been wrong. The polls also appeal in some deeply subjective way to the curious journalistic belief that there is a supreme value in being first with a story, even if it's not right. Why wait for the result of the election when at modest cost and a less than modest risk of error one can tell what it will be a few hours, days or weeks before!

This is very silly. Children are taught that they must wait until Christmas Day to learn the nature of their gifts. We are presumed to be adults; we can also wait. There is no point whatever in predicting with inaccuracy what, in a few hours or a few days, will be known for sure. And this is especially so when the polling — the general fascination with who is ahead, who is behind and who will win — has replaced solid reporting on what the election is really about.

Realization that grownup people can wait and may, in all reason, prefer to wait will not come easily. A few years ago I was invited by one of the networks to comment on the results on the morning after an election, itself very possibly a questionable exercise. The studio, which had been in service throughout the night, looked like the underground command post of the Eighth Air Force at High Wycombe after a particularly difficult operation. The excitement was still high; a gubernatorial race in Ohio was close and as yet undecided. I was asked tensely my view as to the probable outcome. I replied that I wouldn't dream of offering it; it was profoundly stupid to be so concerned; in a mere hour or so all would know for certain. Rarely have I had such an adverse reaction. My host's voice quavered in anger; I thought I saw tears in his eyes; clearly I had been subversive of everything for which he stood, including the way that he made his living. Only with difficulty did I avoid expressing my regrets.

But I still stand firm. I plead for a deeply negative public response to the present preoccupation with electoral tactics and strategy. I propose that all who are questioned on their voting intentions or on how, on coming out of a polling booth, they have voted give, with all solemnity, a totally false reply. Let us hear instead about the issues; let us be informed when candidates seek to avoid them; and let all political strategists remain far back in the background of the campaign, where they belong.

9

ARE THE RICH
A DIRTY SECRET?

(1985)

This started as a letter to The New York Times *but was published as an Op-Ed piece. As in the previous letters and elsewhere on numerous occasions, I here urge that when we do something for the affluent at the behest of the affluent, as often we do, we be sufficiently honest to say so. Rarely have I been associated with an effort with so little likelihood of success.*

To The Editor of *The New York Times:*

There are few matters in which Americans have taken more pride over the last two centuries than their commitment to plain speech. All have heard it: we are a down-to-earth, plain-spoken people; we abhor evasion or cant. And with this have gone two other claims: we believe ourselves wisely alert to political motivation and chicane. And we are deeply attached to the thought that more income is more enjoyable than less. I would now like to urge that our supposedly forthright habits of speech be allowed to express what we all know to be true about politics and money.

Specifically, we accept that politicians and political parties come to power with an obligation to their supporters, and this normally involves improving their supporters' income. Yet such a thing may not be mentioned. Or if mentioned, it is subject to indignant denial and rebuke. Thus, the administration of Mr. Reagan assumed office a bit short of five years ago, and was reaffirmed in power last year, with the strong support of the more affluent members of the American public — company executives and corporate PACs (political action committees), the financial community, our more successful entrepreneurs, the otherwise comfortably rich as a class. There were many others, to be sure, but to those just mentioned Mr. Reagan was the most visibly beholden. From them came the large sums of money by which in our democracy political persuasion is all too extensively accomplished, and those so contributing were obviously in line for tangible economic reward.

Here, however, our commitment to candor came to an end. Three basic policies were early put in place by the administration — the supply-side tax reductions, an astringent monetary policy, a large increase in military expenditures. All had a wonderfully favorable impact on the upper-income brackets. All, politically, were a wholly normal reward by Mr. Reagan to his constituents. This, however, was not, could not be said. Even Democrats were unnaturally reserved.

The supply-side tax reductions, with their large absolute benefit in the upper-income brackets and the companion cuts in social expenditures, could not be seen as a service to the rich. Mr. Reagan angrily denounced a few vagrant statements to this effect as demagoguery. Cutting taxes was purely a design for invigorating the economy, *incentives* being the magic word. There was a major sensation in 1981 when Mr. David Stockman, the budget director, conceded that all this was, in reality, a cover for reducing the taxes on the affluent. Public admission of the most predictable of political motivations became an occasion for shocked surprise. Mr. Stockman was called severely to account. The American reputation for plain speech, indeed!

The suppression of our much celebrated candor is even more complete as regards monetary policy. Such policy is held to be neutral as between rich and poor. In fact, it works through high interest rates, which restrain the bank borrowing by which bank deposits, the most used form of money, are extensively created, and such interest rates, it will not be doubted, are very welcome to those who have money to lend. Those who have money to lend normally have more than those who do not have money to lend. As economic truth, this stands with the possibly apocryphal theorem of Calvin Coolidge that when many people are out of work, unemployment results.

Nor is this all. While rewarding those who lend money, monetary policy creates the unemployment that curbs union claims. And its high interest rates attract from abroad the funds that bid up the dollar, discourage exports, make imports cheap, keep farm prices down. We would not only redeem our reputation for clear speech, but have a much better understanding of monetary policy, if we recognized both its service to the affluent and its highly regressive effect on workers and farmers.

A more complex set of motivations is involved in the third major policy of the Reagan administration, the huge increase in military spending. The bilateral dynamic of the arms race, the oft-mentioned conservative fear of Communism and liberal fear of being thought soft on Communism, the bureaucratic power of the Pentagon, are all involved. But if we look deeper, we see that no one since the days of

President Eisenhower has doubted the powerful economic interest of the industrial half of the military-industrial complex. Weapons expenditures reward well-paid executives, technicians and stockholders, and their economic interest is sustained in Washington by a remarkably effective array of well-lubricated lobbies, now commonly called consultants. A budget policy that combines severe curtailment of social programs with large continuing weapons expenditure reflects the interest of the affluent in having more money. And once again this is little mentioned.

Such were the earlier services to the affluent by the Reagan administration. They continue now in the proposed tax reform bill. The cover story is simplification; that is all. The important intent and effect, as so far revealed, is a further major reduction in the top personal income tax brackets. However, this must not be said and so far it has not been said. At most, it can only be whispered.

There is, it is clear, a basic asymmetry in our political discourse. One can be for help to the poor — the hungry, the homeless, those without jobs or prospects. But one cannot be publicly for a policy on behalf of the rich. We have such policies; they are a wholly predictable aspect of our political alignments; it is only that they may not be admitted. The rich in our time have become a dirty secret. There must be that cover story, however improbable.

This effort at evasion is derogatory even of the affluent, for it implies that they are somehow disreputable. It is not thought intrinsically wrong under our system to have money and want more; it is not un-American. Nor was it considered wrong in the past. Dr. Johnson thought the pursuit of wealth one of the least harmful activities in which men until then had been engaged.

What is astonishing is this attempt to conceal obvious political and pecuniary motivation behind unconvincing protestations as to some implausible public good. That, to repeat, is to reject our proud claim to clear thought and plain speech. And surely the disguise succeeds only with those whose beliefs are unduly available.

10

MAYHEM AT
HARVARD STADIUM

(1977)

A deeply felt statement on organized athletics. I feel even more strongly about basketball, in which in college, since I am six feet, eight and a half inches high, my participation was sought and briefly gained. I've never since been to a game.

September 13, 1977

To the Editor of *Esquire* Magazine:

In your September issue you show a picture of the spectators at a recent Harvard-Yale football game in the minutes immediately before all present were exterminated by an exceptionally well-guided missile. I was, clearly, among them. You rejoice for the resulting gain to the Republic, but the gain was less than you and many of your readers will think.

I could not have been there, for I last attended a football game in the autumn of 1934. I was then persuaded to this depravity by a friend who had not previously wished me ill. Through an unendurably tedious afternoon under highly disagreeable weather conditions, the Harvard team, wearing an eccentric shade of red, shoved at a Dartmouth team wearing an uninteresting shade of green. And the Dartmouth team, in turn, shoved at the Harvard team and, as I recall, seemed stronger. The action took place on a desolate stretch of mud at a great distance from our seats. At the end of the game both teams were filthy and went off, I assume, to bathe. No identifiable skills were involved; the luck was of the peculiarly obvious kind — who lost his grip on an obviously slippery ball, who lost his footing on an obviously slippery landfill. I had found similar but greater interest in watching an aging professor negotiate the Widener Library steps with a large armful of books after a bad ice storm. The exceptionally dreary nature of the proceedings was lost on the nearby spectators because most of them were drunk. I'm told that the last forty-three years have brought no appreciable change, except that in some places (though not at Harvard) there is plastic grass.

I'm sorry that so many of my friends got hit by your weapon, and I note with interest that it was, in fact, a blimp. But people with so little judgment as to how to use their spare time were bound to suffer sooner or later or, this choice being available, both.

· 11 ·

DEPARTMENT OF
AMPLIFICATION

(1966)

Americans serving overseas must learn to react well to all contingencies — and also always be alert to save their government money.

December 29, 1966

To the Editor of *The New Yorker:*

In your issue of November 5, in the "Talk of the Town" — a heading that I gather should not in this instance be taken too literally — you tell of the wife of an American official in New Delhi who called the United States Embassy to ask that someone be sent to remove two cobras that had taken refuge from the rains in her garden. Snake charmers were dispatched; they piped diligently, but no snakes were forthcoming.

I do not write to question this story. On the contrary, during my service as United States ambassador in New Delhi a few years back, the established procedure was as described. That is not to say it was commonplace; the appearance of a snake at an American dwelling was sufficiently rare to have considerable conversational value. Rare or not, the snakes had a firm hold on the imagination of all our people. Near the Embassy staff headquarters in those days was a large rocky outcropping, which has since been blasted away and replaced by a swimming pool. A suggestion was once made that it be called Bunker Hill, after my predecessor, Ellsworth Bunker, now United States ambassador-at-large. But our people continued to call it Cobra Hill, after its presumed tenants. The official snake charmer was not, in my day, an employee of the Embassy. He was retained as a specialist on a fee basis at so much a snake. My successor, Mr. Chester Bowles, though an old Roosevelt New Dealer, was also a successful businessman and a New England governor, and I rather doubt whether he has altered this prudent system of compensation. The point is important for explaining why, in your story, no snakes were found.

During nearly all my stay in India, the minister counselor, deputy chief of mission and general manager of American activities in New Delhi was Mr. Benson E. L. Timmons III. A Rhodes Scholar, a trained economist and currently our ambassador to Haiti, Mr. Timmons belies the leisurely reputation of the professional Foreign Service officer by being a man of unbending vigilance where public money is involved and a relentless enemy of all forms of carelessness, laxity, hocus-pocus and fraud. In the summer of 1962, Mr. Timmons began to believe that the government of the United States was being snared by its snake charmer. He was especially suspicious of the ability of this skilled and dauntless man, whenever called, to lure large, handsome and exceedingly lethal-looking specimens out of the shrubbery and into the gunnysack he had brought for the purpose. The snake was always displayed when our man claimed payment; in the interest of safety (as in the recent case), the operation was conducted circumspectly, with all onlookers at a respectful distance. Mr. Timmons concluded that the American people were paying over and over again for the same snake.

His suspicions were never verified. A decent as well as a stern man, he merely warned that on the occasion of the next alarm the gunnysack would be examined *before* operations began. All that is known is that there was a drastic decline in the rate of recovery. Indeed, it fell from 100 percent to zero percent for the one or two incidents during the remainder of my tour. At zero — and here is the deeper significance of your story — it evidently still remains. So I imagine it may be in Haiti if snakes are a problem in that beautiful but beset land.

U.S. EMBASSY GEESE

(1965)

In New Delhi in front of the lovely Edward Durell Stone Embassy Chancery there was, in my time, a large, iridescent but sadly vacant pool. Reaching into my Canadian past, I thought how much it would be improved by the presence of some Canada geese. With the assistance of the Smithsonian Institution in Washington, four were obtained, two of which went to the New Delhi zoo, two to the empty pool. Here my defense against a hostile critic.

June 7, 1965

To the Editor of *The New York Times:*

Though I am compelled to speak from general knowledge, I must sharply question the New Delhi dispatch of your Mr. J. Anthony Lukas, under date of June 5, in which he accuses one of the Canada geese, formerly of the Chancery fountain, of having bitten an old lady. These geese are my friends; indeed, I installed them in the pool, and we came to know each other well. They are proud and aristocratic, rather contemptuous in bearing, even away from an embassy, and sometimes a trifle mean. But they would never, never bite an old lady. One bit an automobile one day — and broke his neck doing so. That is the kind of bird they are.

· VI ·

A BOOK OF PREFACES

I AM ASKED once a month, sometimes once a week, to introduce some writer's work — occasionally that of a friend, more often that of some would-be scholar of whom I've never heard. My excuses for not doing so are warm, compassionate and transparently fraudulent. Here, out of admiration and affection, are a few from the times I gladly yielded.

1

JAMES MILL:
The History of British India[*]

(1968)

For anyone with an interest in and concern for India, James Mill is absolutely essential. When this great book was republished a century and a half after its first appearance, I reread it with great and, because of my years in New Delhi, appreciably more informed interest. Not all of what I say of it would meet with Mill's approval.

James Mill was born in 1773 near Montrose, Scotland, of poor parents — his father was a cobbler and small landholder. Although not rich, his parents were ambitious for their son, and his mother in particular was determined that he should have a good education. After attending local schools, he went to the University of Edinburgh under the patronage of Sir John and Lady Jane Stuart, with whom he is assumed to have lived as, more or less, a member of the family. It was in Edinburgh that he began to develop what was to be his enduring passion for the Greek classics. It was his intention to prepare for the Church, not from any known interest in its work but because it was an accepted means of social and economic advance for impoverished Scottish youth at the time, as for many years thereafter. He first served as an itinerant preacher but in 1802 abandoned this vocation and went to London with Sir John Stuart.

Mill's early years in the English capital were less than happy. Initially he became a journalist and editor of two literary journals, did a translation and began his career as an essayist. But before long he had sufficient income to contemplate marriage, and therewith his life took a sharp turn for the worse. He ignored and probably disliked his wife, although this did not prevent him from having nine children by her, of whom John Stuart, named for his patron, was the oldest. The burden

[*](New York: Chelsea House Publishers, 1968.)

of providing for this vast brood darkened the middle years of Mill's life and, presumably, affirmed his agreement with his friend Thomas Malthus on the dangers of overpopulation. His problems were further intensified because after 1805 he had given up his other regular sources of income to concentrate on *The History of British India*. He expected, when beginning the book, to complete it in three or four years. It took twelve. He sustained himself and his family during this time with miscellaneous journalism, editing, translations and hack literary work. He also produced, among other more substantial volumes, his pamphlet *Commerce Defended*, in which he strongly attacked the notion that the economic interests of the nation are safeguarded by the landowning classes, his position being sharply at odds with earlier and more tolerant attitudes toward the landlords.

As work on *The History* continued, a new and powerful influence entered Mill's life in the form of Jeremy Bentham. This association began in 1813 and was in every respect symbiotic. Mill was audience, editor and exponent of Bentham's ideas. Bentham found in Mill an avid disciple for his doctrines, one whose mind was extensively prepared by his own reading and thought. To further the association, Bentham bought a house for Mill and his family to live in not far from his own and made concessions on the rent he charged them. The two men often went together to walk in the country but in 1814 had their first quarrel over Mill's evident preference for the company of Joseph Hume.

The History was finished in 1817, at about the time the association with Bentham was coming gradually to an end. The book brought a sharp change in Mill's life, for, its criticism of British government in India notwithstanding, it led to his employment by the East India Company. The Company paid him well, and Mill rose rapidly in its service. His financial problems were by way of being solved by 1821; with his salary at £1000 a year, he could regard himself as quite rich. Though his responsibilities were considerable, he was able to discharge them in just six hours a day. In the time remaining, he engaged in a wide range of discussions on contemporary issues, wrote and revised *The Elements of Political Economy* (1821) and contributed to the *Westminster Review* his memorable injunctions to public virtue as he defined them. During these years he also saw coming to maturity the most notable achievement of his life, one for which, with some reason, he took full credit, namely, his son John Stuart Mill. His son (a man of mellower wisdom) succeeded him not only as a political economist and Utilitarian philosopher but also in employment at India House. James Mill died in 1836.

With *The Pilgrim's Progress*, *Wealth of Nations* and possibly now *The Education of Henry Adams*, *The History of British India* is one of the most famous, most mentioned, most unread books in the English language. Everyone knows James Mill was working on it while he was rearing and educating his more famous son; thus the book is intimately a part of the history and legend of John Stuart Mill. Many, studying the Mills, must have thought it a work they might one day read, but for a long while few have.

Partly this has been because of inaccessibility. The available editions are deep on the library shelves. The one here reprinted with annotation by Horace Hayman Wilson dates from the 1850s, and the original was in a type well designed to try the eyes. (The ample and important footnotes were all but microscopic.) And, of course, it is a work of formidable length and thoroughness; it is not for the person who wants to read and relax.

In recent times it has also fallen under the heavy cloud that covers colonialism. All right-thinking people now disapprove of colonialism; accordingly, some at least do not much read or write its history. This would be an inauspicious time to bring out the definitive work on the Belgians in the Congo or the French in Senegal. All of this is unfortunate and a very poor reason for ignoring a classic of British and Indian history.

In the first place, *The History of British India* is a great piece of English prose. It is not an easy book, but it is stylish and lucid. It draws on what may well have been the richest scholarship of the day; James Mill's enormous erudition was divided, more or less equally, one imagines, between his famous book and his famous son. And there are passages whose organ tones are worthy of Gibbon or Macaulay and that all but put Churchill to shame. Consider these early paragraphs:

> From the time when Vasco da Gama distinguished his nation by discovering the passage round the Cape of Good Hope, a whole century had elapsed, during which, without a rival, the Portuguese had enjoyed, and abused, the advantages of superior knowledge and art, amid a feeble and half-civilized people. They had explored the Indian Ocean, as far as Japan; had discovered its islands, rich with some of the favourite productions of nature; had achieved the most brilliant conquests; and, by their commerce, poured into Europe, in unexampled profusion, those commodities of the East, on which the nations at that time set an extraordinary value.
>
> The circumstances of this splendid fortune had violently attracted the attention of Europe. The commerce of India, even when confined to those narrow limits which a carriage by land had prescribed, was supposed to have elevated feeble states into great ones; and to have constituted an enviable part in the fortune even of the most opulent and powerful; to have contributed largely to support the Grecian monarchies both in Syria and Egypt; to have retarded the downfall of Constantinople; and to have raised the small and obscure republic of Venice to the rank

and influence of the most potent kingdoms. The discovery therefore of
a new channel for this opulent traffic, and the happy experience of the
Portuguese, inflamed the cupidity of all the maritime nations of Europe,
and set before them the most tempting prospects.

One wonders how anyone, in a matter of five sentences, could more
successfully have conveyed the excitement, the sense of high drama,
with which the great trading adventures to the Indies were launched.

British rule in India is also one of the greatest achievements of the
time — of the two centuries that it lasted, until Indian independence
in 1947. The attitudes that make it, for the moment, an unfashionable
subject of study and interest will pass. And this will be as true in India
as in the Western world. The British succeeded the Mughal dynasty —
that of Babur, Akbar, Jahangir, Shah Jahan and Aurangzeb — which
came from Central Asia and established itself in India upon the defeat
in 1526 of Ibrahim Lodi, who was also of an alien dynasty. (The Indians,
in time, adopted the Mughals as their own.) The British did not, as did
their predecessors, exchange their old kingdom for the new. Nonetheless British administration from abroad was a model of compassion
and concern for the masses as compared with the despotism and anarchy it replaced. Despite the excesses of Clive and his near contemporaries in Bengal, the British were unquestionably regarded as liberators
in their time. And to this day what was British India is appreciably
more prosperous than those parts that remained under the rule of the
princes. But independence was eventually won in India, as elsewhere,
by the cultivation of animosity against the imperial power. And there
was much snobbishness, insult and indignity to nourish it, all of which
is remembered. When these memories fade, the accomplishments of
the British administration will once more be featured.

For these accomplishments were, indeed, great. British rule in India
was, first of all, an extraordinary exercise in the art of administration.
A mere handful of men — the Indian Civil Service never had as many
as a thousand British members at one time — carried the responsibility
for government. They had the support of a few regiments of British
and a rather larger number of Indian troops. Men, on the whole, were
selected carefully, impressed with the importance of their task, paid
well by the standards of the time and given large responsibility and
commensurate authority. The collection of revenue, the maintenance
of order and the administration of justice were in the hands of the
collector — the regional administrator. When famine threatened or
Muslims and Hindus clashed in the villages, the problem was his. All
of these administrators were young, many of them in their twenties,
and they governed hundreds of thousands, even millions, of people.
While there were doubtless petty tyrants and perhaps a few thieves,

nearly all involved were honest and dedicated. It has been commonly observed of British rule that it did very little — that it was law-and-order government and nothing more. This is unjust. It irrigated vast areas to protect against the threat of famine and built a comprehensive railway system to get the food from the places of surplus to those of deficit. It began to build an educational system. Not many other governments at the time did more, and few others did so much so well.

Mill's *History* is the basic document on eighteenth-century colonial administration. But it also affected what happened in the next hundred years, for his criticisms of British administration, which he enumerated in detail, were influential in the reforms that followed. And so was Mill himself, for one consequence of his writing of the book, as I've said, was his employment by the East India Company, in which he came to have an important role. The diligent read him as they prepared for examinations for the service, or as they took ship for the subcontinent, or during the course of the long journey there. These latter uses of his book were, it must be said, of mixed advantage, and note must also be made of its negative consequences.

However erudite he may have been, James Mill had some serious shortcomings when it came to writing about the civilization of India. For one thing he had never been in the country of which he wrote at such length. In the preface he argues that this was an advantage; had he visited India, he could have seen only a small corner of that vast land, and for this he would have sacrificed his larger view. That is a small marvel of defensive pleading; it would have been a warmer, more sympathetic book had Mill experienced Indian life and culture for himself. Also, Mill did not know the relevant Indian languages, and translations of Indian classics were much less commonly available in the early years of the nineteenth century, when he wrote, than they are now. He also excuses himself on this, but he would not have excused any man who essayed to comment on the Greek or Latin poets without a knowledge of Greek or Latin. He discusses the *Mahabharata* under this handicap and the further and more serious one that, at the time, it had not yet been rendered into English.

He had two other faults. To this day men regularly return from India in one of two extreme states of mind. Either they are enraptured by everything Indian or they wish to see nothing ever again of the country and its sloth and misery. So it was also in Mill's time, and, without having been to the subcontinent, Mill threw in his lot with the latter group. He was determined to show that Indian culture was barren, perverse and objectionable, and equally determined to prove this to be so in all particulars. He made clear his suspicion of those who confessed their admiration; their scholarly credentials and good sense were in doubt. "The Brahmens," he advised, "are the most audacious, and perhaps the most unskilful fabricators, with whom the annals of fable have yet made us acquainted." Taking issue with admirers on a less exalted matter, he observed, "From the frequency and care with which the Hindus perform religious ablutions, the Europeans prone from partial appearances to draw flattering conclusions, painted them, at first, as in the colours of so many other virtues, so likewise in those of cleanliness. Few nations are surpassed by the Hindus, in the total want of physical purity, in their streets, houses, and persons."

More than simple bias is involved here. Mill was the prophet of a faith that made it difficult, perhaps impossible, to understand the civilization of India. He was a Benthamite, and not for just one season or one country. If a man's moral worth was measured in England by the practical utility of his actions, so it must be in India. If one tested policy by the greatest good for the greatest number in Europe, so also among the masses of Asia. If one realized the greatest good by competitive individualism in one place, so in the other. And by these tests there was little in the indigenous culture of India that passed. As one measured government in Westminster, so in the capital of the maharajah, nizam or nabob. Caste, accommodation to the hot climate, the conservatism of an agricultural economy, the social customs of the villages and the inherently predatory character of landlords and rulers were all outside the range of Mill's faith and hence unworthy of any effort at comprehension.

But not everything can be blamed on Utilitarianism. He also had a tendency remarkable even in an Englishman (or a Scot) of his time to measure religion, marital customs, manners, the personal hygiene mentioned above, by his own standards. No carefully nurtured sense of humility kept him from knowing what was right. And, his education notwithstanding, Mill was in many ways a very narrow man. He was a fine writer; accordingly, one must grant him a feeling for the graces of English and classical prose and verse. This apart, he must have been nearly devoid of aesthetic sense. In consequence, the magic of Indian temple architecture and sculpture escaped him entirely. And so did that of the art and architecture of the rulers. Nominally Mill's bias was directed against the Hindus, but in practice it embraced also the ruling Muslim dynasties. The last of these, the Mughals, were among the greatest patrons of architecture and painting the world has known, and one of them, Shah Jahan, who built, along with much else, the Taj Mahal and the Red Fort in Delhi and who supported one of the world's great schools of painters, is rivaled only by the Medicis. None of these achievements, if they were known to Mill, were deemed worthy of more than passing mention. Most went unmentioned.

.   .   .

What redeems these failings? In the first place, only a comparatively small part of his work is about Indian India. Most of it is about British India, and here Mill's Benthamite faith, coupled with his uncompromising honesty and candor, is not a handicap but an advantage. He judges British rule in India by the standards of the time, and he judges it with all of the moral authority and certainty of a man of belief. Nothing is more sacred than his own convictions; one cannot imagine that many in positions of authority were spared his criticism. A few years before Mill wrote, affairs being in their typically shocking condition in the Kingdom of Oudh (the important state centered on Lucknow on the Ganges Plain), the then governor general, Sir John Shore, evicted the ruler, who had but recently succeeded to the throne. The local mismanagement was a highly cooperative enterprise in which many participated, but the governor general had been persuaded that the nabob was the focus of the trouble. This is Mill's comment on the background of the action: "Great industry and skill had been employed in prepossessing the mind of the Governor-General with the most unfavourable opinion of the young Nabob, as a man between whose character and the interests of the English an irreconcilable contrariety was placed." He then goes on to describe the means by which the ruler was deposed. It was accepted by all that he was the son of the old nabob and a menial woman of the seraglio. But he had been acknowledged by his father, and under Muslim custom and law this was sufficient. Now it was held that his mother went home at night to a husband and that the boy had been purchased unborn for five hundred rupees as a putative son by the old nabob, who felt himself insufficiently supplied with progeny. Contemplating the history and the motives involved, Mill, in a fine concluding passage, attributes innocence, stupidity and injustice to the exalted British official without pausing for breath:

> It is impossible to read the account of this transaction, drawn up by the Governor-General, and not to be impressed with a conviction of his sincerity, and his desire to do justice. But it is easy also to perceive how much his understanding was bewildered; and impossible not to confess that he decided against the unfortunate Nabob the great question of a kingdom, upon evidence upon which a court of English law would not have decided against him a question of a few pounds.

Standards that might be meaningless or even bigoted when brought to bear on Hindus and Muslims were not at all bad for judging the conduct of eighteenth- and nineteenth-century Englishmen.

The other redeeming feature of this edition is Mill's editor, Horace Hayman Wilson, who also continued *The History of British India* from where Mill had left it. An Orientalist and professor at Oxford, Wilson was as persuaded of the depth of Indian culture as Mill was of its sterility. And while he is not without respect for Mill in his particular areas of competence, Wilson did not believe that these extended to Oriental languages, literature, art, manners, philosophy and religion. He not only felt obliged to correct Mill in these matters but, as any reader of his comments will quickly sense, rejoiced in the opportunity. Accordingly, we have in these volumes both Mill's views on India and the vigorous opposing views of his editor.

One will ask what is the meaning of *The History* for modern India — or for modern India and Pakistan. It is not insignificant. Both of these lands are profoundly Asian; it was a measure of the power as well as the quality of their culture that it kept its character and integrity through two centuries of strong British rule. India, as Gandhi insisted, is to be found in its villages. I do not suppose that a transmigratory visitor returning to a village in Bihar or Orissa after an absence of a thousand years would find much that had changed. But there is also a super-structure that is immensely British. I have mentioned the Civil Service. The parliament, the police, the law courts, the army, the universities, the newspapers and the industrial and commercial life are all in their essence according to the British model. Mill's *History* is a chronicle, possibly the best that we have, of the original transplantation of this model. It is not only an admirable and even unique document on economic, political and cultural imperialism, but it provides an early record of the institutions of government, education and economic life that are most conspicuous to the visitor in India to this day.

The book has another high relevance. People often ask what they should read before going to the subcontinent; I always suggest E. M. Forster's *A Passage to India*. If one knows this great novel, nothing will come as a surprise. It pictures as no other the clash of the two cultures, Eastern and Western, and the uncertainty and ambiguity of the lives of those who live between them. Indian society exists between the two worlds and has the insecurity that comes from an uncertain identifi-cation with each. So does Indian administration. So does Indian diplo-macy. All this explains India's approach to economic development and modern technical achievement. When the Japanese adopted, they adopted — confidently and fearlessly. So, one senses, did the Chinese. But the Indians remained far longer in suspense and indecision.

Mill, I think, provides the clue. The Japanese could select what to take from Western civilization, as could the Chinese. Economic orga-nization, technology, the industrial ethic, were taken over completely. Language, art, other culture, social and family life, could remain in the traditional mold. But in India the powerful and dominating British culture, of which James Mill was such a superb and supremely confident exponent, offered much less choice. Benthamite concepts of government and economics were believed to be the natural order of things. So were English manners, English ethics, English social customs, even English food. So, of course, was the English language itself. It was not so much that they were imposed as that their superiority was taken for granted. Having to adopt much, the Indians adopted fearfully and often rather badly. They wished to conform, but they sought also to stay apart.

Here in this great book we see, in marvelous panoply, how enormous was the task. Accordingly, we come to understand the sources of the insecurity that Forster so wonderfully evokes, why Indians today often seem more Westernized than they are. And we also understand the underlying commitment to traditional Indian attitudes and values that the visitor — the modern engineer, agronomist, politician, diplomat — is so often so puzzled or disconcerted to discover in what he thought were wholly Westernized, wholly modern men. We see here the reasons that Europeans and Americans often find Indians, as they say, difficult; they are unprepared for this continuing commitment to early traditions for which, in other Asian countries, they would be completely braced.

The story of the tasks that eighteenth-century Englishmen took on in India in all their variety and complexity will carry the reader through this book, for it is rich in interest itself. But in getting the measure of the imperial tasks and accomplishments, the reader will also win as a result an understanding of the psychology and behavior of modern India or, more precisely, of the behavior and thought in that thin but dominant stratum of Indian society that once was juxtaposed to the Raj.

2

ANTHONY TROLLOPE:
*Barchester Towers**

(1983)

This was the introduction to an early offering in a new Penguin series. I first discovered Trollope while looking for a defense against Dickens, to whom, like so many young in my day, I was prematurely and excessively exposed. I never fully recovered from Bleak House *and* Barnaby Rudge. *Then I discovered I could escape to Trollope; my sense of my debt to him has never diminished.*

Anthony Trollope was born in 1815 with, someone has said, a pen in hand. His father was a financially disastrous barrister, and, in consequence, support of the family came from his mother, Frances Milton Trollope, who accomplished an even more extravagant flow of books than eventually would her son, though with the considerable difference that nearly all of them, if not forgettable, are certainly forgotten. The great exception is *The Domestic Manners of the Americans,* published in 1832, the result of an adventuresome sojourn in the border states. Its picture of the natives is of a people only a few infirm steps up from barbarianism. It was, needless to say, not well regarded by the relatively few Americans at the time who were given to English literature; in an enduring tradition as regards commentary on the United States and the more perverse foibles of its citizens, it found a much better response in England.

Anthony Trollope was educated at Winchester and Harrow and thereafter in his early life was, like James and John Stuart Mill, sustained by the Civil Service. He rose to a senior position in the Post Office, is credited with the invention of the pillarbox (to non-Britons, the ordinary local mailbox) and was importantly involved with various of the negotiations that resulted in the international exchange of mail under the aegis of the Postal Union.

*(Harmondsworth, England: Penguin English Library Edition, 1983.)

Almost everyone, whether a reader of his books or not, has heard of Trollope's writing habits: he arose very early in the morning and, with his watch before him, ticked off some twenty-five hundred words at the rate of a thousand words per hour. Then he had breakfast and went to the Post Office. In describing his routine, he told also of the scrupulous attention he paid to what he had written: he never, he said, sent a manuscript to the publisher without reading it over carefully first. For a long time after his death Trollope was neglected, and much of that neglect seems to have been caused by what he wrote of himself in his *Autobiography*, which was published posthumously in 1883. There he told of his severe discipline while writing, and he listed, mercilessly and more or less to the penny, the revenues from each of his books. No good writer, it was said or anyhow felt, should be so predictable in his work habits or give such knowledgeable attention to his personal pecuniary affairs. Genius is always a trifle dissolute and, in financial matters, distinctly careless. Always it is subject to waves of inspiration and despair.

Happily, attitudes have long since changed. Trollope has been forgiven his discipline and his diligence; he now ranks fully with the most admired novelists of the Victorian era, and it is quite possible that no other, Dickens excepted, has a larger contemporary following.

After a couple of unsuccessful novels set in Ireland (where he had become a postal inspector), he discovered Barset, and there followed the novels of Barsetshire, of which *Barchester Towers* was the first. Then he went on to the noted Irish Member of Parliament Phineas Finn, and after tracing the history of *The Eustace Diamonds* and the wonderfully devious Lady Eustace, he took up the politically and socially complex life of the greatly influential Pallisers. Whether concerned with the politics of Westminster or those of the cathedral close in Barchester, Trollope remained consistent. The issues, including such less than heart-rending matters as how the minor coinage would be arranged were Britain to have a decimal currency, were always unimportant; important only was how the game was played and who would win. Trollope anticipated the modern American television commentator I have described elsewhere, who, not wishing to be bothered with the tedious questions of what is right and who is wrong, sees politics purely as a spectator sport. In fact, in real life Trollope was politically much involved. He deeply suspected Conservatives, and after resigning from the Post Office in 1867, he stood for Parliament for Beverley as a Liberal. Fortunately he was defeated; the House of Commons, even then, might have interfered with his writing.

A familiar figure in the London clubs and an enthusiastic hunter — in the season he went out three times a week, and horses, foxes and dogs appear with great frequency in his works — Trollope continued to write prodigiously through failing health until his death in 1882. It is one of the more rewarding experiences of the modern Trollope addict, of which there are thousands, that he or she can still come up with a volume that other Trollope fans have not read or did not even know existed.

As may be imagined, there has long been debate over which is the best of his novels. There will never be a decision; such controversy is a harmless pastime and for professors of English literature a useful source of lecture material. Were I asked, I would retreat to Trollope's own judgment, which is that *The Last Chronicle of Barset* is truly the most ingenious, compelling and otherwise most impressive of his stories. The Reverend Josiah Crawley, permanent curate of Hogglestock in that book, is a marvel of portraiture and psychological conflict.

But what cannot be in doubt is that *Barchester Towers* was the work that first informed the world of the Trollope genius. Perhaps it should be read after *The Warden,* a lovely little novel altogether less ambitious in its reach, which introduces the reader to the Barchester scene, the clerical life of the cathedral close and many of the people who reappear in *Barchester Towers*. But that isn't necessary. Having bought or otherwise come upon this volume, you can start right in; Trollope gives you all the background you need. You have before you one of the delights of life.

Barchester Towers, like some of Trollope's other works, is a novel of politics, here between the two parties of the diocese and the cloister. The conflict is intense, preoccupying, often mean and, as noted, quite devoid of issues, this being the special Trollope touch. Vaguely in the background is the difference between High Church liturgy and traditions and the crudities of the Low and modern Churchmen. But the issues, like those in the parliamentary novels, do not obtrude, and the reader is never involved with them. His or her concern is not with what is right but with who will prevail. The contest between the Grantly faction and the Proudies, including the superbly depicted Reverend Obadiah Slope, is entirely over who will emerge as the dominant power in the community. Some clerical patronage is at stake — who will be warden of Hiram's Hospital, who will be the new dean of the chapter — but the possession of these prestigious and well-paid posts is far less important than the manifestation of influence that is involved in granting them. It is that — who is on top — that counts.

The struggle presents two of Trollope's greatest heroes or, as pedants may prefer, antiheroes. These are the aforementioned Slope, the bishop's chaplain and clerical man-of-all-work, and Mrs. Proudie, the bishop's wife and the true power in the Proudie party. In interest Mr. Slope and Mrs. Proudie far outshine Archdeacon Grantly, the leader of the opposing traditional and altogether more reputable forces. Here, either by accident or by design, is one of Trollope's miracles. The author is wholly on the side of Grantly; so, as the story progresses, is the reader; but it is with Slope and Mrs. Proudie (and the poor bishop, who is their instrument and victim) with whom the reader becomes involved. One cares a great deal less what happens to Grantly, his wife, the scholarly Mr. Arabin or Eleanor Bold, the widow to whose asserted beauty and much more convincing income the unmarried members of the clerical community are greatly attracted.

In fact, there is no great suspense as regards Slope. Trollope allows you to marvel at his instinct for self-promotion, his energy and efficiency in the use of the small powers of his position. But he leaves the reader in no doubt that the Reverend Obadiah Slope is one of the most ruinous political operators of all time. Slope should someday return and consort with Richard Milhous Nixon.

Mrs. Proudie's skill and resource are in sharp contrast with Slope's, and this too is evident from the outset. In a perverse way, as the pages pass, one begins to admire this incredible woman. Much later, in *The Last Chronicle*, Trollope killed Mrs. Proudie off, in response, as he tells in his autobiography, to a conversation overheard by chance in his club in which she was severely condemned. Rising into view from a concealing high-backed chair, he responded to her critics by saying he would oblige them and dispose of her in an early issue of the magazine in which the story, as was then the custom, was being serialized. She was greatly missed, not least by Trollope.

As Trollope devotees have quarreled over which is the best of his books, so they have expressed strong, even combative, views as to what is good and bad within his novels, not excluding *Barchester Towers*. Thus — a small point — his names have been much attacked as being too unambiguously comic — the physicians Dr. Fillgrave, Mr. Rerechild, Sir Omicron Pie; the farmer Farmer Greenacre; the upwardly mobile Lookaloft family. I'm all for Trollope. He knew that one man's too obvious search for laughter is another man's fun. Also the names, Sir Omicron possibly excepted, have a good English sound. There must, somewhere in the world today, be a pediatrician called Rerechild.

More serious is the question of whether in this book the author talks too much. For what it may be worth, I think he does. He digresses at length on women, tradesmen, farmers, politicians, the clerical scene. Some of this chattiness is richly informative on Victorian mores and manners. Some is very wise. His observation that if honest men do not scrounge for money, thieves will get it all should no doubt be in the minds of all authors when they sit down to bargain with their publishers. But some of his talk is a bore. The last two or three chapters of *Barchester*

Towers suggest somehow that he had difficulty knowing how to stop. The accomplished reader will cause his or her eye to scan and, on frequent occasion, slide over these passages. You should read just enough to see whether it catches and retains your attention; if it doesn't, then you can move on to where the story resumes, and without the slightest feeling of guilt.

Finally, there is the problem of Trollope on love and marriage. These are not exactly commercial encounters and transactions; Trollope always tells how much his men and women love each other. Allowance must also be made for the different manners and constraints in such matters in the clerical world and in the last century. But after all possible concessions, Trollope's love passages are still unconvincing. His people often fall in love on the very first and very casual meeting, especially if money or a clerical living is involved. They then agree to marry on the third or fourth deeply hygienic encounter. It is assumed by all that Eleanor Bold will marry Mr. Slope merely because she is polite to him, has allowed him to call a couple of times and has received a letter from him. She falls in love with Mr. Arabin in the course of an equally fugitive exposure. So it is with all of Trollope's lovers. He had no time for the long courtships that, in practice, were normal in those days. It should perhaps be noted that when Trollope's people become lovers, this has none of the modern connotation of bed and sex. It means only that they will now call each other by their first names and maybe kiss.

On the other side, and overwhelming such faults, if these they be, are the Trollope accomplishments. There is the intricate and beautifully crafted political game to which I have adverted. Also the wonderful portraits not alone of Mr. Slope and the Proudies but also of Mr. Harding, the former warden of Hiram's Hospital, of the bizarre Stanhope family and of the less than sympathetic archdeacon.

There is, as well, the superb sense of scene. Trollope said late in life that he had roamed over the streets and lanes of Barchester and Barset until they had a reality for him greater than that of any city or county in England that was more visibly on the map. This can readily be believed, for he takes his reader with him. I can close my eyes and see it all, too — the cathedral, the palace, Hiram's Hospital, Plumstead, St. Etwold's, Ullathorne and on out to Puddingdale. So can every reader. Among other things this is a singularly lovely countryside, with an exceptionally fine, mellow and affluent architecture. One is surprised on hearing at the big party at Ullathorne that the roads are so bad. Miss Thorne's party (like the earlier one at the bishop's palace, it should be added) is another of Trollope's triumphs. The reader also attends and at Ullathorne enjoys it all from noon to dark.

And, ultimately, there is the fun. Neither *Barchester Towers* nor the later Barset books could rightly be called works of comedy. These are serious people seriously engaged with life. The scene and portraits are real. But lurking just below the surface is Trollope's rich sense of the absurd. And sometimes, as when he deals with the Stanhope family, the browbeaten bishop or Mr. Slope, it comes fully into the open. If there is little to be said for Trollope's love and courtship, there is much to be said for the deeply amusing language in which the effort is couched. Mr. Slope's slightly alcoholic speech of proposal to Eleanor Bold is the pre-eminent example. Here it is in full:

> "Beautiful woman," at last he burst forth; "beautiful woman, you cannot pretend to be ignorant that I adore you. Yes, Eleanor, yes, I love you. I love you with the truest affection which man can bear to woman. Next to my hopes of heaven are my hopes of possessing you. . . . How sweet to walk to heaven with you by my side, with you for my guide, mutual guides. Say, Eleanor, dearest Eleanor, shall we walk that sweet path together?" . . .
>
> "Ah! Eleanor," he continued, and it seemed to be his idea that as he had once found courage to pronounce her Christian name, he could not utter it often enough. "Ah! Eleanor, will it not be sweet, with the Lord's assistance, to travel hand in hand through this mortal valley which his mercies will make pleasant to us, till hereafter we shall dwell together at the foot of his throne?" And then a more tenderly pious glance than ever beamed from the lover's eyes. "Ah! Eleanor —"
>
> "My name, Mr. Slope, is Mrs. Bold," said Eleanor. . . .
>
> "Sweetest angel, be not so cold," said he, and as he said it the champagne broke forth, and he contrived to pass his arm round her waist.

The first thought of anyone writing an introduction to a book such as *Barchester Towers* is to envy the reader, for he or she, one presumes, is coming to this great novel for the first time. What a pleasure awaits! But I have a second thought. Before writing these words, I read the book once again — it occupied me for a long airplane trip across the United States and for odd hours in a hotel on the West Coast. It could have been for the fifth or sixth time. So far from envying the Trollope novice, I found myself feeling blessed. I was enjoying it even more than on earlier encounters. So, dear reader — as Trollope himself salutes you a shade too often — if you have been here before, welcome back. *Barchester Towers,* not alone among Trollope's works, is meant to be read at, say, ten-year intervals over a whole adult lifetime.

3

GLORIA STEINEM:
*The Beach Book**

(1963)

Gloria Steinem, as here told, I like very much. When she compiled this highly frivolous collection of essays, she had not quite discovered the women's movement, and I knew her as a writer with a fine comic sense. Thus my effort here to show a little of the same. A preface for any one of her more recent books would have had to be perhaps even a trifle ostentatiously solemn.

Except that I like this book and the woman who put it together, I could seem a most improbable person to write the introduction. Not a dozen times in the past fifty years have I gone to the beach for as much as overnight. On those occasions, with the single exception of a visit to a beach near Puri, in India, where the main attraction is an excellent hotel set well back from the sand, I have always come away confirmed in the view that a beach is a most unpleasant place to spend time. Still, I am better qualified for this small literary exercise than may be imagined. For, as is so often the case, with pain has come perception. I think I understand the place of the beach in our culture.

One might suppose that it had none. On a hot day, which is when many people go, it is too hot to be tolerable. For some, a darkened skin is a status symbol, but for a certain number of my fellow Democrats and those who are leading the modern Republican revival in the South, a white skin remains a singular and perhaps their only source of distinction. There is nothing intrinsically attractive about the look or the smell of decaying fish or the flayed chicken bones, sandwich crusts, truncated frankfurters and oiled paper that careful picnickers have interred and that the waves and stray dogs have returned to public contemplation. Nor do those who bring this food to the beach really enjoy it in the first place; their teeth grit on the sand. Along most of

*(New York: Viking Press, 1963.)

the East Coast of the United States and all of the West Coast, the water is usually too cold for swimming. Walking in the sand barefoot is debilitating and sometimes painful; with shoes on, it's even worse.

But these discomforts are, in fact, the first clue in the explanation of why Americans flock (as the newspapers say) to the beach. For it is these annoyances and others that inhibit all forms of activity and thus make the beach appealing to the physically and intellectually inert. The sun makes it difficult to read, and, anyhow, ordinary sunglasses don't have your prescription. I have told how exercise is proscribed. Beaches are often not much to look at, and since they are public property, there is no incentive to improve them. Desecration is possible, but that requires no effort. Our liberalized attitudes do allow a certain amount of sedentary lovemaking, which, in highly exceptional cases, may be encouraged by seminude beach attire. But again, one imagines, there is that terrible gritty sand. You cannot talk on a beach, for there is nothing to prop you up, and, outside of a Hollywood bedroom, no one has ever carried on a worthwhile conversation lying down. At a place called Wellfleet on Cape Cod, I once saw my friends Dwight Macdonald, Mary McCarthy, Harry Levin and Arthur Schlesinger, all stretched out on the sand and, most improbably, talking only at intervals.

This is what explains the attraction of the beach in our society: total physical and mental inertia are highly agreeable, much more so than we allow ourselves to imagine. A beach not only permits such inertia but enforces it, thus neatly eliminating all problems of guilt. It is now the only place in our overly active world that does. In even the most austere modern living room there are a television, a stereo, a slide projector, a sofa, a telephone, a portable bar, cards, the family photograph albums and possibly some books. Some of these things can be escaped by moving out to the backyard, but there one encounters the great suburban clichés — barbecues, crabgrass and neighbors. In bygone days the well-to-do could go to Europe or to the porch of a summer hotel, and the steamship lines shrewdly exploited the inner longings of their potential clients by always showing their passengers in a state of well-blanketed collapse. Now on a modern jet there is barely time for a meal, and the seats go back only just so far. A motel can have even more distractions than a living room.

I once knew a man who made the rounds of all the winter resorts — Mont Tremblant, Sun Valley, Klosters, the Palace Hotel in Gstaad — and at each he rented a room overlooking the ski slopes and sat there. But, to my surprise, he told me one day that he wasn't happy. The social pressure to do something — at least take the ski lift up and see the view — was relentless to the point of being uncomfortable. Eventually he married an energetic divorcée.

It is true that as an opportunity for total inertia even the beach is in decline. Some people have always insisted that they are on the sand for a purpose, namely, to soak up the sun, but they are exceptionally restless souls with a special need for some surrogate sense of function. The real danger, as usual these days, is electronic — transistor radios, tape recorders and unduly portable television sets. People, one hears, are taking these to the beach in increasing numbers. Presumably they are under the impression that they want distraction, not realizing that what they really want is to escape distraction. Given enough such electronic environment, they will soon find it better to be distracted at home. The older Asian cultures have raised the art of sitting — under a pipal tree, by a well, in a field, on a sidewalk, in a Zen temple, even in the middle of a Calcutta street — to a level of high accomplishment. Inertia, people have learned, is possible far from the ocean. There is a clue here; one can imagine a trend. A beach, it will soon be revealed, is not a place but a state of mind. The Ford Foundation is said to be financing a small study on the subject.

4

R. A. BUTLER:
*The Art of the Possible**

(1971)

This is another exception to my otherwise stalwart stand against the autobiog-
raphy; no other recent book by a British politician is as good.

After a long career in British politics, service as chancellor of the exchequer
and a near approach to the post of prime minister, R. A. (Rab) Butler became,
as I say in this piece, master of Trinity College, Cambridge. There, with the
acquiescence of the fellows of the college, he made me one of their number, and
we remained friends until his death. Just before his last illness, arrangements
were under way to have him come to Harvard for a long visit, something he
much wanted to do. It was our grievous loss.

The political memoir is the most common, though not necessarily the
most distinguished, of modern British art forms. A dozen or more
appear every year; one judges that no British politician is so obscure
or so tedious that he does not at least contemplate a message to posterity.
Against all the rules of journalism — there is thought to be some convention against aggravated abuse of the reader — the London Sunday
papers publish generous extracts for what must be the world's most
indifferent audience. The books themselves are then read in fragments
by other politicians looking up their own names in the index.

A spectacular exception to this disenchanting prose has, however,
recently appeared. It is this autobiography of R. A. (now Lord) Butler,
and, not surprisingly, it was greeted with enthusiasm, which, considering the genre, must have been combined with a major element of
surprise. I was in England at the time of its publication there, and I
don't remember seeing a single unflattering review. Such prizes as are
awarded for this kind of book it won.

*(Boston: Gambit, 1972.) This preface was to the American edition; the book had earlier
been published in England by Hamish Hamilton.

There was good reason for the approval. Though a member of an old academic family — Lord Butler is now master of Trinity College, Cambridge, and his family has been continuously associated with the university since 1794 — he had a remarkable public career of which to tell. He entered the House of Commons in 1929 from Saffron Walden and remained there, showing an unusual affinity for major office, for the next thirty-five years. He was involved, successively, with India (where, before returning to become a Cambridge master, his father had been a senior officer in the civil administration), education, the Exchequer and the Foreign Office. Though a junior minister at the time and not himself deeply involved, he has never made secret his belief that the Munich agreement was inescapable: Britain needed to gain time to mobilize arms and public opinion both at home and abroad for the war against Hitler. In a moving passage in this book he restates this view and, characteristically, does not omit to agree with John Wheeler-Bennett, who said in *Munich: Prologue to Tragedy* that the action was required "to save our own skins" and "because we were too weak to protect ourselves — we were forced to sacrifice a small Power to slavery."

In 1953, Butler was the acting prime minister following Churchill's stroke; three years later, under rather more difficult circumstances, he was again acting head of the government when the Suez crisis did in Anthony Eden. Eden departed for Jamaica but did not immediately resign; as Butler tells, "The only method of communication [with him] was by telegraph to the Governor, who then had to send a messenger on poor roads all the long distance to Ian Fleming's home at Golden Eye." Where, one wonders, was James Bond?

However, Butler made his greatest claim in more important and much less dramatic matters. As chancellor of the exchequer — the post he held longest — he was instrumental in modernizing the economic views of the Tory Party. He made Keynesian economics official; public intervention in the economy became a matter not of ideology but of practical judgment. The press, in turn, celebrated the similarity between the economic policies of Butler and Labourite Hugh Gaitskell by inventing what must be the most unlovely word in the history of modern politics — Butskellism. Recent Tory governments have shown a marked tendency to revert to ideological type, but nothing in the resulting experience suggests the unwisdom of Butler's magnificent indifference to party doctrine.

A good many people have played an important part or had a strategic view of great events, and they have managed, nonetheless, to say nothing very interesting about them. This is where Butler is the great exception. Uniquely among autobiographers, British and American, he writes to rejoice the reader and not himself. He also follows the truly remarkable rule of not bothering to repeat what people already know. (Most of those who want to read about elections know which ones were won or lost. Butler assumes knowledge of such details.) He is always perceptive, on occasion biting, and he sees both his own role and that of others with poorly concealed amusement.

This last, the humor, has importance beyond the book. It is one of the much debated mysteries of British politics why Rab Butler never became prime minister, for he was in competition with markedly less able men. Part of the answer, one cannot doubt, is here: he could never view himself with the terrible solemnity of the truly ambitious politician. Determined party leaders are always a little suspicious of those who are amused, so it is the solemn men who make it. Not surprisingly, their memoirs are terrible, while the rare ones from such as Butler are much better or, as in this case, very, very good.

5

SHIGETO TSURU:
*The Collected Works**

(1976)

This comment helped launch the Japanese edition of the published papers of Shigeto Tsuru, of which there are thirteen volumes. Japan has produced no better economic scholar, and certainly no one more diligent or influential in the field. On the occasion of his fiftieth Harvard reunion, in 1985, he returned to Cambridge; it was my particular pleasure to escort him to the platform on that Commencement Day, where he received a greatly merited honorary degree.

In the autumn of 1945, well after the shooting was over, I went into Japan; like others with advanced degrees, I saw the hostilities only from a safe distance. One of my assistants on a mission to assess the effects of the air war was Paul Baran, who was already there. He and Paul Sweezy were two of the three most distinguished Marxist scholars of that generation, and Baran quickly located — perhaps he had already done so — the man whom almost all would list as the third in the trio, Shigeto Tsuru. We met in a very grim city at a very grim time.

It was, in fact, a reunion, for I had known Shigeto at Harvard in the 1930s. My preoccupation at that time had been with agricultural economics, a rather plebeian subject. His was a much more prestigious association with economic theory, including Marxist thought. Harvard graduate students and instructors of my generation told each other that Shigeto Tsuru would surely become one of the great figures in economics; not always is youthful judgment so good.

The years of the war were painful ones for Shigeto. There could have been few people in the world with less sympathy for the military ambitions and adventures of the Japanese government. Nonetheless, when the conflict started, he sensed that he had no choice but to go back to his own land; only if he did so could he work effectively af-

*(Tokyo: Kodansha, 1975–1976.)

terward for change. So he returned. He did not enjoy his brief period
of military service; later he endured in some civilian role — I'm not
sure that he ever told me quite what. When peace came, he made
himself available as a volunteer friend and counselor to those Americans who hoped, as he did, for a new and harmonious relationship
between the two countries. There could, I believe, have been none
more qualified.

It is not often that people separated by half the circumference of
the globe maintain a close association, but for the thirty years since the
end of the war, I have continued to count Shigeto Tsuru and his wife
among my closest friends. In a true friendship, as this has surely been,
no accounting is kept of benefits. But there are exceptions to all rules.
In this case the balance is very much in my favor, for, in an act of
almost unparalleled generosity, Shigeto Tsuru has constituted himself
over the years the guardian of my books in Japan — the man who
supervises translations and keeps a highly professional eye on the product. As all know, the distance in language between English and Japanese
is very great. So, accordingly, is the service he has rendered to me. I
wish I could claim to have done as much for some colleague. It would
help me to think of myself, as I think of Shigeto Tsuru, as a wonderfully
unselfish man.

This is my personal gain. There is another and larger gain, which I
have shared with many others. It derives from the remarkably disciplined and fertile imagination Shigeto has brought to economics and
politics. I've said he began as a Marxist. But for him this was not an
intellectual harness but an emancipation from the conventional classical
tradition in economics. And his work has continued to be refreshed by
new evidence and thought. Always when I have encountered something
he has written, I have known immediately that my knowledge of the
subject, great or small, would soon be richer than before. He is one of
those rare people who neither writes nor speaks unless he has thought
the matter out in full and documented his conclusions — in short, provided the reader with something on which to rely. I speak here with
some assurance; my interest in the shortcomings of growth as the measure of the achievement of the economic system, which was first outlined in *The Affluent Society,* has closely paralleled his concern for the
impact of industrialization on the quality of life in Japan.

I'm honored to have had such a companion. I have read or listened
to him on these subjects with particular interest and involvement. But
I must add that I have never read anything of Shigeto Tsuru's, however
incomplete my ability to judge, without feeling myself to be in the hands
of a master.

His competence is combined with a quiet, charming confidence that
is almost equally a Tsuru trademark. The United States is a young

country. In earlier days and even to some extent now, American scholars have had an inferiority complex in relation to the older and more
self-assured academic tradition of Europe. And Japanese economists,
from a yet younger industrial civilization, have perhaps shared some
of the same feelings. But not Tsuru. Certain in his own knowledge and
achievement, he has always walked with a quiet assurance through the
larger community of world scholarship. I have heard him lecture in
France and in the United States as well as in Japan. In all three countries
it has always been the same — he invites acceptance, not argument.

While there have been facets of Shigeto Tsuru's career with which
I have been less acquainted — his service to the Japanese government,
his years as a university president, his subsequent journalistic career,
his role as one of the most influential figures in Japanese public life —
I have sensed at second hand how important these have been. Let me
add, however, one very different final word: like other American economists, I have never encountered a Japanese scholar or a Japanese
politician without inquiring when he last saw Tsuru. I have yet to meet
one who didn't know him; nor have I ever met one who didn't speak
of him with respect and affection. Perhaps that is because the Japanese
are more polite and better mannered than most. More likely, it proves
that prophets can be *with* honor in their own country as also in the
world around.

· VII ·

A TRAVELER'S GUIDE

THE MODERN TRAVELOGUE is our most redundant literary form, for its authors describe what, in this well-traveled age, the available readership has already seen extensively for itself. I would like to think that these pieces offer a slightly different view.

THE UNITED STATES

(1971)

This article was written originally for The Times *of London as one of a series of slightly informal travel guides, and it later appeared in* New York *magazine. A few weeks after the latter publication, when my wife and I were returning from Mexico via John F. Kennedy Airport, the local head of customs materialized on the steps of the plane, grabbed our hand luggage, got the rest from the carousel and saw us by the customs inspectors and to a taxi. "You, Professor Galbraith," he said in explanation, "are the first writer in history ever to say anything nice about customs officers."*

The position of the Democratic Party, some favored areas apart, has declined since this was written, and Amtrak services, or some of them, have improved to the point where Amtrak itself is under severe Republican attack as a threat to the free enterprise system.

The reader is reminded, perhaps unnecessarily, that this piece was written fifteen years ago. Accordingly, there is a marked obsolescence in the references to persons and personalities of the time, a fate that, in the case of many, no one can greatly regret. By nearly all of the substantive observations on the American scene I still firmly stand.

A wise Englishman once wrote that no one should ever visit the United States for the first time. It was not that he would find life there dangerous or even all that expensive. Rather, he would listen to the locals, a kindly term by which Americans themselves denote the indigenous peoples employed in their many overseas enterprises, and return with an excessive number of erroneous beliefs. The Englishman was right. Among all the world's races, some obscure Bedouin tribes possibly apart, Americans are the most prone to misinformation. This is not the consequence of any special preference for mendacity, although at the higher levels of their public administration that tendency is impressive. It is rather that so much of what they themselves believe is wrong. By contrast, what is written in this guide, although American in source, may safely be believed; thereafter the prospective traveler is urged again to exercise the utmost skepticism.

Of the general manners and customs of the Americans very little need be said; all visitors will almost certainly have already made the acquaintance of American tourists. Most will have known Americans employed in foreign lands by General Motors, Ford, International Business Machines, Squibb or the Central Intelligence Agency, and a fair number will themselves have worked for one or another of those manifestations of American enterprise. The American at home is indistinguishable from the American abroad, although the latter invariably has the impression that travel has given his personal culture a richer and more burnished gloss.

The traveler to the United States will do well, however, to prepare himself for the class-consciousness of the natives. This differs from the already familiar English version in being more extreme and based more firmly on the conviction that the class to which the speaker belongs is inherently superior to all others.

Each class believes itself to be, by endowment, the natural ruling class. American businessmen believe that their bluff, practical wisdom, made manifest in dealings of seemingly inordinate intricacy and combined with their knowledge of modern management techniques and interpersonal communications, makes them the acknowledged leaders of the Republic. Lawyers feel the same way from the demanding and painful experience of guiding the aforementioned businessmen through complexities that neither the clients nor their lawyers understand. American scientists assume their own superiority from their knowledge of nuclear physics, modern biology, the procreative tendencies of mankind and the possibilities and limitations inherent in the computer. Other intellectuals react in the same fashion to their more perceptive view of the intentions of the Pentagon or the tendencies of American imperialism. Trade union leaders see a like advantage in their freedom from the hang-ups of the intellectuals, their practical appreciation of pecuniary income and their association (though it is admittedly tenuous) with the masses. Journalists make similar claims on similar grounds. Military men see much value in their tough-minded, uncomplicated view of Communism, and, as will be noted presently, among the American ruling classes, they do, in fact, do a great deal of ruling.

In the United States all business not transacted over the telephone is accomplished in conjunction with alcohol or food, often under conditions of advanced intoxication. This is a fact of the utmost importance for the visitor of limited funds who is also (should this ever be true) paying his own expenses, for it means that the most expensive restaurants are, with rare exceptions, the worst. Since what is served there is a secondary consideration, little attention is paid to it. Also, no known economic law acts to keep down the cost of the meal. Those who frequent these resorts are transacting business, soliciting business, reminding people they are in business or getting drunk under the excuse of doing business, and so all costs can be charged to an expense account or, at a minimum, taken by each of the participants for the group as a whole as an income tax deduction. Cheaper places — the traveler should have such names as Nedick's, Chock Full O'Nuts and Horn & Hardart in mind — are for eating, and, accordingly, the food is given attention. Nutburgers and Kaiser Stoneless Peaches, American delicacies popularized by the late Evelyn Waugh, are much sought after by visitors. They are hard to find.

The United States is very large, and, unlike Australia's, its population is scattered inconveniently over the entire area. This means that all but the most eccentric tourist will have to settle for a visit to New York, Washington, San Francisco or Los Angeles, one of the national parks (usually the Grand Canyon) and New England. Under this limitation, he or she will see very little of the countryside, but about this nothing, unfortunately, can be done. Unless the visitor is willing to suffer indignity or expense far beyond the tolerance and means of the ordinary tourist, he or she must travel by air, and, at the height flown by modern aircraft, all terrain looks alike, except that Algeria is brown, Brazil green and Canada in winter a grayish-white. Alone among the civilized nations, the United States lacks an acceptable system of rail passenger transport, which is the only economical and comfortable way of gaining an impression of the landscape. The visitor should have this shortcoming in mind when he is informed, as he often still is, of the blessings of American private enterprise. Railway passenger travel in the United States was at first left to private management — the only important country to try this experiment. It didn't work. There is now a system of rail passenger service called Amtrak, but it operates on the principle that, being partly public and thus a form of socialism and thus wicked, it should be bad enough to discourage people from using it. Except to passengers with deep ideological convictions, the whole idea seems unfortunate.

The visitor from Europe, unless especially advised to enter through Boston, Philadelphia or Washington, will come by way of John F. Kennedy Airport into New York. On landing, he will encounter scenes of indescribable chaos, but this cannot by any means be attributed to the American genius for confusion. London, in need of a new airport, has just emerged from a solemn and sometimes angry discussion as to where it should be. New York, having a similar need, has decided not to build one — not, at least, in the near future or within easy range of the metropolis. This is, in fact, extremely rational — some think, in the case of New York, uniquely so. Airplanes are admirable for the minority inside but hideous for the majority outside and below. The New York decision honors the rights of the outsiders rather than those of the insiders. It means that, after much disorder resulting from congestion, air traffic will be distributed to other cities; some people could be forced back to trains; some will avoid New York completely; and some businesses will move away. This will adversely affect the growth of the city, which, by common consent, is already too large. The good sense in this matter should buoy up the traveler during the hours he dwells either over or in JFK.

He will also, perhaps to his surprise, be cheered by the U.S. customs and immigration officials. These middle-aged and generally amiable bureaucrats assume that all who come through their gates are minor smugglers whose visas have no doubt involved perjury, but they are resigned to such frailties. In every respect they are in pleasant contrast to the lackadaisical or officious juveniles who, in a manner of speaking, welcome the traveler at Heathrow in London and react with suspicion to anyone whose skin is dark.

The City of New York is currently undergoing a grave experiment that affects the comfort and, on occasion, the safety of even the most casual visitor. The experiment consists in seeing whether a city of that size can be operated on a far smaller amount of money than would make its life tolerable and a still smaller amount than would make it agreeable. The richer New Yorkers, many of whom are very rich indeed, are cooperating with an enthusiasm that the affluent rarely show for social experiment, and at great personal expense. They are paying for private security guards in unprecedented numbers and costly private schooling for their children; they are contributing an appreciable share of their personal property to burglars, sacrificing their liberty of movement after sundown and accustoming themselves to the sight and smell of garbage beyond anything ever experienced during a dustmen's strike in Great Britain. And they are accepting numerous other costs and inconveniences in order to show that private affluence is consistent with public squalor. Even among those who doubt the success of the experiment, a strong feeling prevails that existing federal rather than higher local taxes should pay the city's bills. However, the federal government is more deeply concerned at the moment with street safety in Saigon. An unhappy situation.

New York City is the stronghold of the liberal Democrats; the state as a whole, other things equal, prefers Democrats to Republicans. Alfred E. Smith, Franklin D. Roosevelt and Herbert Lehman, the great Democratic leaders of the first half of this century, all became governors of

New York. However, the present [1971] governor, the elected state officials (with one exception) and the senior senator are Republicans, and the recently elected junior senator, Mr. James Buckley, was elected as a Conservative and now calls himself a Conservative-Republican. He got in principally because two liberals ran against him and split the opposing vote. The most durable reason that the Democrats, despite their majority, do not now elect their slates in New York is important, and it is much, though evasively, discussed. It is because, contemplating their majority, they have thought it possible to win with their most tedious candidates, these being preferred by the wealthy, pedantic and often rapacious men who provide the money for the campaigns and the New York state party with what is very loosely referred to as its leadership. Surprise is felt recurrently that the people, as distinct from the fat cats, find the candidates so selected repellent. However, hope lingers that at the next election the voters will be more receptive, and this hope is controlling. (? consoling)

The social structure of New York City at the present time defies description. It is further complicated by the aforementioned tendency of all the American castes to consider themselves thrice-born. Ostensibly at the top are the artistically and socially sensitive, as distinct from the ordinary, rich. These number perhaps three thousand and achieve their position by their patronage of the arts, liberal politicians and the currently fashionable social panaceas. Of late, some caution has developed over association with anything that might be considered too radical, bringing with it criticism of what has been called Radical Chic. Support of population control is still thought to be safe. In this circle, distinction is associated with the decoration of one's apartment and one's body; in consequence, the interiors, the women and some of the men have an unfortunate tendency in their appearance to reflect professional advice. All of the members of this caste may be recognized by the fact that they call Leonard Bernstein Lenny, and the European visitor can readily gain admission by using this nomenclature.

Below the patrons of the arts, politics and social progress come the practicing artists — theatrical producers and directors, actresses, actors, writers, journalists, columnists, redeeming-social-content pornographers, musicians, painters, sculptors, architects, film directors, dress designers, television performers and, at the extreme fringe, an occasional network executive. The cultural tendencies of this community, which numbers in the tens of thousands, are universally deplored in the United States and throughout the world. They are also universally imitated. The lifestyle attempted by a socially underdeveloped artist in the Communist countries is what he imagines exists in New York.

Nearly all of the races of the world — blacks, Puerto Ricans, Jews of diverse origin and date of disembarkation, Irish, Italians, Chinese and

Anglo-Saxons, called WASPs — live in greater or lesser juxtaposition in New York. Once, the visitor was told rather repetitively that this city was the melting pot; never before in history had so many people of such varied languages, customs, colors and culinary habits lived so amicably together. Although New York remains peaceful by most standards, this self-congratulation is now less often heard, since it was discovered some years ago that racial harmony depended unduly on the willingness of the blacks (and latterly the Puerto Ricans) to do for the other races the meanest jobs at the lowest wages and then to return to live by themselves in the worst slums.

Two famous New York institutions deserve a word. One is the United Nations, which, it was once hoped, would make New York the fledgling capital of an eventual world-state. The UN is currently important as the place where statesmen take their crises when imagination fails them as to other action and where parents take their children when they wish to demonstrate or implant vision. Otherwise it is a world apart, impinging on the life of the city only as the automobiles of the diplomats are illegally parked.

The other notable New York institution is Wall Street. Legend has it marching Americans against Communism in Indochina, defending American imperial interests everywhere else and holding the line against socialism at home. Somewhat inconsistently, it, in fact, provided the largest part of Senator Eugene McCarthy's financial support when he ran for the presidency in 1968 in opposition to the Vietnam war and succeeded (with the support of Mrs. Johnson and a great many others) in persuading President Lyndon Johnson not to stand for re-election. University undergraduates, Americans for Democratic Action, which is the vehicle of the Establishment left, and the peace groups were more prominent than Wall Street in the McCarthy campaign, but balancing cash against vehemence, they may have been no more influential. However, the great majority of Wall Streeters go to the suburbs at night often rather tired and give no thought to running the country.

Until the late 1960s, a younger Wall Street generation, the progenitors of growth funds, performance funds, hedge funds, go-go funds and other instruments of popular enrichment, were greatly valued for their bold genius in managing other people's money. They even achieved a measure of social acceptance, and the more reckless were invited to appear on television talk shows. It has since been discovered that their success depended to a regrettable degree on the fact that the market was going up. The slump in 1970, following the previous boom, put about half of all the brokerage houses in serious financial trouble. This was aggravated, in turn, by extreme mismanagement. Although frequently pictured as the focal point of a uniquely fearless free enterprise, the Wall Street houses and the Stock Exchange promptly and unhesitatingly petitioned the United States government to establish a billion-dollar corporation (the Securities Investors Protection Corporation) to bail them out of any further difficulty. This is part of a general American tendency of which the alert visitor will soon become aware. Government loans to aircraft companies, government subsidies to supersonic travel and government underwriting of industrial research and development as well as government protection of investors are held in high regard by most American conservatives. Although socialism is disapproved in the United States, an important exception is made when it is needed by the rich.

On going from New York to Washington, the visitor whose information is only slightly obsolete will assume that the natural bridge between the two cities is the American Establishment. This, he will have heard, rules in both places.

For much of the twentieth century he would have been right. Although numerous tasks of government — running the Department of Agriculture or the Department of the Interior, administering welfare and social insurance and heading such regulatory agencies as the Federal Trade Commission, the Federal Communications Commission and the Interstate Commerce Commission — were undertaken by non-Establishment talent (or, in the case of some older regulatory agencies, by nontalent), the prestige and power of the Establishment were elsewhere enormous. This is no longer so.

The Establishment consists of New York and Washington lawyers of impeccable attire who combine a deep concern for the public interest with a profitable preoccupation with the needs of their large corporate clients. Associated with them are the presidents of the Ford and Rockefeller Foundations, a few exceptionally articulate business executives and bankers, the presidents of the older private universities and a number of very presentable college professors who are recruited for their ability to give the Establishment truths a solid basis in economic and political doctrine. (The first chairman of the Establishment was the late Dr. Nicholas Murray Butler, for more than a generation the president of Columbia University. He was succeeded in the 1920s by the late Henry Stimson, secretary of state under Herbert Hoover and secretary of war under Franklin Roosevelt. He, in turn, was succeeded in 1945 by John J. McCloy, a lawyer like his predecessors, a Republican, a wartime official under Roosevelt, high commissioner in Germany during the Occupation and later chairman of the board of the Chase Manhattan Bank and chairman of the Ford Foundation. His successor-designate in the late 1950s was Dean Rusk, then president of the Rockefeller Foundation, but upon Rusk's becoming secretary of state, David Rockefeller, a banker, was advanced to Establishment chairman.)

In the early 1960s, the position of the Establishment could not have seemed more secure. In 1961, Mr. Rusk took over at the State Department, succeeding Messrs. Christian Herter and John Foster Dulles, both Establishment figures, and the latter eminently so. Douglas Dillon, a vice chairman who had served in the State Department under President Eisenhower, became secretary of the treasury. Allen Dulles, long in charge of the CIA, was retained in office by President Kennedy. McGeorge Bundy became head of the National Security Council in the White House. Robert McNamara, something of an outsider, was solidly encased at the Pentagon with Establishment lawyers and advisers. Outsiders who were so unwise as to associate themselves with foreign policy were either kept at a safe distance or, as in the case of Chester Bowles, soon sacked.

Power in the United States government is — or has been — more concentrated than is often imagined. If you have the Pentagon, the CIA, the State Department, the Treasury and the man who coordinates those agencies at the White House, you have it all, and all these the Establishment had. Although it never formally avowed the British socialist doctrine of the seizure of the commanding heights, the American Establishment was manifesting the same sound instinct.

Sadly for its members' self-esteem, it is now, in the 1970s, out of office and under a heavy cloud. The fortunate are practicing law or selling corporate bonds; a few, like Mr. Dean Rusk, are in exile. (He is teaching in Athens, Georgia, which is the American equivalent of Ulan Bator.) The presidents of Columbia and Harvard Universities have departed office following local demonstrations. The so-called *Pentagon Papers* extensively documented the inner thoughts of a great many of these men, and they were widely held to have lacked prescience. Recently there have been numerous suggestions that the Establishment should never again be entrusted with public responsibility.

Its present low estate has little or nothing to do with party politics. Most of its members are Republicans, but, in their years of eminence, even when the Democrats were in power, they were said, occasionally by themselves, to be "lending their talents to the administration." Something must be attributed to President Nixon, who is a distinctly non-Establishment Republican. His polemical style has always offended Establishment Republicans, who privately call him crude. And he has always cultivated the support and affection of those members of the party whose wives wear sensible shoes, who ask what the country is coming to and whose suspicions are aroused by the self-assurance of the Establishment and the way its selflessness and high-minded concern for international affairs are combined with extreme affluence. On taking office, Mr. Nixon made clear his attitude in a manner uniquely discomfiting to Englishmen by nominating Walter Annenberg as ambassador to the Court of St. James's. Since World War II, this post above all others has been sacred to a senior member of the Establishment, and Mr. Annenberg does not even belong.

The more important factor in the rising disesteem of the Establishment has been its support of the Vietnam war. The latter is, possibly, the most grievous disaster in American history; the visitor to the United States must be prepared for a distaste for this enterprise beyond anything he may have imagined. As the architect of foreign and military policy and a defender of the war, the Establishment has come in for heavy blame. Many of its members think this unfair. They have long believed that its views are made right by the sheer eminence of those who hold them. Responsibility, in effect, annuls error. It was sufficient that the Vietnam policy was made by men of excellent reputation. This being so, it was not to be expected that anyone would question whether the intervention was necessary or wise. A most unfortunate way of proceeding.

While Calvin Coolidge is best remembered for his observations on economics — for his forecast that the stock market would fluctuate and similar thoughtful prognoses — much of what is believed about the United States government can, conveniently, be gleaned from his presidential memoirs. There he notes that the Congress passes the laws and the President executes them, that is, the laws. In practice, however, the procedure in legislation, administration and appropriation of funds is quite different, as, indeed, many informed Americans would now concede. (Numerous such Americans are content to teach the established myths and relay them to foreigners while holding that to believe them personally would suggest hopeless naïveté.) Thus, the initial decision in favor of an invasion into some new part of Indochina or a new antimissile system to defend the Republic is taken not by the Congress or even by the President but by the military authorities, after discussion in the case of invasions with the intelligence agencies and in the case of weapons procurement with the weapons firms. The decision is then, in the common phrase, sold to the President, who retains limited powers of modification. The action is thereupon ratified by those members of the Congress who join the longest service in the legislature with the least tendency to be critical of military initiatives or needs. Objection from others in the Congress or from the public, while expected, is, unless extreme, ignored. The agencies that take these decisions — the Department of Defense and (though less important) the Central Intelligence Agency — are located not in the District of Columbia but in the nearby Commonwealth of Virginia. This is a matter of more than passing importance, for the visitor is still likely to be told that the principal seat of government is in Washington, D.C.

Less portentous questions of policy and public administration do originate with government departments located in the older capital and, from time to time, with the President and Congress. For this reason, but rather more because of tradition, the President and Congress continue to attract a good deal of attention. Vigorous effort is now being made to retrieve for the legislative branch some of the power over war, peace and the purchase of armaments for so long exercised as a matter of moral right by the Pentagon and the collateral bureaucracies. Intellectuals expect the effort to fail. (American intellectuals, it may be here noted, always associate prescience on public issues with profound pessimism. This the visiting pundit is advised to remember if he expects his own views to be taken seriously.)

The Congress of the United States consists of two houses — the Senate and the House of Representatives. The Senate has unlimited debate; in the House, debate is ruthlessly circumscribed. There is frequent discussion as to which technique most effectively frustrates democratic process. However, a more important antidote to American democracy is American gerontocracy. The positions of eminence and authority in the Congress are allotted in accordance with length of service, regardless of quality. Superficial observers have long criticized the United States for making a fetish of youth. This is unfair. Uniquely among modern organs of public and private administration, its national legislature rewards senility. The same principle is applied to the leadership of its principal crime-prevention agency, the Federal Bureau of Investigation. Although crime has been increasing in the United States for some years, those most concerned about law and order — by another interesting departure in the field of public administration — do not suggest that Mr. J. Edgar Hoover, the permanent head of the FBI, is in any way responsible. In fact, Americans of fundamentalist conviction hold, quite generally, that God has begun according immortality to man and has started in Europe with General Francisco Franco and at home with Mr. Hoover.

Nonetheless, the congressional gerontocracy is currently under attack and so also, even more surprisingly, is the head of the FBI. He has, quite possibly, been a victim of the sexual revolution in America. Until recently the thought of his extensive dossiers detailing sexual or fiscal delinquencies was sufficient to keep even the boldest politician silent and cooperative. The larcenous still worry. But the others often now feel that the release of a few lurid episodes from their personal sex histories would add luster to otherwise pedestrian personalities. So they can attack Mr. Hoover with impunity. Still, learned men do not expect this effort or that against the seniority system to be any more successful than that against the Pentagon.

They are probably wrong. In recent times, the Senate has come to enroll some of the most talented citizens of the United States. And the quality of the members of the House has been greatly improving. Much of the power of the military in the cold war years stemmed from the circumstance that it was not challenged. Now the generals are at war with Indochina, with the Congress and with the country as a whole — war on three fronts. Two have always been thought a maximum. For this reason as well as on past form, the Congress and the country will eventually win.

It is a mark of the modern eminence of the Senate that the leading Democratic aspirants for the presidency in 1972 are all members. Until recently, senators were thought, by their training there, to be under-achievers, and the single senator to be elected to the presidency direct from the Senate in the first four decades of this century, Warren Gamaliel Harding, served powerfully to confirm that suspicion. Apart from Edward Kennedy, whose statements that he is not a candidate the country always regards as less than firm, all of the presently leading Democratic contenders come from conservative, traditionally Republican states — Edmund Muskie from Maine, one of the two states that never voted for Roosevelt; George McGovern (the most liberal of them all) from South Dakota, which has been called the most conservative state in the Union; Birch Bayh from Indiana, a putative stronghold of the silent and conservative majority; Harold Hughes from the traditionally Republican state of Iowa. One reason for this is that Americans may, perhaps, no longer be as conservative as the columnists assume and the comfortable wish to believe. But a more important reason is that to be elected in those states a Democrat has to be remarkably good.

The Democrats are at this time the normal governing party in the United States or so regard themselves. They now have a majority in both houses of Congress and would also have the presidency did they not seem to be war-prone. (All wars in this century have begun under Democratic auspices.) It follows from the normal Democratic ascendancy that President Nixon and his colleagues are regarded as temporary intruders in Washington — some observers have compared them to a military encampment in an occupied city. However, they are treated with extreme courtesy by former office holders who served under Kennedy and Johnson, many of whom have retired to profitable law practices in the city and who need the good will of the Republicans for fixing cases before the federal agencies and lobbying for legislative inaction in opposition to the public interest. Mark Twain described the Congress of the United States as the only native American criminal class. This is no longer so, but the appellation has much relevance to the Washington bar. Those erstwhile officials now in the law firms play an active part in the affairs of the Democratic Party, where they favor, in principle, reforms that do not reflect adversely on their own past records or affect adversely the interests of their more remunerative clients or the larger party contributors. Such reforms are few.

The visitor to Washington will encounter two drastically divergent views of what the White House should be like. One, essentially mon-archial, holds that it should be a place of glamour and excitement, a symbol of the majesty of the state, a showcase of the nation's culture. This view is principally praised by New York and Washington liberals who are accustomed to being invited to the White House or wish they were. Sensible Americans regard it as so much nonsense. The second and sounder view is that the less heard of the White House, the better. In a republic the average citizen should be able to recall the name of the President and possibly that of his wife but never the names of his children or principal assistants. The White House under President Nixon is dull and the President, his family and staff seem excellently endowed to put this dictum into effect. Except for Dr. Henry Kissinger, the President's adviser on foreign affairs and an exception both because of his academic background (he is from Harvard) and his party-going proclivities, all of the President's advisers are unknown save that they also have German names, although they are not thought to function with Teutonic efficiency. In making the White House boring, the Nix-ons have shown themselves, perhaps inadvertently, to be true repub-licans.

President Nixon is frequently called to task for being inaccessible, a complaint that has come especially from his Cabinet officers. The crit-icism is inappropriate. The American bureaucracy has become so enor-mous that it requires a large staff in the White House just to keep in touch with its multitude of activities. Cabinet officers naturally report to this theoretically subordinate staff. And if legislators, reformers, lobbyists, job seekers and those in a position to practice bribery through campaign contributions are knowledgeable, they, too, go to the relevant man in the White House. Cabinet officers thus being well down the bureaucratic ladder, it would be unnatural as well as difficult for a busy man like the President to bother with them. The American Cabinet, all visitors should be warned, conducts no business. It assembles only for public relations purposes and to hear presidential homilies. Years ago, when a function such as education needed emphasis, people spoke of raising it to Cabinet rank. This terminology is now obsolete, although to speak of lowering an agency to Cabinet level is still unusual.

On leaving Washington to tour the country, the politically concerned visitor will think he should look into the operations of the state gov-ernments and otherwise inform himself on regional and local questions. That impulse should be resisted; the difficulties are grave, and this is an area where nearly all accepted knowledge is contradicted by the facts.

Thus, as all students of American history are aware, the conventional wisdom is that the Democratic Party is strong in the Deep South, drawing its strength from its ancient commitment to keeping the blacks in their place, a pursuit more often referred to as the defense of the Southern tradition. The Republicans, created by and in the image of Abraham Lincoln, are the emancipators. In practice, the Southern Republicans appeal to the hard-core supporters of white supremacy; this is the thought, so called, behind President Nixon's Southern Strategy. And Democrats are increasingly being elected with black support. A growing number of blacks in the South are themselves contending for public office, almost invariably on the Democratic ticket, the party of their ancient oppressors. The reason is that the improving tendencies of man in civil rights have been valuably reinforced in the South by the need to be nice to black citizens whose votes are being solicited. In consequence, all Democratic candidates speak much more respectfully of their constituents, black and white, and last January several new Democratic governors in the South went out of their way to cite their own enlightenment on the question of race. The new governor of Georgia, Jimmy Carter, recently proclaimed that in his state the politics of racial discrimination were over. Even Alabama's George Wallace, of highly resistant reputation, is visibly shifting his concern from the plight of the oppressed white supremacist to, at a minimum, that of the downtrodden blue-collar worker.

Moving west, the visitor should glance down briefly at Texas. Topographically it is without interest; politically it is the last part of the United States where the two major parties, Republican and Democratic, compete through open conservatism for the support of the rich. (Because oil revenues are extensively exempt from income taxes, the state has an exceptionally large number of residents who are refugees from the federal tax system.) Being so visibly conservative, the leading Texas Democrats are not highly regarded in the rest of the country except as possible sources of campaign funds. Sensing this, John Connally, recently the governor and once considered by many the most influential Democrat in the state, has gone over to the Republicans and is now secretary of the treasury under President Nixon. The visitor will find many Democrats bearing up under the loss with courage and fortitude.

Perhaps partly because they have so little prospect of power, Texas liberals are among the liveliest and least inhibited in the country. (In the United States, though power corrupts, the expectation of power paralyzes.) They have their own newspaper, *The Texas Observer*, a well-researched journal that more orthodox Texas statesmen feel should not have the protection of the First Amendment.

The visitor will be told that the politics of California, the most populous of all the states, are possibly the most eccentric in the Union and certainly the most incoherent, but California is, in fact, the best governed. Electoral contests for the state legislature are fought with a vigor that elsewhere is seen only in races for the United States Senate. The state government is administered by a proud, competent and honest civil service. The school system is one of the best in the country, and the California university system is, by a wide margin, the best in the world. In recent years, the University of California has been the object of repeated attack by Governor Ronald Reagan. Governor Reagan, a one-time film actor, was, it is less well known, a pioneer trade union leader in Hollywood and a founding member of Americans for Democratic Action, which, in his time, was considered by many of his present supporters as rather more inimical than the Communist Party of the U.S.A. There are a great number of them who really believe that his move to the far right was in response to conviction. Considerable damage to the universities is said to have been done by Governor Reagan. A recent survey shows, however, that by all conventional measures of distinction, the University of California at Berkeley (only one of some eight units in the state system, which, in turn, are supplemented by numerous state and junior colleges) remains substantially ahead of Harvard, its nearest competitor.

Berkeley is, perhaps, the best place for the visitor to reflect on the role of the university in American life. It was at Berkeley in the mid-1960s that the student eruption called the Free Speech Movement first occurred, and it was from there that it spread around the world. In consequence, the universities became, for a time, one of the most powerful political influences in the United States. It was the universities — not the trade unions, not the free-lance intellectuals, not the press, not the businessmen, although, as I've said, they helped to a greater degree than is commonly understood — that led the opposition to the Vietnam war, that compelled the retirement of President Johnson (the war apart, an excellent President), that forced the pace of the withdrawal from Indochina, that started the battle against the great corporations on the issue of pollution and that, in the congressional elections of 1970, helped defeat a score or more of the most egregious time servers, military sycophants and hawks.

As the visitor comes back over the Great Plains and prairies, he or she enters the heartland of the country. Here church, farm and family still rule. Here support of the Republican Party is not a political exercise but an act of public piety. But here, also, as I've noted, the Democrats have been making great gains in recent years.

While the matter is open to considerable dispute, there are some who hold that Chicago, which was for long the symbol of crime, violence and misgovernment, is now the best-governed large city in the United States. Only, it is said, his crude enthusiasm for law and order in the ghetto and for Lyndon Johnson and Hubert Humphrey at the Democratic Convention in 1968 has kept people from recognizing that Richard Daley is a very great mayor. It is beyond doubt that Chicago streets are cleaner than those of New York — and that the new skyscrapers and highways are expensive. However, truth is one thing and paradox another, and allegations concerning the progressive and humanitarian tendencies of the Chicago city government should be treated with reserve. The educational system is inferior to those in other large cities; children in Chicago average a year or two below children in New York in reading achievement. And just behind the new office buildings with their glittering façades is, perhaps, the most angry and unpleasant ghetto in all the country. Chicago remains a poor place for the poor.

The visitor should return home to Europe by way of New England. This is entirely agreeable. Boston remains, after San Francisco, the most pleasant city in the country; both managed to escape, although only narrowly, the worst depredations of the urban highway builders. The new Boston Government Center is one of the more interesting examples of urban design since Rockefeller Center was built in the depression years of the 1930s. People come to visit it, which is very remarkable where modern architecture is concerned. In the political geography of the United States, Massachusetts, like Wisconsin and, of late, Minnesota, has long had an importance wholly disproportionate with its population. Along with the rest of New England, the commonwealth is considered the original home of ethnic politics. In fact, however, the largest minority, the French Canadians, has never had a candidate for major office. The Kennedys have always been careful to eschew the Baroque oratory and style usually associated with Irish politicians. A quintessential (and increasingly rare) Yankee, Leverett Saltonstall, was one of the most successful vote getters in modern times. And in 1966, the state elected the first black to sit in the United States Senate since Reconstruction, although blacks represent only a tiny minority of the population.

A surprising amount of the rest of New England remains unspoiled, and Vermont, the most beautiful state in the Union, has further distinguished itself by being one of the first (along with Hawaii) to abolish advertising along its highways. Finally, for going home, Boston's Logan Airport is much better and more peaceful than New York's JFK.

A VERY SPECIFIC GUIDE
TO THE ECONOMIC FOLKWAYS OF
AMERICAN BUSINESS AND BUSINESSMEN

(1977)

Another guide. This one was written expressly for business visitors from abroad, but I would like to think that some Americans may also find the rules useful. After nine years I still adhere rigorously to all of them.

Part of my recent life has been spent outside the United States, mostly in England and Switzerland, and there I have been called upon with some frequency, generally by businessmen, to comment on affairs at home. This I have done with a confidence enhanced as always by distance but also with the feeling that there should be a firm set of rules for interpreting modern American economic folkways. Such rules are needed because the approved belief is often — perhaps usually — at a 180-degree variance with the American reality. Foreign executives talk regularly with American executives and are thereby reassured in the conventional error. In consequence, I have decided to set down what the European or other overseas businessman should have in mind when meditating on the American economy, as, given its weight in the world, almost everyone engaged anywhere in business is required to do.

I have come up with ten rules. I had hoped there might be ten; maybe truth has its own arithmetic.

1. Under all circumstances official American economic forecasts should be mistrusted and, if possible, ignored. Only the crop projections from the Department of Agriculture have any validity. The reason is that government forecasts cannot be in conflict with what the administration currently in office needs to have happen. No government forecaster can say unemployment will worsen, inflation become more severe or that economic growth will give way to recession. Yet these things, alas, do occur. It follows that our official forecasts are right only when things go right.

There is a further and chilling possibility, which is that high officials make cheerful forecasts because they actually expect things to get worse. They fear that unemployment or inflation or both will increase. So they say things will get better in the next quarter in the hope that this will lift spirits and make things improve.

2. Mistrust likewise the forecasts of all private American economists. These, unlike the official forecasts, frequently have no compelled error. The econometric models on which they are based incorporate and assess the effect of movement in economic variables in accordance with past experience, and they are the product of much careful and intelligent effort. But none incorporates factors shaping the economic outlook that are *not* part of past experience, and economic life, sad to say, is a process of constant adjustment to things that have never happened before. No econometric model before 1974 allowed for the effect of an oil embargo or of a massive increase [or later a decrease] in petroleum prices. With one possible exception, none before 1969 allowed for the depressing effect of a big drop in the stock market. None can foretell the success or failure of, say, an incomes policy.

Also remember that were the future known, there would be no need for forecasts. No one could get attention for what everyone can know; forecasting the hour of tomorrow's sunrise is not a remunerative line of work.

Remember, too, that a great many private economists make forecasts in a random way not because they know what will happen but because, being economists, they are supposed to know and are expected to say. They must, sometimes disastrously, live up to their professional image.

3. Bear always in mind that the value of any recommendation on economic policy can never be judged by the applause it produces, for that applause comes from the articulate, and they, all but invariably, are the affluent. It does not reflect the wisdom of the action, only the effect of the action on the well-to-do. What most helps those who least need help is rarely what is of most value to the economy.

4. Bear also in mind — a companion point — that many American economists shape their advice so as to enhance the approval it evokes. And, as before, it is the well-provided who are heard. Since their approval is the only reward being sought, professional corruption is not necessarily involved. An economist does not have to be in the pay of the high economic establishment to be subject to its influence, although compensation is frequently an encouragement.

5. Remember that the state of American business confidence where government policy is concerned has no visible relation to economic performance. That is because what improves the confidence of the American business executive is what improves his sense of personal well-being; what improves his personal well-being is what improves his after-tax income.

Thus, a reduction in the upper-bracket income tax is extremely good for business confidence but does little or nothing for economic performance. All American executives are already working with an intense devotion to duty; they always do. Nothing more can be expected; hence business performance will not improve just because they get to keep more of their own money.

6. Be aware that, given a choice between love and his own long-run economic interest, the American business executive will vote out of love. The historical evidence on this general rule is more than powerful; it is irrefutable.

Businessmen voted heavily for Herbert Hoover, whom they loved, and against Franklin D. Roosevelt, whom they did not love. But business was better, the business prospect far brighter, under Roosevelt than under Hoover. None of those who ran against Roosevelt — Landon, Willkie, Dewey — made a plausible case that he could improve on Roosevelt's performance, but all had, from the heart, powerful business support.

Since Roosevelt, love has continued and extended its triumph over self-interest. Business was exceptionally good under Harry Truman, and businessmen rewarded this performance by voting in 1948 for Thomas E. Dewey. They loved Eisenhower more than Kennedy and Johnson, but employment and economic growth were both better under Kennedy and Johnson. In 1971, Richard Nixon imposed comprehensive wage and price controls, which American businessmen abhor. They nonetheless voted resoundingly for his re-election in 1972 and further affirmed their affection with massive transfusions of cash. In 1976, they endorsed the far from satisfactory economic performance of Gerald Ford — according to the impeccable testimony of *Fortune* magazine, by an eight-to-one margin.*

The lesson here for the overseas businessman is especially clear: do not ever be influenced by the rich, warm and usually self-denying political affections of your American colleagues, for they will grievously warp your business judgment. Except in the United States, where it is inevitable, love and business should not mix.

7. Keep in mind that American businessmen expect to win elections even when they lose, and often do. Following the Carter victory last autumn, Gabriel Hauge, chairman of Manufacturers Hanover Trust Bank in New York and an articulate and thoughtful spokesman for the businessmen who had voted for Gerald Ford, addressed a stern letter to the President-elect through *The New York Times*. Mr. Carter had, Mr. Hauge said, done well to "back away" from his pre-election promise of standby wage and price controls. Now there were other

*And the same was true in 1984, massive deficits notwithstanding, for President Reagan.

steps that businessmen required. Mr. Hauge stressed, especially, that Mr. Carter should bring into his Cabinet the kind of confidence-inspiring men whose poor economic performance had just lost the election for Mr. Ford. Many believe that Mr. Carter was persuaded.

8. Remember that, traditionally, American businessmen, and especially those in high executive positions, have a strong sense of impending disaster. Almost any public action they dislike will, they solemnly warn, precipitate economic ruin. Such predictions are made because those making them are incapable of finding any other way of attracting attention. Let all bear in mind Adam Smith's deathless observation that "there is a great deal of ruin in a nation."

9. Especially avoid according any attention to American business warnings that the free enterprise system is in peril in the United States, and particularly if such warnings come from high corporate executives. Outwardly the American executive is a solid, affable, confident chap; inwardly he is given to mild paranoia. After a lifetime of effort and struggle he has reached the top of a great enterprise, and at this point he is called to account in Washington by politicians who, as he sees it, are caught up in the anticorporation rhetoric that won them election. For reasons that have their roots in outdated economic religion and the congenital obtuseness of public relations men, he thereupon deliberately sets himself up for their attack by defending his company — huge, potent, bureaucratic — as a superb microcosmic manifestation of classical economics. Such a contradiction between his faith and the reality is joyously exploited by critics — men of no comparable achievement, income or assets. The American business executive is forced to the conclusion that the system — free enterprise itself — is truly in grave danger. What is really in danger is the classical defense of capitalism.

10. I come to my final rule. It applies not only to the United States but to all the industrial countries in our time. Where governments, elections and personalities are concerned, you should always minimize, never exaggerate, the likelihood of substantial economic change.

There are two reasons for this. First, in public affairs circumstance is far more influential and ideological preference far less important than is commonly supposed, especially by economists and businessmen. And second, all modern governments are vast bureaucratic organizations with their own dynamic, and these organizations, more than presidents, prime ministers or chancellors, are now in control.

BRAZIL

(1980)

On my last trip to Brazil I kept this rather substantial journal; it was never published. Conceivably it tells more about the country and the events of my journey than one needs to know. But my editor liked it, and I enjoyed writing it.

My pioneer observations on Brazil's indebtedness are still generally valid, but the decaying military dictatorship of 1980 has now given way to a still tenuous democracy, as is the case elsewhere in Latin America.

NEW YORK — AUGUST 17

After twenty-two years my wife and I are again visiting Brazil. Inevitably, I have been invited to give some lectures, but since everyone is anxious to inform a lecturer to his own purposes, it is not a bad way to learn something about a community. I used to make it a rule never to visit countries where military governments are in power, but the Brazilian generals have recently offered an opening to democracy, so, as often happens, I am able to organize my principles as required.

There is also the circumstance that my books sell in some quantity in Brazil, and where books go, an author can surely follow. Not that publication in Brazil has always been without problems for me. Ten years ago my novel, *The Triumph*, came out in Portuguese in Rio de Janeiro. It told of an old Latin American dictator in his last days of power; of how he was replaced by a vaguely leftist convocation, which aroused the gravest suspicions of the cold warrior club in Washington; of the devious brilliance with which the dictator's son was brought back from the University of Michigan by the State Department, installed in office and surrounded with dollars and arms for his protection; and of how it turned out that the little bastard, as he almost certainly was, had fallen in with the wrong people at Ann Arbor and become a Communist. Since his old man had owned all the significant wealth of the country, the son had only to deed it over to the people and the revolution was complete. After some twenty thousand copies of the book had been sold in Brazil, as it was reported to me, it was read by some unnaturally literate colonel, who thought my words had local application. There was a stinging rebuke for the publisher, and sales were discontinued.

We are traveling on a Varig DC-10, which is pleasantly uncrowded. The tourist-class passengers have several seats apiece on which they can stretch out for undisturbed sleep. First class is not so comfortable. Our check-in was accomplished in just under four minutes; the food is completely palatable; departure was prompt; on all other matters Varig functions with Teutonic dispatch.

RIO DE JANEIRO — AUGUST 18

We arrived on time this morning and then waited an hour and a half for our baggage, which evidently had followed us by sail. The various responsibilities of the airlines are a metaphor of our time: man can master without difficulty the complex technology of the air, but the social organization required to remove clothing, toilet articles and contraband from the plane's hull and transport them to the terminal is beyond him.

Newsmen and television technicians converged on me at the airport to ask what I thought of Brazil, of the inflation rate, of the government's policies in general. I replied that I didn't think it appropriate to prescribe fully for any country's economic problems until I had been there for at least a week. They were deeply dissatisfied.

Rio de Janeiro, when finally achieved, was dense with fog, smog and particulate matter and crawling with Volkswagen beetles. When it emerged into the sunshine, the city was as beautiful as I remembered it, although the beetles remained. My first lecture this evening (after some sleep) was at Mendes University, and the questions that followed made it a lively affair. One line of inquiry concerned Brazil's external debt, now between $50 and $60 billions with proportionately heavy debt service. To this I was able to respond that whatever the disadvantages of debt, it is better than the deprivation that would have existed had it not been incurred. And if a debt cannot be paid, this need no longer be acknowledged. Instead a conspiracy develops between the debtor, who does not wish it known that he is in default, and the creditor, who does not wish it known that he has made a stupid loan. So, after exceptionally solemn negotiations, it is announced that the debt has been extended, rolled over or refinanced. Sometimes it is said that all three have been done. Such methods successfully conceal the basic fact, which is that the borrower is broke and cannot pay.

I was asked why I had been so willfully backward that I had not accepted the now relevant economic doctrines of either Karl Marx or Professor Milton Friedman. I agreed that there was a certain affinity between the two. The ideas of both men are anchored solidly in the past — Friedman's in the world of Adam Smith and eighteenth-century post-mercantilism, those of Marx in violent, predatory nineteenth-century capitalism. Bureaucratic corporations, trade unions, changing work habits, the democratization of public and private consumption, OPEC, urbanization and the welfare state have all been relentless forces for change and have rendered obsolete all who do not accommodate to it, socialists and old-fashioned classical economists alike.

RIO DE JANEIRO — AUGUST 19

The Caesar Park Hotel, where we are staying, looks out on Ipanema Beach, which is a few densely populated miles south of the old city center. The hotel also overlooks the surf riders, who are determined but incompetent. They await a large wave from the Antarctic (the beach faces south), maneuver themselves on top of the roll and are then immediately thrown off. They do not improve with practice.

This morning we toured the city, visited some Baroque churches — interesting but not completely remarkable by European standards — and I met for lunch and dinner with a small cross section of the Brazilian academic and business establishment. At lunch the talk turned to energy, which Brazil is trying, with some success, to organize and conserve. Cars, if relentlessly numerous, are much smaller than in New York, and motor fuel is several times as expensive. By law the latter must be a mixture of alcohol (20 percent) and gasoline, the alcohol coming from corn and sugar cane. However, it requires energy to propel the tractors that plant and harvest these crops and more to manufacture the alcohol. What is called the energy balance (a somewhat disputed calculation) is around 65 percent, which is to say that the production of 100 units of alcohol uses up around 65 units of equivalent energy for a net gain of 35 percent. Since alcohol use is confined largely to automobiles, alcohol supplies only a very small share of Brazil's total liquid fuel consumption — somewhere around 4 percent. A few cars are equipped to run exclusively on it and are so labeled on the back; they are said to give their owners a feeling of distinction. Brazil's petroleum reserves lie below a layer of hard rock through which seismographic exploration operates with some difficulty. Exploration is proceeding, as also offshore drilling, but with limited hope.

Twenty-two years ago Rio gave the impression of a city that had greatly outgrown itself. The water supply was a random thing; streets were as filthy as those in New York; it was faster, on the whole, to walk than to telephone. All seems infinitely better now; this morning a uniformed force was out on the beaches, picking up cigarette butts. In the evening I came back to the hotel with the mayor, a Berkeley engineering graduate of, to me, astonishingly recent vintage. He agreed that there had been improvement but was principally impressed with what remains to be done. (The hills surrounding Rio, as also those adjacent to other Brazilian cities, are still climbed by the *favelas* or slums, the houses reflecting the extremely informal architecture of the inhabitants, and public services such as street paving, water supply, electricity and schools being extensively absent. The lack of electricity is especially serious, for that means there is no television.)

RIO DE JANEIRO — AUGUST 20

Today I combined a tour of the adjacent countryside, a luncheon in the hills out from and above Rio and a lecture to the Brazilian Academy of Sciences with, for most of the day, the kind of terminal headache that I am required, doubtless for reasons of character, periodically to endure. The lecture, addressing the current problems of the advanced industrial countries (and the interesting tendency of the socialist world to share with us in misfortune), is not of present consequence. As I have already learned to expect, the questions afterward were on how to deal with the Brazilian inflation, how to deal with the Brazilian debt and (one not previously mentioned) how to deal with the prospect of Ronald Reagan. Reagan fills even the conservatives here with concern, while Jimmy Carter seems appreciably more popular than he is at home. The Republican stand on the Panama Canal has led to the fear that Latin America will again be regarded as a colony, the sympathy for Somoza to the fear that we will again be forthrightly on the side of dictators as the traditional bulwarks of democracy against Communism. Reminding my audience that I had supported Adlai Stevenson, Eugene McCarthy, Hubert Humphrey, George McGovern and, more recently, Edward Kennedy and had predicted publicly that all would win, I responded with the estimate that Reagan would not make it.

A business executive told me of a recent conversation with the Brazilian minister of aeronautics. He had commented in passing that Brazil should always invest in the very highest technology. "Not so in my line of business," said the minister. "We do not intend to have a big war. Since our only possible enemy in a small war would be Uruguay, Paraguay or Argentina and all have second-class planes, all Brazil needs is a second-class air force." A very sensible man.

Talk turned to the need to get nuclear arms under control and of the Strangelove fraternity that rejoices in hardheaded study on how everyone, everywhere, can be destroyed. My luncheon companions look with fear on these nuclear chess players, as, indeed, they should. Nothing would do more for our Latin American alliances than to subdue such foolhardiness.

Rio is usually observed from the sea or from the space adjacent to the beaches. One must go to the hills, some protected as parks and others from earlier times as a source of the water supply, to see how small its available land space really is. The dense vertical building that distinguishes and, in a way, graces the city is the consequence. That this vertical living is not disliked is evident in the distant valleys; here, too, suburbanites live not in separate houses but in small skyscrapers.

Tomorrow we go to São Paulo.

São Paulo — August 22

A day has been lost in intercity movement and other distractions.

When we were here before, São Paulo looked like Los Angeles. Now it seems a perpetual Manhattan, although the skyscrapers are not so closely packed; they stand at random over the urban acreage, which looks like a well-filled asparagus bed. Each is essentially the same — a rectangular block with continuous rows of windows in the two long sides and blank walls at the ends. In an unsuccessful effort to differentiate, the window sashes and blinds are painted in different colors. Occasional departures from the standard style are often worse.

During television interviews and the question-and-answer period after my far from brilliant lecture last night at *Estado de São Paulo* (the Brazilian *New York Times*), the subject of inflation recurred endlessly. I am being instructed in the intricacies of indexing in Brazil, indexing being the more or less automatic adjustment of wages, salaries, pensions, savings account interest and other payments to keep them abreast of rising prices. It doesn't work very equitably; savings accounts this year, for example, are scheduled for a 45 percent increase in interest, but this, given a 100 percent inflation rate, means a 55 percent loss in real value. There is, of course, political agitation on the subject, and so there could be concessions. All would be simpler with stable prices.

At dinner after my lecture in the handsome quarters of the newspaper a local professor summarized the progress of economic discussion in his country: "Once we talked only of the low price of coffee. Now we talk only of the high price of everything."

São Paulo — August 23

Yesterday, as a good citizen, I responded to a request from our consul general, a former associate in India, and met with a group of businessmen at the Consulate. Then I had lunch with the heads of many of the local multinationals. Then a press conference. Then a large lecture, following which at least a hundred people came up with books to be signed, my local publisher having thoughtfully established a booth in the foyer. When all was over, there was a small dinner that lasted until midnight. Were I younger and not fully conditioned, I would not have survived. It was an instructive day.

Years ago in the prime of the Foreign Service club — when the State Department was a place for gentlemen from Princeton, Harvard and Yale — São Paulo was the kind of post to which the United States sent socially superior but fully committed drunks. None stooped to a knowledge of business or economics, which is the chief reason for having representation in such a place. Now the Consulate and associated Trade Center are manned by sensible, informed and, I judge, hard-working men and women of no social distinction of any kind. This is progress.

Yesterday morning I spent some time once again defending Professor Friedman. In the afternoon with more enthusiasm I defended myself. The case against Friedman was that he has been adopted by Latin American dictators, notably in Chile and Argentina, so, *pro tanto,* he must be a rather repressive type. I conceded that his system — control the money supply and you control all — worked against inflation in a highly organized world only as it caused extensive idle plant capacity and much unemployment. It is thus that it arrests corporate price increases and counters the wage pressure of the unions. To inflict such suffering one must have a fairly stern government. But I exempted Friedman personally from any such repressive instinct. That dentistry is painful does not make the dentist a sadist.

I ran into trouble myself because I said that modern industrial economies should make greater use of indirect taxation on high-end or luxury consumption — expensive meals, clothing, automobiles, entertainment, hotel rooms and the like. Taxes should no longer be the same on items as a whole. Clothing, automobiles, even food, depending on the nature and the price, can be the greatest of necessities or the greatest of luxuries. Taxation must be graded to price, not levied uniformly across the board. There are no adverse incentive effects from such taxation; it is hard to oppose on political grounds. An angry interlocutor told me that I was being irresponsibly hostile to the rich, to which I responded, as I have often before, that social tranquillity in all modern societies is advanced by screams of anguish from the affluent. These persuade the poor that the rich are suffering, too. He was, I think, far from convinced.

The differences in income and living standards in Brazil are appalling. And I sense that even among the affluent the discrepancies are a more than casual source of worry. This does not, needless to say, extend to the point of their giving up anything they really enjoy. It does require that the doors of all important-looking cars be kept locked from the inside to discourage kidnappers and hijackers. And the Marine guard at the American Consulate makes it a practice to call the consul at intervals over the radio telephone to be sure that all is well.

Today was something of a holiday. In the morning we drove through miles of urban wasteland to an artist colony called Embu on the city fringe. There were some quite good paintings there and many depressing artifacts. Artists are the most agreeable of shopkeepers; they don't really expect you to buy and are surprised and grateful when you do. In the afternoon, at the Museum of Modern Art, we saw a stunning exhibition of Indian featherwork. Headdresses, neckbands, earrings and other items of apparel, including some superbly decorated and (I suppose) poisoned arrows, were on display in perfectly symmetrical colors. I had not previously thought of feathers as an art form. The exhibition might come to New York; if so, it should be seen.

Around 100,000 people from nearby rural areas and from the densely populated low-income states of northeastern Brazil move into São Paulo and its environs *every month*. The resulting social problem is enormous; so also is the contribution to economic development: an eager work force, gratefully available at low wages. I will have a later word on this.

BRASÍLIA — AUGUST 24

São Paulo is immeasurably vast, but it is related to all other cities. Brasilia must be seen to be believed, and even then it is hard to comprehend. Square mile upon square mile of rectangular six-story apartment blocks with a vast acreage of reddish soil between and all graded to the grandeur of the politicians or bureaucrats living therein. Toward the center a mass of government departments, banks, hotels and embassies, each category occupying its allotted space. The banks, many of them with an official function, are towering and numerous, but all are smaller than the Bank of Brazil, the local equivalent of the Federal Reserve, a great skyscraper with black cancerous nodes hung on its sides. All these structures look down on a large artificial lake, some forty or fifty miles around; and the entire city, including a number of other lakes, is the achievement of the last twenty-five years. Something over a million people, all employed by the government and its supporting service industries, now inhabit what, in the 1950s, was an exceptionally barren stretch of semidesert land. There should be no doubt: Brasília, however it is viewed, is one of the prodigious achievements of the century. At the peak of construction, 100,000 workers were employed.

Contrary views are offered from the moment of arrival. Better, one is told, that the bureaucracy be leavened and watched by a mixture of other occupations; the pure distillate is bad. When the city was planned, the automobile was indispensable, but now, with gasoline scarce and expensive, the expanses are too great and the streets too wide; better that more things were within walking distance. I myself sense another and deeper error. Architects have almost always relished space; it is their monument. Ordinary people, in contrast, relish intimacy. Certainly there is nothing intimate about Brasília.

BRASÍLIA — AUGUST 25

A lengthy television interview last evening was not a success. A beautiful young woman interviewed me on economics, although she had not previously encountered the subject. Before each question she had a long conference on what to ask and after each answer another long conference on what I had said. The whole effort took some hours. One question, after much discussion, was "Professor, what is truth in politics?"

I am attending a series of seminars at the University of Brasília; these, in service to my vanity, are, extensively, a survey of my own economic writing. I am expected to comment in an authoritative way on what I meant to say. Today a professor told me that of my various books the one he liked best was a small pamphlet entitled *How to Control the Military*.

I learned that it is dangerous for a swimmer to dive too deeply into the new lakes; trees, some houses and a few derelict automobiles were never cleared from the bottom.

BRASÍLIA — AUGUST 26

The American Embassy Residence, where we went for dinner last evening, is several miles out of town with a fine view of the city and airport. I was again impressed with the workmanlike quality of our official representation. In the past our diplomats placed great emphasis on the social graces in both their own operations and those they entertained. This allowed for much personal enjoyment and, as earlier noted, frequent intoxication. Last night's gathering, by contrast, was of intelligent and sensible people. We learned from the wife of the Australian ambassador that she had recently backpacked across Brazil from Brasília to Belém and from there had gone on to New York; she observed that that kind of travel puts one in closer touch with the country.

In the planning of a city from scratch it seems inevitable that something would be forgotten. I asked about that. In Brasília it was space for a cemetery and provision for libraries. Both oversights have since been corrected.

BRASÍLIA — AUGUST 27

Dinner last evening was at a large private house across one of the lakes. The building of the lake had required, in turn, the building of a lengthy bridge where none previously had been needed; a professor accompanying us said it was the Brazilian way of stimulating public-works investment. I have now met a fair number of Brazilian public officials. They are knowledgeable, articulate, intelligent, very serious and were mostly trained at one American university or another. Around seven hundred Brazilians are now studying in the United States at government expense.

Attention at dinner was on the Republican Party platform, which was currently under discussion at the convention in Detroit. I was somewhat handicapped in its defense, for I hadn't read it. One observation: "For the people who wrote that platform, Latin American policy is a minor footnote to anti-Communism. Is it really their belief that only the Somozas can save us from Communism? Or from Fidel Castro?"

Brazil has nine months of compulsory military service, which is said to be hard to evade, but the military presence in Brasília — as also in Rio and São Paulo — is almost totally invisible. It does become evident a few miles out of town in an enormous structure, dwarfing if anything the Pentagon, that is called locally Fort Apache; the roads near it are full of recruits engaged in one form of exercise or another. All are identifiable, if in no other way, by their haircuts, which are achieved by placing a flower pot firmly over the head and then clipping the hair closely up to the rim.

BRASÍLIA — AUGUST 28

Although my lectures came formally to an end yesterday, I met this morning for a question-and-answer session with the students of the University of Brasília. This was in the main classroom building, a structure down by the lake that is one classroom and a walkway in width, three low stories high and 750 meters (around a third of a mile) long. Although adult audiences in Brazil are preoccupied with inflation and the overseas debt, student questions run almost exclusively to the depredations of the multinational corporations. This morning no other subject was raised. When our meeting was over, my audience moved out into the sun and into the huge parking lot, where they got into Volkswagens and Fiats and some lesser products of multinational crime and drove contentedly away.

This afternoon we visited the Foreign Office, the most successful of the architectural innovations in Brasília. It stands in a water garden and encloses a sweeping reach of space, a scattering of Brazilian painting, sculpture and old lithographs giving it the appearance of a newly finished but still unoccupied museum. This emptiness is a great relief. Approaching the building, one shudders that it might be completely filled with diplomats.

Lunch today was, as might be expected, on foreign affairs. Some Foreign Office people thought the Carter administration negligent as regards Latin America; no longer was the latter central to North American thought. I argued, especially as regards Brazil, that this was a good thing. Once our pre-eminence in wealth and power bred a certain condescending paternalism to which Latin America, in turn, had become accustomed. As increasingly Brazil approaches the United States on terms of economic equality, it is this paternalism that is missed, but is it really wanted? I believe I was somewhat persuasive.

BELO HORIZONTE TO OURO PRETO — AUGUST 29

Belo Horizonte, where we arrived last night, is the capital of the State of Minas Gerais and fifty minutes by air from Brasília on the way to Rio. The city has a population of around two million and is the center, among other things, of an extensive mining industry. All of this I tell, for I did not previously know any of it myself. Brazilians are much better informed about Pennsylvania and Pittsburgh.

The beauty of the horizon from which the city gets its name cannot be seen either by night or by day. By day, however, the city, which spreads up and down over numerous hills, has something of the aspect of San Francisco.

Today, after the usual session with the press on inflation, I met for a seminar with local government planning people and businessmen. The question here, as elsewhere, is how to cope with the huge continuing influx of peasants and farmers into the city. Housing, water, electricity and other municipal services fall perpetually behind. And the consequence of not coping is the terrible hillside *favelas,* which people build for themselves and which are without services of any kind. There was considerable criticism at the seminar of the central government — of its rigidity and reluctance in yielding to local initiative. One felt at home.

In the late afternoon we drove for a couple of hours to Ouro Preto over a countryside of no compelling beauty, some of it badly brutalized by open-pit mining. Away from the mines the soil is a deep red from the iron, and it lies raw and barren by the roadsides. Only the low, distant, bluish mountains have beauty in this land.

Ouro Preto, in colonial times the capital of the state and now under the protection of UNESCO as the Williamsburg of Brazil, lies in a valley between low hills. Churches and white colonial houses cover the valley and climb the hillsides. Over the next valley there is a heavy cloud of smoke from one of the fires that scorch this area in the dry season.

OURO PRETO TO BELO HORIZONTE — AUGUST 30

Ouro Preto was once a major gold-mining center; thus its name — Black Gold. It now has a population of around forty thousand, much reduced from its great days, and is, one judges, the only city in Brazil so favored. The numerous churches are richly Baroque and range from interesting and extravagant to unsightly. One had originally been exclusively for slaves, special mercy being required for them. To save on

carving, many local graves have only a number; the survivors can readily remember that the loved one is at #77; others don't need to know.

We visited a gold mine, one of the few still operating in the area and
deriving, I judge, more of its revenues from visitors than from what
is mined. We were lowered down to no great depth on an inclined
railway and guided through the rooms and galleries. Once two thousand men toiled in these passages; now there are only twelve. There
are several hundred acres of floor space underground; the galleries
are vaulted in a kind of elementary Gothic and are not only impressive
but rather beautiful. The walls sparkle in the electric light, although
not with gold. Some of the galleries end in luminescent pools of water.

To get the gold, the rock is pounded and crushed in a lengthy
Cuisinart-like process that, miraculously, gets rid of the dross and keeps
the infinitesimally small residue of metal. Many tons must be mined
for each trifling ounce. Last month, a good one, the mine produced
just under six kilograms, or around twelve pounds of gold; in poor
months the yield has gone down to two hundred grams. An enormous
effort is being expended to fill a very few teeth.

On the way back to Belo Horizonte I learned how Brazilians manage
weekend travel. To cut down on gasoline consumption, service stations
are forbidden to sell any fuel on Saturdays and Sundays except to taxis
and a few other commercial vehicles. If one is going on a weekend
trip, the obvious thought is to take along a spare can of gas, but that,
too, is forbidden, and it invites cremation in case of an accident. So
travelers pack containers of alcohol, which is legal and safer, and when
the tank is down by a third or so, they add it to the previous mixture.
Thus they can get home. A man who hadn't remembered to bring some
alcohol and who was running out put in three bottles of Seagram's VO
and a bottle of Jack Daniel's. These didn't work at all well, for they
contain a great deal of water. While your average lush will take it, water
isn't acceptable to an engine.

BELO HORIZONTE TO SALVADOR — AUGUST 31

This morning, Sunday, the boulevard in front of our hotel in Belo
Horizonte was forbidden to motorists and became the track for a bicycle
race. The cyclists went around and around the central strip, pedaling
furiously. One, more clever than the rest, rode a motorcycle, although
perhaps he was an official. Another circled aggressively the wrong way.

SALVADOR — LABOR DAY

Salvador is on the Atlantic in the heavily populated, still impoverished northeast, and it was the first capital of Brazil. Important rem-
nants of the old colonial city remain to be seen and are inadequately
protected against the intruding skyscrapers. Of the Baroque churches

one, San Francisco, is perhaps the most extravagantly decorated of any in Christendom. There is a fine exhibition of religious art in an old monastery. Bahía State, of which Salvador is the principal city, was — and remains — extensively affected by African culture. At a big dinner last night in an old sugar mill a large troupe from the neighborhood gave a superb exhibition of African-influenced music and dancing, which was orgiastic, athletic and, at times, appropriately suggestive of some distant, mystic jungle. One dance was a choreographic immolation of the white masters — greatly deserved, it was said.

The rural economy of Bahía now depends on cocoa, this having replaced coffee as the leading crop. Brazil produces more cocoa in some years than does Ghana. Sugar is still of importance; natural rubber, which is currently cheaper than synthetic because of the high price of the oil stock from which the latter is made, is being encouraged. Iron mining, copper mining and refining and petrochemicals are the industrial priorities in what still is, industrially, an undeveloped region. In rural Bahía, as elsewhere in the northeast, far too many people struggle far too unsuccessfully to make a living on the land. So they go to São Paulo.

Last night I had an interesting talk with the governor on the social consequences of sugar. Sugar is the most antidemocratic of crops — a few rich masters, a great many workers planting and harvesting the cane at miserable wages or none at all. Everywhere it has been cultivated, Hawaii possibly excepted, it has left behind a legacy of poverty and social discontent. Fidel Castro should make his nightly obeisance not to Marx but to a stalk of cane.

My lecture this morning on the nature of rural poverty was to a good audience in an old, handsomely restored lecture hall of the university. The question period was not a success. The electronic system for the simultaneous translation into Portuguese was on the same wavelength as that of a new local radio station. I had to estimate the general thrust of the questions, mixed as they were with music and commercials, and frequently confined myself to agreement or approval of what was said. According to a woman who listened in, I was heard to endorse a line of canned soups, an underarm deodorant and a newly designed tampon.

After lunch with local industrialists and development officials, we toured the huge petrochemical installation and are now on the plane back to Rio to connect for New York. It remains only to say a word on the development of Brazil.

This, like the building of Brasília, has been prodigious. In the last two decades a backward agricultural country has been transformed into one of the first ten industrial nations of the world. The growth rate in some years has been in the 10 to 15 percent range; comparison with Japan is by no means inappropriate, and, it might be added, a sizable Japanese settlement has added appreciably to the achievement.

Such growth has been the result of a combination of government leadership and investment, private-sector initiative and eager rural labor, reinforced by the profound belief that development is a good thing. The Brazilian government has had a huge part in the effort; some 60 to 70 percent of all industrial investment has been by the government or government-sponsored banks. And the government role continues; rather more than half of all airplane travel in Brazil, I was told, with no evident way of checking, is on tickets purchased by one or another public agency. Not outside the socialist world has the government participated so comprehensively in economic development. Brazil is no triumph of private enterprise.

In the south and most of all in São Paulo, however, the government activity has been both the lodestone and the framework for a strong private development, which has come from both the large multinationals and the local firms. A substantial part has been financed by the big inflow of funds from other countries, which (along with payment for petroleum) has resulted in Brazil's impressive national debt.

Most of all, the development must be attributed to the aforementioned army of willing workers, fresh from the greater privation of the farms, notably of the northeast, who have been and remain eager for any kind of work at almost any wages. The new Brazil has been built on the backs of the recently arrived workers from the countryside. Since the rural areas are still poor, still overpopulated, this inducement to development will continue. It reflects a common and far too little noticed phenomenon on the world scene. Singapore, Hong Kong, Germany, Switzerland, Austria, France and our own cities of the industrial North have all been sustained by erstwhile rural workers from within the country or from abroad for whom anything in a city, however bad, still seems better than what they have fled. It is the least celebrated feature of modern capitalism.

ARGENTINA

(1986)

This piece, originally published in The New Yorker, *is the natural sequel to the one preceding. In both Brazil and Argentina, as elsewhere in Latin America, the legacy of dictators has been debt, and that debt and democracy are now in deep and dangerous conflict. But along with the indebtedness, there is the further and even more serious legacy of economic and political contention of which I here tell.*

No one, I suppose, travels to another country without some expectation as to what he will see, hear or otherwise learn. In the case of a recent visit to Argentina, my expectations were perhaps more than usually firm. I was last there in 1958 on an assignment from the Carnegie Corporation to meet with economists on the university faculties of a half-dozen or so Latin American countries — Peru, Chile, Argentina, Uruguay, Brazil, Costa Rica and Guatemala. Nothing about American academic life is more rewarding than the travel it arranges for its more fortunate members. On that earlier journey, I went one night with a number of other economists to dine at a large and somewhat boisterous restaurant in the La Boca district of Buenos Aires. In the course of the evening a woman of the place sat down beside me and asked why I looked so sad.

"He is an economist," one of my Argentine colleagues informed her, "and an economist naturally thinks about our inflation."

Twenty-eight years ago the inflation rate was between 20 and 30 percentage points annually. More recently, and until the heroic efforts at stabilization, it had been well over 1000 percent a year. Obviously, I could expect to hear much about inflation.

I knew also that I would hear much about the Argentine overseas debt. This, now amounting to around $48 billion, is smaller than that of Brazil at an estimated $103 billion or that of Mexico at $96 billion. But it, too, would be a central subject of discussion.

As had many others, I had been following the history of this indebtedness. It goes back to the days when the large international banks —
Citibank, Chase Manhattan, Manufacturers Hanover and the unfortunate Continental Illinois — were speaking well of their own success
in "recycling" the Saudi Arabian and other OPEC oil revenues. This
recycling consisted of passing along as loans to Latin American and
other countries the deposits lodged in their care. I had also noted, as
I had when studying the problem in Brazil, the innovative semantics
of the banking industry as these loans ran into trouble. Once loans that
could not be repaid were said to be in default; by the more casually
spoken they were said to have gone sour. Now they were rescheduled
or rolled over. Then, if not kept current, they became problem loans.
And if the default continued, they were reclassified as "nonperforming
assets." The language of modern banking has its special fascination
and mystery. Certainly no one has recently said of the South American
loans that unwise bankers made foolish loans to irresponsible or incompetent governments, a circumstance that does not enhance the
likelihood of prompt repayment.

I went to Argentina with a further thought in this matter as to the
American precedent. In the 1830s, a number of American states —
Pennsylvania, Louisiana, New York, Mississippi, among them — borrowed prodigiously to build canals, turnpikes and railroads and to
establish banks. Around $200 million, perhaps more, was so bor-
rowed — a huge amount in the heavy dollars and by the small popu-
lations of the time. Much of this money was recycled from the surplus
savings of Britain — from the greatly more affluent British financiers
and citizens. After the panic of 1837, these loans went extensively into
default. Some states eventually paid; others, not without indignation,
rejected all responsibility for what was held to be an indefensible financial aberration. This precedent was repeated after the Civil War,
when states and localities accorded guarantees and subsidies to the
railroads they hoped would come their way. When the railroads went
into bankruptcy, as did such distinguished enterprises as the Union
Pacific, many of the guarantors declined to make good. Overseas as
well as domestic investors went again through the wringer.

But default was not confined to the United States. British investors
are still awaiting a return on their equity investment in the Grand Trunk
and Grand Trunk Pacific Railways in Canada, which were taken over
after World War I by the Canadian government, along with another
ailing property, the Canadian Northern, and made into the Canadian
National Railways. None of these problem loans, it should be noted,
proved permanently damaging to American or Canadian credit.

There was also earlier and less than encouraging experience with
Latin America. In 1890, the great British banking house of Baring
Brothers and Company found itself with £21 million in defaulted Ar-

gentine loans in hand. It was threatened with bankruptcy, and the Bank of England had to mount a historic rescue operation. In the 1920s, American banks and investment houses lent money both freely and injudiciously to Latin American governments. A loan appreciation of the National City Company — the ancestor of Citibank — that later came to light reflected the mood of the times:

> PERÚ: Bad debt record, adverse moral and political risk, bad internal debt situation, trade situation about as satisfactory as that of Chile in the past three years. Natural resources more varied. On economic showing Perú should go ahead rapidly in the next 10 years.

After the 1929 crash these loans, not surprisingly, went, in the primitive language of the time, into default.

Nor is the record of seemingly more responsible governments perfect. In the years following the First World War, the debts of our wartime allies and others came to be considered a serious burden on international commerce and well-being. Calvin Coolidge was adamant on repayment: "They hired the money, didn't they?" But Herbert Hoover granted a one-year moratorium, and later in the New Deal years the loans, those of Finland apart, went into default. The Johnson Act, prohibiting further such loans, was passed in rebuke in 1934, but no enduring harm was done to the credit of the borrowing countries. One goes to South America today with the feeling that the precedents in international finance as regards debt repayment are not impeccable.

My recent trip to Argentina was once again under philanthropic auspices; my wife and I were the guests of the Arturo Illia Foundation, an Argentine scholarly organization devoted to the institution and perpetuation of democracy and remembering in its name Argentina's last democratic president. It has close relations with the present government and derives support from the Friedrich Naumann Foundation, a German endowment that contributes to good works in Argentina.

The beginning of our journey was not wholly auspicious. Our departure from Boston was on a dark autumn Thursday under a heavy fall of rain; our plane was very late arriving at Kennedy Airport, and we made our connection to Aerolineas Argentinas with only minutes to spare but in time to discover that the flight to Buenos Aires had been canceled some days earlier. No one from the airline had thought to tell us. We spent the night at a hotel near JFK, and the next morning the phone rang constantly as callers ranging from the protocol officer of the President of Argentina to the American head of Aerolineas Argentinas expressed their sorrow at this oversight. While waiting, we read and went for a long walk around the airport parking lot.

Our arrival in Buenos Aires was on Saturday afternoon, the day following our eventual evening departure. A small delegation of reporters and television people sought my views on various economic matters while a huge and unruly crowd welcomed Valeria Lynch, the Argentine pop star, as she is called, and effectively blocked all airport egress.

By the time we had accomplished the several-mile drive into the city through heavy traffic and along a nicely landscaped boulevard defaced by randomly placed billboards and were comfortably settled in the Plaza Hotel in downtown Buenos Aires, a full twenty-four hours, less two for the change in time, had elapsed since we had left our lodgings in New York. Argentina, one still feels, is not next door.

Our hosts had arranged for a day of rest before serious business began, but economic discussion was well under way by the time we reached the hotel. We were specifically advised, as a practical matter, on the recent passage from the peso to the austral. The old bank notes survive; it would have cost too much to print new ones. The last three zeros are simply ignored. Thus a ten-thousand-peso note had become ten australs. (Some notes had been stamped to this effect.) In the days just before our arrival the austral had actually gained a bit on the dollar.

"Argentina does have one piece of good fortune," said one of our hosts reflectively as we sat stalled in the dense afternoon traffic. "We have enough oil."

For our day of recreation we were taken on an airplane ride of around an hour and a half to the Iguazú Falls of the Rio Iguazú on the border between Argentina and Brazil, a land of tropical aspect and vivid red soil. The falls are higher than Niagara but less voluminous. The main cataract plunges, nonetheless, with a highly impressive roar, and, by way of variety, there are twenty-odd smaller ones. The water, unlike the fairly fresh blue of Niagara, carries an infusion of the surrounding soil and is slightly brown, as is also the rainbow that one looks down on from the top of the falls. Improving greatly on Niagara is the seeming absence of any trace of human habitation. It is just as the first Europeans, who were attracted for several hours — some say days — by the roar, first saw it in the sixteenth century.

Our day ended back in Buenos Aires with a long dinner and evening discussion of the Argentine economy with two extremely well-informed businessmen.

On Monday following our visit to Iguazú, I had a morning meeting and luncheon with the minister of economy, Juan Sourrouille, and a dozen or so economic officers of the government. In the ensuing days there were seminar sessions with government, university, foundation and other variously employed economists, and two luncheon meetings, one with leading bankers and another with industrialists. One day I had breakfast with members of the Argentine-American Chamber of Commerce and lunch in the massive American Embassy Residence with Frank Ortiz, our ambassador, a distinguished career officer who had assembled more senior American officials. Some of the latter we met again the same evening for dinner and an extensive discussion with President Raúl Alfonsín at the presidential residence, which is on a ninety-acre stretch of parkland on the edge of Buenos Aires. On three other evenings I gave lectures on economics and arms control to various audiences, including one at the University of Buenos Aires Law School, where I was also awarded an honorary degree. The session on arms control was before a small but rather tensely involved audience. Noting the smaller turnout for this topic as compared with those for economics, one of my hosts pointed out that in Argentina there is no "real peace bloc." People feel safely distant from the nuclear dangers of the Northern Hemisphere. The nuclear winter, which Argentine crops and cattle would surely not survive, is not yet seen as a clear and present threat. This misconception I tried in my lecture to correct.

There were some easier moments. We walked down Calle Florida, the great shopping street reserved for pedestrians, and looked at the diverse and well-stocked stores. On our last day we were taken on a six-hour boat trip around and through the Paraná Delta, an extraordinarily intricate system of waterways adjacent to Buenos Aires. And one morning I had a two-hour visit with Jorge Luis Borges, who was exuberantly pessimistic about all Argentine politicians — and soldiers — and their works.

Over the week as a whole, however, economics was the preoccupying topic. It was not easy, viewing the shops just mentioned, the massive new office buildings, the dense motor traffic and the generally relaxed and well-dressed crowds of Buenos Aires (where almost half of all the people of the republic now live), to think of this as a country of chronic economic crisis. (Around Buenos Aires there is a vast underclass in the shanty towns, as they are called. These the visitor does not see.) But talking with economists, one certainly cannot feel there is any lack of understanding of the problem. Argentina has a notable tradition in economic research and instruction; Raúl Prebisch, who has since died but who was absent in Chile during my visit, was one of the great pioneers in the economics of Third World development. There have been or are many others. It is one of the more evident and unhappy curiosities of our time that two countries which are especially well supplied with economic talent, Israel and Argentina — two countries with, someone has said, the most economists per square mile — have had, at least until lately, two of the most ostentatiously mismanaged economies. Perhaps in the case of Israel, with its great military need and preoccupation, there is some excuse. For Argentina, one of the most richly endowed countries of the world and subject to no hostile threat, real or plausibly imagined, there is no similar justification.

. . .

The explanation of the modern Argentine problem, especially the propensity to inflation and latterly also to economic stagnation — minimal or no economic growth — goes back a half century to a major change in the way the role of the state in economic matters is perceived, something that is, to this day, not fully appreciated in its economic consequences as regards countries like Argentina. In neither Argentina nor other countries was inflation a clear and omnipresent danger until the 1930s. The gold standard was taken generally, although not quite consistently, for granted. Any undue pressure of purchasing power on the economy from the earnings and expenditures of workers, businessmen, public employees and the military caused prices to rise. Gold then flowed out as the country in question became an expensive place in which to buy and an easy one to which to sell. A crisis, later to be called a depression, then a recession and finally, in pursuit of economic nicety, a growth adjustment, put things right, though in an indubitably painful way. From the diminished foreign and domestic demand and the greater overseas competition came diminished sales, unemployment, business failures, reduced farm income and lower public revenues, all of them combining in varying measure to reduce the competing claims on the economy. The Great Depression, which, along with other more complex causes, reflected the collapse in income flowing from the speculation and plush foreign and domestic lending of the 1920s, was a painful example of this process. So was the condign suffering it imposed on workers, farmers, businessmen and the citizenry at large.

The influential voice bringing the old design to an end was that of John Maynard Keynes. His *General Theory of Employment Interest and Money,* published in 1936, held in effect that the government, not the automatic mechanism of the gold standard and the market, should henceforth control and arbitrate the various and competing claims on the economic product. If these claims were too great, they would be brought within the current capacity of the economy by higher taxes or reduced public expenditure. And if, as in the stagnant world of the depression years, they fell below the ability of the economy to provide, the government would supplement them — add spending of its own for presumptively useful purposes or for people in need. Or through tax reduction it would allow more private expenditure, all with the purpose of bringing the system back to capacity operation. From this latter action came the enduring identification of Keynes with deficits in the public budget — deficit spending. But he believed it was equally essential, if purchasing power or aggregate demand were in excess of capacity, that the economy be restrained in a humane way by the government and not by the detached cruelty of depression and recession. The latter were seen as threatening the very survival of the system; Marx, not without hope, had said that the capitalist crisis would sound the death knell of capitalism.

From this great change has come the modern problem of Argentina, of other Latin American countries, of Israel and, for that matter, of the United States as well. It was assumed by Keynes, or anyhow by his followers, that the actions required to correct too much and too little demand would be opposite but equal — basically symmetrical. And the needed actions would be equally feasible for all governments. Alas, what was economically symmetrical proved not to be politically symmetrical. The politics of expansion — increased public expenditure, tax reduction — turned out to be highly agreeable; those of curtailment — tax increases, reduced public expenditure, wage and price restraint — were politically repellent. And while they might be possible for strong governments, they are not so for weak governments pressed by the poverty of their people. They have especially not been possible in recent decades for governments in Latin America, including in Argentina.

According to everyday explanation, the recent Argentine inflation was the result of the unlicensed printing of money; if the printing presses were somehow stopped, the inflation would be over. It is not at all that easy. The deeper and more intractable causes of the inflation are claims on the economy far in excess of the capacity of the system to supply — claims by businessmen seeking higher earnings; by trade unions seeking more wages and benefits; by the military protecting its turf; by numerous public industries, many under the auspices of the military, operating at astonishing losses; and by the civilian public services. (Approximately 20 percent of all employment is provided by the government, including the military.) Finally, there are the claims from overseas by the international banks — the foreign creditors.

In the past, the Argentina government yielded to most of these claimants — yielded to business, the unions, the military, the public enterprises and the public sector. (Instead of repaying foreign creditors, it frequently evaded their claim by simply borrowing more.) It was politically far too difficult to increase taxes, impose business price and wage restraints, reduce military and other public spending, enact higher charges and ensure greater efficiency in the money-losing public enterprises, which in some cases might mean their forthright excision. For as long as they were available, the loans from abroad eased the situation; otherwise the various competing claims were simply accorded the income they sought. The total being in excess of the capacity of the economy, prices were bid up or pressed up by wages, and at a steadily accelerating rate.

The money needed to satisfy these claims was, indeed, borrowed from — created by — the central bank. But this was a detail — in all respects a consequence, not a cause. And everything became vastly more difficult when, in the late 1970s and early 1980s, the easing flow of overseas loans came to an end and repayment was demanded instead.

Among the claims on the economy there was one that thereafter did not get met. That was for funds for new investment. No one spoke for that; it was suppressed by high interest rates. In the absence of new investment (and even the insufficient replacement of the old), the result was economic stagnation in what is, potentially, one of the richest countries in the world.

The matters just mentioned were the ones under discussion in Buenos Aires while we were there — how to reconcile downward the various claims on the Argentine economy, how to negotiate downward the claims of the external creditors, how to revive domestic investment and growth.

In June of 1985, some months before our visit, a major step was taken toward the accommodation to its capacity of claims on the economy. This was the Austral Plan, by common consent an exceedingly well-thought-out design. Its most publicized but, in some respects, least important feature was the introduction of the new currency, the austral, already mentioned. Complementing this was a series of steps addressed specifically to the various claims. The first was a freeze on wages and prices, with the double purpose of limiting the increase in the money income and the resulting money claims of business and labor and altering expectations as to inflation. This would protect businessmen, unions, public workers and others, making it unnecessary for them to ask for more income to cover themselves and insuring their real purchasing power as prices went up.

The Austral Plan also included an increase in taxes, along with an effort to make tax collections more effective. Also a reduction in public expenditures, including for the military — the military budget has been cut by around a third in the last two years. Tariffs on imported goods were raised, as also the fees and prices charged by public enterprises. In a new and much discussed move a compulsory savings plan was put into effect: individuals and firms are paid to postpone present spending against the promise of a larger later return. My visit followed by a few days one by Franco Modigliani, the 1985 Nobel Prize–winner in economic science, a popular and much respected figure among his economic colleagues, not made less so in Argentina because of his Italian origins. He was critical of the forced savings plan, and his comments received wide press attention. I held, when asked, that it was worth a trial. No one can charge undue influence to North American visitors if their observations tend to cancel each other out.

A final and crucial step will be to win postponement in one form or another on foreign-debt repayment. The urgency of this has been reduced somewhat by temporary or "bridge" financing arranged through the International Monetary Fund, and during my visit there was much discussion of possible further help, as recently proposed by Secretary of the Treasury James Baker, from loans by the World Bank that would be directed specifically to new investment.

The initial response to the Austral Plan was, as the international press has noted, exceedingly favorable, and this was affirmed when the Radical Party of President Alfonsín won a substantial, though by no means overwhelming, mandate in the next congressional elections. The mood during all my conversations, including those with the president, was strongly optimistic, although the latter, inquiring as to those with whom I had been meeting, told me that my sample was distinctly biased in favor of supporters of the plan.

The difficulties, nonetheless, are gravely evident. All the above-cited claimants on income have their spokesmen, some of them their political parties, and in Argentina, as everywhere else, it is taken as a manifestation of political weakness, even of bad faith and cowardice, if leaders and spokesmen soften their demands on behalf of their constituencies. Though when I was there prices and wages were being held by the freeze, there was no apparatus for enforcement of the controls, and some price inflation — 2 or 3 percent per month — had continued. Real wages, being held constant, had thus declined. Sooner or later, the price and wage ceilings will have to be lifted, or they will become ineffective and irrelevant. There could then well be an upward thrust of both prices and wages.

To ensure against this, demand and supply need to be in close balance when the controls are lifted. This requires that the tax increases and the public-expenditure reductions be effective, that the budget claims on behalf of the public enterprises be reduced by then and that the overseas claims be eased. All of these steps, as I've sufficiently noted, are replete with political difficulty. Additionally, the years of inflation and unpopular and resented governments have greatly weakened the tax system and left a legacy of comprehensive experience in tax avoidance. This is especially the case with the affluent, who for years have been moving their money into foreign bank accounts and investments as an escape from both domestic inflation and taxes.

During our visit the erstwhile Argentine military leaders were on the defensive in two trials, one in the civil courts for the infamous human rights abuses in the past years of military rule — the mass deaths, disappearances and tortures — and another within the military itself to establish responsibility for the ill-advised and highly incompetent operation against the Malvinas, elsewhere known as the Falklands. However, there is still an evident need for caution where the military budget is concerned. The generals have shown their willingness to move in on politicians in the past; they have some eighty thousand troops at their command. That a country like Argentina, devoid of any plausible enemy, must support such a large and expensive military establishment is one of the absurdities of the age. But it is an absurdity protected by the weapons of those who are served by it.

The publicly owned industries — steel, railroads, petroleum, ordnance, a host of lesser enterprises — are also a problem. Once the socially owned corporation was seen as the benign fulfillment of the socialist dream. Now no longer. In France, Spain and Italy socialist governments now spend a major part of their time and energy seeking ways to reduce the costs of sustaining archaic money-losing firms that have been unloaded by private enterprise or to dispense with them entirely. So it is for Alfonsín's Radical Party in Argentina. One of the officials with whom I talked in Buenos Aires noted with evident sorrow that the yield of the forced savings plan in the early months was falling well below the deficit in the state-operated railway system.

The IMF has urged, as a condition for its continuing help on the Argentine balance of payments, that Argentina reduce its deficit in the government budget to 4.5 percent of Gross National Product. Argentine government economists think 5 percent a more reasonable and possible target. (By way of comparison, the deficit of the United States is now around 5 percent of Gross National Product.)

What is reasonable and possible depends, in fact, on what is cut, a distinction that the IMF has not always made in the past. Its demand for "austerity" has regularly been taken to mean reduction in social programs — those on behalf of the old, the impoverished, the handicapped and the ill. There is no justifiable case for such savings in Argentina or for any democratic government that tries to make them. As regards cuts in military spending and the public enterprises, the case is very strong.

There remain the claims of the foreign creditors, the international banks and their smaller acolytes who joined in the once seemingly imaginative opportunity presented by these loans. It was a grave miscalculation; creditors do not ordinarily escape miscalculation without cost. And an easing of the terms of repayment — the extension more or less indefinitely of such repayment, combined with lower interest charges, perhaps even a moratorium — could well be in the interest of the banks. Were the claims on the Argentine economy thus eased, it would increase the chances for success of the present stabilization effort and enhance the chance of later repayment. If the stabilization effort fails and inflation resumes and accelerates along with the accompanying economic stagnation — the denial of investment that goes with inflation — the banks have a very good chance of getting nothing at all.

The Argentine economists and officials, as also the bankers and industrialists with whom I talked, were overwhelmingly committed to a negotiated repayment. Once, in a large meeting, when I asked if there was support for a unilateral suspension of payments until stabilization was assured along the lines recently proclaimed by Peru, I was rather sharply rebuked even for the question. But there was also agreement that, along with the other demands on the economy, this one, too, had to be reduced. There is the added problem that, unlike other claims, it must be met with currency earned by an excess of sales to foreign countries over purchases. The Argentine trade balance is, at present, favorable, in considerable contrast with that of the United States. But Argentine agricultural products, which make up by far the largest part of that balance, are in competition with great world surpluses in wheat, corn and other crops, and they must contend with the strong protectionist measures by which the European Economic Community countries and the Japanese government aid their farmers and with the American abundance, which largely keeps us from being a market. (Only the Soviets, with their enduring agricultural problem, come strongly to the rescue.) This circumstance also requires a liberal attitude on loans. Our bankers should also have in mind that the foreign currency that the Argentinians spend on loan service and repayment does not get spent on American manufactured goods, with resulting employment and reward in the United States. The banks, in light of their past errors, should not expect too exclusive a claim on Argentina's overseas earnings.

One evening in Buenos Aires I went on *Tiempo Nuevo,* a widely watched discussion program on television. My interrogator, a notably self-confident man, pressed me as to my views on the Argentine prospect for economic stabilization and resumed economic growth. I carefully declined prediction but affirmed my hope for success. This hope he strongly discounted; there had been too many failures by too many Argentine governments in the past. He could not condone wishful thinking. I warned him, perhaps a trifle sharply, of the occupational disorder of great television figures and numerous other public persons, which is to associate intelligence with a mood of extreme pessimism. He should struggle to rise above such a tendency. Next day on Calle Florida, people stopped me to tell of their approval, and President Alfonsín sent me word of his. But returning on the plane to New York, I did not, in fact, find myself wholly sanguine. The week had provided impressive evidence not only of the intelligence of the Argentine effort but also of the obstacles to achievement. I had no doubt, however, but that we should hope for success and, with the leverage available to us, particularly on loans old and new, give our best support.

INTRODUCING INDIA

(1974)

To have served as ambassador to India is to have acquired a kind of tenure in Indian-American relations. One continues to be sought out by Indian students, scholars and political leaders when they come to the United States, something that I find far from unrewarding. And, as I say here, one is thought an indispensable source of advice by all prospective travelers to the subcontinent.

The following was written as a foreword to a collection of essays edited by Frank Moraes and Edward Howe, a book that was itself meant as an introduction to that wonderfully interesting land.

Ever since I went to India as ambassador, I have functioned as a minor oracle and guide for an appreciable fraction of all the people contemplating a journey there, and I decided some years ago that I should codify my advice. This is it. The rather simple points made here are what most aided my own understanding. I doubt that they are terribly original; most knowledge involves not invention but sorting out from what other people know the things you should believe yourself.

The first question one is asked by the prospective visitor to India invokes my central point. That question is "What should I see?" This inquiry is usually made as regards an intended tour of two or three weeks; sometimes it is made in anticipation of a stay of two or three days, although then with the only slightly apologetic addition, "I realize, of course, that I can't see *everything* in that time."

Once, no doubt, Americans visiting Europe or Englishmen crossing the Channel asked the same question. But that must have been some time back. It is not a question one can ask about a whole continent, and it is the beginning of wisdom about India to realize that it is not a country but a subcontinent or, for that matter, no less than Europe, a continent. Within it, between greatly blurred boundaries, there are not one but many nations.

Geographically, the point is beyond dispute. The contrast between the Himalayas and the plains of the Ganges River is a good deal greater than that between the Alps and, say, the south of Spain, and much more abrupt. There is high country in south-central India that is like England, and not far from a town called Wellington one can go riding on the Downs. Nearby is a terrifying hill with numbered hairpin turns. Going down, one comes to coffee plantations and at the bottom to rubber trees, rice paddies and palms. This is all in an hour or two of driving. In western India there is a great desert from which the sand blows for hundreds of miles in the spring to darken and, oddly enough, to cool Delhi. In Assam to the far east it rains every hour or so, several hundred inches in the course of a year. It is high country, while, to the south, Bengal is barely above the ocean water level. Some of it often is not.

Differences in geography are easy enough to grasp. And a country can accommodate a nearly unlimited number of them and still qualify as a country. It is the differences in language, social and economic behavior, art, architecture and religion that make India many nations.

Since long before history became reliable, invaders have been sweeping into the subcontinent from the north and west. Some overran nearly the whole area (the far south was often spared) and remained; some made brief incursions and departed. The imperial power of those who remained was not usually durable; the central authority soon weakened, and imperial satrapies and feudatories became independent states.

India's rulers, great and small, have rarely been permissive, at least about the things they thought important. (Measured by results, they were right. Religious conversion went into a serious decline when those in charge ceased to use death and eternal damnation as a threat and education, medicine and food as a bribe.) In consequence, the invaders and the later local despots implanted their preferences as to language and religion in the parts of the country they governed, and their courts reflected their personal artistic and architectural traditions. The last of the inland invaders, the Mughals, came from Central Asia and deposed the previous intruders in 1526. They were among the most inspired builders and patrons of the arts of all time. The contrast between their palaces, tombs and mosques in central and northern India and the temples of the older Hindu tradition in the south is especially sharp.

On the swords of the great northern invaders came Islam. And added to the durable and still poignant diversity that this brought to the subcontinent was the earlier or later work of the Buddhists, Jains, Sikhs and Christians. Alongside the different social and artistic traditions of courts and rulers were placed the different religious traditions of the various faiths.

Last of all, from over the sea, came the Europeans, and most notably the British. They were the first invaders in historical times to establish hegemony over the whole continent; it is mostly owing to the British that we think of India as one country rather than as a federation of many. Although the Europeans left their mark on the design and architecture of the big cities — New Delhi, Bombay, Calcutta and Madras — this Westernization would doubtless have been accomplished in time by Intercontinental, Sheraton, Caltex and the automobile. The British cultural impact, which was political and moral rather than artistic, was also horizontal rather than vertical. It captured not a region but a stratum. To this important point I will return.

Thus the many nations of India. Some are reasonably close in language, art, architecture and tradition — as close, perhaps, as France to Italy. Such might be a fair description of the relation between the great northern state of Uttar Pradesh, which centers on Lucknow and embraces the old Muslim Kingdom of Oudh, and the neighboring states of Bihar and Bengal. But Madras, Mysore and Kerala in the south are culturally more distant from Uttar Pradesh than Germany is from Spain. Germans and Spaniards use a roughly similar alphabet; the language of the south of India is as mysterious to a northerner as Arabic is to an Austrian. The difference between the Cologne Cathedral and the Alhambra is certainly not greater than that between the Red Fort in Delhi and the great temples of the south.

No less important is the difference in the social temper and economic organization of the several Indian nations. Most Indians make their living by scratching it from the soil. The Indian village has the dignity and stability of an old culture, but life for most of its inhabitants is meager and brief. This, however, is not everywhere the case. In the Punjab in the northwest farmers ride tractors, use fertilizers and grow abundant crops of the new high-yielding varieties of wheat. On one thing Hindu, Sikh, Christian and Buddhist gods agree: in practice, as distinct from principle, those who have the most should get the most. In consequence of this rule and their own intelligent efforts, the Punjabis now have a standard of living, or in any case a mode of life, that is probably superior to that of the surviving small farmer on the Appalachian plateau in the United States. They supply to the rest of India the wheat that once came from Kansas, the Dakotas and eastern Washington. Bengalis and Madrasis are much poorer, and here another comparison with Europe is apt. For, as do the Greeks and the Italians when contemplating the Swiss or the Swedes, those in the Indian south concede to the northerners their superior industry and wealth while avowing, in their turn, their own more eclectic culture and wisdom.

The meaning of this is that one does not visit India or know India. One visits a part of India — what elsewhere would be a nation-state. One should be content to know something of that part; it is better to know something of something than nothing of much. No one is apologetic about trying to understand the Dutch while being happily ignorant of the Irish.

Few living Americans or Europeans have traveled over as much of India as have I. It is a great inducement and a matter of considerable personal economy to move about at public expense. For a long while I found myself delighted by my continual sense of discovery; then I became depressed at how little I still seemed to know. When I came to understand that I was ambassador not to one country but to many, my morale improved. So it will be with the visitor who goes to India and comes away feeling that his personal voyage of discovery is somehow incomplete.

I've been speaking so far of the regional diversity of India. There is also diversity on the social plane — a horizontal diversity that divides Indians into great, mostly noncommunicating layers, and this, too, must be understood. I am not speaking of the caste system, the great Indian cliché. Indians respond to Western curiosity about caste much as do self-righteous Americans when asked about racial discrimination: Alas, yes, it did exist, and the attitudes still survive, but progress is being made. I've always thought Indians a trifle too apologetic about caste. The most remarkable feature of Indian cultural, social and economic life has been its genius for survival. Before there were schools or universities, a tradition that required that children be trained or made learned in the occupational knowledge of their parents was not a bad substitute, and this the caste system accomplished. But the survival of caste attitudes is not my interest here. By horizontal diversity I refer to the line that divides village India, which is most of India, from modern urban, bureaucratic and intellectual India.

Most Indians live in the villages and directly or indirectly draw their living from the land. They pay taxes. Some of the sons go off to the cities or to the army. Almost all listen to transistor radios. They vote in numbers that make Western electorates seem indifferent. Yet the Indian village is not much governed by either New Delhi or the capital of its own state. Nor is it governed in any actual sense by itself. It lives by an accepted code of behavior, not by formal law. This is safer. The people of India learned centuries ago to hope for the least possible attention from higher levels of government, for until well into British times all governments were instruments of spoliation. They sent armies to recruit and pillage and tax collectors to extort. The self-sufficiency of the village was its strength; to be left alone was its greatest good fortune. The lesson of centuries is not soon unlearned.

The remainder of India — the upper horizontal slice — is, by comparison, very small. This is the India of the Civil Service, the Rajya

Sabha and Lok Sabha and the great business houses of Birla and Tata; the India of the Five Year Plans and the steel plants and disputes over the relative roles of the public and private sectors; the India of newspapers, airplanes, armed forces, foreign policy, concern over the United Nations and about Kashmir; the India of the chief ministers of the states and the municipal corporations of Bombay, Calcutta and Madras. In this world everyone of major importance quite literally knows every other one by sight and name; introductions are rarely necessary, one to another. Their world is also complete and self-contained — so much so that most foreigners and a great many Indians come to think of it as all there is. For understanding India that is the greatest and perhaps the most common mistake of all.

For eventually one comes to realize that much can happen in this small horizontal stratum while nothing changes in village India. Atomic power plants are built; the bomb is debated; a new Five Year Plan is discussed; a treaty is concluded with the Soviet Union; across the desks of the civil servants move great piles of files, the paper gray and dog-eared. Village India is not affected. It would be a mistake to dismiss modern India; it has vitality, an abounding and sensitive pride, an undoubted undercurrent of self-righteousness and a marked capacity for self-deprecation and humor. But, extensively, its wheels turn by themselves.

There are, to be sure, points where the two Indias come together. The fertilizers and hybrids that are making the Green Revolution are the result of such a conjunction. So is the near elimination of malaria, an accomplishment that might cause a good many people to enter a minority vote for DDT. [There recently has been some resurgence of the disease.] And there are other places where the future of India still depends on joint effort. This is notably so in the case of birth control. Knowledge of birth control methods comes from the modern sector — the upper slice — and so far it has not crossed the chasm. But, sadly, it is in the villages that the babies are born. No fact concerning India is so important — so all-embracing — as the resulting relentless expansion in population. It is the ultimate constraint on every chance for escape from the rending poverty that exists on all sides.

The regional diversity of India is obtrusive; even the shortest stay will sufficiently persuade the visitor as to how much more there is to see and to learn. The horizontal diversity is seductive; it causes people to imagine that, having experienced the small world of modern India, they have experienced all. As I have said, this is an error common to both foreigners and many Indians. I had been long in Delhi before I realized how urgent could be the discussion of economic planning, village development, schemes for health and educational betterment, encouragement of village crafts and, of course, family planning, and how slight would be the consequence. Such discussion is an art form of the modern slice — or, at best, an expression of its conscience and concern. The reality is the absence of any levers for moving the great village mass — the absence, on occasion, even of means of communication with the India of the millions.

Thus the several and diverse nations of India. It is no small task, the effort at comprehension. I trust that this brief introduction will slightly aid that task — and slightly ease the pain when the reader discovers how much there is to study and how much he or she has still to learn. Whatever happens, if my own experience is any guide, it will be an enchanting adventure.

6

RUSSIA

(1984)

This essay was first published in The New Yorker *in the autumn of 1984 and tells of a journey to Moscow and Leningrad in March of that year. There were two Russian responses. One of my hosts wrote to tell me that Soviet hospitality did not, as I say here, have to be returned to Russians visiting the United States; Americans could be generous or not as they chose. And a high Soviet official told me that he had shown my piece to then Foreign Minister Gromyko. Mr. Gromyko said it was "informative."*

The New Yorker *checking staff, celebrated in all literary circles for its pursuit of truth, ascertained the number of items in the Hermitage and Winter Palace Museums here mentioned and concluded that, at the rate of three minutes each, it would take eleven years for us to view them all. I replied that my claim of only seven years might not be mathematically exact; it was, however, what, with whatever error, I had been told.*

Over the past twenty-five years I have made four visits to the Soviet Union, always with many of the same purposes in mind. I have the normal curiosity about another huge part of the globe, its markedly different social, political and economic systems and — especially in Leningrad — its compelling art and architecture. Also, I've long believed that much can be learned in Russia about one of the basic tendencies of the modern economy and polity, West or East. That is the present-day commitment to vast organization — in the West, to the great modern public agency and the large, inevitably bureaucratic corporation; in the Soviet Union, to the even more enormous socialist apparatus that combines the structures of government, industry and commerce.

The approved view, celebrated in the political rhetoric of capitalism and Communism alike, holds that a total difference separates free enterprise from socialism. The fact is, though, that if steel, chemicals or automobiles are to be produced on a large scale, there will be somewhat similar organizations for doing it, whether in the capitalist or the socialist world. Additionally, these enterprises will stamp their special culture — hours, discipline, hierarchy — on the surrounding communities. A high official of Fiat told me many years ago that any problem encountered in the manufacture of Fiat automobiles in Turin was likely to occur a few months later in the operation they had initiated in Togliattigrad in the Soviet Union, labor negotiations notably apart. Thus my feeling that one can learn something — much, I think — of the difficulties of what can perhaps be called the age of organization by observing their comprehensive manifestation in the Soviet Union. *The New Industrial State*, a book I wrote some years ago, which, in part, celebrated the similarities between the two systems, had a substantial circulation in the United States and also, in Russian translation, in the Soviet Union. Critics in both countries disapproved of its contention that there is a tendency toward a bureaucratic convergence of the two economies. I did not find this wholly discouraging.

My further, and more pressing, concern in my visits to Russia has been to associate myself with the general goal of maintaining civil communication between the United States and the Soviet Union. I am not attracted by the Soviet system, but I am committed to the need for arms control — to the thought, one I have frequently expressed, that after a nuclear exchange the ashes of Communism will be indistinguishable from the ashes of capitalism, even by the most perceptive ideologue. But it is a prerequisite for the control of nuclear weapons that there be a modicum of confidence and trust between the two countries. An important contribution to this trust would be a muting of the political rhetoric on both sides; many of the people I encountered on my most recent trip singled out for particular mention President Reagan's reference to the Soviet Union as an evil empire. And, like others, I also feel that something can be accomplished by movement between America and Russia, including interchanges in the sciences and the arts. The people and the purposes of both countries seem far more ominous in political and military report than in firsthand observation and account. The latter impression is of men and women on both sides engaged in the everyday business of life, with a similarly expressed fear of war, a similarly expressed desire that they and their children be allowed to live in peace.

My first visit to the Soviet Union was in 1959, in company with two Yale professors — Lloyd Reynolds, the greatly distinguished economist and long-time chairman of the Yale economics department, and Michael Montias, a slightly younger, Russian-speaking scholar. Our purpose, supported by the Ford Foundation, was to visit the economics departments and research facilities of the universities from Tashkent in Central Asia to Kiev in the Ukraine and from Tbilisi in Georgia north to Leningrad. This we faithfully did, and it is at least possible that in consequence we did not see the very best of Soviet economic talent, which is drawn relentlessly into the practical work of the vast economic apparatus of the state or the closely associated economic institutes. We also visited numerous industrial establishments, as in Russia or China one feels obliged to do. To the best of my recollection, I have never inspected a factory in a serious way in the United States.

The late 1950s was a time of optimism for the Soviets, and also for Americans. We were asked repeatedly if we didn't concede that the Soviet Union would soon catch up with and eventually surpass us in economic performance, and we would find ourselves replying that our own prospect was not bad. A mild competition would then develop over who could give the greater glow to his country's future. One day in Moscow, as I've often told, I thought to change the terms of this competition. Asked if we took seriously the Russian intention of over-taking us in economic output, I expressed amazement. I adverted to the already frightful automobile congestion in New York City and the incipiently lethal air pollution in Los Angeles and expressed shock that the only goal of a planned economy was to replicate the excesses of an unplanned one. Our hosts were not deterred; obviously, they said, there might be special problems as regards automobiles. It is extremely help-ful to a candid exchange of views in the 1980s that neither capitalism nor socialism can be said to be working so very well.

A journey to Leningrad and Moscow in 1964 is also vivid in my memory. I was with a delegation to discuss, among other matters, the possibility of closer cultural relations and interchange. My companions included David Rockefeller, Norton Simon, James Michener and Buck-minster Fuller; the chairman of our group was Norman Cousins. The special attention of our hosts was focused on Rockefeller; he was the embodiment of the American ruling class and the only one singled out to see Premier Nikita Khrushchev. But also commanding attention was Buckminster Fuller, whose diverse ideas on art, architecture and urban design and on sociology and contemporary anthropology led to a re-quest from the Russians that we adjourn our meetings so that he might give a special lecture. It far exceeded the meetings in interest.

One night on that visit we were taken on a ship up the Neva River to Lake Ladoga, and on the way back I had a long conversation with an articulate and charming woman scholar from one of the Soviet institutes, who had earlier worked at the United Nations. (We met again on my most recent trip.) She told me that, on balance, Soviet readers get more from their newspapers than Americans do from theirs. Amer-icans, from long habit, read quickly and superficially and accept what they thus read as fact. The Soviet citizen, out of a tradition reaching back to the days of the czars, reads in depth; any important news story is appraised for what it says, what it probably omits, the purpose of publication, the nuances to be caught. In consequence, Russians emerge with a deeper perception of what is happening in their own country and in the world. I was not convinced, but I found myself greatly attracted by the argument.

My trip this year, like one in the mid-1970s, was by invitation of the Soviet Academy of Sciences and its several institutes — in particular, the Institute of the U.S.A. and Canada, headed by Georgy Arbatov and usually called the Arbatov Institute. A well-known figure in American-Soviet relations, Arbatov had once been our guest in the United States for a weekend devoted to a televised discussion in Vermont.* I was invited partly because of my role as co-chairman, along with George Kennan and Donald Kendall of PepsiCo, of the American Committee on East-West Accord. This Washington-based organization, of which Robert Schmidt, a Minnesota businessman, is the president, has an influential panel of participants, including Averell Harriman, J. William Fulbright, William Attwood, Robert McNamara, George Ball and Joan Warburg. Its purpose is to try to keep our relations with the Soviet Union in a rational mode, reflecting the inescapable fact that the alternative to coexistence is now no existence at all.

My wife was with me on this latest journey, and we arrived in Moscow from Zürich, by way of Swissair, in early March. In what may be something of a custom for invited visitors to Russia, we paid our own airfare and had an understanding that we would return to Soviet visitors in the United States the hospitality we received. March is the rather reluctant beginning of spring in Moscow; there was still a vast expanse of well-used snow. The Sheremetyevo Airport is, in its basic aspects, like Logan in Boston or the Zürich Airport from which we came; only when one encounters the immigration officers does a difference emerge. In Switzerland, where I go to write and in past times used to ski, these functionaries are ostentatiously bored and perfunctory. It is known that if someone gets into the country illegally, the local police will sooner or later catch up with him or her; that is *their* business. American officials are more conscientious; they look with respect at their computer screens, although, one feels, they do not expect to see much of anything. The Soviet officers, in contrast, take their work seriously; youngish men, they leaf through the passport slowly, page by page, and compare the picture carefully — glancing up and down — with the person offering it. Sometimes they ask a visitor to remove his hat. The whole procedure takes several minutes; one of our hosts, who was waiting to greet us

*See "A Different Journey . . . into Television and the Economic Past," page 285.

just outside, made an amused, slightly apologetic reference to bureaucratic necessity and routine.

One drives from the airport into Moscow with the feeling, as in
approaching cities in the western United States and Canada, that land
here is a casual resource. Large stretches of unused and ungroomed
space lie between the great rectangular apartment blocks. For miles
around the city these are the dominant feature of the landscape. Every
account of life in the Soviet Union, and especially in Moscow, tells of
the shortage of housing; the returning visitor's overwhelming impression is of how much has been built in these last few years.

For this visit we were lodged in the National Hotel, an elegant structure from czarist times. It is just off Red Square, and our windows
provided a sweeping view of the Kremlin and through all the early
daytime hours of the nearly endless procession of people on their way
to pass through Lenin's tomb. The line moves rather briskly; it is apparent that, with so many to be accommodated, no one can be allowed
to linger very long at the bier.

For activity, a ten-day stay in Russia is roughly the equivalent of a
normal two months in Cambridge, Massachusetts. Exploitation in a
socialist country is given a new and poignant meaning. On the day after
my arrival I had an informal seminar with academy research workers,
followed by a lecture and another seminar. These were at the Arbatov
Institute, which occupies well-worn buildings (and a palace that was
once in the possession of a Russian prince) in the center of the city.
Thirty or forty rather senior scholars attended my lecture, a somewhat
smaller number the seminars. The general topic was the state of the
American and the world economies, but during the sessions and in
private conversations afterward there was much informal mention of
the problems of the Soviet economy. If one is not thought to be scoring
points against the system, such talk can be admirably candid. Nor is it
always unduly solemn. On this visit, in contrast with earlier ones, difficulties were frequently referred to with a touch of wry humor.

On ensuing days I had meetings at the Institute for World Economy
and International Relations of the Academy of Sciences in a huge many-
storied structure three or four miles from Red Square. It has a staff
of some seven hundred, and one of my hosts expressed the thought
that this might be more people than could be employed usefully in any
known field of research. All around are centers for the study of various
social subjects, not excluding the economy of the Soviet Union itself.
Then came a meeting with the head and a senior officer of the State
Bank — the rough equivalent of the Federal Reserve System or the
Bank of England — which is housed in oaken and marble magnificence
in the building that in prerevolutionary times was the Moscow branch
of the central bank.

Later on, I had a meeting with officials of the Writers' Union, a special session with my Soviet hosts to summarize my impressions, a meeting at the offices of Progress Publishers, which brings English and American writing (including some of my own) to Soviet readers, and what was by all diplomatic standards an exceptional evening at the American Embassy, where a huge group of Russians and resident diplomats had been assembled by Ambassador Arthur Hartman and his wife to be entertained by Pearl Bailey. (She was joined at the end by volunteer Russian singers and dancers from the audience who were of no slight talent and enthusiasm.) Other evenings were given over to dinners, the opera, the ballet and the puppets.

One morning we journeyed out of Moscow to the great Soviet center for cardiological research that is headed by Yevgeny Chazov. In recent years Dr. Chazov has become widely known in American and world medical circles for his leadership in drawing attention to the medical consequences of nuclear war.* I relayed greetings that I carried from American colleagues in this work, and we discussed our common efforts to extend awareness on the impossibility of nuclear confrontation. (Along with a visit to a couple of leading foreign policy specialists at the Central Committee of the Communist Party, this was one of my few departures from economics during my stay.)

After talking with Dr. Chazov, we were taken over part of the huge center — a complex of buildings, hospitals, clinics, laboratories, lecture halls and libraries that cost well in excess of $100 million. I ventured to ask the doctor who was guiding us (and who had worked at the Mayo Clinic) if it wasn't better to attack heart disease at its source. Smoking and unnecessary weight are both visibly common in the Soviet Union; another doctor told us that about 40 percent of all Russian men were overweight. I got the impression that preventive measures are a more difficult problem.

On a relatively relaxed Saturday we drove again into the Russian countryside to visit the churches and monastery of Zagorsk, which is one of the residences of the Patriarch. The great church was densely packed with highly responsive worshippers. On a Sunday evening the Embassy had another large gathering, this one to see works of modern Ukrainian art. I used the occasion to give the economic officers some impressions from my visit; I did not have the feeling that all of my discoveries were wholly new to them.

We ended our journey with three days in Leningrad, on one of which there was a seminar with Academy of Sciences members, mostly to discuss the urban problems of the two countries. It was agreed, how-

---

*With his American co-founder, Dr. Bernard Lown, he was awarded the Nobel Peace Prize in 1985 for the organization International Physicians for the Prevention of Nuclear War.

ever, that our primary attention while we were there would be on the less solemn aspects of the city. We went to the ballet (a particularly fine performance of *Romeo and Juliet*) and to the circus, and we spent the rest of our time on a far from leisured tour of the museums — notably, the Hermitage and the Winter Palace. Our guide told us that if we devoted three minutes to each of the objects currently housed therein, it would take us somewhere around seven years to see them all. This seemed a reasonable calculation.

That the Soviet economy has made great material progress in recent years — certainly in the near decade since my last visit — is evident both from the statistics (even if they are below expectations) and, as many have reported, from the general urban scene. One sees it in the appearance of solid well-being of the people on the streets, the close to murderous traffic, the incredible exfoliation of apartment houses and the general aspect of restaurants, theaters and shops — though these are not, to be sure, the most reliable of indices.

The first of the economic problems of the Soviet Union comes directly from this affluence or relative affluence: it is the formidable burden that the infinitely numerous, incredibly diverse requirements of the modern consumer-oriented economy place on a socialist planning system. In its early days the Soviet economy had to produce only the exceedingly limited range of consumers' goods of a decidedly elementary living standard — simple foods, plain clothing, fuel, some housing, rail transportation and the raw materials and machinery that supplied or sustained this production. There was not a great deal else. This — in concept, at least — was not an unduly onerous task for central economic planning, although in the chaotic days following the First World War and the Revolution, even this presented serious difficulties and led temporarily to a partial return to the market with the New Economic Policy of the 1920s.

Now the modern consumer economy, East or West, calls for the production and distribution of a truly stupefying number and variety of products, and it is by success in accomplishing this that, in substantial measure, the success of an economic system as a whole is judged. Diverse foods, clothing in some variety and style, drugs, dentifrices, cosmetics, sporting goods, toys, bicycles, automobiles and their supporting repair services, hospitals and health maintenance, entertainments — the list goes on and on. The yellow pages of the New York telephone book tell of what is required in the United States, and the same things are required in only moderately less measure in the Soviet Union as well. It remains the socialist rule, if not quite the fact, that all these goods, all the needed raw materials, all the machinery and equipment for production, will be supplied in accordance with a comprehensive designation of quantities and time and not in response to prices in the market. When one reflects on this vast apparatus, one wonders not that it has major areas of failure but that it works as well as it does. Certainly none of the founding fathers — not Lenin, assuredly not Marx — could have foreseen the burden that modern consumer requirements would place upon a socialist planning apparatus. One is tempted, as I once was when viewing our own quite massive corporate structure, to the metaphor of the bumblebee. In principle, with its heavy body and slight wings, it cannot fly; against all the expectations deriving from its design, it does.

Partly the Russian system succeeds because, in contrast with the Western industrial economies, it makes full use of its manpower. While insufficient motivation may well be a source of inefficiency in the Soviet Union, unemployment, our most persistent (and painful) source of social inefficiency, is not. Nor, needless to say, do the Soviets have our Veblenian leisure class — the considerable number of people who are released by material well-being from manual or mental toil, although not perhaps from a certain indignation at being so characterized. However, Soviet economists were rather quick to point out that while all labor is employed, not all is well employed. Not a few people are kept on the rolls against possible need or simply because this is the easiest, least controversial course.

Addressing the problems imposed by the consumer culture, I asked one leading economist where the system now works least well, and he identified three areas of failure. One is insufficient investment in infrastructure. (The Russians not only have several of our problems but, in conversation, take over our nomenclature as well.) He especially noted too little expenditure on roads and highways and on warehousing and other storage facilities. Next he mentioned the tendency to overemphasize more glamorous as opposed to more urgent lines of production. "There is far more credit to be gained from producing an automobile than from producing the screws that are necessary to repair it." The final problem on his list was that presented by the mixture of products from the multiproduct firm. A shoe factory produces both heavy boots and women's shoes, but it is far easier to make the boots than to deal with the more careful workmanship and the style differences required for the shoes. So it is by the boots that the company fulfills its plan, while it is the shoes that are chiefly wanted — a small but compelling example of the problems of socialist planning in the consumer economy.

There is an interesting thought here for the United States. A military doctrine that has been articulated with much emphasis and some passion in Washington in recent years holds that by escalating spending on weaponry, we can so overstrain the Soviet economy that the Soviet leaders will cry for a halt. This, not to overstate matters, is mindless nonsense. By its nature, military production is an exercise in central planning; it is so for us as well as for the Soviets. In this competition we force upon them more of the planning in which they are manifestly experienced, and we are forced to the centralized planning that no one suggests is our special forte. Meanwhile we fail to see that it is our greatly various civilian production that has beome the valid test of economic achievement in Russia — a test that they have much difficulty in passing.

Since the Russian system functions less than perfectly, some Americans have gone on to suggest that it is in crisis — in danger of collapse. This I strongly doubt; nor, I think, is it the view of competent observers generally. It may, indeed, be that a certain stability is provided by the huge bureaucratic apparatus and its own inertia. Changes are certainly under discussion, but one senses that they are by way of repair and improvement. During my stay in Moscow and Leningrad four possibilities for reform were especially mentioned.

The first is the now ancient question of centralization and decentralization — ancient because it was being debated with seeming urgency when I was first in the Soviet Union in 1959. How much authority should be accorded the industrial enterprise — the large firm in particular — in matters of manning, investment decision, product mixture, production methods, worker motivation and much more? How much authority should be — or must be — retained by the ministries in Moscow?

One gains the impression that almost, though not quite, everyone is for decentralization — in principle. Much more in the way of flexible and local initiatives is wanted in the system. Against this movement stands the great dynamic of centralization, the powerful tendency for central authority to intervene when anything goes wrong: There is also the compelling fact that power is enjoyed for its own sake; it is not something that the central bureaucracy easily surrenders. I said that *almost* everyone favors decentralization. There remain some active theoretical exponents of strong central control. It is by such control, it is held, that a socialist economy works. Commenting approvingly on the present pressure for decentralization and the discussion it is provoking, one Soviet economist said that there were others, if not many, who would give me a different view.

Agricultural policy is the second matter under active debate, and this, too, is hardly new. As has always been the case, one could start intense discussion by asking why Russia, which was once called the breadbasket of Europe and which has vast reaches of arable land, is now a major importer of grain. In commenting on this on my recent journey, I noted that this situation was hardly a source of sorrow to the United States — or to Canada, Argentina and other supplying countries. I could have added that it is a highly effective design for keeping American farmers and their congressional representatives on the side of trade with the Soviet Union and in opposition to various forms of trade embargo.

During previous visits reference to the agricultural problem brought mention of inadequate fertilizer supplies, inefficient distribution and use of fertilizer, the low quality of farm machinery — difficulties with what my fellow economists, with a certain professional inelegance, call farm-production inputs. The primary reference this time was to prices — to the fact that, for political and social reasons, farm prices and resulting income have been kept too low in relation to the prices of other consumers' goods. The point was stressed by several economists with whom I talked, and especially by an exceedingly well-informed agricultural economist, a veteran of several years' service in the United States. It is not, I judge, that the Soviets fear that higher food prices will provoke the kind of protest they have brought in Poland in recent years. (One of my hosts asked, "Where do you Americans get the idea that we have any real influence on Polish economic policy?") Rather, stable food prices have a highly symbolic importance: they advertise the basic stability of the economic system. Such is the store set by this symbolism that the price of bread has not been increased since 1947. Now, it is being held, symbolism must give way to reality — to the need to return more money to the agricultural sector and thus better incomes to those who work on the collective and state farms. Accordingly, it is said that farm and food prices will be raised — gradually.

At the State Bank meeting and on one or two other occasions a third problem came up for discussion. This is the Soviet version of yet another American and Western European disorder — inflation. When, in the Soviet Union, the spendable income exceeds the available supplies of the more sought-after goods, queues form at the shops. We saw these one day as we drove past a large shopping center on the edge of Leningrad. Standing in a queue is an uncomfortable thing; the shortages that induce it are seen as a failure of the government or the system. I asked my hosts if it wouldn't be wiser to distribute a little less income in relation to the supply of goods, since wages, after all, are under state control. In consequence, people would attribute their inability to buy to their own failure to earn enough rather than to the failure of the economic system to supply the desired goods. Surely that would be better for the reputation of the system.

A senior financial official agreed — indeed, was exceedingly firm on the need for a change along these lines. Talking of the tendency for income and demand to exceed supply, he sounded very much like Paul

Volcker, the Federal Reserve chairman, reacting to the American deficit. He was equally explicit on the difficulties involved. All rewards and incentives — all payments for increased productivity, all raises in wages to attract workers to disagreeable or low-prestige jobs — increase the flow of income. These payments are all easily raised; meanwhile the pressure to keep prices stable is strong — hence the disparity between purchasing power and the supply of goods at the going prices. The Soviets, too, have their peculiarly intractable form of inflation.

The fourth problem, which, again, has its counterpart in the United States and the other older industrial countries, is the shortage in the supply of labor for the tedious, disagreeable or backbreaking jobs. In the United States the situation would be acute in fruit and vegetable harvesting, in many of the service occupations and even in factories if it were not for Mexican, West Indian and other migrants, legal and illegal. We greatly deplore this movement into the labor force but would be in desperate straits if it didn't occur. The British solve a similar problem in labor supply with West Indians, Pakistanis and Indians, the French with Algerians and Portuguese, the Germans with Turks and Yugoslavs, the Swiss with Italians and Spaniards. Indeed, no Western industrial country manages without such workers.

The Soviet Union has the same difficulty regarding agricultural workers, people for such unpleasant jobs as street cleaning in the cities and, one economist suggested, even clerks in retail trade. Higher pay is not the answer; no level of pay is sufficient to induce a college professor or even an elementary school teacher to take up work on the roads or on a collective farm. I remarked that countless millions in China and India would be delighted to come north, in the manner of the Mexicans into the United States, and do this unpleasant work. Rarely have I made a suggestion that was less enthusiastically received.

It is hoped in Russia that the much debated educational reform will reduce the number of young people seeking white-collar employment and do something to make hard labor more honorable and attractive. I did not confess my own doubts. All societies applaud the stolid, diligent manual worker; in all of them the applause comes from those who have escaped such toil and seek escape for their children as well. Severe, tedious physical effort is everywhere a soul-rewarding thing — for other people.

In Leningrad, as I've said, I met for a morning with members and professors of the Academy of Sciences who had a particular interest in urban affairs. We had no trouble in agreeing on another problem common to our two countries — the enormous cost of the great modern metropolis and the way this cost has been increased by the huge movement of people from rural communities into the cities. In three areas the Soviets have found better solutions than ours, and the differences are ones on which we would do well to reflect. The streets of Moscow and Leningrad are much cleaner than those of New York or Boston. There is no doubt that they are much safer. And the transportation of people, both by bus and by subway, is far more efficient. Ever since Lincoln Steffens returned from his 1919 journey to Russia to tell Bernard Baruch, somewhat too optimistically, "I have been over into the future and it works," Westerners have been cautious about applauding Soviet achievements, the ballet and opera apart. A diligent convocation always stands ready to charge that the reporter has succumbed to propaganda, hospitality or a Potemkin effect. On the subject of basic urban services one can accept the risk.

It had been my intention while I was visiting Russia this time to concentrate on economics. I'm committed, as I've said, to all available steps to end the arms race, but that is an effort one pursues primarily at home. My hope, instead, was to try to contribute a little to the understanding and confidence that are essential before real progress on arms reduction is possible. However, one cannot be in Moscow or Leningrad and escape the issue of nuclear weapons and war. Along with a request for an appreciation of Senator Gary Hart — this was just after his New England primary victories — it came up in every discussion. As nuclear war is now a besetting fear in the United States, so it is in the Soviet Union. Perhaps more so. For the Russians, one senses, it is much more nearly a present threat. For the last century and more, American wars have been fought a long way from home. We are in a small, indeed nearly unique, enclave on the earth's surface that has been exempt from military ravage and disaster, and our temptation is to assume that somehow we will escape in the future. Not so the Russians. Their experience, from Napoleon to the First World War and the civil war and on through the Second World War, has been with military invasion and devastation. That, not escape, is their norm. Accordingly, the warlike talk from the Reagan administration and the Pentagon in these last years may have had an even greater resonance in the Soviet Union than in the United States. The Russians could well be even more frightened than are we. Almost no one during our time there failed to ask us if it was our government's intention to let the missiles fly one day. I responded with a plea for a calm and common expression in both our countries of the will to survive.

7

THE SCOTCH:
AN EXCURSION
BACKWARD IN TIME

(1984)

This was written in 1984 for a Reader's Digest *series on the origins and accomplishments of American ethnic and tribal groups and was published in abbreviated form, as befits* Digest *practice, in 1986. Frankly, I consider the complete essay superior to the published version. Brevity is to be praised only when it culls out the dross, and this I was taught as a writer not to put in. The piece parallels, at several points, my own earlier book on the Scottish clans with whom I grew up in Canada.*

It is a measure of the lack of ethnic self-identification of the Scotch or Scots that there is no agreement as to what we should call ourselves. In North America the reference is most frequently to the Scotch, while in Britain it is to the Scots. In all probability, it is on this continent that we are more nearly correct. The early British reference was commonly to the Scotch; Dr. Johnson, when he went with Boswell to the Highlands and the Hebrides in 1773, so spoke, and there could be no higher authority than the author of a dictionary. It seems likely that reference to the Scots came into use in Britain in the last century at least partly because the word Scotch had been pre-empted by the whisky with which our race is closely, some have thought damagingly, associated. The older usage survived outside the British Isles, although not in all cases because the competition from alcohol was less significant.

Our lack of self-identification as a race extends to politics and lesser folk rites. American politicians over the decades have appealed to, and for, the Irish, Italian, Hispanic, black, Jewish and Polish vote, but no aspirant of record seems ever to have sought that of the Scotch. Partly this is because we have no politically cohesive sense. Also, we prefer to think that we are the ones who make the appeals to the other ethnic groups — a supposition that will, no doubt, be open to grave question. In any case, that anyone would don a kilt, attach a sporran and, mem-

orizing a few lines from the Gaelic or Robert Burns, ask for our support
we would consider sublimely ridiculous. Certainly we would vote against
him or her.

In various parts of the American Republic clansmen do gather to
celebrate St. Andrew's Day, and there are notable assemblies for the
music, dancing and sporting events that make up the Highland Games.
All know or have heard of our most challenging contribution to athletic
achievement, the tossing of the caber, described by the uninitiated as
a man in a skirt balancing and then heaving a telephone pole. We have
also a certain penchant for clan history, an exercise which in the case
of my own family has not always been rewarding. We trace in ancient
times to one Thomas Galbraith, chief of the clan, who, for unspecified
misbehavior, was duly hanged. And the rest of our story seems to have
been written almost entirely from high-court records, with recurrent
mention of the crime of *hamesuchen,* or the knocking-off of one's guests
when they are asleep under one's roof.

The movement of the Scotch to America has extended over nearly
three centuries. Some, perhaps only a few hundred, found it wise to
leave their homeland after the Jacobite risings of 1715 and 1745, and
in my Canadian youth the more nostalgic clansmen still assembled of
a Saturday evening to drink and inflict violence on each other in memory of the Massacre of Glencoe and the Battle of Culloden, respectively
and roughly 230 and 175 years earlier. The Canadian village of Glencoe
was a few miles distant.

The first large-scale migration, a half million or more between 1730
and 1770, came not directly from Scotland but by way of Ireland. The
Scotch-Irish had been encouraged and compelled by the English to
reside in Ulster and then, in response to mercantilist, that is, protectionist, economic policy, were denied the English market for the wool
and its products on which their livelihood depended. Moving on to
New England, they went, not without some local encouragement, to
the three northern states, where the names of such towns as London-
derry, Vermont, Belfast, Maine, and (possibly) Dublin, New Hampshire, celebrate their provenance.

Many more of the Scotch, a huge migration for the time, went to
Pennsylvania, where the Quakers valued them initially as a buffer against
the Indians along the borders of the settlement to the west but came
eventually to believe that the Indians were more benign. Tension in
the 1770s grew to the point where a Scotch-Irish expeditionary force,
the Paxton Boys, marched on Philadelphia to voice their political demands and their highly motivated hostility to the Indians. They were
persuaded to peace (except against the Indians) by, among other ne-
gotiators, Benjamin Franklin. In Pennsylvania, as wherever the Scotch-

Irish went, they took their pot stills with them, the symbol of their commitment to their favorite beverage. This had the further commercial advantage that in a time of primitive transportation, it substantially reduced the bulk of the surplus grain — first barley and later corn — that had to be conveyed to distant markets. As the available land was taken up in Pennsylvania, the Scotch-Irish migrants went south and extensively into the Carolinas.

In the late eighteenth and early nineteenth centuries the great movement to the Americas was from Scotland itself. On the Lowlands of Scotland are lands as bountiful as any on earth; anyone who doubts it should one day drive across the great bridge over the Firth of Forth above Edinburgh and travel on to St. Andrews. It is also a countryside of surpassing beauty. But the Highlands are a different story: life there has always been gray, grim and precarious, and over the centuries the wisest have left. It was Dr. Johnson again who said, "The noblest prospect which a Scotchman ever sees, is the high-road that leads him to England." However, from around 1770 to the middle of the last century and later, the yet more noble prospect was the American colonies — soon to be the United States — along with Canada and, a little later still, Australia and New Zealand. By the time of the American Revolution there were enough Highlanders in the colonies to make up a noticeable part of the fighting forces, and it is an unfortunate but compelling truth that they fought on both sides. An anomaly in historical motivation kept many of the recently arrived Scottish settlers loyal to the English crown.

The occasion for the exodus from the Highlands was the Highland Clearances. For centuries the rural inhabitants — the crofters — had grubbed a living out of the resistant soil without security in their tenure and recurrently without food in their mouths. Then, beginning in the 1770s, the lord's pleasure was withdrawn, and they were extensively evicted to make way for sheep. High wool prices motivated the expulsion; so also, it has been said, did the belief of the landowners that the sheep, the Great Cheviots, moving over the hills were more beautiful than the natives they displaced, a highly plausible possibility. In the enthusiasm of the moment villages were burned; the foundation stones can be viewed to this day. In Sutherland in the far north, the particular case being the village of Strathnaver, it was later alleged in the courts that the agents of the Duchess of Sutherland and her husband proceeded with such efficiency and dispatch that elderly and infirm residents were not removed before their dwellings were put to the torch.

Of the dispersed, some were resettled along the coasts of Scotland, and an astonishing number found the fare or other means for transport to the New World; perhaps more surprisingly, they survived the journey. They were followed in the 1840s by many who had remained behind, for in those years the potato blight brought a hunger to the Highlands no less acute than that in Ireland.

It is another indication of how poorly in comparison with the Irish we Scotch celebrate our history and our hardships that the Irish famine is known to all, while on the Clearances and the failure of the Scottish potato crops the received history is all but silent. This, however, is partly because the movement from Scotland was numerically far smaller — through the last century for which official United States government tabulations are available only a fraction of that of the Irish or, for that matter, of the English, Germans, Scandinavians or others. (In the decade following the famine — 1851 to 1860 — a recorded 38,000 Scotch came to the United States; from Ireland there were 914,000. In the same decade, by way of comparison, 952,000 came from Germany and 253,000 from England and Wales.) But the Scotch were aided in forgetting their own history by the happy fact that, within a generation, all, almost without exception, were richer and far better housed and fed than had been their ancestors for centuries. So they blotted out the anguish and kept in mind only the kilt and the pipes.

Coming to the United States and Canada — migration to the two countries cannot wholly be separated, for many came to New England by way of New Brunswick and Nova Scotia and others to Upper Canada by way of New York — the Scotch, unlike the Irish or the Italians, did not congregate in a dense urban mass. Rather, they spread out over the countryside. This, and the fact that most (though by no means all) were Protestants, contributed to the loss of identity I earlier mentioned. Italian and Irish Catholics living cheek by jowl in close religious communities in a city — quite often in a sordid slum — kept each other conscious of their ethnic roots. Not so the urban Scotch. There were, however, settlements in farm areas that were liberally populated by Scottish clansmen. To these they brought the horses and cattle for which Scotland is noted — the Ayrshire, *Scotch* Shorthorn and Aberdeen Angus (often wrongly called Black Angus) cattle and the stylish, white-stockinged Clydesdale horses. Along with the livestock they also brought a variety of traits much celebrated in our literature and extensively derived from circumstances that allowed of no other. Thus the Scottish settlers were thought to be hard-working; early American agriculture did not tolerate those who were otherwise. (At the earliest opportunity, many of us deserted the hard toil of the farms with celerity and great joy.) The Scotch were said by everyone to be thrifty; there are no alternatives to thrift in the absence of money. So it was on the early farms.

The townspeople, more often of English extraction, thought the

Scotch dirty, just as in Minnesota and Wisconsin in the days of Thorstein Veblen the Norwegians and other Scandinavians were held to be. To assert superior cleanliness is a way of asserting class or ethnic superiority. In the absence of bathrooms a low level of personal hygiene is normal. However, among the Scotch some were thought even by their own to carry this tendency to extremes. A neighbor of ours in Ontario took his wife once each summer — they were affectionate but childless — for a picnic on the northern shore of Lake Erie; it was their annual one-day release from work. While she spread out the picnic dinner, he went up the beach and out of sight to bathe. One year, much celebrated in local legend, he returned from his lonely immersion without his waistcoat; it had disappeared. His wife went up the beach with him to search but without success. The following summer he came back from his bath rejoicing. The missing garment had been found; it was under his underwear.

The Scotch brought with them their undoubted (if less than unique) concern for education. From this came a commitment to the public schools, a belief (one I still affirm) that there cannot be competent learning without firm discipline and, in time, a great exfoliation of colleges and universities under Presbyterian and other Scottish auspices, including Knox College in Illinois, Macalaster College in Minnesota, Carnegie Tech (now Carnegie-Mellon) in Pittsburgh and, not to be overlooked, Princeton University in Princeton, New Jersey. Mention of Carnegie-Mellon leads on to mention of Andrew Carnegie, who made money in the steel business to sustain philanthropy, a situation that has now been reversed, as it is the shareholders' philanthropy that currently, in appreciable measure, sustains the steel mills. From Carnegie came (along with other endowments) the Carnegie libraries, quite possibly the greatest single inducement to literacy and reading since Caxton himself.

In reaction, perhaps, to their age-old tendency in the Highlands, the Scotch in this country earned the reputation of being exceptionally law-abiding. And, indeed, American history records the name of no great Scottish criminals; it tells of no notably malignant Scottish gangs; we were not celebrated by Lincoln Steffens for controlling city governments in our own rapacious interest, although, no doubt, exceptions can be cited. The Reformation came powerfully to Scotland, partly in response to the preaching of John Knox, partly in consequence of the financial and licentious abuses of the clergy and laity whom he assailed. A commitment to both personal honesty and sexual rigor survived to my own time. Sexual concourse among the rural Scotch in all but the most aberrant cases was confined to the safely married, and even there it was viewed with some slight doubt by the very righteous. Divorce was unknown. Youthful romance did, however, have a certain matter-of-fact aspect, and in *The Scotch*, a modestly anthropological study of my clansmen in Canada which I published some twenty years ago, I told of my own experience in the matter.

When I was emerging from adolescence, and from reading Anatole France, I learned that, given great affection, unlicensed sexual trans- actions were more defensible than I had previously been allowed to suppose. One day the object of my love, a compact golden-haired girl who lived a half mile away, came over to visit my sisters. They were not at home, and we walked together through the orchard and climbed onto a rail fence that overlooked a small field where our purebred Scotch Shorthorn cattle were pasturing in front of us.

With the cows was a white bull named OAC Pride, for the Ontario Agricultural College, where my father had bid him in at an auction. As we perched there, the bull served a heifer that was in season.

Noticing that my companion was watching with evident interest, and with some sense of my own courage, I said, "I think it would be fun to do that."

She replied, "Well, it's your cow."

In considering the role and contribution of any ethnic group, the temp- tation is to turn to the great men and women of that race who have made it in military careers, politics, the arts, industry and banking, science and, if more dubiously, in sports. It is a temptation, however, that risks grave error. For one thing, great achievement has come from all the races; it is wrong to imagine that there is anything exceptional about any one. And by what measure, in any case, would one total up and assess the relative contributions? One does note that the Italians have a holiday for Columbus, and with Americans of African descent we now join to remember Martin Luther King, Jr. Unlike the Irish, the Scotch do not even have a parade. Two of Lincoln's generals, Grant and McClellan, were of Scottish descent (I concede that "Scottish" is perhaps more satisfactory than "Scotch" in this usage), but while Grant was certainly the best, McClellan was presumptively the worst. When Grant's reputed ethnic tendency to drink led to a complaint to the President, Lincoln asked that the nature of his beverage be ascertained so that some might be given to the other Union generals. In later years Douglas MacArthur was both applauded and decried. He was cele- brated beyond compare by his admirers, but that admiration did not extend to Harry Truman, who, to considerable applause, gave him the sack.

There is another problem. Four of our Presidents — Monroe, the aforementioned Grant, Hayes and Wilson — were of Scottish stock, and six more — Jackson, Polk, Buchanan, Andrew Johnson, Arthur and McKinley — were of Scotch-Irish derivation. This is an impressive score. But only a detailed examination of lineage and bloodlines would tell how great were the other ethnic infusions and admixture in these men. Because they lacked ethnic identification, and in the absence of any religious bar, the Scotch married into the other races without the slightest restraint.

The Scotch from Patrick Henry on were certainly numerous among the founding fathers — those who signed the Declaration of Independence and framed the Constitution. Daniel Webster, Henry Clay, John C. Calhoun, Stephen Douglas, Mark Hanna, Thomas Benton and Chauncey Depew illuminated the Congress of the United States and, in one or two cases, dangerously assailed its ears. Paul Douglas of Illinois, John McClellan of Arkansas and George McGovern of South Dakota were more recently in the Senate; Charles Robb of Virginia and Scott Matheson of Utah are among the current governors. While speaking of public figures, I must also mention Alexander Haig, once a general and secretary of state and later still a noted polemicist. With a partner of the same name he could also be a famous brand of beverage.

Archibald MacLeish, perhaps the best known and certainly the best loved of American poets, made a proud point of his Scottish origins, and he is in the company of Dwight Macdonald, the king of curmudgeons, and in descent from Washington Irving, Edgar Allan Poe and Herman Melville, all of whom had Scottish forebears. Taking, as some would insist, the long step from literature to journalism, the Scotch abound — Horace Greeley of *The New York Tribune*, who urged the young to go west; James Gordon Bennett of *The New York World*, who himself preferred to go to Newport, Rhode Island, and was a pioneer of the yellow press; Joseph M. Patterson, whose *New York Daily News* upheld the hand of Franklin D. Roosevelt; and the man who spared no effort to bring it down, Colonel Robert Rutherford McCormick of (and then identical with) *The Chicago Tribune*. Currently in this tradition, and not exempt from the controversy it has engendered, is Rupert Murdoch.

Oddly, in light of our solemn, even dour, reputation, we have been numerous and great in Hollywood — Elizabeth Taylor, John Forsythe, Helen Hayes, Charlton Heston, Warren Beatty and Shirley MacLaine all have clan connections. So did David Niven, one of my great friends over the years, who loved to tell of getting caviar from a Black Sea ship caught in Valetta Harbor by the wartime blockade and serving it out to his Scottish regiment on Malta during World War II. A "Jock," as he called him, protested sourly, "That *fooking* jam tastes of fish."

It is in industry, especially that involving mechanical innovation, that most clearly we have excelled. As Carnegie gave us steel, so Robert Fulton gave us the steamboat, Cyrus McCormick the reaper, Samuel

Colt the revolver, Samuel F. B. Morse the telegraph, Alexander Graham Bell the telephone and Donald Douglas the transition from train to everyday air travel. Truly an impressive list. Of Scottish origin also were (and are) the Mellons of Pittsburgh, who, besides banking, brought us the modern aluminum industry and Gulf Oil. The latter company traces originally to the great Spindletop discovery and one J. M. Guffey. Years later, after seeking and receiving financial help from the Mellons to enlarge his enterprise, he was, according to legend, found sitting disconsolately in a Pittsburgh hotel. Asked what had happened to his oil business, he responded with four of the saddest words in the English language: "They throwed me out." The story may not be true, but it shows that, on occasion, the Scotch have held their own even with the Irish.

For the financial achievements of the Scotch one must go back to yet earlier times — to London and Paris and the resulting American resonance. William Paterson from the Lowlands was the founder in 1694 of the Bank of England and, in descent therefrom, the Federal Reserve System some two centuries later. A few years after Paterson John Law, also from Scotland, arrived in Paris and sold the regent, a decidedly vulnerable man, on the idea of a bank with note-issuing powers. From this was derived the Mississippi Company (Compagnie d'Occident) to exploit the extensively nonexistent gold deposits of Louisiana. In the years between 1716 and 1720, this initiative produced one of the wildest speculative episodes in all history and the forcible promotion of migration to New Orleans and the lower Mississippi. We can therefore give ourselves credit not only for the presence of our own race in this country but, through Law, for quite a few of the French as well.

As we seem to have succeeded in business and also in the sciences, with Edwin McMillan, Robert A. Millikan and Irving Langmuir, Nobel laureates all, so there are areas where we have been outpaced. In economics Adam Smith and James and John Stuart Mill are founding fathers. But the most influential of the modern generation of American economists — Paul Samuelson, Simon Kuznets and Milton Friedman, to mention three Nobel Prize–winners — are Jewish. So is Martin Feldstein, whom many think of as the stubborn defender of fiscal responsibility under Ronald Reagan. In economics the Scotch have evidently given way to a greater ethnic talent.

So also in athletics. Scottish names are far from prominent in football, baseball and basketball, although I do read much of John McEnroe in tennis. In Europe we have a reputation in soccer but principally for the grave alarm that is occasioned by the prospective arrival of the Scottish fans. It seems likely that our race has been among the first to

discover that four days after an athletic event there is a greatly diminished interest in who won or who contributed to the winning; instead,
all turn their attention, in a feckless way, from the past to the future.
Making money or even writing verse has a more durable claim on
popular esteem.

At curling and golf, two indigenous Scottish pastimes, the Scotch
have excelled. The names of Arnold Palmer, Jan Stephenson and Tom
Watson are notable in the world of golf. But our commitment to this
sport is far from universal. Golf is played with a club and a ball that
are both too small. Having investigated the game, I can attest that the
hitting of the ball and its resulting direction are entirely in the realm
of accident. And moving across the course in a golf cart, as is now the
custom, must also be the most sedentary, even sordid, of all known
forms of athletics.

Doubtless there will be dissent from this last finding; this it is the
Scottish nature in religion, politics, philosophy, economics and personal
relations proudly to allow. Such tolerance, indeed, we would love to
believe, is our best and, one hopes, most lasting contribution to the
American polity, culture and scene.

8

A DIFFERENT JOURNEY
...INTO TELEVISION AND
THE ECONOMIC PAST

(1977)

Three and a half years, most will think, is a long time to devote to a mere
television series — one that will be over and gone in a matter of thirteen hours
and then largely forgotten. I would not have agreed to participate had I guessed
in advance how long I would be involved in The Age of Uncertainty. *Yet*
I look back on the experience with pleasure — a different culture, colleagues
and co-workers half my age, a glimpse one would never otherwise have had of
the birthplaces of Marx and Thorstein Veblen, the house of Adam Smith, Death
Valley and the headquarters of NORAD inside Cheyenne Mountain in Colorado.
The final product was viewed with some skepticism in Britain, favorably in the
United States, warmly in a dozen or so other countries and with the greatest
possible enthusiasm in Japan, where the companion book sold something over a
half-million copies. It is hard not to admire the intelligence of the Japanese.
    This piece was written for The New York Times Magazine *to introduce*
the series to the American television audience.

Until the summer of 1973, we didn't think that an ordinary television
set would receive any recognizable pictures at our farm in southern
Vermont; an effort to get the moon landings with an aerial hung up
in a tree had been a visual disaster, and only Cronkite's voice had let
us know the astronauts were there. But the Watergate hearings came
in strong and clear, and it was while watching them that I received a
phone call from Adrian Malone of the BBC in London.
    Malone and his talented team of directors, production assistants,
cameramen, soundmen and all the infinity of other trade unionists who
make television films had recently completed *The Ascent of Man*, their
noted series on the history of science, with Jacob Bronowski. Would I,
they were wondering, be interested in giving similar theatrical expression to the history of economic ideas? I looked at John Dean there on
my screen, reflected on his exceptionally conservative stage presence

and was personally encouraged. Without knowing what a theatrical image of the quantity theory of money would be, I more or less accepted.

For the next three and a half years, with some time off while locations were being sought or reconnoitered, my own education in the relationship between economics and television was substantially advanced. The result of our effort — *The Age of Uncertainty* — emerges in the United States this week; it has already been aired, as I learned to say, in Britain, is currently being shown in Canada and will eventually, one hopes, go around the world.

As the basic theme of the series, we early decided we would contrast the great certainties of thought in the last century — when capitalists knew that they were boss, socialists that they had a highly workable alternative, imperialists that they had a mission, rulers that they were meant to rule — with the great, though not unrewarding, uncertainties of our own time. In the division of our labor, I would supply the ideas and the words; their presentation would belong to the BBC. By the time the project was over, I had written two books — one on the history of money, one with the same title as the series — from which the television scripts were drawn. Both the books and the scripts owe much to my BBC colleagues, who pressed me constantly, just as my Harvard students might well have done, for amplification, clarification and more interesting detail. And I contributed some — if fewer — thoughts on locations and illustrations. For me, at least, the collaboration was wonderfully instructive and also a great deal of fun.

The modern economist, moving between family and equally demanding computer, regards the historical and literary digressions of economics as an unscientific waste of time. Our concern with the history of economic ideas thus took us into a sadly unfashionable field of learning. Because of this, I suppose, we planned to divide our presentation between the ideas — those by which, as Keynes averred, we are all ruled — and their practical consequences. First the men and the manifestation of their ideas in their own time; then, in later programs, the influence of those ideas on such institutions as money and the modern corporation, the potentially fatal competition between economic systems, the metropolis, the population and other pressures that hold the Third World in its poverty.

Our last program was a discussion by and among those with a specific responsibility for these concerns — our audience was allowed to see, in fact, how today's leaders perform. To stage what would be shown as a two-and-a-half-hour conversation we invited for a weekend of filming in Vermont Henry Kissinger; Georgy Arbatov of the Academy of Sciences of the Soviet Union; former British Prime Minister Edward

Heath; Shirley Williams, a Labour Member of Parliament; Jack Jones, head of the Trades Union Congress of Britain; Ralf Dahrendorf, then of the London School of Economics but with a long experience of the European Economic Community; Kukrit Pramoj, until a short time earlier the prime minister of Thailand; Katharine Graham of *The Washington Post* and others. A morning's exchange between Kissinger and Arbatov may be as close as any of us will ever come to sitting in on a summit negotiation on arms control. And on nuclear proliferation there was the most enlightened comment in years. "We Thais," Pramoj observed, "do not intend to have those nuclear weapons. We are a very, very careless people and we don't want any such things around — we might let one drop."

The major problem in planning this series was not, as some will imagine, how to simplify and avoid oversimplification; most economic ideas can, in their true essentials, be put in understandable form without sacrificing meaning. The most difficult problem was selection: On which relatively few men should we focus?

Fortunately, there is no dispute as to who was the founding father of economics. It was Adam Smith (1723–1790), and he is also, by a safe margin, the most enchanting figure in the history of the subject. His *An Inquiry into the Nature and Causes of the Wealth of Nations* was published in the year of American independence, but unlike many of his liberal friends, Smith did not favor devolution, as it would now be called in Britain, for the American colonies. He wanted them to stay in the British Empire, elect their proper quota of members to the Parliament at Westminster and have it understood that when the American population exceeded that of the British Isles, there would be a new Constantine capital in the West. We concluded, after careful consideration, that that capital would be in Indiana. The film shows the Houses of Parliament and Big Ben situated amidst ample parking space in downtown Indianapolis.

Smith was incapable of either forgetting or failing to find use for a fact. *Wealth of Nations*, in consequence, is a massive compendium of information on the economic world of his time. Unknown to his followers, who have rarely read their prophet and are not overly given to humor, it is also full of sly fun: "The late resolution of the Quakers of Pennsylvania to set at liberty all their negro slaves, may satisfy us that their number cannot be very great." But, above all, *Wealth of Nations* contained the germinal concepts that economists were to recover, restate, refine and, on occasion, offer as their own for the next two centuries — how prices are set; how income is distributed; how the driving power of self-interest is best released; the gains achieved from specialization (called "the division of labor"); the importance of encouraging this division by expanding freedom of trade; the proper and for him, of course, limited role of the state; the famous and still applicable canons of just and efficient taxation. Much of Smith had been anticipated by earlier writers, but *Wealth of Nations* put it all together. The book was an immediate best seller, and, in contrast with more recent times, the reputation of its author seems not to have suffered thereby.

For millions who have never read him, Smith is the prophet of uninhibited capitalism. Next came Karl Marx (1818–1883), perhaps a little better read by the faithful, who proclaimed the end to which capitalism was heading. But he did more than that. Marx's writing is rich in insight. Joseph Schumpeter, the most sophisticated conservative of this century, began his *Capitalism, Socialism and Democracy* by calling Marx a genius, a prophet and, as an economic theorist, "first of all a very learned man."

John Maynard Keynes (1883–1946) is the third inescapable figure in the history of economics. He brought the full power of self-confidence, writing skill and analytical ability — a most formidable coalition — to bear against the belief that depression and mass unemployment were inevitable. In Marx's system these crises, each one more devastating than the last, would bring capitalism to its crashing end. Keynes, at least temporarily, discredited this conviction.

He also brought style to economics, something that is greatly needed. He was a patron of the theater, an ardent book collector, a member of the Bloomsbury group and the husband of Lydia Lopokova, star of Diaghilev's ballet. Finally, and more important, Keynes revitalized the subject.

A marked, although not necessarily useful, characteristic of economists is their preference for rationalizing inadequate economic performance instead of doing something about it. In the 1930s, the most eminent economists succeeded in coming to terms with mass unemployment, idle plant capacity and persistent price deflation in much the same way as their professional descendants (now called Keynesians) have come to accept a combination of inflation and unemployment as something to be cured three or four years hence by divine intervention, assisted, perhaps, by better labor-management relations. Keynes's assault on professional comfort initiated a period of activism and innovation in economic policy that lasted into the 1960s. It also had a curious effect on how he is remembered. He felt that the depression and unemployment of the 1930s threatened personal liberty, democratic government and the free-market economy, all of which he cherished. But his highly motivated desire to save the existing social system earned him an unparalleled reputation as a radical.

.   .   .

As to the antecedents, acolytes and successors of the three men I've just mentioned, they also largely selected themselves, although here almost every economist, either out of genuine concern or to show acuity of scholarship, will be able to cite some omission. David Ricardo (1772–1823), the wealthy Jewish stockbroker whose handsome country estate was recently purchased by Queen Elizabeth for Princess Anne, took the ideas of the master, separated them from Smith's great mass of fact and hardened them into unsentimental law. Two of the statutes were the iron law of wages — the case that man, by his propensity to breed, would always bring his compensation down to the lowest level that would sustain life — and the labor theory of value, which held that the worth of a product was determined by the amount of labor embodied therein. These kindly propositions were not only a legacy to capitalist thought but a major gift to Marx as well. The system starved the workers and took from them the value they created. And this Ricardo, who was no socialist, affirmed.

Deep in my heart, I have always thought Ricardo overrated; he owes some of his reputation to the obscurity of his prose, which engendered the belief that great treasures of thought must be concealed therein. A perhaps greater figure was Ricardo's contemporary and friend Thomas Robert Malthus (1766–1834). He anticipated Keynes with the view that depressions might be caused by an organic deficiency of purchasing power, a theory that Ricardo rejected, as did all reputable economists for the next century, but one that is now generally accepted. And Malthus held that population, by increasing geometrically, had an ineluctable tendency to outrun the food supply, which, at best, increased only arithmetically. This articulates an anxiety that, after 150 years, is still exceedingly acute in the poor lands of what is now called the Third World.

In further descent from Adam Smith, I gave only passing attention to James Mill and the prodigiously learned John Stuart Mill. They systematized, elucidated, clarified and persuaded rather more than they invented. I by-passed Jeremy Bentham, the great Utilitarian philosopher and reformer, one reason being, as later in the case of Hegel, my own deficiency in interest and knowledge. Also, much of what Bentham urged sounds utterly commonplace now — no one in the Senate would get headlines today for asserting Bentham's immortal thesis that the purpose of government must always be "the greatest good for the greatest number." And, finally, there is the circumstance of his last wishes. Before he died in 1832, at the age of eighty-four, Bentham instructed that his body be dissected in the presence of friends. This touching ceremony went forward as ordained, and, in accordance with further directions, his skeleton was reconstructed and a wax head put on top. The resulting resurrection, dressed in Bentham's clothes, was then placed in a glass-fronted cabinet in University College, London, where it remains. For a man who did so much for his own memory, it seemed hard to do more.

I will also be rebuked for omitting detailed reference to Alfred Marshall of the University of Cambridge, who, for forty years, until his death in 1924, presided in saintly eminence over economics in all the English-speaking world. Marshall taught and greatly systematized the subject, and his huge textbook excluded the undiligent and unworthy; but no really great innovation, either in ideas or policy, bears his name.

Marx's two great disciples were, of course, Friedrich Engels (1820–1895) and Vladimir Ilyich Ulyanov (1870–1924), known to history and all but his friends as Lenin. Engels, like Marx, Lenin and the other revolutionaries of the last century (it is almost impossible to think of an exception), was of comfortable middle-class origins. In his case, radical thought was combined with remunerative multinational textile manufacture, making him particularly affluent. For Marx, Engels was friend, financial angel, admirer, collaborator and protector in the world of practical affairs, in which Marx was notably feckless. From Marx's notes, Engels finished the last two volumes of *Capital*, and scholars think that his contribution was not much less than that of his mentor.

Lenin's additions to socialist theory have always seemed to me slight; twenty years ago, I spent much of an autumn in Geneva reading his collected works, most of them a dreary waste. But his strategic sense was sure. Marx was contemptuous of agriculture and saw in capitalism the virtue that it rescued peasants from the idiocy of rural life. Lenin, in contrast, saw the importance of the peasants and promised them land. The Russian Revolution was saved when the peasant-soldiers deserted the czar and broke ranks to go and get what they had been promised. Marx was also generally uncritical of colonialism; to him it was a step along the path that, by way of capitalism, led on to the establishment of socialism and communism. Lenin, on the other hand, saw colonialism as a factor that prolonged the life of capitalism; capitalists and also workers in the industrial lands, or anyhow their leaders, rode on the backs of the Indians, the Chinese and the other colonial peoples. In consequence, he took the revolution to what we now call the Third World. Lenin was primarily a man of action, not a theorist. His greatest achievement, as my Harvard colleague Adam Ulam has persuasively argued, was not even the Russian Revolution, the kicking-in of a rotten door, but the conquest of the ensuing anarchy and administrative chaos, which must have been without parallel (assuming such things can be measured) in all history.

Along with the problem of selection for the brief television hours allotted went the problem of countering the revisionism to which all the economists just mentioned have been subject, a work less of scholars than of popular myth. Thus Adam Smith is now the cult hero of all free enterprisers. In fact, he had no faith in the deeper competitive commitment of businessmen, and he made that point in an oft-quoted passage: "People of the same trade seldom meet together, even for merriment and diversion, but the conversation ends in a conspiracy against the public, or in some contrivance to raise prices." He also warned strongly against corporations, then called joint-stock companies, for he believed their instinct was either to lassitude or to monopoly. Had Smith been called before the Senate Subcommittee on Antitrust and Monopoly in any recent time, his testimony would have been a sensation.

Revisionist attitudes about Marx have gone much farther. A personally kindly man, though given in later life to harsh words for those with whom he disagreed, he was launched in the newspaper business by German industrialists and was sustained as a foreign correspondent by the devoutly Republican *New York Tribune* for an important part of his life. He was expelled from Prussia in 1843 for criticizing the czar and for advocating a more secular approach to divorce, a free press and the preservation of the ancient right of the people to go into the forest to collect dead wood. Not a radical platform. His immediate program, put forward (with Engels) in 1848 in *The Communist Manifesto*, is less than Draconian — a progressive income tax; public ownership of railroads and communications; extension of public ownership in industry; cultivation of idle lands; free education; and better soil management. Marx did foresee and proclaim the violent end of capitalism, but that was inherent in the contradictions of the capitalist system. Admittedly, he was not averse to advancing the day.

Marxists have, however, reinterpreted Marx to justify any line of action, no matter how sanguinary, that has since seemed necessary. And non-Marxists have held him responsible for all that governments operating in his name have done since his time. Apart from the excesses of the Paris Commune of 1871, where there was much vicious and bloody slaughter on all sides, no one in Marx's lifetime was killed or even jailed by his partisans, although some were sequestered for professing his faith. After the British broadcast of my program on Marx, an overwrought conservative asked in the BBC magazine *The Listener* how one could mention the man without telling of all that has since been perpetrated in his name. The rule troubled me deeply, for, rigorously applied, it would be hard on Jesus: every British church service would have to end with a reference to what was being done in His name in Northern Ireland.

An even more serious revisionist problem arose with the one great American on my list. He was Thorstein Veblen (1857–1929), who, with Henry George, is one of the two American economic writers first published in the last century who still command an audience. There have been recent French and English editions of his *The Theory of the Leisure Class*; the book continues to sell well to this day. Professor Harry Levin of Harvard has called Veblen the most underrated writer of the last seventy-five years, and in the field of economics there is still an acute sense of guilt that his worth was not recognized in his lifetime. During his active years he moved, often involuntarily, from Cornell to Chicago to Stanford to Missouri to Washington, D.C., to the New School for Social Research in New York, and was never accorded the conventional honors of the profession.

To understand Veblen in context, one must begin with Herbert Spencer (1820–1903), the English sociologist and philosopher who enchanted the American plutocracy with the notion that, like Darwin's higher primates, they reflected the survival of the fittest. (The phrase actually comes from Spencer and not, as commonly supposed, from Darwin.) "The American Beauty rose," the first John D. Rockefeller told a Sunday school class one rewarding morning, "can be produced in the splendor and fragrance which bring cheer to its beholder only by sacrificing the early buds which grow up around it." This same struggle and sacrifice, he went on to say, operates with equally wondrous effect in economic life, and, he added, this "is not an evil tendency in business. It is merely the working-out of a law of nature and a law of God." The fortunes of the rich and the short, mean lives of the poor, it followed, were justified by the overall advance in quality they brought about.

This superbly contented world Veblen joyously took apart. The tribal customs and rituals of the affluent, he said, were, like those of the Papuans, the proper subject of anthropological study. Newport, Rhode Island, was important not as a place of residence but as a manifestation of conspicuous consumption — Veblen's greatest phrase. The Vanderbilts and Mrs. Stuyvesant Fish were important only as the most conspicuous consumers.

As to the way the conspicuous rich got rich, there is not much doubt. Rockefeller made his money less by building the oil industry than by monopolizing it. The elder Morgan did the same in steel, and it was said of Elbert Gary, his man in charge of operations, that he never saw a blast furnace until after his death. Until World War II, the Mellon grip on aluminum was so tight that the metal had a scarcity value more remarked than that of silver, of which there was an embarrassing excess. In 1940 and 1941, when large quantities of aluminum were suddenly needed, this monopoly came close to costing the RAF and the United States Air Force their existence. Of the railroads, Vanderbilt was a builder but also a monopolist. Daniel Drew, Jay Gould and Jim Fisk of Erie fame were looters pure if by no means simple. Not many thought Theodore Roosevelt, a Republican, guilty of overstatement when he called such men the "malefactors of great wealth."

But in recent times these reputations have undergone a remarkable improvement. Public relations — the work, for example, of Ivy Lee for Rockefeller — had a little to do with it. Philanthropy did more; mention of the Rockefellers, Guggenheims and Mellons now brings to mind foundations, museums and art galleries. Public service and politics have greatly helped. Whatever his merits as a statesman, Nelson Rockefeller is not regarded as a predatory figure. The children, grandchildren and art galleries have, in effect, beatified the ancestors, who are now thought of as builders and public benefactors. To them and not to the farmers, construction gangs or the self-effacing entrepreneurs who never made the Newport scene now belongs the credit for making the country great.

Coming to the institutions that emerge from the ideas, even well-motivated critics, the existence of whom I reluctantly concede, may find my selection arbitrary. That is partly the fault of television. A book can have all the chapters it needs; in a television series there can be only thirteen programs, a quarter of a year.

As a subject, money and its uncertainties was an easy choice. So also the economics of the metropolis and the modern corporation. The corporation is, I think, the greatest force for change in our time. People serve it devotedly. It is at war with narrow nationalism. It has also effectively disenfranchised its capitalist owners, established a close symbiotic relationship with the modern state and arranged, among other things, to be helped, sheltered or taken over when anything goes wrong. To tell of its history and achievements, rewarding and otherwise, we created Unified Global Enterprises, or UGE (an initial H is understood), a dynamic multinational that combines the more spectacular history and the more dramatic personalities — James Glow, Jr. (the Last Glow); A. F. Glow (the After Glow); Harold McBehan, the supreme exponent of dynamism; Howie Small, the technocrat — of a dozen or more American and world giants.

I did not deal with the welfare state, the environment or the unions, and I slighted the whole question of how to reconcile reasonably stable prices with reasonably full employment. Anyone who had succeeded in avoiding my views on these issues up to now had, I thought, earned the right to remain undisturbed.

I did deal with the ideas underlying colonialism and with the continuing equilibrium of poverty in the Third World. Attitudes on colonialism have also been subject to an especially compelling revisionism; all now agree that it was an exercise in undisguised rapacity, cupidity and exploitation. Some of the British had certainly in mind to make money in India, but the little band that ruled the country viewed the moneymakers with undisguised contempt. Their mission was prevention of famine, preservation of communal peace, enjoyment of their prerogatives as rulers and, above all, enforcement of the rule of law.

The important fact, however, is that people would rather be ruled badly by themselves than well by foreigners from afar. Even had our management in Vietnam been a triumph of justice, honesty and economic progress, we still would have been in trouble, although perhaps less so than from relying on Diem, Ky and Thieu. The modern view of colonialism does not allow for any affirmative achievement to be noted. I had one prominent supporter for my case that even good performance is rejected. This was from a one-time Vermont resident — he lived there in the years just before the Philippines came our way — and he warned against the prospect with trenchant force. (He assumed, of course, that all colonialists would be white.)

> Take up the White Man's burden —
> And reap his old reward:
> The Blame of those ye better,
> The hate of those ye guard —

He, of course, was Rudyard Kipling, of Brattleboro, Vermont, and we filmed his warning in his study, which is largely unchanged from the time when he wrote *Captains Courageous* and *The Jungle Books* there. Most Englishmen were, I believe, surprised to learn that Kipling had lived, if temporarily, in the United States, and the surprise extends to virtually all Americans.

To get things as they were, not as they are now imagined, is, I suppose, the problem of all history, and it is only modestly more difficult in political economy than elsewhere. Against this were some quite extraordinary, and to me unexpected, advantages from having the support of the camera on such matters.

Marx, when he was young, was a romantic idealist — an attitude from which the rest of his life was in some sense an escape — and his system is distinguished by its rich appreciation of man's involvement in the broad currents of history. The romanticism is wonderfully affirmed by a camera trip over the Brothers Grimm countryside of the upper Moselle, in which he wandered as a boy. The historical involvement can be visualized when one sees the great Roman ruins in his birthplace in Trier, which, as Augusta Treverorum, was the foremost Roman bastion against the German tribes — the Rome of the north.

Theater also has its value in affirming social issues — a greater value, I believe, than solemn scholars are likely to concede. Henry Ward Beecher removed the guilt of his affluent Brooklyn congregation by telling them that "God intended the great to be great and the little to be little." It makes a distinct impression to witness an actor saying so from his pulpit.

I argue in the series that it was World War I (not World War II, in which my generation had its moment of glory) that was the great turning point in the influence of the social classes. Before 1914, the traditional ruling classes in alliance with the new business power were certain and secure. After the massive stupidity of the trenches, they were discredited forever. To this day, nothing illustrates that stupidity as does a camera tour of the battlefields and cemeteries of the Somme. In Western Europe at least, nothing remotely so hideous survives from World War II.

The greatest difficulty in television is the need for condensation; it is a Procrustean bed in which not only the legs are trimmed off but also all else, except sometimes the head and the heart.

For a year, as we traveled and filmed, I regularly lay awake each night wondering how the requisite points could be made in fewer words. And I remained in bed early each morning to continue the paring. Then I went out in the daylight to the camera to learn that what I had written was still too long. For three days in a hotel in New Haven, Connecticut, I tried to get into five minutes my explanation of Irving Fisher's equation of exchange — how prices vary with the quantity of different kinds of money, the velocity of its circulation and the volume of transactions. At any decent university any professor of merit would, with a little effort, make it last for at least three classes. Maybe a term. Fisher was an economist, eugenicist, mathematician, inventor, Prohibitionist and speculator — he lost between $8 million and $10 million in the 1929 crash, a considerable sum, as I noted, even for an economics professor. To say all this and much more I had maybe fifty words. One of the dangers in condensation is that you tend simply to list things, omitting everything that is amusing and thus ending up with only what is solemn.

However, television demands that you keep a balance between eye and ear. While writers assume almost automatically that pictures are inherently simple-minded and everything that can be done with words should be done with words, pictures — visual images — are the case for television. They are also what attract and hold attention. Thus the need for condensing the words. I never noticed any uncontrollably vast crowds trying to get into my hour-long lectures at Harvard or any great tendency for students to linger after they were over. Before I started the BBC enterprise, I sought the advice of my friend and neighbor in Switzerland, David Niven. I imagine that no one speaks more intelligently on these matters out of such long experience. "The series will succeed," he said (I somewhat paraphrase), "in accordance with their success in keeping your face off the screen, thus making it minimally welcome when it does appear." For my journey into television that was, I think, the wisest guidance of all.

· VIII ·

A PROCESSION
OF HEROES — AND
SOME BYSTANDERS

ALL OF THE MEN here discussed I met at one time or another, Muhammad Ali Jinnah and Mahatma Gandhi excepted — a statement that is at least a minimal exercise in name dropping. But nearly all that I tell of them here comes from the work and writing of others, almost none from my own, usually brief, acquaintance.

WINSTON CHURCHILL AND
FRANKLIN D. ROOSEVELT*

(1985)

This and the review-article following celebrate the Churchill style. They tell how language can be a weapon, a way of subduing opposition, a genuine source of power.

I suggest in the first of these comments that Churchill must have had for at least some of his vast literary effort some "supremely talented ghosts." When the review first appeared, his one-time daughter-in-law, Pamela Harriman (Mrs. Averell Harriman), wrote to correct me sharply on the point. Churchill was above and beyond imitation; all this was his. I happily accepted the correction. Then, in his recently published diaries, John Colville, once and for long Churchill's aide, challenged any historian to distinguish between Churchill's prose and that of those who had learned to replicate it. Pamela slightly relented. I do doubt that any politician who is truly dependent on ghosts can ever be very persuasive in his writing. For one thing, he will not be able to tell good writing from bad or the literate helper from the hack.

In the years of these letters — if I may begin on a mildly personal note — I thought myself rather close to wartime affairs in Washington. In 1940, I was on the staff of the National Defense Advisory Commission, the first of the wartime agencies. Then, for two intense years, I was in charge of all price-control operations. Then, later and briefly, I was in the Lend-Lease Administration and the preparatory agency for UNRRA. Finally, in 1945, I was a director of the United States Strategic Bombing Survey in Europe and Japan. In all these years I, like others, took pride in my access to privileged if not terribly secret

---

*This was a review, originally published in England in *The Times Literary Supplement*, of *Churchill and Roosevelt: The Complete Correspondence*, Volume I, *Alliance Emerging*, Volume II, *Alliance Forged*, Volume III, *Alliance Declining*, edited with a commentary by Warren F. Kimball (Guildford: Princeton University Press, 1984).

information and made evident my pleasure in my superior knowledge. (My memory retains vividly a greatly off-the-record meeting of younger officials at the Mayflower Hotel in the autumn of 1940; there a well-placed Army intelligence officer just back from England told us that the RAF had suffered grievous defeats from the Luftwaffe, that it was only sensible in our planning to assume that Britain was finished.) In the years since the war, I've been a fairly diligent reader of the memoirs and more formal histories of the time.

I tell all this in order to say that neither from that early experience nor from the ensuing books — Churchill's memoirs and papers being the only possible exception — did I learn as much as from these three volumes. No one from now on can possibly pretend to a knowledge of the larger events of these years who hasn't read them. Nor should anyone who wishes such knowledge suppose that he or she faces a painful obligation. On the contrary, the books are strongly addictive. One stays with them far into the night, always curious as to what the next letter or telegram will say, how a particular issue, difference or conflict will be resolved.

Much of the credit for this compelling interest lies with Warren F. Kimball, who is professor of history at Rutgers University. Though loosely described as the editor, he has, in fact, written in the headnotes to the exchanges a superior account of military, political, economic and personal affairs as they bore upon action and decision in the months and years from September 11, 1939, when Churchill took office at the Admiralty, to April 11, 1945, when, from Warm Springs, Georgia, Roosevelt sent the last of the letters before his fatal stroke. Anyone writing in competition with Roosevelt and especially with Churchill risks a damaging comparison. Professor Kimball's comment is in no way overshadowed; instead, his explanations of the context, which in the aggregate are almost as long as the letters themselves, emerge as an informed, thoughtful, literate and altogether indispensable guide to the correspondence.

Professor Kimball's effort is not flawless. He is a trifle too eager to find disagreement and conflict between the two principals; a major lesson in these volumes is how few such conflicts there were and with what tolerance and wisdom those that developed were composed. He could have given a little more guidance as to the personalities and competence of the supporting casts, especially on the American side. Most readers will wish to know more about those who were drafting the Roosevelt letters or seeking to intrude their views or policy needs. (On this a later word.) There are also occasional small typographical or spelling errors, although they are decidedly fewer than in the correspondence itself. These last Professor Kimball scrupulously notices and corrects.

·   ·   ·

The first and most important thing that is evident in these volumes is the difference between the two leaders in the eloquence, force and style of their letters and messages, a matter that, perhaps out of respect and affection for Roosevelt, some of the American reviews I have seen have not sufficiently stressed. Churchill, throughout these years and notably in the period before the attack on Pearl Harbor and again after the American forces in Europe became dominant, was very much the junior partner, the pleading voice. Roosevelt had the money, the supplies, the merchant ships, the planes and the troops. But this difference, one is compelled to believe, was extensively offset by the skill, reach and eloquence of Churchill's persuasion. Every letter has his literary trademark, is replete with the Churchillian flourishes. One cannot suppose that he wrote all of them himself; he must have had some supremely talented ghosts. But one cannot doubt that he placed his own special imprint on each communication. Here, worth citing in full, is his letter of congratulations to FDR after Roosevelt's defeat of Wendell Willkie in 1940:

November 6, 1940

From Former Naval Person to President.

I did not think it right for me as a Foreigner to express any opinion upon American policies while the Election was on, but now I feel you will not mind my saying that I prayed for your success and that I am truly thankful for it. This does not mean that I seek or wish for anything more than the full fair and free play of your mind upon the world issues now at stake in which our two nations have to discharge their respective duties. We are now entering upon a sombre phase of what must evidently be a protracted and broadening war, and I look forward to being able to interchange my thoughts with you in all that confidence and goodwill which has grown up between us since I went to the Admiralty at the outbreak. Things are afoot which will be remembered as long as the Eglish language is spoken in any quarter of the globe, and in expressing the comfort I feel that the people of the United States have once again cast these great burdens upon you, I must avow my sure faith that the lights by which we steer will bring us all safely to anchor.

Roosevelt's letters, in contrast, are in bureaucratic prose, grammatical but wooden. When he is tempted to a Churchillian flourish, it is not very exciting. This is his first letter after the attack on Pearl Harbor and the American declaration of war:

December 8, 1941

For the Former Naval Person.

The Senate passed the all-out declaration of war eighty-two to nothing, and the House has passed it three hundred eighty-eight to one. Today

all of us are in the same boat with you and the people of the Empire and
it is a ship which will not and cannot be sunk. FDR

Churchill is stronger not only in style but on substance — on high
military strategy, to which Roosevelt but rarely addressed himself, and
on the international political matters with which much of the correspondence is concerned. For this last he evidently had, in Anthony
Eden and on down into the Foreign Office, much more competent
support. The State Department, in contrast, was then headed by Cordell
Hull, many of whose concerns — with eventual trade relations and like
matters — bore only indirectly on the war. Or they were a digression
or obstruction. Then in the last months Hull was succeeded by Edward
Stettinius, a man of great personal beauty but deeply dimmed perception; his appointment was made on the plausible theory that a vacuum
was better than an obstacle. And behind Hull and Stettinius in those
years were the old State Department professionals, self-regarding aristocrats who were profoundly though proudly incompetent as regards
the practical problems of the day. So for support on foreign policy
Roosevelt had to rely on Harry Hopkins, Admiral William Leahy and
others of his personal staff. Accordingly, along with his eloquence,
Churchill frequently had the advantage of a better-considered case,
one more in line with controlling circumstance and one to which, in
the end, Roosevelt repeatedly came around. The reader has, obviously,
to guess to which of the great wartime initiatives the Churchill prose
and persuasion contributed. One cannot read these letters without feeling that on the destroyer deal, Lend-Lease and the conferences that
brought the leaders together on a host of lesser matters they were very
important. They were clearly less influential when it came to military
decisions; here Roosevelt had the trusted and effective support of General George Marshall. In consequence, superior aptitude notwithstanding, Churchill failed in the exchanges having to do with some of the
great military issues, notably his Mediterranean and Balkan ambitions
and his grave reluctance as to Overlord, the frontal attack into and
through France.

Overall, these letters run heavily to political questions — to personalities, developments and decisions in North Africa, Italy, France, Greece,
Poland and, as the war drew to an end, in Germany. (Churchill, especially, made clear his desire to keep political matters away from the
military and in his own hands.) Two issues dominated this correspondence and, indeed, account for a fair proportion of the total exchange.
One was how to deal with and manage de Gaulle, whom both leaders
disliked but whom Churchill was disposed to remember as the French-
man who did not surrender in 1940 and who was, partly in consequence, the most effective French leader. Roosevelt, out of his own

personal aversion, resisted de Gaulle until nearly the end, although here perhaps the old guard in the State Department with its ties to Vichy was also important.

The other preoccupying political problem was Poland. The volume of correspondence on this is huge and in roughly inverse proportion to the influence over Polish affairs that either leader was able to exercise. Hungary and Czechoslovakia are scarcely mentioned in these letters, and Romania and Bulgaria rate only passing references toward the end. Certainly no one can doubt the superior capacity of the Poles to make themselves heard. Ultimately, of course, neither Roosevelt nor Churchill had any real effect on the outcome; here, as elsewhere in Europe, the controlling influence was the occupying armies, and in Poland they were Stalin's.

Another continuing theme is how to persuade Stalin on the numerous matters on which he needed persuasion — on the need for postponing the second front, on the huge and at times insufferable risks attending the convoys to Murmansk, on Poland and on the rather smaller but much debated issue of where to have the meetings of the Big Three. In all these the surface fact was the extreme personal stubbornness of Uncle Joe, or U.J., as he was always called by the two correspondents and which, it appears, he eventually heard about and did not like. The deeper fact, by no means unacknowledged in these letters, was the vastly greater burden of combat and death that was assumed by the Russian armies until very nearly the last days of the war. One is reminded again and again of how two of Hitler's decisions shaped the eventual outcome, decisions on which those who are inclined to discover some enduring mark of genius in Hitler's rule, however evil, should reflect. One was his decision to attack Russia and bring her huge armies into opposition; the other, a mere five months and a few days later, was to declare war on the United States and thus to ensure that American attention would be focused primarily on Germany, not on Japan. Rarely, if ever, have leaders in their wartime needs and policy been so favored by an enemy, and Churchill, at least, leaves no doubt as to his awareness of his debt.

Along with politics in the liberated countries, de Gaulle, Poland and Uncle Joe, there is shipping. Questions concerning the allocation of merchant-shipping space and landing craft to various oceans and operations and reports on the course of antisubmarine activities come regularly into the letters. So, in a curiously blurred, amorphous and indecisive way, do various problems with China, Chiang Kai-shek and the China-Burma-India Theater. They are blurred at least partly because they do not focus on Churchill's underlying commitment to India and to preserving the Empire.

As noted, the meetings — in Argentia, Newfoundland; Casablanca; Quebec (twice); and in Teheran and Yalta with Stalin — are much discussed. Everything, even the details of living accommodations, engaged the personal attention of Churchill and Roosevelt, perhaps as a relief from the heavier questions with which they were concerned. A recurrent problem was how to keep down the number of people attending the conferences, an effort that resulted in total failure. In Washington, as also one supposes in London, nothing so distinguished an official — not high military rank, not Cabinet position, not assumed self-importance — as an invitation to attend. Nothing was so terrible as to be left behind. In the end, subordinates came by the planeload to what for most, as all concerned with summitry must know, were days of elaborately camouflaged unemployment.

Domestic policy and politics intrude on these volumes but, as between the two politicians, in a highly asymmetrical way. Churchill used the War Cabinet and the House of Commons as a buttress to argument. Repeatedly, when he needed a modification or change of policy, he would plead his difficulties with his Cabinet colleagues, the need to make a statement about the matter to the Commons. Churchill does not persuade the reader, and one doubts that he persuaded Roosevelt, that he was ever in much real trouble. Roosevelt, in contrast, had far more serious political problems in the Congress, with the electorate at large and in the two elections he had to fight during the years of this correspondence. Though he does not often mention them, they are vividly evident as constraints on what he can say or do. The reader will emerge from these letters with the feeling that Churchill, the leader of the lesser power, was far more secure in his authority. This, too, strengthened his hand.

A few final thoughts remain. One, as I've earlier said, is the great, indeed overriding, fact that both leaders preferred agreement to conflict. Success consisted in minimizing disputes, not in winning them. As one reads these books, nothing is more certain than the satisfaction each principal felt in dispatching a letter that said, "I agree." Or in confining action to the few amendments that would make agreement possible. Had it been otherwise — had there been the normal desire of politicians to win their case — the history of these years would have been different and far less happy.

One is also impressed with the extraordinary number of matters they — again Churchill more than Roosevelt — kept wholly and solidly in mind. Neither was young; both had recurring episodes of ill health. But only in the last months — after the 1944 election — does one sense a decline in Roosevelt's perception and personal competence. And Churchill, of course, is strong to the end.

Finally, were it not so normal in such matters, one would be impressed with how little either leader ever reflects on the horror over which he presides — the personal terror of the foot soldier privately contemplating his probable death, of the B-17 or Bomber Command pilot knowing he may not return from his mission, of the merchant seaman looking out on the waters of the Arctic, which he will most likely soon enter. Or the ordeal of civilians in cities under attack. Of such matters there is no mention. Instead there is a serene quality about these letters that extends to the citing of casualty statistics and merchant-shipping losses and is altogether remote from what those immediately concerned endured. It has long been assumed that in resisting Overlord, Churchill was moved by his terrible memories of the Western Front, but this he nowhere makes explicit. Perhaps this serenity and detachment is inevitable. War requires that both leaders and historians close their minds to the reality of conflict and resort to their own form of psychological denial of the awfulness of man's aggression.

FURTHER ON CHURCHILL
AND THE CHURCHILL STYLE*

(1978)

I must relent somewhat as regards the early words in this essay. As have all authors, I have noted the recurrent instinct of publishers to clandestine operations — to the release of books, if not in secret, then with greatly thoughtful reticence. However, it has not been, I must say, my personal experience and complaint. And I now find that I have been a little unfair to these Churchill volumes. The individual books were published with decently reticent publicity. The series as a whole, including the ancillary volumes, was issued mostly for libraries and Churchill scholars, so it required and got less public notice.

Publishers, as all authors feel compelled to tell you, regularly publish books in deep secret, and considering the quality of much of the stuff that gets into print these days, one can only be grateful. But there are occasions when this compulsive commitment to literary overclassification denies the public interesting reading material, more interesting perhaps than anything similarly suppressed by the CIA or the National Security Agency. The biggest loss of which I know is the fifteen books of Winston Churchill's papers, released up until now in exceptionally clandestine fashion. I've rarely encountered anyone, the wage hands of the publisher apart, who knows about them, although there must be a fair number of students of modern British and European history who are sorry their public libraries cannot afford them. The production to date costs $270 and requires around three feet of shelf space. Individual volumes can be purchased, but I feel genuinely sorry for anyone who doesn't have access to them all. Certainly anyone of the requisite literacy who is being rewarded by the current government concern for

*This was a review, originally published in *Esquire*, of *Winston S. Churchill*, Volumes 1–5, edited by Randolph Churchill and Martin S. Gilbert (Boston: Houghton Mifflin, 1966–1977).

the well-being of the rich should get all the books for personal perusal.

The production, as again I prefer to call it, is a double-track operation, so far consisting, on the first track, of five main volumes of extracts from Churchill's public and private letters, speeches and official papers and from the responding communications and comment, all linked together by a highly competent and readable narrative that tells where Churchill was at the time and of the political, personal or literary context. Then on the second track are up to three companion volumes for each of the principal ones, and these consist of letters to and from Churchill, more of his official papers and a great many letters and documents from the archives of contemporaries that express views, invariably strong and often adverse, on Churchill's personality or judgment. These companion volumes I liked best of all. For the seven books containing material up to 1914, the editor was Randolph Churchill. After his death in 1968 from various self-destructive assaults, the job was taken over by Martin S. Gilbert. The senior Churchill, wherever he is, must be reflecting on his extraordinary luck in both editors.

I was introduced to the project years ago, before anything was published, when Randolph Churchill showed up one day in Cambridge, Massachusetts, with the manuscripts on his father's early parliamentary career and asked me to look at that part of the connective tissue having to do with economics. In the period in question, Winston Churchill was heavily involved with tariff policy — he was a deeply committed free-trader — and with Lloyd George in the pathbreaking first steps on social insurance and the welfare state. I started with the economics parts and went on to be captured by all the rest.

Some of the fascination is in the history itself. More is in the political and bureaucratic conflict that swirled constantly around Churchill and of which he was truly a master. His skill in these sordid arts depended, in turn, on a very commonplace qualification: a deeply fearsome certainty that he was unquestionably right. Nothing else, I've observed over the years, is so important for winning battles in Washington. The men who wanted to bomb North Vietnam were absolutely certain that it would end the war; those who were opposed only doubted it. Churchill's confidence did not desert him even when he was irretrievably wrong, as in his belief that the old guard feudatories who fought the Bolshevists after the Russian Revolution — Denikin, Kolchak, Wrangel — were on the wave of the future or that British India was forever. Churchill lost those battles.

He also lost some battles when he was right. He has been greatly blamed because as chancellor of the exchequer he brought Britain back to the gold standard in 1925 at the prewar price of gold and the prewar parity with the dollar. When bought with the expensive pounds, British goods, coal in particular, were not competitive with those of foreign producers. So British prices had to come down, and one consequence was the coal-miners' strike and the General Strike of the following year. Churchill, as these papers show, was, in fact, deeply suspicious of the official, orthodox and Establishment pressure that forced this decision, and he resisted it nearly to the end. The problem, as he later noted, was that on economics his self-assurance was not as great as on other matters. These were his thoughts as of 1927 on the financial mind at work, functioning (so to speak) just as generally it still does in the United States today:

> The financial policy of Great Britain since the war has been directed by the Governor of the Bank of England and distinguished Treasury permanent officials who . . . have pursued inflexibly a strict, rigid, highly particularist line of action, entirely satisfactory when judged from within the sphere in which they move and for which they are responsible, and almost entirely unsatisfactory in its reactions upon the wider social, industrial and political spheres.

A further element in Churchill's power was his use of language as a weapon. And, in the end, it is this that makes these books so wonderful. That so many millions of words came from one man in one lifetime is remarkable but not, perhaps, totally astonishing. Churchill headed a history-writing organization that kept on producing (and also making money) even when he was in the most demanding of ministerial offices. He used assistants — and used them even for his more casual articles. What *was* astonishing was his ability to give the papers so produced a vital touch, to implant an air of excitement both in what he wrote himself and in what others had drafted for his amendment and revision. This depended, in part, on his own ability (and also, one presumes, that of his staff) to find, select and organize material so that even the most hostile opponent would be attracted by the information offered, the instruction provided. It also depended on an inventive, if often extravagant and sometimes reckless, use of adjective and metaphor. And, of course, it owed a great deal to the resource and flow of the language itself. Here he is, speaking on the BBC in 1935 to oppose legislation according greater self-government to India. (For some inexplicable reason, it was originally transcribed in verse form.)

> Sir Samuel Hoare has thrust upon Parliament
>   the most bulky bill ever known.
> If it was as luminous as it is voluminous,
>   it would indeed command respect.
> But what is this India Home Rule Bill?
>   I will tell you.
> It is a gigantic quilt of jumbled crochet work.
> There is no theme; there is no pattern;

there is no agreement; there is no conviction;
there is no simplicity; there is no courage.
It is a monstrous monument of shame built by the pygmies.

We have all this extraordinary writing because Churchill's career, or much of it, antedated the political and bureaucratic use of the telephone; politicians and public servants in his time persuaded one another by letter and document. Churchill's telephone transcripts would not have been nearly as good as his written words. Henry Kissinger is currently standing himself to considerable legal expense to keep his calls from being published. On purely literary grounds that is probably well advised.

It's hard to think of any misfortune that could be as devastating for a politician as the release of his official prose. But Winston Churchill survives — and brilliantly. In 1953, he received the Nobel Prize in literature.

3

CHARLES DE GAULLE*

(1966)

This review has considerably less to do with Charles de Gaulle than with the eloquence and general historical style of David Schoenbrun, who was in his time a voice of information and authority on the air waves. It is a bit harsh. But books by journalists are frequently reviewed by other journalists, and journalists are often friends or, at a minimum, realize that they must coexist. So the resulting reviews are often unnaturally and sometimes even pathologically favorable. An occasionally adverse comment helps, though in a very minor way, to right the balance.

There is a widely accepted classification of books into books and non-books, but it is also valuable to divide them into independently propelled vehicles (such as the bicycle or motorcycle) and sidecars. The first come from people who are concerned primarily with writing a book, although this, needless to say, is no guarantee of quality. The sidecars are the work of more occasional scholars, like the late Errol Flynn, Sammy Davis, Jr., and Art Linkletter, who have their careers solidly grounded in seduction, entertainment or children and who write on these subjects strictly on the side. Not all of this effort is negligible, as the survival value of the works of Caesar, Cellini, Saint-Simon and, by some possible calculation, Fanny Hill duly attest. But, as a general rule, the writer involved is subject to a certain amount of literary discredit, which, in view of his strong position elsewhere, doesn't usually matter. He accepts this in exchange for a certain amount of money.

Since the pioneering days of Vincent Sheean and John Gunther, foreign correspondents have been great perpetrators of the sidecar.

---

*This was a review, originally published in *Book Week* of *The New York Herald Tribune*, of *The Three Lives of Charles de Gaulle: A Biography* by David Schoenbrun (New York: Atheneum, 1966).

Their profession takes them, as a matter of course, to interesting places at exciting times, and they know all the great men. Though perhaps more sensitive to discredit than most, they are accustomed to writing, and also they usually need the money.

Mr. Schoenbrun was for many years the Paris correspondent for CBS. His current book is a sidecar, drawing on his long association with Charles de Gaulle, and I hope that he makes a great deal of money out of it, for otherwise he won't compensate for the damage to his literary reputation. The debit is, in fact, heavy. He sets out to tell the story of de Gaulle in each of his three great roles in modern France — professional soldier, his country's savior, in the more or less secular sense of the term, and statesman — but he writes under the burden of severe handicaps, which, sadly, he doesn't surmount.

His worst problem is unfamiliarity with the first law of modern English literature, which is that a man who tries to write fancy language will fall on his face and the one who tries to write like Winston Churchill will fall the flattest of all. Here is Mr. Schoenbrun in the very first pages — it is a prologue entitled "Incarnation and Reincarnation," and he is describing the scene at Churchill's funeral: "London's weather was at its majestic worst, but Londoners were at their adverse best as they waited patiently for General de Gaulle to pay his last respects to Winston Churchill, so that they could follow him into the hall to bid farewell in their turn to the man who incarnated England in its darkest and finest hours."

This, he goes on to tell, rang down the curtain on a fine period of history, "an epic that is not likely to be performed again, the last of the passion plays of the neo-Dark Ages of pre-Thermonuclear man."

And, alas, this is only the warm-up. Before the author even gets out of that prologue, he has made de Gaulle the "lone ranger of the Western plains" and then "a tower of babelizing contradictions." In Chapter 2 — its title is "Advice and Dissent" — the author gives his considered view of the events that were to destroy France in 1940. They moved "with the fatality of a Greek tragedy, in the essential meaning of true tragedy, which is the evitability of the inevitable." That's what he says.

It seems to me that in the later chapters the writing becomes a little less gluey. The author, one feels, is a sensitive man and couldn't stand it himself. But unhappily this allows attention to pass to content, which is generally limited on de Gaulle's early military career and rather episodic even on the years when he led the Free French. As the book proceeds, there is more, and one begins to get some sense of the man whom, with much reason, the author admires. De Gaulle is intelligent, vain, more adaptable politically than the legend holds, remarkably able to recognize reality, as in Indochina and Algeria, but remarkably nostalgic on France's European role and still very angry (as he had been during World War II) with the British and Americans. This is sound, if not exceptionally surprising. Sadly, one must dredge it out of material that shows an equal disregard for novelty: "Suez was almost a death blow to the Western Alliance, which has never been the same since." "Kennedy knew that he would face no more powerful and dangerous adversary than the Soviet leader."

The author also has a habit of mixing together great events with minor diplomatic and foreign office trivia and, on occasion, with stories that the biographer of Clara Bow would have thought too slight. Thus he tells of a visit he made to de Gaulle in his capacity as president of the Anglo-American Press Association not very long after both had assumed their presidencies. The author asked de Gaulle if, for old times' sake, he could call him "General." This de Gaulle graciously conceded and then insisted on calling Schoenbrun "Mr. President." The author then got confused and started calling de Gaulle "Mr. President." De Gaulle was amused. The story could not really have been retrieved short of having them call each other Dave and Charlie, with a slap, each by the other, on the back. (This matter of mode of address comes up again toward the end of the book, when Mr. Schoenbrun reproduces a lengthy interview with President Eisenhower in the finest Eisenhower idiom. It begins, "You know, de Gaulle and I got along fine personally. . . . Of course, he and I were never Charles and Ike.")

Mr. Schoenbrun also has a habit of tossing off a generalization or nonfact as though it were certified truth. For example, he has a badly wounded de Gaulle in World War I being evacuated to a hospital "just the day before the British Expeditionary Force, which was to rush up and stem the German advance, landed at Boulogne." This was neither the intended British role, if that is what the author means, nor what they did. Sir John French's orders were to conserve his minuscule force, and he accomplished this by a strategy of retreat that might have seemed cautious to Quintus Fabius Maximus and certainly seemed so to his own ultimate commander, Marshal Joffre.

Finally, there are the clichés. These march through the book like the German army marching through Paris, rank upon serried rank, the plumed columns relieved only by the occasional appearance of the hackneyed or the trite. (As will be seen, I found myself captured and committed to the art form.) On every page there is an example; one becomes involved, as in a game, with finding it. If anyone thinks I exaggerate, here is a selection I compiled by opening the book at random and choosing one from that and each of the next four pages.

PAGE 233: "De Gaulle was not the responsible captain on the bridge of the ship of state."

PAGE 234: "Future historians will have a mass of testimony, pro and con, to pore over."

PAGE 235: "De Gaulle saved what was still left to save of the honor, democracy and unity of France on the brink of the abyss."

PAGE 236: "General de Gaulle raised his long arms, looked up in the air as though invoking the heavens to bear witness."

PAGE 237: "I am convinced that de Gaulle believed in the nobility of his cause."

I am convinced that the noble course for me now is to pursue the matter no further.

4

JOHN MAYNARD KEYNES*

(1984)

In 1937, I went to the University of Cambridge for several terms to study under John Maynard Keynes. Sadly, that was the year he had his first heart attack, and he didn't teach or even appear. I finally encountered him in Washington during World War II; once, when I was directing price control operations, he came to my office, as I tell here, to give me a memorandum he had written on the pricing of pigs. It is, alas, one of the few documents missing from his collected papers.

I was asked by several people after this piece was published if I had read all twenty-nine volumes in the collection. (Actually thirty, for one was in two parts.) Quite a few I had read before they were assembled; more I now read with interest, even fascination; some I scanned, a word replete with ambiguity. But coming to some, I resorted to sampling, which, I prefer to believe, was greatly judicious. When the truth is inescapable, not even an accomplished liar (which I trust I am not) should evade it.

One of the astonishing and little-examined aberrations of academic, professional and business life is the prestige that is accorded without thought to the specialist. A highly practical design by which a person of everyday energy or competence is enabled to make a useful or anyhow identifiable contribution to intellectual, scientific or economic pursuits somehow becomes something intrinsically more significant than broader, more diverse knowledge or greater effort. In medicine the specialist is considered much superior professionally and socially to the general practitioner; one notes, these days, the effort to show that

*This was a review, originally published in *The New York Review of Books*, of *The Collected Writings of John Maynard Keynes*, edited by Elizabeth Johnson and Donald Moggridge (New York and London: Macmillan and St. Martin's Press and Macmillan and Cambridge University Press for the Royal Economic Society, 1971–1984).

the family doctor can really be quite a reputable fellow in his or her own way. In academic life one hears fleeting praise for breadth of scholarship, but no one doubts that scholarly depth is much better. The businessman has long been advised to take care of his own business. One of our more improbable metaphors holds that a cobbler should stick to his last. I have never encountered anyone who knew what a last is or was.

Whatever the case in other disciplines, there can be no doubt that in economics, specialization is the parent not only of boredom but also of irrelevance and error. Certainly this is so in all practical matters. Widespread influences, many from far outside the field as it is commonly defined for classroom convenience, bear on every important economic decision. So it is in monetary policy, tax policy, prices and wages policy, trade policy and all other government and private decisions. But the specialist, by his or her training, righteously excludes what it is convenient not to know. The specialized economist is thus spared the relatively modest expenditure of energy and intelligence that would bring most of economics and much of the relevant politics, social relations and psychology within his grasp.

The question of specialization in intellectual matters and its mind-saving role are central to an appreciation of John Maynard Keynes, by far the most influential economist of the twentieth century and, with Smith, Marx and possibly Ricardo, one of the three or four greatest economists who ever lived.

Keynes rejected specialization. His life and effort were guided by as diverse thought and experience as that of any person in modern times. Passing into the British Civil Service in 1906 with not the highest distinction in mathematics and economics — "The examiners presumably knew less than I did" — he became concerned with the trivial intricacies of currency and banking in India. On this he wrote a monograph, *Indian Currency and Finance,* and then immediately broke with professional practice. Any scholar of moderate capacity could have learned all that there was useful to know about the subject in around three months, perhaps less, and then, in the modern professional mode, have remained with it for most of his life and been celebrated in a modest way as its leading international authority. But Keynes's genius, many now feel his eccentricity, led him quickly to other matters, and no one ever went so far into so many. In each he was to find something that improved or expanded his knowledge of other subjects.

In no necessary order of importance his vocations and avocations included the following: his public career in the Treasury during two wars; his long association with King's College, Cambridge, of which he was the highly successful and, as a speculator, one must believe exceptionally lucky bursar; speculation with his own money, at first disastrous, then remunerative; the chairmanship of a major insurance company; journalism; support for the arts, leading to the establishment of the Cambridge Arts Theatre and the Arts Council of Great Britain; his adequately celebrated friendship with Lytton Strachey, Vanessa Bell, Virginia Woolf, Duncan Grant, Leonard Woolf — the Bloomsbury group; his equally celebrated love, first for men and then for Lydia Lopokova, whom he married ("Was there ever such a union of beauty and brains/ As when the lovely Lopokova married John Maynard Keynes?"); his interest in agriculture and particularly in pig farming, a subject on which he submitted a thoughtful paper to me on our first meeting when I was at the Office of Price Administration in the early days of World War II.

Finally, though much else might be mentioned, there were his books — his polemic against the Versailles Treaty and his volumes on economics, including, most especially, *The General Theory of Employment Interest and Money*, published in 1936. (His title eschews commas.) No one contemplating all this will think that Keynes denied himself knowledge from the full range of life and work. Bertrand Russell once thought he was spreading himself a bit thin, but he soon retreated from this position. Keynes's intellect, he said, was the "sharpest and clearest" he had ever known; he could run the risk.

That Keynes overspecialized will not occur to anyone contemplating the twenty-nine volumes of his writings now published, an enterprise of vast proportions accomplished with skill, imagination and great editorial conscience and fortitude. The first fourteen volumes reprint his major works and the discussion and defense that these provoked. The rest, labeled *Activities*, consist of letters, papers, public documents and published articles concerning and in support of his public, academic and personal preoccupations, including the letters, documents and editorials of others that elicited Keynes's comment or response.

I do not suppose that anyone will ever sit down and read all of these books unless, God forbid, it is for yet another life of Keynes, of which, for the time being at least, we have had or are having enough. Many of my generation have the advantage of having already read most of them, *A Treatise on Probability* generally apart. Some, like Keynes's two-volume *A Treatise on Money*, must now be read again with the knowledge that Keynes himself extensively abandoned the conclusions he reached there; few scholars have ever so jealously guarded the right to change their minds when argument or experience told them they were wrong. Some, particularly his *Essays in Biography* and *Essays in Persuasion*, are small works of art; his memoir of Mary Paley Marshall, wife of Alfred Marshall, in *Essays in Biography*, is one of the most engaging and affectionate pieces one is ever likely to read. He tells of Mary Marshall as the first woman lecturer ever in economics at Cambridge and how, after her husband's death, she became the "tutelary goddess" of his books and "of the rising generation of students." "So," Keynes continues, "in her seventy-fifth year, defying the University Regulations, by which it is now thought proper that we should all be deemed to be deceased at sixty-five, she was appointed Honorary Assistant Librarian of the Marshall Library of Economics; and so she continued for nearly twenty years." He goes on to tell how, as she approached ninety, she was induced to give up the bicycle that, with a blithe contempt for Cambridge traffic, she had ridden daily to work all those years. (In Cambridge at the time it was known that Keynes himself had confiscated it.)

Finally among the books, there is *The General Theory,* to which I shall return.

The material included in *Activities* cannot be so easily characterized. Some of it is fascinating; some is of purely historical interest, which is the nonhistorian's way of saying it is of very little interest to virtually anyone. Keynes was much in Washington in the war years, and to an American reader there are passages here that rank with Isaiah Berlin's brilliant reports on the contemporary scene and still others that are rich in interest for survivors among the younger economists who were in Washington at the time. The young men were then locked in a struggle with their older professional colleagues and especially with the business executives who had descended on the capital with a passionate commitment to business and economic policy as usual. There was a war, but that should not be the reason for any undue extension of government controls or the source of other inconvenience. Keynes was not so disposed; here is part of a 1941 letter to Walter Salant, then in the government and for long after a leading figure in the Brookings Institution:

> There is too wide a gap here in Washington between the intellectual outlook of the older people and that of the younger. But I have been greatly struck during my visit by the quality of the younger economists and civil servants in the Administration. . . . The war will be a great sifter and will bring the right people to the top. We have a few good people in London, but nothing like the *numbers* whom you can produce here.

Other letters and reports in *Activities* have to do with currency balances, payments problems and the personalities and attitudes of wartime Washington officials, many of whom are now, mercifully, forever forgotten. In writing to some of the less brilliant stars in this constellation, Edward Stettinius being a prominent example, Keynes abandoned the sterling truth of the Salant letter, as my generation would have seen it, and was, as needed, repellently flattering. In these years some squalid hack had written a book about Lend-Lease on which

Stettinius then placed his name, and Keynes wrote admiringly, but fulsomely, to the alleged author. He cannot have supposed that his note would ever be published.

But one should not dwell on such aberrations. The letters and documents detailing Keynes's positions over the years are in wonderfully forthright and clearheaded prose, with few concessions to political thimblerigging. On such matters as Britain's return to gold in the 1920s or the effort to escape devaluation in 1931, he refutes with unrelenting vigor the fashionable (and disastrous) beliefs, so called, of the grave members of the financial establishment in London. These were the men who, in pursuit of high principle, were willing to risk the social and political effects of severe deflation in order to keep the pound on the gold standard at its old parity. Here, and powerfully, Keynes's wider perspective on social and political consequences led him into dissent. One sometimes wonders, on reading these volumes, if anyone of opposing views escaped his correction. Certainly Winston Churchill as chancellor of the exchequer in 1925 did not. Speaking of Churchill's decision to return to gold, Keynes asks, "Why did he do such a silly thing?" and then answers his own question: "Partly, perhaps, because he has no instinctive judgment to prevent him from making mistakes; partly because, lacking this instinctive judgment, he was deafened by the clamorous voices of conventional finance; and, most of all, because he was gravely misled by his experts." That rather takes care of everyone. It is now known, incidentally, that Churchill did doubt the wisdom of the action.* It was, indeed, the error of the clamorous financial establishment and the experts.

Because there is so much of Keynes (including quite a bit that is peripheral), anyone trying to cover the entire range is tempted away from his central contributions — the matters on which he changed both economic and political thought and the course of history. In any consideration of the man and his work, three achievements, two of major and one of less durable effect, stand out.

The first, chronologically, was his powerful tract against the reparations clauses of the Versailles Treaty, *The Economic Consequences of the Peace*. Its argument that Germany could not, within the framework of the existing international monetary and exchange relationships, meet the claims made upon it is at least debatable. Étienne Mantoux, the son of Paul Mantoux, the great French economic historian, published a persuasive case against Keynes in 1944, a few months before his own death in World War II. If Germany had lowered its living standards —

---

*As a previous essay in this chapter tells. See "Further on Churchill and the Churchill Style," page 306.

what is now so casually and amiably called by the financial establishment a resort to austerity — the requisite trade balance might have been developed. The decisive question then, as in the debtor countries now, was whether the political structure of the new republic could take the strain. (It was also necessary then, as now, that other countries take the goods.)

What is less in doubt is the effect of Keynes's book on the public and political attitudes that came out of the war and the peace. Germany, partly and perhaps primarily as a consequence, ceased to be regarded as the offender in the 1914–1918 conflict and became, by wide if not complete agreement, the unfairly abused victim. In contrast, after 1945 Germany was held responsible, not least among the Germans themselves, for the devastation and death.

A further consequence of Keynes's book was that reparations after World War II were taken not in monetary claims but in kind. Perhaps — it was certainly my view at the time — this was worse. One had to know the reaction of the workers of a German industrial town to the removal of the equipment that accorded them their livelihood to see how depressingly cruel this alternative to Keynes could be.

The second and more important effect on history came seventeen years after *The Economic Consequences*. This was *The General Theory*. Unlike nearly all of Keynes's other writing, this volume is deeply obscure; perhaps had it been otherwise and had economists not been called upon to debate his meaning and intentions, it would not have been so influential. Economists respond well to obscurity and associated puzzlement. But the essential point in *The General Theory*, though intricately disguised, is wholly clear: the modern economy does not, as the once accepted theology held, tend automatically to optimal performance.

This, coming as it did after six years of depression and an even longer period of poor economic performance in Britain, cannot now seem an altogether astonishing point. Nonetheless, it broke in on the established structure of economic thought, as it was termed, with a glass-shattering effect. Not some recurrent and self-correcting aberration of the business cycle was here involved; in the absence of corrective action by the state, grave unemployment would be the norm. Production did not create its own sufficient demand; holding on to money — liquidity preference — could intervene to reduce demand. Then output would spiral down until privation forced a spending of revenue that was in balance with the supply of goods. Here equilibrium — the underemployment equilibrium — was re-established. There was much more than this, but this is the hard core.

It was again Keynes's eclecticism — the greatly questionable rejection of specialization — that helped him to this conclusion. Had he been a serious specialist, he would have excluded wage behavior, investment behavior and the business cycle from his analysis as being the business of other people. Given the flexible prices and costs of the competitive firm as commonly assumed, the equilibrium would still have been optimal.

It was also the paradoxical consequence of Keynes that he led to a new specialization in economics, one between microeconomics and macroeconomics — "micro" and "macro," in the regressive inner jargon of the economics profession. Microeconomics, as all know, deals with the presumptively still optimal performance of the firm, macroeconomics with the presumptively nonoptimal tendencies to underemployment or inflation of the economy as a whole. Specialization again disguises the high certainty of nonoptimal microeconomic performance — bureaucratic and other failures in the modern corporation — with a high probability of macroeconomic effect. The Keynesian lesson that all economic life is of a piece was quickly lost in the new accommodation to professional simplification and classroom convenience. But the notion of optimal overall performance did die forever. Nowhere has its death been celebrated so dramatically as in our own time by the Reagan administration, with its huge and stolidly defended Keynesian deficits. Keynes, should he return, would be astonished.

The third of Keynes's great contributions was to the Bretton Woods system, specifically the International Monetary Fund and (as it is called) the World Bank. The volumes about them in this collection contain a truly phenomenal discussion of postwar trade, employment, commodity, financial and other policies. There is also extended discussion of the policy toward Germany after its defeat in World War II, including a strenuous objection to the Morgenthau plan for the deindustrialization of the Reich. All this is richly documented and supported by vigorous, lucid argument and much forthright common sense.

These books were written during the years after Keynes had suffered his first severe heart attack and was threatened by the recurrence that eventually killed him. One cannot believe that he ever spared himself. Central is Keynes's hope for a stable, internationally managed monetary system after the war, with stable exchange rates providing a secure and predictable basis for international trade.

In anything like its original form and intent, the monetary system envisaged at Bretton Woods did not survive. What was hoped would be a stable relationship between currencies gave way to the reality of increasingly diverse internal economic policies or nonpolicies, some of them reflecting the freedom from fiscal orthodoxy that was allowed by Keynes and his general case that internal economic well-being and employment should not be sacrificed to external exchange stability.

The conflict between the two is still not fully accepted, certainly not by those who talk glibly about creating a new international monetary system. Stable or predictable exchange rates will never be possible so long as individual countries have different rates of inflation (or, more improbably, deflation) based on different monetary, fiscal and wage/price policies. This is recognized in some degree with respect to the poor countries of the world; they get instructions from the IMF on their fiscal and monetary policies without regard to how damaging the implementation of those policies may be. The surprising thing is how well international trade survives instability; it would be especially surprising to Keynes.

What came out of Bretton Woods differed in substantial, though not — as it turned out — decisive, measure from Keynes's proposals, but they, too, would have been a casualty of the diverse policies of economic sovereignty. This diminishes but by no means excludes interest in the discussion in these volumes of prospective international monetary arrangements; along with much else, one is reminded how concerned and responsible such discussion was at the time. Keynes and Bretton Woods raised false hopes, but these hopes were, nonetheless, the product of an intense interest on the part of the entire international community. It is a mood that seems all but archaic now.

5

SCHLESINGER,
SORENSEN,
JOHN F. KENNEDY*

(1965)

This review was written for British readers of The Observer, *some of whom, as indicated, thought these books by my friends a trifle too long. Perhaps more than a review, this is a defense. The hero here is John F. Kennedy. But like many heroes in the past, he is in competition for attention with his biographers.*

In the twenty years since the books first appeared, there have been enough Kennedy volumes to fill a small library. Looking again at the accounts by Sorensen and Schlesinger, I'm inclined to think that they are still the best and give as valid a picture as any since.

Theodore Sorensen was President Kennedy's closest adviser and co-worker, not only in the White House years, but for a long time before. Arthur Schlesinger knew Kennedy as a contemporary and casual friend before 1960, but they were not previously allied in political activities. Nor was he as close to the President in the White House as was Sorensen. The President regarded him, I think, less as an assistant than as a distinguished colleague to be consulted on points of history, used as an emissary to the liberal and literary community and assigned to particular tasks in the field of Latin American and United Nations affairs.

Each of these men has now written of the Kennedy years, and each in his book reflects his own particular experience and qualifications. Sorensen has far more to say of the campaign for the presidency, and he has a more intimate personal view of what happened afterward. He is not in doubt as to who of the President's entourage or appointees were inadequate, incompetent or devoted pre-eminently to themselves in their service. But he deals with such handicaps with the restraint of

*This was a review of *Kennedy* by Theodore C. Sorensen (New York: Harper and Row, 1965) and *A Thousand Days* by Arthur M. Schlesinger, Jr. (Boston: Houghton Mifflin, 1965).

a careful lieutenant. The commonplaces that all politicians use in speech — the obeisance to honesty, morality, intelligence and general political righteousness — slip more than occasionally into his text. In consequence, he is not at his best on the domestic issues, with which he was most concerned. On foreign policy, including the meeting with Khrushchev and the missile crisis, he is brilliant.

Mr. Schlesinger, on the other hand, has little to say on the presidential campaign. And though he deals at length with questions — Latin American policy in particular — with which he was especially involved, his book is much more that of a professional historian. He seems always to have the relevant facts at hand, and he is all but unique in his ability to order them into an engrossing narrative. He also brings a skeptical and informed judgment to bear on a wide range of matters from economics to foreign policy.

Unlike Sorensen, and reflecting his own greater degree of detachment, Schlesinger does not suffer gladly those, not excluding the fools, of whom he disapproves. Where Sorensen feels a certain commitment to the commonplace, Schlesinger has a modest obligation to the unimportant. The activities of the United States government are enormous in their variety. No one can tell about everything it did even in the brief span of three years, but Schlesinger is, at least slightly, impelled by his historian's conscience to try. He does not deal with design controversies within the Battle Monuments Commission or proposals for a bold new approach to prostitution in federally aided housing, but he touches on almost everything else.

Yet, admitting that an adequately disagreeable editor could have been useful here and there on both books, I cannot think that critics who have complained of their length have any case. Both men have written out of a deep sense of obligation to the man they served. Kennedy's accomplishments in those three short years were important. And they opened the way for much further and needed change. Surely it would have been unworthy and even irresponsible to have confined this history, as some British critics have recommended, to the few glamorous events — the meeting with Khrushchev, the great row over steel prices, the two Cuban episodes — that make particularly good or compelling reading.

In both books, not surprisingly, I found my attention strongly attracted to the accounts of those enterprises in which I was myself involved. My interest flagged slightly as I passed on to the exploits of Secretaries McNamara and Rusk, and it fell further as I came occasionally to someone I didn't know. It might have weakened yet more had I lived throughout the period in Stoke-on-Trent. So I will concede that the English reader should not feel bad if he doesn't get through both books right away. But historians would have reason to feel bad if either author had limited himself to what is fascinating to those only distantly involved.

It was the English critics, or some of them, who rebuked Mr. Sorensen for writing too much. The Americans, or some of them, abused Mr. Schlesinger for writing about the wrong things. He was far too candid. Was it right to cause heartaches for people still in office? Was it proper to reveal the intentions of a man now dead? Was it wise to discuss the substance of confidential conversations around the conference table?

Of course it was right. The only people with serious grounds for objection are those who reflect the oldest desire of public servants, especially those concerned with foreign policy, which is to have a license for decorous inaction or error. (I cite my own sordid example. Whenever, while in public office, I awakened to the knowledge that I had done something supremely silly, I found myself immediately speculating as to whether the whole matter could be made or kept secret or, at a minimum, kept out of the newspapers.) No one has suggested that any of Mr. Schlesinger's revelations are inaccurate. He is not accused of revealing military secrets. Surely public officials should not be protected from the publication of adverse comment on their performance while in office. Surely such comment by a President is particularly important; who was in a better position to judge? Journalists, scholars, commentators, publicists, anyone with a responsible concern for national affairs, should never join with their natural enemies to espouse secrecy and reticence.

Nor is there anything but good in reporting the conversations of public officials, including chiefs of state, after the fact. A man who will clam up because he is afraid that what he says will later be quoted is too craven to have anything worth saying. And that applies to visiting heads of state as to all others. The public official who lowers his voice and pleads for strict confidence is invariably getting ready to say something damaging to the public interest. If he fears he will be quoted, maybe he won't say it. So much the better.

Both Sorensen and Schlesinger served in the executive branch of the government, and as they write of these years, their natural opposition is the permanent official Establishment, especially in the field of foreign policy. This is highly visible in the case of Schlesinger, always discreetly in the background in the case of Sorensen. In the Establishment view, Kennedy was an annoyance. He was an idealist, not the practical friend of the regressive Latin American hierarchies; he didn't have the same reflex commitment to the cold war as did Dulles; he couldn't bring himself to sweep the terrors of nuclear conflict under the rug; he could never be put off by a formula or slogan, however sanctified by use.

I am not sure that here Messrs. Sorensen and Schlesinger are completely accurate in the selection of their target. My own impression is that the permanent Establishment would have accepted leadership. And the President has the right to appoint secretaries, under secretaries, numerous assistant secretaries and lesser officials to help provide this leadership and assume its risks. That is the *raison d'être* for political appointees. Quite a few of the people Kennedy appointed, however, did not think it their function to provide leadership or to absorb political criticism; they thought it their purpose to give the permanent Establishment a lesson in caution, cold war clichés and personal contentment.

The ideal situation for anyone in public life is one that provides protection in the present by secrecy and in the future by forbearance. Writers such as Schlesinger are a source of serious discomfort; those afflicted by what they write feel justified in excoriating them. But oddly enough in a world where so much goes wrong, some things go right. Reward and distinction nearly always accrue to the candid. Those who for a time are celebrated for discretion — for suppressing the truth — are forgotten. We should be glad that things are so arranged.

6

ROBERT KENNEDY ON
THE MISSILE CRISIS*

(1969)

Neither at the time nor afterward did I think the missile crisis the great and successful episode in our history it was thought by some. It showed, on the contrary, how fragile, almost negligible, is the issue of our existence when it passes under the control of domestic political exigency.

The heroes I here celebrate are the Kennedy brothers, Adlai Stevenson and the others who resisted the seemingly brave but, in reality, cowardly calls to go to, or over, the brink.

On Saturday, October 20, 1962, I had just arrived in London to give a lecture and, such things not being possible in New Delhi, had gone to see a Peter Ustinov play. When I came out of the theater, the papers had big black headlines about a Chinese invasion of India, and I made a suitable mental note that another political ambassador had been caught absent from his post at the moment of need. I wasn't therefore especially surprised when, about three o'clock in the morning, the duty officer at the London Embassy awoke me with a message from President Kennedy conveying the same thought in rather sardonic terms and asking that I return forthwith to India. This I did. On arriving, I learned, however, that it was the Russians in Cuba, not the Chinese in the Himalayas, who had induced the President's message. He wanted me to persuade Prime Minister Nehru to react sympathetically and use his influence accordingly.

Though I did so, there could have been few Americans, in or out of office, who were less involved than I in the missile crisis of the days following. The Chinese were making great progress in the mountains.

---

*This was a review, originally published in *Book World* of *The Chicago Tribune*, of *Thirteen Days: A Memoir of the Cuban Missile Crisis* by Robert F. Kennedy (New York: Norton, 1969).

Someone had to worry about an infinity of questions, including the military reaction of the Indians, the foreign policy of Bhutan, and how to keep under wraps our own crusaders (fortunately not numerous) who saw in India's involvement with China an exciting new break-through in the cold war. Additionally, our communications system with the State Department was monopolized by the Cuban crisis, as was the attention of everyone in Washington. I knew only what the headlines told until long after the fact.

When I did have time to worry about what was happening back home, it was, as ever, about the peculiar dynamics of the White House crisis meeting. This has the truly terrible tendency always to favor the most reckless position, for that is the position that requires the least moral courage. The man who says, "Let's move in with all we have and to hell with the consequences," will get applause, and he knows it. In reality, he is a coward who fears that in urging a more deliberate policy, he will invite the disapprobation of his colleagues or will later be accused of advocating a policy of weakness. Normally, also, he is aided by his inability to foresee, or even to imagine, the consequences of the action he advocates. In contrast, the man who calls for caution, a close as-sessment of consequences, an effort to understand the opposing point of view, especially if Communist, and who proposes concessions must have great courage. He is a real hero and rare.

I would have worried more in 1962 had I then known with what classical precision these tendencies were working themselves out in Washington. We know it now from this fascinating memoir by a central participant that recalls those perilous days. The generals, with the major exception of Maxwell Taylor (who later and sadly succumbed to the advocates of sanguinary action in Vietnam and so blotted the end of a well-regarded career), were all for the easy heroics. So was one group of civilians, who, like the generals, yearned to be known as men of hard-boiled masculine decision. They urged not air raids on the missile sites but, for purposes of scholarly gloss, a "surgical strike." There can, in history, have been few more appalling examples of the self-deluding power of words. Those concerned knew about air power, or should have. They knew, accordingly, that there was no way of bombing the missile sites without attacking all of the surrounding acreage and almost certainly missing some of the missiles. The medical counterpart of a surgical air strike would be an operation by a surgeon with cataracts and wearing ski mittens, who, in moving to excise a lung cancer, was fairly likely to make his first incision into the large intestine.

On the other side were the men with enough moral courage to consider the consequences — Robert Kennedy, Robert McNamara, George Ball, Adlai Stevenson and, before all, the President himself. In particular, there was Adlai Stevenson, who suggested trading some obsolete nuclear weapons in Turkey (which the President had already twice ordered removed) for similar action by the Russians in Cuba. (It has since been said on ample authority that the President would have removed those missiles if that had been necessary for a peaceful bargain. And they were taken out almost immediately after the missile crisis.) As one reads this memorandum, it is nearly impossible to imagine anyone opposing these views — and those who did must now have a certain problem in explaining it to themselves.

The most chilling thing about this book is the reflection it prompts on what would have happened if the men of moral courage had not been present — or if the President's disposition had been not to uphold but to overrule them. And it is disconcerting to consider how the political position of an administration, one more moderate than its Republican opposition, was juxtaposed to the survival of the country, even of mankind. I don't know what insanity caused the Soviets to send the missiles to Cuba, and especially after showing commendable caution about the deployment of this gadgetry in far less dangerous locations. But once they were there, the political needs of the Kennedy administration urged it to take almost any risk to get them out; temporizing would have been politically disastrous. Yet national safety called for a very deliberate policy — *for* temporizing. In the full light of later history, it called for an even more cautious policy than the one that Kennedy pursued. Again we see how frayed and perilous are the threads on which existence depends.

Robert Kennedy, perhaps it is needless to say, wrote this memorandum himself, and it is done with economy of style and no slight narrative power. With all his other talents, he was a very good writer. This makes it especially sad that the publisher, no doubt in order to retrieve an investment in the manuscript, has made it a monument to bloated bad taste. To what should have been a compact and powerful booklet, he has added not one but two unnecessary forewords and a random medley of photographs — an Air Force RF101 in flight, a Navy F8U at rest, Dean Rusk about to take off. He has then put great white spaces between the highly artificial chapters and about a half inch of paper between the lines of type. Finally, all available documents, omitting only the original articulation of the Monroe Doctrine and the final act of the Punte del Este Conference, are included, also between wide margins. The result is essentially a pamphlet, but it has been made available for what would be an adequately triumphant price for the average book. If in the Norton publishing firm there is a Mr. Norton, Virginia, he should be ashamed of himself.

7

CHESTER BOWLES*

(1971)

Chester Bowles, who died in the spring of 1986, had a twenty-year battle with Parkinson's disease, an affliction that left him almost totally disabled and without means of vocal communication. History has not, I think, been as gracious as I had here predicted and hoped. The combination of long illness and long silence, together with the Reagan reaction against so much of that for which he stood, took him both off the scene and out of the history. This all who knew his efforts and his achievements must truly regret.

Truth, not unconvincing humility, is the greatest virtue, and, accordingly, I may observe that I am better qualified than any man alive to review a book on the public life of Chester Bowles. He succeeded me in *de facto* responsibility for price control in World War II. (I was in charge of prices until just before he became head of the Office of Price Administration as a whole.) He preceded and followed me as ambassador to India. We worked together in the presidential campaigns of 1956 and (in lesser measure) of 1960, and in the early months of the Kennedy administration in 1961. He is a friend, which is a disadvantage only if the book in question is bad; only then do you have to consider whether the author should get the truth from you or someone else. This, fortunately, is a good book. It is the story of a fascinating career in public office — one combining brilliant successes with sudden, sad and sometimes heartbreaking setbacks, when the author succumbed to men who were, by an infinity, his inferiors.

A case could be made, and I am more than prepared to make it, that Bowles was the best civilian administrator of World War II. When

*This was a review, originally published in *The New York Times Book Review*, of *Promises to Keep: My Years in Public Life, 1941–1969* by Chester Bowles (New York: Harper and Row, 1971).

he took over at OPA in mid-1943, the price, rationing and rent policies that were to serve for the duration were well established, as was the basic organization. We had done well enough in a technical way. The trouble was that our public, and especially our political, relations were atrocious, and the whole stabilization policy was in mortal danger as a result. On price control I had shown an outstanding talent for alienating politicians and business executives. Leon Henderson, who had departed some months earlier after rendering brilliant, innovative service in setting up the agency, had shown a more modest ability of the same sort. A number of my colleagues and subordinates also had a genius for angering anyone they encountered — usually by a moving display of superior moral tone. When Bowles took over, he proved to be equally unyielding in his defense of the public interest in general and of price control in particular, all the while holding the lobbyists at bay. But at the same time he won the grudging respect of the Congress and the positive affection of the public. He was candid, persuasive, compelling. Although there is a business myth to the contrary, OPA was, to the end — as the polls unequivocally told — the most beloved of the public agencies. People, not surprisingly, knew it was on their side.

It is my impression that Bowles is now regarded as the best, or anyhow the most imaginative, governor of Connecticut in the years after the war. And certainly he was something different and exceptional as an ambassador. Although the governments of the United States and India have a natural talent for annoying each other, Bowles overcame these handicaps on his first tour and raised his job to that of unofficial counselor and confessor to the Indian government. (All of us who followed lived off the capital he had accumulated.) This too, considering that ambassadorships are positions of some grandeur but slight power, was no minor accomplishment.

The Bowles achievements were built, first of all, on a quick and wide-ranging intelligence, which is monitored by the unsentimental views of his very intelligent wife. This intelligence drives an almost painful desire to make things happen. And for making them happen, Bowles has, in turn, a nearly unlimited faith in the possibilities of public persuasion. No one, in his view, is so benighted that he is beyond reach of a convincing memorandum or a good, long, persuasive talk — although it is possible that, on mature reflection, he might wish to make an exception for Dean Rusk, the Alsop brothers and Senator Robert A. Taft.

The qualities that account for Bowles's successes are, as might be expected, clearly in evidence in this book. Its primary emphasis is on the policies for which the author battled and the arguments that he deployed. He had a much greater ability to get a problem into comprehensible form than most men in public life; where FDR paraphrased to make an issue seem understandable, Bowles always kept the real situation in view. The result is a long book, but it could have been longer still; a more careful effort to relate the week-to-week happenings in which the author participated or of which he had highly privileged knowledge would have made it even better.

So much for the success story. A possibly more remarkable and engaging feature of this memoir is the way Bowles deals with his failures — his defeat for re-election as governor in 1950; the Byzantine operation by Democratic State Chairman John Bailey and his hoplites that awarded the 1958 Senate nomination to Thomas J. Dodd, a statesman whom historians will celebrate only for his spacious cupidity; and, most heartbreaking of all, the appalling decision by President Kennedy to throw Bowles out of the State Department in the autumn of 1961 after he had proved himself the only man with an inclination to change the men and policies that already, at the Bay of Pigs, had shown an exquisite potential for disaster. But while this part of the story is fascinating, I am not at all sure that it leaves the right impression. Bowles is at great pains in all of these episodes to understand his own role, and he ends up each time putting a great deal of blame on himself. Although this is morally commendable, and a model for LBJ to emulate in his forthcoming memoirs, it is far too easy on his friends and also his enemies.

The truth is that Bowles's liberal friends failed him in moments of crisis. His courage and his conscience repeatedly took him into dangerous territory. And his idealism and faith in persuasion (a persuasion that could be uncomfortably prolix) made him seem too good to be effective. So men concerned with their own safety or with trying to prove that, though liberals, they were practical, tough and hardheaded left him in the lurch. And the way was open for the triumphs of his enemies — in their time, Tom Dodd and Dean Rusk.

The failure of the liberals in 1961 was particularly unforgivable. Chester Bowles was the first member of the liberal establishment (unless I could make some claim) to come out for Kennedy, and JFK responded by designating him his foreign policy adviser. Bowles then became under secretary of state under Rusk, a man who had never previously met Kennedy and who had made no effort on his behalf. After taking office, Bowles moved with characteristic energy to introduce new faces into the department and the embassies, to retire the time servers and the more egregious of the cold warriors, to reform the aid program and the Latin American policy and, above all, to break away from the frozen militarism of the Dulles era. In consequence, he came quickly to be regarded by old guard diplomats as a threat to all they held dear and, worse still, to their jobs. So, with Rusk's acquiescence and perhaps help, they decided to get rid of him, and they succeeded.

Bowles was sacked on the grounds that the department wasn't working — it wasn't responding promptly and imaginatively to the great issues of the times — and that, of all things, it was his fault. On an otherwise pleasant Sunday afternoon, following a football game earlier that weekend in New Haven, Rusk called in his under secretary and gave him a press release announcing his promotion to ambassador without function. Prior to that time the captive columnists of the Pentagon and the foreign policy establishment, in accordance with the peculiar ethics of this branch of journalism, had done a very competent job of fingering Bowles for extinction.

So much Bowles tells, and with a remarkable absence of rancor. He doesn't tell of the failure of his friends — Galbraith, Abram Chayes, Tom Hughes, possibly Arthur Schlesinger and other liberals — to rally adequately to his side. We did protest in one way or another, but we should have responded to the advance warning from the columnists with indignant threats or promises to go too. If the department couldn't abide Bowles, we weren't likely to accomplish much.

While he exculpates his friends, Bowles does express mild discontent with the performance of his own appointees, who, though they didn't double-cross him, at least deserted his cause with a celerity they had never revealed in handling their official duties. I've elsewhere celebrated the most enchanting case — that of Phillips Talbot, whom Bowles, with some encouragement from me, took from an obscure academic job involving educational exchange and put in charge of the India, Pakistan and Middle East section in the department. It was an area, we thought, where the Dulles treaties, supplies of arms and attacks on neutrality had been especially inimical. Talbot, a charming and agreeable citizen, turned out to be one of the most contented cold warriors of them all. He deserted his patron and presently, when Bowles went back to India, became the man to whom Bowles reported. In that position he righteously but consistently undercut the ambassador on arms to the subcontinent before ending his own career in Athens as envoy to the Greek colonels. Bowles confines himself in the book to saying that he had been made unhappy by Talbot. He is almost equally gentle with John Bailey, Dean Rusk, U. Alexis Johnson (who was appointed deputy under secretary over Bowles's objections and who served as adjutant general for the defenders of the Dulles legacy) and the White House people who cooperated in his ouster. Possibly he is too easy on Kennedy, for certainly the President, on this occasion, was wrong.

Here, I think, is another reason for Bowles's failures. He was too nice, and people, knowing this, didn't fear him sufficiently. Over the years two men of broad political experience, Averell Harriman and Chester Bowles, have advocated roughly the same policies. Both early on reached the conclusion that knee-jerk anti-Communism was not a policy, that we must learn to live with the Communist world, that to allow the Pentagon to dominate foreign affairs was an inspired formula for disaster. Both were liberals who rejected cold war liberalism. Both were very much disposed to translate their beliefs into action. Even in the days when to be sensible along those lines exposed a man to serious criticism, Harriman's views were treated with respect by hostile politicians, bureaucrats and columnists, while all, by contrast, jumped on Bowles. This was at least partly because Harriman wasn't and isn't so nice; his disapproval of men and policies is categorical, rarely a secret and influential. Washington is a place where men praise courage and then act on elaborate personal cost-benefit calculations. There was cost in getting crossed up with Averell Harriman but not with Chester Bowles.

This provides occasion for reflecting on an old problem. It is already certain that, as the historians will decide matters, Bowles will not finish last. On the contrary, he will finish well ahead of his competition. But it is also clear that, as things are now arranged, nice guys do get tripped up along the way.

LYNDON JOHNSON*

(1971)

There have been few men whose acquaintance, perhaps I can say friendship, I enjoyed more over the years than Lyndon Johnson — until the terrible trauma of the Vietnam war. As I indicate in this piece, we had somewhat similar backgrounds. We were of nearly the same age, arrived in Washington at nearly the same time, had in those days the same singleminded commitment to Franklin D. Roosevelt. Johnson's initiatives on behalf of civil rights and against poverty were greater — on civil rights, needless to say, far greater — than those of FDR. One measure of their effect is the controversy they still provoke, the inspired attempts still being made to show that the accomplishments against poverty did not, in fact, end it. (Mention is never made of how much there would now be in the absence of that effort.) Annulling this in the Johnson history was the Vietnam war. Perhaps this review does something to put the record right. It does, in any case, celebrate both the political prestidigitation and the accomplishments that we all so admired.

Around Iona Station, Ontario, in the early part of this century my father, William Archibald Galbraith, was a man of about the same public stature, I would say, as Samuel Ealy Johnson in the neighborhood of Johnson City, Texas. He was a farmer as well as a part-time politician and probably a bit poorer than Johnson. The Ontario Agricultural College, which I attended in the same years that Lyndon Baines Johnson was at Southwest Texas State, was no better calculated than its Texas counterpart to give a student a sense of academic superiority; I stirred some unjustified local resentment years ago by describing it as perhaps the least transcendent and certainly the least expensive center

*This was a review, originally published in *The Saturday Review*, of *The Vantage Point: Perspectives of the Presidency, 1963–1969* by Lyndon Baines Johnson (New York: Holt, Rinehart and Winston, 1971).

of academic excellence in the English-speaking world. In the ensuing years I have lived comfortably on the fringe of the Harvard and New England establishment, though with only a fraction of the intimacy of association that LBJ has had with the Washington (and Dallas, Houston, Fort Worth and Austin) power elites.

The reason I make these comparisons is that early in the pages of his book Lyndon Johnson says that he has always been disadvantaged and, to a degree, persecuted by the Eastern aristocracy and meritocracy because of his unfortunate rural background. The reviews of the book by various members of the Eastern literary community could easily intensify his feelings. I am able to remind him that this one is by an equally authentic member of our particular counterculture.

Partly for this reason, no doubt, there is a great deal in the book I would commend or defend. One of the first reactions of the critics to the proofs, I hear, has been the feeling that very little is new. It is not so. New to all of us who have known, listened to and (more often than not) rejoiced in LBJ's polemical skills over the years is the soft-spoken kindness of the volume. He is simply not sore at anyone; he treats everyone (almost everyone) with a kind of avuncular magnanimity that is nearly without parallel in political memoirs and is totally without precedent in his own past practice. Only the most careful reader will get a whiff of the vintage Johnson — as when he comments on Clark Clifford's urging consideration in 1968 for 500,000 to a million *more* men for Vietnam; or when LBJ's relations with Robert Kennedy are described as usually "cordial though never overly warm"; or when Townsend Hoopes, who left the Pentagon to become an outspoken opponent of the Vietnam war, gets omitted entirely from the index and rates only a generic mention in the text as one of several uninformed lower-echelon Pentagon civilians; or when Senator Fulbright is called more difficult to please with peaceful gestures than Ho Chi Minh.

New also is the picture of Johnson as Hamlet, a man tortured by the call of public duty on one hand and a rending aversion on the other to anything smacking of ambition or interfering with family, grandchildren, fireside or ranch. It is hard to believe how badly LBJ always wanted to escape from the distractions of politics and public office. In point of fact, no one will.

The most surprising manifestation of this unexpected trait was in 1964, when Johnson, by then President, had great difficulty deciding whether to run for a full term. He says he didn't make up his mind until the Democrats had been in convention for two days at Atlantic City. It was a state of the presidential mind that, in our innocence, none of us along the boardwalk ever suspected. Had his decision gone the other way — had Lady Bird, whom he credits with persuading him, been instead adverse — the effect when it reached that convention hall would have been less than that of a hundred-foot tidal wave over the waterfront, but not much.

When LBJ is concocting a whopper of this glorious magnitude, you can clearly sense the glow of professional pride. Perhaps one should be less admiring than I am. It is art for art's sake; you find that it doesn't always interfere with the truth. In this case, only a few pages on, he details the Byzantine or, more accurately, the Johnsonian (for one doubts that anyone in Byzantium was quite his equal) maneuvers by which in the weeks preceding his decision he had worked to win general support for the vice president he wanted and to ensure that it wasn't Robert Kennedy, whom he didn't want. (In another imaginative passage he explains that personally Bobby was just fine and most welcome, but he would have weakened the ticket down in the border states.) For someone who wasn't sure he was running, hadn't yet surrendered to his wife, this was surely unnecessary work. I can testify that it took up a good bit of presidential time, because, for a brief moment in 1964, I was a broker on this matter between the President and Robert Kennedy. I discharged my duties with such inspired impartiality that I convinced each principal that I was the hopeless dupe of the other.

Besides the news of LBJ's comprehensive rejection of worldly ambition, much more is new. He took almost no interest in what the Democrats were doing at Chicago in 1968. He had no thought of firing (or easing out) Bob McNamara as secretary of defense. And much more. One must understand LBJ's rather special approach to history: his test is not so much what happened as what he believes he can persuade other people to believe, and he is ever an optimist. Accordingly, to say that his book is without originality is to reflect a very narrow view.

There is another and more substantial virtue to this memoir — one that reflects Lyndon Johnson at his best. He has organized the material not chronologically but by the major efforts of his administration — civil rights legislation, federal support for education, help to housing, the war on poverty, the model cities program and defeat of the Communists (usually referred to as aggressors) in Panama, the Dominican Republic and Vietnam.

His account of everything except the defeat of aggression is wonderfully stamped by the Johnson personality and shows why, on domestic issues, he was (or could have been) the most effective Chief Executive since FDR. He had, as he here makes clear, a superb sense of priorities — of the urgency of the problems of race, the cities, education, medical care and the poor. He was far better than John F. Kennedy (perhaps even than Franklin Roosevelt) in winning the requisite response from the Congress. Toward the end of the book, in one of its best passages, he outlines the Johnson techniques for wringing action from a reluctant congressman. No one can doubt that it is by a master of the craft. It was hard work, which he did not delegate. He got on the phone himself — or got the backslider down to the White House for some intense education. He also made sure that the congressional leaders were informed of legislation in advance and got proper credit when it passed. And, finally, when he got what he wanted, he put excellent men in charge. His appointments at the Departments of Housing and Urban Development and Health, Education and Welfare — Bob Weaver and especially Robert Wood, Charles Haar, John Gardner and Wilbur Cohen — were among the best public officials and administrators ever. The book takes an earthy, energetic pride in these achievements, and the pride is justified.

The Johnson competence was not, of course, confined to domestic matters. If his own intelligence and experience were involved, he was equally good on foreign policy. One example greatly impressed me. Back in the Eisenhower years the United States had entered into an agreement (Public Law 480) to supply India with grain against the deposit of rupees. The action combined compassion with alleviation of our own wheat surplus. It also always worried me, for it appreciably reduced the feeling of urgency with which Indian politicians and officials approached the problem of the domestic food supply, but I never got beyond speeches warning of the danger. In 1966, when the Indians again had a bad year, they appealed to Johnson for help. The President sensed the danger, and he supplied the food but this time under short-term arrangements of considerable uncertainty. The criticism both at home and from India was bitter, as he here tells. However, his knowledge of agriculture and politicians had been unerring. He helped at least a little to increase the sense of compulsion behind the Green Revolution in India.

Alas, on all foreign policy issues this personal knowledge was not available. There will be many explanations of Lyndon Johnson, and since he is a complicated man, most people will feel that the explanations must be complicated, too. It is my thought that a simple one will survive: he was excellent on the problems of which he was personally in command and which included, in particular, anything having to do with the United States alone. He failed when he had to rely on advisers. Until he became vice president, he had not seriously bothered his mind with most questions of foreign policy. So here he relied not on himself but on the cold war civilians and the military, and it was fatal. This book confirms my view.

By 1963, when Lyndon Johnson became President, it was evident, not to a few but to many, that the automatic anti-Communism of the old foreign policy establishment, including the old Dulles group in the

State Department and their allies in the Pentagon, was a formula for disaster. These men saw Communism as an all-embracing conspiracy reaching out to every country on earth. Believing this, they attributed to the Communists any violent reaction to grievance anywhere in the world. They dismissed contrary evidence as erroneous and contrary opinion as naïve. Since they viewed any spread of Communism as inimical to the American interest and believed that all disorder was caused by Communists, there was a powerful case for American intervention whenever there was any insurrection anywhere.

The danger of this view was widely accepted. It was the principal reason President Kennedy had not intended to continue Dean Rusk as secretary of state. It was the subject of the first conversation I had with Johnson as President on the day after Kennedy's murder. That we were being victimized by this doctrine was taken for granted by Arthur Schlesinger, Richard Goodwin, Carl Kaysen, more cautiously by Averell Harriman, by such senators as Wayne Morse, Ernest Gruening and William Fulbright and by numerous others. The problem was not the doctrine but how to deal with it in a bureaucracy and a country that had been so dangerously oversold on the simplicities of the cold war.

Sadly, Lyndon Johnson bought both the bureaucratic advisers and the doctrine, and he remains firm on the subject in this book. In 1964, some American children in the Canal Zone raised the flag in front of the high school. Riots followed, and the Panama government used the ensuing disorders for another try at revising the unequal treaty on the canal. Rusk promptly saw the long arm of international Communism operating by way of Castro in the disorder. LBJ still does: "Irritation over the unfortunate flag incident was understandable, but the Panamanian students' reaction had served as a trigger to obviously well-planned anti-American demonstrations." It was easy to blame the Communists, not the ancient grievance over the canal. After the military descent on the Dominican Republic in 1965, there was an unparalleled effort to identify as Communists those who had led the insurgency and thus occasioned the action. It failed. As later writers have sufficiently established, the disciplined Communist cadres imagined by Washington simply did not exist. But they are back and powerfully in command in this book.

Regarding Vietnam, the doctrine of the omnipotent, centrally inspired, all-pervasive Communist conspiracy gets its full play. It is vital to a larger strategy of justification for our involvement in that unhappy country to which LBJ, one senses, has given a good deal of thought. The first element of this justification consists in giving the responsibility for the Vietnam war firmly to John F. Kennedy. The opening paragraph of the third chapter begins:

As Air Force One carried us swiftly back to Washington after the tragedy in Dallas, I made a solemn private vow: I would devote every hour of every day during the remainder of John Kennedy's unfulfilled term to achieving the goals he had set. That meant seeing things through in Vietnam as well as coping with the many other international and domestic problems he had faced. I made this promise not out of blind loyalty but because I was convinced that the broad lines of his policy, in Southeast Asia and elsewhere, had been right. They were consistent with the goals the United States had been trying to accomplish in the world since 1945.

I have always thought that my Kennedy friends who held that JFK would never have done what Johnson did in Vietnam were being unfair; one cannot have the knowledge that allows one to compare what a dead man would have done with what a living one actually did. This book squares the accounts.

The next part of the justification consists in assuming that there is external inspiration for *everything* that has happened in Vietnam. It is all part of a larger Communist strategy; there is no civil war. The Viet Cong are scarcely mentioned; nationalism is not a factor. The question that arises as to who guides the ultimate international strategy now that Moscow and Peking have fallen out is resolved, not too satisfactorily, by identifying international Communist aggression with Hanoi and not going back of that small capital. But the military ambition of international-*cum*-Hanoi Communism remains great. It extends to Malaysia, Thailand and beyond — though no longer to the beaches of Hawaii. At the time of the Indonesian coup, General Suharto and his colleagues were encouraged to fight for their lives against the Communists by the knowledge that we were in Saigon, only a thousand or so miles away. So the conflict with Hanoi still has global implications. And were it not for the outside intervention, South Vietnam would always have been as peaceful as a church social — and especially under the democratic government we helped to create. There has been speculation as to whether this history had to be rewritten in light of *The Pentagon Papers*. On this I have no opinion. But the chapter on how successfully we promoted free elections in Vietnam could have done with some updating.

The third element of the justification, the initial error of intervention having been covered by the need to abort the international conspiracy, is the protection of American lives. Some boys having been sent there, more were always needed to give them help; bombing was always needed for their protection. The decisions to send reinforcements were consistently unanimous, a not surprising result since dissenters among LBJ's advisers were first excluded and then encouraged to depart. George Ball was an exception. He gets some mild praise here as a devil's advocate but also as a man who, however reluctantly, went along.

The final element in the justification was the continuing intransigence of Hanoi. Repeated overtures were made to them; their response
was invariably negative. Of this intransigence, Mr. Johnson is clearly
convinced. And he is almost convincing. (I confess that I have never
fully shared the contrary belief that the North Vietnamese would have
seized any excuse to rush to the conference table.) But we were bombing
them, as LBJ makes clear, to make the war costly — to make them see
the greater wisdom of negotiating. The refusal of a country to respond
to peace overtures under such circumstances might be intransigence;
it could also be a refusal to be intimidated. Intransigence we deplore;
refusal to knuckle under to force we understand and applaud. We
understand it even better when we view Vietnam as one country and
not two, and when we suppose, also, that the North Vietnamese see
themselves as the custodians of the national interest in opposition to
the forces that once upheld the French and are now being upheld by
the Americans. No more than our original need to intervene do these
possibilities get debated in this volume.

The fact is that, like the effort itself, LBJ's defense of his Vietnam
policy is a misfortune, but it demonstrates the larger truth I have
already mentioned: where Lyndon Johnson's own knowledge and instincts were decisive, he was a good President. And he is good enough,
as memoirists go, in telling about it. He was misguided when he got
into the hands of the cold war strategists, and he still is when recalling
Vietnam.

9

AVERELL HARRIMAN*

(1971)

In earlier essays in this book I wondered why God, when He chose to award immortality, began with J. Edgar Hoover and General Francisco Franco. That speculation is now otiose. No one will wonder adversely as regards Averell Harriman; ninety-five at this writing, he is a monument to the wisdom of divine judgment in this important matter.

I will return to the Dulles errors and aberrations here mentioned in a later review dealing with the brothers and their sister.

In May of 1959, I was in the Soviet Union, as was Averell Harriman — a visit of which he tells in this book. One day we went together to see the Zim auto works on the outskirts of Moscow. As we were being ushered through the plant, word of the visitor spread along the assembly lines. Workers by the scores and then by the hundreds abandoned their machines to surround Harriman, first to shake hands and then to demand a speech. It was evident that they knew, as by now do most Americans, that he is a very great man and, among oher things, our most effective exponent of Soviet-American coexistence — for which one may read "existence."

Harriman's reputation depends on a nearly total lack of interest in doctrine, combined with a passionate concern for practical results. It is nearly fifty years since he first went to Russia for the highly practical purpose of taking up a manganese-mining concession under Lenin's New Economic Policy. Ever since, when he has thought it possible to work something out with the Soviet government, he has tried. When he has thought the Soviets wrong or overreaching, he has said so (he has been equally unsparing on his own government), and as Harriman's

*This was a review, originally published in *Life* magazine, of *America and Russia in a Changing World* by W. Averell Harriman (New York: Doubleday, 1971).

friends and co-workers have long known, he has never been able to leave people in any doubt as to his meaning. During World War II, he was deeply concerned with getting the Russians the equipment they needed to defeat Hitler's armies. And he was equally determined to keep peace within the Grand Alliance. But he was also the first man to warn influentially that after the war Stalin would stake out a major claim in Eastern Europe. This he neither excused nor defended. He was not for starting a new war, but he was for bringing all of our considerable bargaining power to bear in opposition. It was said in those days that Harriman was generally adverse where the Soviet Union was concerned.

In fact, then — as before and since — he was merely adhering to his conviction that with the Soviets much can be accomplished by honest, friendly, unsentimental negotiation and nothing at all by hostile rhetoric, warlike threats or efforts to persuade their leaders of our infinite capacity for kindness. This belief dominated his efforts to get peace in Laos and to win Soviet support for peacemaking in Vietnam and his crowning achievement, the partial test ban treaty. (He also had a lot to do with getting the treaty through the Senate.) We should pause on occasion to be grateful for the perils that no longer afflict us. One of these is radioactive fallout — indeed, the term has almost disappeared from use. The thanks are due on our side chiefly to Averell Harriman.

But he is not without recognition on the Soviet side. It speaks well for the Soviet leaders that, his candor notwithstanding, no other American has so enjoyed their confidence and respect. And it says something for Soviet society that the workers that day in Moscow were so well able to identify a friend.

This book is Harriman talking about a half century of doing business with the Russians. It is clearheaded, balanced, candid and interesting. It is, in fact, exactly like a Harriman conversation, which, in some sense, it is. The book began as a series of lectures given at Lehigh University, and it includes questions put by the students, along with Harriman's replies. Its principal fault is in being too short, which is also in character. Harriman's interest has always been in making things happen, and it still is. To dwell at any length on the past, and particularly on his own role therein, seems to him a ridiculous exercise in personal indulgence.

The peculiar genius of American foreign policy over the past two decades has consisted in putting the wrong man in charge. Being frightened of the Soviets, we have assumed that safety lay with someone who was a doctrinaire enemy of Communism — who was powerfully gripped by its omnipotence and wickedness. More remarkably, real expertise in foreign policy has been thought to be associated with such an attitude. We could not have been more wrong. As this book makes clear, such a selection in the case of John Foster Dulles brought the perils of brinksmanship; the fraudulent promise of liberation for Eastern Europe, with its tragic consequences for the Hungarians; the incredible condemnation of neutrality as immoral; the military pacts with the indigent nations of the world, which brought security neither to them nor to us and burdensome expense to both; and, with all else, our habit of excessive reliance on military power. It could be said that it brought the culminating disaster of the Vietnam war. The trouble with those who are wedded to doctrine is that the doctrine is likely to be proved wrong and the marriage persists.

Better by far that we have practical men. It would have been best of all, in these past years, if we had had Harriman. He had the background, the experience, the political stature, the respect of other world leaders, the unparalleled skill as a negotiator and the habit of bringing negotiations to a successful conclusion. (A great many diplomats have an existential view of negotiations; the pleasure is in the process.) And on the substance of the matters needing negotiation — the hopelessness of our enterprise in Indochina, our need to find some way of limiting the nuclear arms race, the need to live with the Communist world — nearly all now agree that he was right. If he had been secretary of state through the 1960s, he would have powerfully resisted the Indochina adventure. It is hard to imagine that our involvement there would have enlarged and extended against the opposition of so effective a man. If the Vietnam war had been avoided, the Democrats would still be in power. And since he is the most durable and indefatigable of public servants, it is quite likely that Harriman would still be heading the State Department. What a mistake we made; how much we missed!

10

SENATOR PAUL DOUGLAS*

(1972)

One day in the autumn of 1966, I had a call for help from Richard Wade, now a professor at the City University of New York, who was then serving in the re-election campaign of Paul Douglas, the senior senator from Illinois but referred to, on occasion, as the senior senator of the United States. Douglas was in a close race with Charles H. Percy, one of his former students at the University of Chicago. I responded; with Wade I campaigned in a small plane from Carbondale to the Chicago lakefront, primarily in the college and university towns. It was evident by the end of the journey that Paul Douglas's political career was over. Little concerned with foreign policy, he had gone along in a mostly passive way with the Vietnam disaster. This was the cause throughout our tour of numerous hostile questions and reactions. He had become another and different casualty, I felt, of that miserable war. There was a great deal more to him, as I here try to tell.

Joseph Schumpeter, an economist of a slightly earlier generation than Paul Douglas's, a more fashionable but possibly less useful member of the profession, used to tell his classes at Harvard, as I have elsewhere noted, that, as a young man in Vienna, he had set his mind on being the greatest scholar, the greatest lover and the greatest general of his time. He would then add, with an appropriate expression of sorrow, that such were the circumstances of the Austrian Republic following World War I that there was no opportunity for a military career. Douglas, with three different and more conservative goals in life, succeeded in all of them. He was one of the best and most influential economists of his time. He ranks, with Senators George Norris, Robert F. Wagner and the two Robert M. La Follettes, among the most influential legis-

---

*This was a review, originally published in *The Progressive*, of *In the Fullness of Time* by Paul H. Douglas (New York: Harcourt Brace Jovanovich, 1972).

lators of the century. And, enlisting in the Marine Corps at the age of fifty, he had a military career that was not only unique but heroic.

Douglas's autobiography, *In the Fullness of Time*, covers all three professions, and it is fascinating. From an impecunious childhood in Maine, he went on to college at Bowdoin and then to graduate work at Columbia and Harvard. Beginning in 1920, he taught economics at the University of Chicago for twenty years and made this his base for numerous initial forays into the field of social reform. Of his several careers, Douglas recalls his university life with the least enthusiasm. It is possible, although he pleads to the contrary in this book, that he didn't much like it. It didn't absorb his almost unbelievable energy; he was frequently, to use his phrase, out of tune with his teachers, colleagues or surroundings.

At Harvard, Douglas had studied under two of the most eloquent reactionaries of the age — T. N. Carver and C. J. Bullock — and he pictures them with considerable accuracy as narrow and embittered men. (He especially recalls Bullock's course in the history of economic thought, which was described by students in my day as covering the period from Adam to Adam Smith and which came down to the recent past only to denounce such radicals as Herbert Hoover.) In the university as a whole, he found a "deep-rooted provincialism and social snobbery that pervaded both the student body and many of the faculty." This opinion was not lightly held. Philip Stern, who is celebrated in this book as one of the most brilliant of Douglas's staff members, once told me that he had considered it wise to keep his employer in ignorance of the fact that he himself had been to Harvard — or, anyhow, not to make a point of this aberration.

The University of Chicago fares only a shade better. On returning after the war, Douglas found that the "economic and political conservatives had acquired almost complete dominance over my department," that his former friends and allies were dead or had departed and that his new colleagues could not conceal "their impatience and disgust with me." This, one should notice, accords with a major academic tradition: those who uphold the reputable view in a university defend to the death the right of others to disagree. They do not, however, feel obliged to be pleasant about it or to conceal their conviction that the dissenter is, by comparison with true believers, mentally and morally defective. On the whole, both Harvard and Chicago come off badly in this book, and I would say that the strictures were probably deserved in their time.

The years in the Marine Corps were for Douglas ones of unadulterated joy. He discovered, to his pleasure, that he could hold his own, not only mentally but physically, with those who were thirty years his junior. The old, he feels, have much more going for them than people commonly assume — a belief that increasingly I share. Some veterans will wonder if an all but mortal wound could give a man as much pleasure as it did to Douglas. But he makes his reaction sound quite convincing.

By far the longest part of the book, however, is about politics and his years in the Senate; there, at approximately the age when a senior British civil servant contemplates retirement, Paul Douglas began his period of major achievement. The list of the legislative projects with which he was influentially associated is nearly unending — civil rights; Social Security, where his professional authority was great; labor legislation, where he was equally informed; housing; and education. He was against pork barrels, for the Marines, for the Indiana Dunes, for protection of the oil-shale reserves in Colorado, Utah and Wyoming and against the oil-depletion allowance. In nearly every case, he accomplished or helped to accomplish something. Most often he got pretty much what he wanted.

There may, conceivably, be more detail on these efforts than the average informed reader will be able to digest. Douglas tells that, during his three terms in the Senate, he came awake every morning at five o'clock — few things give me such intense pleasure as the discovery that others are hopeless insomniacs — and proceeded to read in detail *The New York Times*, *The Washington Post* and *The Congressional Record*. It is possible that when he wrote this book, he judged the reading appetite of others by his own.

And there are other faults. One can assume, I think, that such splendid figures as Everett McKinley Dirksen, Douglas MacArthur, Robert McCormick and the gallant Senator C. Wayland Brooks of Illinois — all of whom march through these pages — were given to us by a bemused God to inspire our laughter. But Paul Douglas never allows himself even a chuckle; he takes them as seriously as they took themselves. He is also terribly deficient in malice; repeatedly, when he nails someone for truly outrageous behavior, he carefully omits his name.

Then too, although this may be deliberate, *In the Fullness of Time* does not resolve the mysteries of the remarkably complex and contradictory personality of its author. On occasion, Douglas himself confesses puzzlement. A Quaker, he thought the Friends the finest corporate group he had ever encountered. And he found enormous satisfaction in war; he is not altogether sure why. Though he had a deeply ingrained and richly justified suspicion of the motives of the Establishment and Lyndon Johnson, he strung along with both on their most dubious enterprise, the Vietnam war. Douglas has always been intensely anti-Communist out of powerfully libertarian conviction. While open to argument on other matters, he refused to accept that liberty, a strong part of the alternative to Communism in Europe, was not seriously an alternative in the governments we supported in Indochina. However, he does concede that his support for intervention there in the 1950s, when it was urged by Vice President Nixon, was a mistake. All should remember, incidentally, that Douglas, again like Norris and other Progressives, was a domestic senator; the internal problems of the United States were for him a prior and sufficient preoccupation.

Finally, there is the question of how Douglas managed to survive and flourish in association with the Chicago politicians. Perhaps his original selection as the candidate for a Senate seat in 1948 was not inexplicable. When Jake Arvey, the Chicago boss, returned from the war, he obviously had very much in mind the improvement of the Illinois political scene. There was a natural shortage in those precincts of men who didn't steal, and thieves are often hard to elect. But it is still a puzzle how Douglas, this didactic and unbending man, managed for the next eighteen years to remain on reasonably good terms with Ed Kelly, Richard Daley and the associated and righteously flexible myrmidons of the city, county and state.

I have frequently had to do business with the Massachusetts political professionals — saints in the minor scale of their villainy as compared with their brothers in crime from Cook County. The experience has always been mutually unpleasant; I have rarely failed to arouse an occupational, as well as a deeply personal, hostility. Douglas could do business with such men year after year without yielding anything and without arousing intolerable opposition. (His only enduring difficulty, as it turned out, was with Adlai Stevenson.) He suggests in this book that deep, deep within the soul of every politician is a streak of natural goodness — a desire to be better than he is — and to this instinct Douglas tried to appeal. Perhaps; such a streak has certainly escaped my notice. And its existence is surely the best news about Chicago statesmen in some time.

However, these are minor complaints, and the puzzles add to the interest. The book as a whole is a major document on the history of the midcentury. There should be some way of recycling men like Paul Douglas.

THE DULLES BROTHERS
— AND SISTER*

(1978)

My admiration of the Dulles brothers, it will be evident, is restrained. Some repetition in this essay from other parts of this book emphasizes that feeling. Not even the Reagan foreign policy wholly redeems these gentlemen, although it can be said of Alexander Haig that as secretary of state he tried.

Donald Segretti, here mentioned, was one of Richard Nixon's minor political malefactors in charge of election dirty tricks. I am prepared to believe that he has now reformed and is a good and suitably obscure citizen.

My review brought a powerful and sadly ill-considered response from the book's publisher, which, along with my reply, is here reprinted, perhaps more for my own pleasure than for that of the reader. No writer should be entirely denied such gratification, and, I have observed, few are.

Given the general revisionist urge of our times, there is satisfaction in the feeling that the position of the Dulles brothers in history is reasonably secure. They inherited the enormous fund of good will that FDR, our conduct of World War II, the Marshall Plan and such men as Averell Harriman, Dwight D. Eisenhower, George Marshall, Paul Hoffman and Harry Truman had accumulated for the United States. This they then worked to liquidate, each in his own way, with such efficiency and dispatch that no other names are likely to have any similar standing in the effort.

Both men were well attuned to the task. Both, but especially Foster, had impressive self-serving competence. They shared more or less equally a capacity for truly spectacular misjudgment. Both, though again Foster more than Allen, could exclude from view questions of annoying social

*This was a review, originally published in *The New Republic*, of *Dulles: A Biography of Eleanor, Allen and John Foster Dulles and Their Family Network* by Leonard Mosley (New York: Dial Press, 1978).

complexity. For them revolt against privilege, injustice and exploitation and the counterpart aspiration of the masses were not moving forces in history; they were the work of Communists or other troublemakers. The brothers will be thought of, somewhat unfairly, as the classic men of Wall Street — unfairly, because there have always been a great number of Wall Streeters with no similar ignorance of the way the behavior of governments reflects or reacts to the politics of privation and despair.

Both brothers enjoyed major political and bureaucratic success. Their formidable personal skills and personalities apart, it came from a nearly total absence of the self-questioning that characterizes all wiser and safer men. They were also lucky in their timing. They came to office when foreign policy had suddenly become a prestigious and engrossing preoccupation for Americans, outdoing old wealth, elective office, business success and Hollywood in the aura that participation conferred. And because of its relative novelty there was no firm national or political judgment as to what was sensible and who and what were not. As a manufacturer of textiles or chain saws can now become a knowledgeable central banker by the act of appointment, so it then was in foreign policy. Were a man adequately tailored, traveled and mannered and able to affirm in a reliably repetitive way the current clichés on American security needs, he could be an authority. People were taken at their own valuation on foreign policy, and in the case of the Dulles brothers this was very high.

There *were* differences between them. Allen Dulles was an amiable man, capable of basic bureaucratic and tribal loyalties, and these, on the whole, were reciprocated. Foster was self-centered and self-righteous to the extent that he was incapable of elementary loyalty or good faith. There was no one — not even, as this book tells, his attractive and rather goodhearted sister — who might not be sacrificed in the service of his personal convenience or ambition. The excellent and honest Foreign Service officers who saw — and warned — that the Chinese Communists might have a brighter future than Chiang Kai-shek are a monument to this grim trait. Dulles threw them to Joe McCarthy, making unconvincing murmurs of apology as he did. And, from the service of Styles Bridges of New Hampshire, a man known by his colleagues to have an even more refined and intricate instinct for evil than Senator McCarthy, he brought to the State Department an executioner tutored by Bridges to extend the slaughter.

His cultivation of the anti-Communist hysteria of the time; his reckless talk of the liberation of Eastern Europe, which the Hungarians, much to their sorrow, took seriously; his alienation of the neutral countries in his vacuous attack on neutralism; his praise of his own nuclear brinksmanship; his doctrine of massive retaliation; and his self-serving and unreliable treatment of the British (as well as the Israelis, Nasser and the Egyptians) at the time of the Suez crisis, all reflected the Dulles instinct for personally expedient bad judgment and action.

History overtook Allen Dulles. Within a twelve-month period in the early 1960s, he was responsible, as head of the CIA, for two of the most luminous foul-ups in the long annals of inspired public error — the flight of the U-2 at the time of the 1960 summit (after it was known that the Soviets could shoot down the plane and there was wonder why they didn't) and the Bay of Pigs. (All of us who were around at the time had also to contend on a variety of matters with Allen and his coterie of self-assured refugees from more pedestrian employments. My own affliction, among others, when I was ambassador to India, was a schedule of overflights across India from Bangkok to northern Nepal to supply some tribesmen who were supposed to be opening up a kind of miniature second front against Peking.) So Allen Dulles was sacked. It is a measure of his percipience and self-knowledge that he then, and quite unapologetically, wrote a book on the craft of intelligence. One thinks of Donald Segretti on honesty in elections. John Foster Dulles died in time to get an airport.

The reason the Dulles brothers will not be rescued by revisionists is one of the few matters on which this book seems wholly reliable. Mr. Mosley's history takes the Dulles principals from cradle to grave and their more agreeable children somewhat beyond. In line of duty, he interviewed numerous of the old Dulles associates, and these included quite a few vintage cold warriors who still unite in believing, some in hoping, that our relations with the Russians will one day so develop as to retrieve their misjudgment on Vietnam. Several spoke fondly of Allen Dulles, although not of his judgment or his ability as an administrator. All without exception dumped hard on Foster. He was too much to defend.

These conversations, if accurately recalled, are useful. Mr. Mosley has also dug up some interesting family history, which one hopes is true, including some of a harmlessly voyeuristic sort. And there are occasional new items or overlooked details. Once, as World War II was drawing to a close, I went to a meeting with John Foster Dulles and some others at the headquarters of the Council on Foreign Relations in New York to discuss our German policy. With great and adamant certainty, he said that Germany must be dismembered — some of it going to France, some to Austria, some to Poland. I demurred; he contemptuously refused debate. In later years I had difficulty persuading people that Dulles had ever been this far off. Mr. Mosley here affirms that he did, indeed, urge this view and implies that it could have been compensation for the excessively tolerant position of his law firm toward Germany in the Hitler prewar years — one, it should be said, that Allen did not share.

Mr. Mosley has also an easy, readable style, and he can move rapidly as well as biologically, metaphorically and hydraulically to get a chapter under way: "They were tall, strong in muscle and thigh, and tough as old boots so far as cold water and pain were concerned; but the Dulles brothers and their sister were prone to an extraordinary number of illnesses in their lifetime." The less favorable side is that his book is a mine of minor misinformation, and this leads, inevitably, to doubt as to some of his larger and less checkable facts, conversations and conclusions. Dean Rusk was never head of the Ford Foundation. The Russians never dropped paratroopers dressed in civilian clothes to take possession of Berlin in the closing days of the war. (I doubt that they had the clothes.) Hitler, in the last weeks, was not at Zossen but in his bunker under the garden of the Reichschancellery, surely one of the best celebrated retreats since St. Helena. His earlier headquarters was not in Poland but in East Prussia. The Peenemunde raid came *after* the V-2 had been put into production at an underground factory, and it did not appreciably delay the use of the rocket against England. (Mr. Mosley is not, however, the first to fall for this myth.) Noel Field is said to drive through "the placid Swiss countryside" from Collonges into Geneva, which is a lot like traveling across the placid New York countryside from White Plains to the Bronx. Lord Lothian, the British ambassador in Washington, here offers a special visa to Eleanor Dulles nearly five years after his death. Well done, Lothian. She then went abroad and later earned the love of the Austrians by getting them "well over $1 million in Marshall Plan aid." Austrian love comes cheap. Stalingrad, according to this writing, *did* fall to the Germans.

Along with others, Mosley thinks Allen's World War II operations for the OSS in Switzerland were rather brilliant, in striking contrast with his later performance. I suspect Mr. Mosley of depending excessively on the history according to Allen and his approving and self-approving co-workers. In Bern, Dulles was certainly more open and available to anti-Hitler Gemans and far less suspicious of their motives than were the British. But he was also, some then thought, insufficiently suspicious of those Germans who dreamed less of peace than of a glorious combined Allied-German crusade against the Soviets. And there was a decidedly passive aspect to this role; never in war before, as then in the case of the Germans, have so many been so eager, some from deeper love of country, others from conscience or out of a wish for reinsurance, to get in touch with the other side. And, as his own postwar account showed, he greatly exaggerated both the power and the popular appeal of the German resistance. At a minimum the Bern years must be explained; any uncharacteristic competence demonstrated there must be squared with Allen Dulles's later instinct for disaster.

John Foster Dulles was a historic misfortune and so was his brother. Together in such potentially damaging posts at so dangerous a time, they are at least proof of the benignity of the gods: we somehow escaped. On balance, we were far safer with Richard Nixon. That they were a disaster Mr. Mosley affirms. One weeps that some editor didn't take the time to read the book before unleashing it, to use a Dulles-era phrase, on the public.

RESPONSE

March 20, 1978

To the Editors of *The New Republic*:

I was reading John Kenneth Galbraith's review of *Dulles* by Leonard Mosley in *The New Republic*'s issue of March 18 with great pleasure, savoring his customary wit, intelligence and cogency, until I came upon his statement that the book is "a mine of minor misinformation, and this leads, inevitably, to doubt as to some of his [Mosley's] larger and less checkable facts, conversations and conclusions."

A somewhat stronger emotion was aroused in me by his concluding sentence: "One weeps that some editor didn't take the time to read the book before unleashing it, to use a Dulles-era phrase, on the public."

As both the editor and publisher of the book I feel I can't ignore such a parting shot and am therefore, with the kind permission of the author, violating a self-imposed rule of silence of some sixteen years' standing in responding to these alleged errors and strictures which do unjustified and, one hopes, unintentional harm to the reputation of a superb book and a distinguished author.

ALLEGED ERROR (1): *"Dean Rusk was never head of the Ford Foundation."*

Mr. Galbraith is quite right — as is the final, printed version of *Dulles*. On page 470 Rusk is identified as head of the Rockefeller Foundation. I can only conclude that Mr. Galbraith made the fundamental error of writing his review on the basis of advance, *uncorrected* proofs. In view of his long experience at book reviewing, I find this surprising, particularly because every publisher issues a *caveat* when sending out advance proofs, entreating all reviewers to check the printed, final version of the book before making any quotations. (The error was in proof, was caught, and corrected in the published book on both pages 470 and 518, the latter being part of thirty pages of detailed source notes.)

ALLEGED ERROR (2): *"The Russians never dropped paratroopers dressed in civilian clothes to take possession of Berlin in the closing days of the war."*

Mr. Galbraith is wrong. This is documented in the German Military Archives in Coblenz.

ALLEGED ERROR (3): *"Hitler, in the last weeks, was not at Zossen but in his bunker under the garden of the Reichschancellery. . . . His earlier headquarters was not in Poland."*

In the twilight months of 1945 Hitler was moved around considerably before going to earth in the famous bunker. One of his last "forward command headquarters" was at Rastenberg, where Stauffenberg's bomb nearly killed him on July 20, 1944.

But what Mr. Mosley and I are at a loss to know is this: Where in *Dulles* is a mention of Zossen or the Polish headquarters? We would be grateful if Mr. Galbraith would find the reference in the printed book and let us know.

ALLEGED ERROR (4): *"The Peenemunde raid came after the V-2 had been put into production at an underground factory, and it did not appreciably delay the use of the rocket against England."*

Contrary to Professor Galbraith's assertions, the facts are these. There were a *number* of raids on Peenemunde. The first took place on the night of August 17, 1943, conducted by Britain's Bomber Command. The first firing of the V-2 (witnessed by Albert Speer and others) was on June 13, 1942. It was a fiasco.

The second and successful test flight took place on October 14, 1942. Albert Speer, in *Inside the Third Reich*, records: "[T]he final technical data was to be available by 1943, at which point we could go right into production." He goes on to point out that in the autumn of 1943 they were still unable to go into production. General Arnold (in *Global Mission*) says the V-2 did not get into production until January 1944.

In early September of 1944 some twenty-five V-2s were fired at England over a ten-day period, hardly the crushing blow Hitler was looking for.

In point of fact the British raid (according to von Braun and others who lived to describe its consequences) killed scientists and technicians and badly damaged workshops, labs, and houses. Perhaps the British should have hit harder. The American Air Force in 1944 attacked Peenemunde *three* times.

The large underground factory (actually there were several) for assembly of the V-2s was *not* at Peenemunde; one of the largest was at Nordhausen, and there were several others at other locations. The initial British attack encouraged the Germans to *disperse* V-weapon activity from Peenemunde.

ALLEGED ERROR (5): *"Noel Field is said to drive through 'the placid Swiss countryside' from Cologne* [sic] *into Geneva, which is a lot like traveling across the placid New York countryside from White Plains to the Bronx."*

Having given us this peculiar geography lesson, Mr. Galbraith leaves both author and publisher bewildered as to just what passage in the book is at issue as "misleading." If Mr. Galbraith would care to take a look at what the printed book *says* on page 130 he will find:

> They did not stop at the French frontier post at Collonges to find out [if the Gestapo were following them], *but raced on through to the Swiss station 50 meters further on. Once the officials had checked them through, they drove quietly through the placid Swiss countryside into Geneva.*

ALLEGED ERROR (6): *"Lord Lothian, the British ambassador in Washington, here offers a special visa to Eleanor Dulles nearly five years after his death."*

For once Mr. Galbraith is right: Lord Lothian died on December 12, 1940, and was replaced by Viscount, later Lord, Halifax, who was in turn replaced in 1946 by the Right Hon. Lord Inverchapel. It was Eleanor Dulles herself who told Leonard Mosley of this offer. (We should have caught her error of memory.) I might remark at this point that all quotes from Eleanor Dulles (and many others, such as Averell Harriman, Paul Nitze, Admiral Arleigh Burke, Richard Bissell, Jr., etc.) were presented to her in manuscript so she could review them, correct them if necessary, and finally initial them to show that the quotes had been read, checked, and approved. (Harriman asked that some of his comments about Ike, for example, be removed and the author did so.)

I think one ought to stop here. Looking back at the body of the review, one finds Mr. Galbraith, who was U.S. ambassador to India from 1961 to 1963, somewhat confusing about the chronology of his tenure and that of Allen Dulles.

Mr. Galbraith writes of how "all of us who were around at the time" were caused problems by Allen Dulles, in his own case by "overflights across India from Bengal [sic] to Nepal to supply some tribesmen who were supposed to be opening up a kind of miniature second front against Peking. So Allen Dulles was sacked."

History records (and Leonard Mosley sets forth in detail in *Dulles*) that Allen Dulles had already effectively been sacked as a result of his role in the Bay of Pigs in April of 1961. Although he was kept on until

November, he was bureaucratically dead from the moment of the failure. John F. Kennedy announced on September 28, 1961, that he was nominating John A. McCone to replace Dulles.

Ambassador Galbraith might give us a better idea of the CIA mentality of the time if he recalls some of the projects proposed and pressures brought to bear on him by the then CIA station chief in India in the years 1961 and 1962. That particular gentleman is still very much alive and, as Mr. Galbraith may be well aware, has *also* written a book on American intelligence.

Surely Mr. Galbraith knows more about the history of American intelligence in our time than he learned from working on the Strategic Bombing Survey and than he displays in his review.

> James O'Shea Wade
> Publisher
> *The Dial Press/James Wade Books*

And in Reply

April 1, 1978

To the Editors of *The New Republic*:

Mr. Wade should have continued and extended his wise practice of the past sixteen years. His protest fails on seven and a half counts out of a total of five.

Let me note at the outset that I review what publishers send me, in this instance bound proof, as I expect to be reviewed. So numerous, however, were Mr. Mosley's slips that I asked the editors of *The New Republic*, out of compassion, to get the book and see if some mistakes hadn't been corrected. One partial correction did escape their notice: on page 470, Dean Rusk *is* returned to the Rockefeller Foundation, although on page 518, he is still telling how the CIA opened the *Ford* Foundation mail. On all other counts Mr. Wade and Mr. Mosley fail.

Thus, had the Soviets seized Berlin by air with troops in civilian clothes to forestall revolt and the Western Allies, it would have been one of the most spectacular operations of the war, the most discussed event of this much described battle. Considering the size of Berlin, it would have been also on an enormous scale. In fact, the Soviets shelled and fought their way into the center of the city on the ground. The end came on May 2, when the Berlin commander, General Helmuth Weidling, crossed the lines on the ground and surrendered to Marshal Vasily Chuikov. The Western Allies were not very close. Had the history been different, it would not have awaited any discovery from the archives. It would have been known long ago, including to those who, in ensuing weeks, were there.

Hitler, at the time mentioned by Mr. Mosley (in the last days when Allen Dulles was negotiating for the Italian surrender), was not moving around; he was in the bunker beneath the Chancellery garden.

The reference to a Polish headquarters that neither the author nor publisher can locate in the finished book is right there on page 139 of the volume I just bought. And the reference to Zossen that similarly they said they would thank me for finding is on page 230. I now accept their thanks.

The V-2 was not manufactured at Peenemunde, as the book asserts. It was in production elsewhere when the installation was attacked. "The attacks on the V-weapon experimental station at Peenemunde, however, were not effective; V-1 was already in production near Kassel and V-2 had also been moved to an underground plant." (*The United States Strategic Bombing Survey [European War] Summary Report*, 1945, page 12.) I helped direct the teams that made this investigation; that production was not substantially delayed was initially affirmed by Albert Speer in interrogations in which I participated. The rest of Mr. Wade's explanation on this matter is merely confusing.

Collonges, correctly spelled in my copy as in Mosley's book but changed by a *New Republic* printer to Cologne, is a close-in suburb of Geneva. No placid Swiss countryside lies between. Thus there was none to drive through.

I was right about the death of Lord Lothian, as Mr. Wade concedes, and also in saying that Mr. Mosley has Stalingrad falling and Eleanor Dulles acquiring the lasting affection of the Austrians for a mere million dollars, which he gives as the Marshall Plan aid to that country. Thus the score in my favor that I mentioned at the outset. That is because Mr. Wade doesn't mention these last two errors; after Lothian, he says wisely, though belatedly, "I think one ought to stop here."

No reader will have trouble with my chronology on the sacking of Allen Dulles. After mention of the Bay of Pigs, I alluded in a parenthesis to the Nepal nonsense with which I had to contend; this was in the early summer of 1961. I was not, in fact, subject to any embarrassing pressure from Harry Rositzke, the head of the CIA in India when I arrived and one of the least clandestine figures in the history of intelligence operations in New Delhi. He has, indeed, written a very interesting book.

There *was* an error in my reference to those overflights to Nepal. Bangkok as the approximate place of origin got transcribed as Bangladesh, and alert *TNR* editors made that, as it then was, into Bengal. I confess this as a special gesture to Mr. Wade. No one is infallible. The expert critic can sometimes find errors in even the most careful work.

12

GEORGE KENNAN*

(1972)

George Kennan has been my colleague in disparate enterprises over the years: we served together in the State Department after World War II and again during the Kennedy administration; with Donald Kendall, the head of PepsiCo, we were for several years the co-chairmen of the American Committee on East-West Accord in service to civil communication with the Soviet Union; Kennan preceded me by a term or two in the highly agreeable task of presiding over the American Institute of Arts and Letters, agreeable, for it involves giving away to deserving artists, musicians and writers several hundred thousands of dollars at no personal cost.

I speak here of a cold war generation as though it had passed, and forever. Alas!

I don't see how a memoir could be better. Even if you aren't interested in the subject at hand, the language carries you along. And the story — with all action filtered through the finest Kennan introspection — is both important and absorbing. Kennan here tells of the origins of the Korean War; the cold war mystique of Secretaries of State Acheson and Dulles; Moscow in 1952 in the last months of Stalin; how Kennan got thrown out of the Soviet Union for an unguarded remark in a Berlin airport; the McCarthy attack on his old friends; the convulsion of the cold warriors over his Reith Lectures, which proposed disengagement in Central Europe; and his service in Yugoslavia under Kennedy. As all is graced by the Kennan style, all is stamped with the Kennan foreign policy trademark.

The latter consists of an ability to think clearly about complicated matters with an utter independence of mind. He draws on a superb

*This was a review, originally published in *The New York Times Book Review*, of *Memoirs, 1950–1963*, Volume II, by George F. Kennan (Boston: Atlantic–Little, Brown, 1972).

stock of historical knowledge; he makes use of a capacious if sometimes less adequate supply of contemporary information or interpretation, a matter to which I will return in a moment.

The worst thing about all thinking on foreign policy is the narcotic attraction of the fashionable view. "You are so right, Mr. Secretary. It's the way we all feel." For this, Kennan has only contempt, but he also derives no special pleasure — as, despite all effort, I always do — from the feeling that nearly everyone is wrong. Having made up his mind, Kennan then gives the reasons with consummate skill and complete certainty. No one should misconstrue his tendency to introspection. It regularly raises the question that he *might* be wrong. Then, with rare exceptions and I think with much justification, he discards the possibility.

Most of the conclusions that George Kennan has reached over the years involve, in one way or another, the Soviet Union, and they emerge with admirable clarity in this book. He has always thought that the Soviets were primarily concerned with their own internal affairs; he was never captured by the belief that they would invite destruction in pursuit of world revolution. He was sure they would negotiate when there was a chance for mutual reward and would abide by the resulting agreements. He has always thought negligible — a prime Kennan point — their prospective response to sentiment or affection. A conventional war with the Soviets would, he was firmly convinced, be unwinnable and a nuclear conflict insane. In dealing with the Soviet Union, he considers the American military a blunderbuss, the Congress often irresponsible and uninformed, and the political leadership, including that of the State Department, in its obeisance to generals and congressmen, gutless to the point of being obscene. He loves Russia, has always been committed to the idea of peaceful coexistence and leaves the reader deeply puzzled as to how we happen to have survived the diplomacy (and frequent recklessness) of Acheson, Dulles, Admiral Arthur Radford and General Curtis LeMay of the Air Force. Maybe we were more fortunate than we deserved.

The Kennan view has been admirably affirmed by events, and yet I wouldn't want to give him a complete bill of health. He sees the Korean War as the logical response by the Soviets to our decision to proceed with a separate peace with Japan and to retain Japanese military bases. Korea was outside our defense perimeter, and, in Kennan's view, the Soviets reacted by having their clients there try to take it over. It would seem equally plausible (and more recent knowledge suggests) that, in fact, they were discovering, as have we, that clients or puppets, especially in that part of the world, are hard to control. South Korea was weak; we seemed unconcerned; surely it was open to the North Koreans to decide for themselves to march down and make it all one country.

Perhaps they got permission; maybe they just informed the Soviets and then went ahead; maybe the Russians tried to discourage them but the North Koreans didn't listen. Certainly both the great powers have since become accustomed to independent behavior by their client states.

Also, Kennan's world is one of governments in which men have a choice between sensible and stupid actions and are not greatly subject to social imperatives. There is a good example of this view in his treatment of John Foster Dulles. He begins a less than affectionate portrait of the secretary of state with the suggestion that by knowledge, experience, ambition and a certain deviousness of manner he was admirably equipped for his job. (Except for the last I do not agree.) He then explains the Dulles errors as the result of poor character plus an unwillingness to stand up to congressional and military opposition. But surely Dulles had one other disqualifying trait, which was his access to only one piece of social knowledge, namely, the difference between free enterprise and Communism and that good men chose the first and the willfully wicked the second. That deprivation, political oppression and economic exploitation might drive men and governments to solutions distasteful to a Wall Street lawyer was well beyond his range of thought. Kennan is not sensitive to such a flaw.

I think he has also, as have others, misunderstood the McCarthy phenomenon of the early 1950s. He puts full blame on primitives like McCarthy, McCarran and Jenner and the men of the Establishment who were too cowardly to stand up to them. With all this one must agree. But something must surely also be attributed to the way the liberals of the time acquiesced in the standard of guilt. If it could be shown that someone ever had a pro-Communist or a pro-Soviet or even a pro-socialist thought, it was accepted that he was disqualified for public service and from the company of true statesmen. By this standard almost everyone of any intellectual viability had some disqualifying stain. Men were kept busy righteously disavowing what was true but shouldn't have mattered. They were right to blame the man who went around hitting people in the jaw. But they should have asked why so many of their own number equipped themselves with glass jaws to be hit.

Finally, Kennan sees the Congress, along with the generals, as the natural enemy of all sensible foreign policy. I am willing to concede him the generals, those of the cold war generation at least, and I agree that in the years covered in this volume the Congress was frequently a force for irresponsible anti-Communism. But as this is written, the Senate has become a powerful voice urging caution and good sense. It was the experts and the generals who proposed or rationalized the more reckless actions in Vietnam and who destroyed Lyndon Johnson with their recommendations. Meanwhile, over the last half decade,

Senators Fulbright, Morse, Gruening, Kennedy, Cooper, Church, Hatfield and McGovern have been moderate and sensible, more so than the senior officials at the Department of State. On the average, I think we are safer if we keep foreign policy under the influence of men who must be re-elected. It was this need, we should remember, that sent Richard Nixon on his pilgrimages to Moscow and Peking.

All of this is to say that not even Kennan is infallible. And also that it is a privilege to argue with this most brilliant and civilized of students of the public scene.

13

CHAIRMAN KHRUSHCHEV*

(1971)

Roswell Garst was my lifelong friend. An inventor and the commercial progenitor of hybrid corn, he moved, as I here tell, from thought to action with greater ease and speed than anyone I've ever known. So now do his sons and daughters. The Garsts, even more than corn itself, are an Iowa monument.

My association with Nikita Khrushchev was more limited — a single meeting, as I've elsewhere told, at Averell Harriman's New York house during Khrushchev's visit to the United States in 1959. Khrushchev had evinced a desire to meet the American ruling class, which, in his view, was made up of those of suitable solvency. This meeting Harriman arranged; the ticket for admission was the ownership or control of $50 to $100 million, or thereabouts. I represented the proletariat. The high point of the evening was a long question by General David Sarnoff of RCA and NBC as to why Soviet leaders did not allow and encourage American radio broadcasting to their country. He praised the medium as the highest manifestation of Western culture and gave the impression that NBC would willingly take over programming in Russia. Khrushchev, to the delight of even that relatively immune audience, replied that the Russian people might not welcome General Sarnoff's programs. "You see," he said, "things have changed in Minsk since you were a boy."

Kwame Nkrumah was the head of state in Ghana until, unwisely, he left the country for a short tour and was rather enthusiastically dispensed with. John J. Rooney represented a Brooklyn congressional district with marked inadequacy for many years.

At lunch in Iowa about twelve years ago Roswell Garst, the great hybrid-corn man, told me of a meeting he had just had with Nikita Khrushchev. Having saturated the United States market with Pioneer Hybrid Corn,

---

*This was a review, originally published in *Book World* of *The Washington Post*, of *Khrushchev Remembers*, with an introduction, commentary and notes by Edward Crankshaw, translated and edited by Strobe Talbott (Boston: Little, Brown, 1971).

Garst had been looking around for new customers, and the Soviet Union had come strongly to mind. Since the Garsts relate thought automatically to action, he had gone to Moscow, made a sales call on the Kremlin and left samples. But he had not been successful — for Garst, a highly atypical result. A few weeks later, however, the Soviet Embassy in Washington had asked him to return — urgently. Arriving in Moscow, he was taken to see Khrushchev, whose interest in corn had significantly deepened in the interval. The huge ear encased in clear plastic that Garst had left on his earlier visit was prominent on the Soviet leader's desk. For a long afternoon he questioned Garst about U.S. methods of corn culture — techniques of hybridization, land preparation, cultivation, fertilization, harvesting, storage and more. The telephone didn't ring; there were no interruptions; Garst said he began to wonder who was running the country. Finally, he begged to ask a question himself.

"I assume, Mr. Chairman, that you have methods of getting information from the United States — that if we have some new atomic secret, you get it in a couple of weeks."

Khrushchev interrupted, angrily shaking his finger at Garst. "No! No! One week only!"

"One week or two weeks, it doesn't matter," said Garst. "I still must ask, why do you question me about matters that are in our experiment station bulletins, that our Extension Services pound into the heads of our farmers, that are on our radio, in our papers, in Iowa hard to avoid?"

"It's the Russian character," Khrushchev replied. "When the aristocracy first learned that potatoes were the cheapest way of feeding the peasants, no one would eat them. But whatever you say for our aristocrats, they knew their Russians. They put high fences around the potato patches, installed fierce patrol dogs, and the peasants immediately started stealing the potatoes. Soon they had developed a taste for them. You should have kept your corn a secret."

This story was much on my mind last autumn when I began to read the Khrushchev memoirs, as they are commonly called, in the London papers. I imagined that they owed their interest to the murky process by which they were acquired and that, for literary and narrative power, Khrushchev probably ranked somewhere between Kwame Nkrumah and Representative John J. Rooney of New York. I was wrong. After reading the book and a fair number of the American and English reviews, I've concluded that a word should be said for a fellow author. I think that, with exceptions, Chairman Khrushchev has had a bum rap from the critics.

There was, first, the question of authenticity — a greater problem for English than American critics, quite a few of whom have attributed the book to the CIA. That agency can be excluded on very simple grounds: someone with the kind of imagination required to write this volume could not be had for government pay. As a novelist with Hollywood possibilities he would be worth around ten times as much. Even Lyndon Johnson could have doubled the fellow's fee to make him his ghostwriter and come out ahead. It may be that the KGB, which has gotten credit from some reviewers, has less competition when it comes to hiring writers and thus can get this kind of talent, but even those who think it responsible agree that it must have worked very closely with original Khrushchev material.

The critics have also complained that there isn't much that is new, but this is equally true of the memoirs of Dwight D. Eisenhower and Harold Macmillan, and, in contrast to those worthy books, the Khrushchev production is full of perfectly fascinating stories. However jaded the experts may be, I was delighted to read about high-level infighting as it is conducted in the Kremlin, how Britain, Claridge's Hotel and the Right Honourable George Brown looked to a visiting Russian and what a terrible indignity it is to arrive at an international conference in a tiny two-motor airplane, which was what happened to the Soviets in Geneva in 1955. (All the others had four-motor jobs.) Clayton Fritchey, the distinguished and discriminating Washington columnist, believes the best thing in the book is the account of Khrushchev's exchange with President Eisenhower at the latter's "dacha" at Camp David. Each tells how he is constantly pressed by his generals for new and expensive weapons, how bravely he resists, how he explains that money is short, how the generals persist, how eventually he gives in.

I thought the accounts of home life with J. Stalin were even better. No person is so little to be envied as the man who must keep company, even in a democracy, with the panjandrums of state. It gives him a good business address but terrible working conditions, and there is something in the juxtaposition to power that destroys the mind, if such exists. Even brief association, as I can avow, can be bad. But within the last year we have had eyewitness evidence that, unbelievably, life in the dictatorships was even worse. Albert Speer has told of Hitler's endless monologues, lasting all night and relieved only by bad movies. Now Khrushchev tells of the equally endless gatherings at the Kremlin relieved by the same movies but also by the fact that, in contrast with Hitler's court, everyone was encouraged, and on occasion required, to get stinking drunk. (The high Nazis in the last days also drowned their anxieties but not in Hitler's presence or by his command.)

It seems to me, however, that the reviewers can be faulted in a much more important respect. Following the lead of Edward Crankshaw, who contributed the commentary, all have been especially concerned to advise the reader that Khrushchev is a very wicked man, who is also both selective in truth and an accomplished liar. His protestations of discontent with Stalin, love for his fellow man, hopes for peace and claims to incipient liberalism are absurdly inconsistent with his own past. I doubt that anyone able to read needs to be so warned. But as a legacy of the cold war we have a priestly convocation of foreign policy scholars who are deeply worried lest any less percipient citizen be hornswoggled by anything being said by the Soviets. Without wanting to put anyone out of a job, I think they can now safely stand down. The astonishing thing about Khrushchev is not that he was an acolyte of Stalin, or that he is generally deficient, even by current Washington standards, in his approach to the truth, or that he lacks general moral tone. What is amazing is how a man with such a record — who was so much one of the gang and who so remarkably survived — could have done so much to change the course of history when he came to power.

For he did set out to improve relations with the West. He did make those hilarious but generally reassuring journeys, which must have been against all advice from the Soviet Foggy Bottom. He did more than any American politician to propagate the belief that war was obsolete in the nuclear age; our people were much more bound by the cold war party line. He did, with whatever help from Mikoyan and others, make that speech at the Twentieth Party Congress and let the light in on Stalin. He did bring people back from the labor camps, and he evidently approved the publication of Solzhenitzyn. All of this, like much of what he espouses in this book, was inconsistent with his past. It should be a cause not of criticism but of rejoicing. Those who accept the will and instruction of the bureaucracy are likely to be consistent, for the bureaucracy resists the new. Had Khrushchev been a bureaucrat, nothing in his attitudes or actions would ever have changed.

These are hard days for heads of state. And, curiously, it is not the big questions but the little ones that get them heaved out. LBJ was excellent on the big issues of race, poverty and domestic social tension, but he couldn't resist advice to blow it all on a country of no importance to the United States and of which, it is a fair guess, he had no perceptible knowledge before he was forty years old. Nixon, disentangling slowly from Vietnam, seems unable (as this is written) to resist furthering an even more mystifying interest in Cambodia and Laos.

Khrushchev, according to informed Russians with whom I have talked in recent years and who seemed not to be trying to persuade to any particular effect, survived his enormous and risky effort to reverse Stalinist domestic and foreign policy and then was canned because of his inability to keep his hands off technical matters on which he was uninformed, possibly, including among other things hybrid corn. (This book is itself a testament to Khrushchev's tendency to mess into anything and everything with a fine disregard for knowledge.) Public office being as perilous as it is these days, the least we can do is to give the occupants a fair break as authors, which is what they so soon become.

14

HENRY KISSINGER
— AND COMPANION*

(1979)

This is another effort — see my review of David Schoenbrun's The Three
Lives of Charles de Gaulle *earlier in this book — to persuade great radio
and television figures who can't write that they shouldn't write.*

*I had a letter from Mr. Valeriani after this was published, advising me
substantially more in anger than in sorrow that Konrad Adenauer had, indeed,
met Henry Kissinger back during the Kennedy administration when Kissinger,
on assignment from Washington, had made a visit to the chancellor. From this
encounter came the judgment on the career that Kissinger had forfeited in
Germany — a truly astonishing exercise in imagination, mental outreach and
career forecasting. I sent the letter along to* The Washington Post, *where my
review had been published. Wanting to protect me or just possibly Mr. Valeriani,*
The Post *chose not to print it.*

*As a reviewer, though, I don't want to be too hard on Mr. Valeriani. I am,
in fact, a little grateful to him. As all who review books know, it is somehow
refreshing to encounter one without a single saving grace.*

My first thought on picking up this book was that another unfortunate
author had got off to a bad start. And since Mr. Valeriani, Boswell
here to Henry Kissinger and reporter for NBC on State Department
affairs, is, most obviously, an agreeable man, my compulsively sympathetic instinct was to assume there would soon be redemption of a
sort. So when he began with an effusive message of thanks to another
State Department media expert, Bruce van Voorst of *Newsweek*, for
"helping to research and *prepare* [my emphasis] this manuscript," his
display of gratitude fostered the excusing thought that he might be
another master of the spoken word who couldn't write and had hired
a fellow reporter to get him on track. However, this justification was
soon shown to be groundless. Mr. van Voorst also cannot write.

*Review of *Travels with Henry* by Richard Valeriani (Boston: Houghton Mifflin, 1979).

One of their early misfortunes is in the matter of witticisms. It comes in the title of the very first chapter: "The Vit and Visdom of Henry Kissinger." Not good. Then there is damage of a different sort on page 6, where Konrad Adenauer is quoted as saying that Henry Kissinger had "the most compelling intellect" of any man he had ever known and that he could have become a chancellor of the German Federal Republic, his being Jewish notwithstanding, had circumstances kept him in that country. This breathtaking judgment Adenauer must have rendered in his eighties or early nineties on the performance of a relatively obscure Harvard professor, for Adenauer died in 1967, and Kissinger didn't begin to emerge as a statesman until he joined Nixon in the White House in 1969.

In the very next pages yet more trouble accumulates in the presentation of the Kissinger humor. I share the view that my old Harvard friend can be very amusing; his rumbled, self-deprecating asides are both easy and apt. But no one, not Bob Hope, not Mark Twain, not even Harry Lauder, can or could stand having all his funny lines stacked one on top of another for several pages with no regard for context. That is what Valeriani does to Kissinger, although, to be fair, he does intersperse a few questionable efforts of his own. Thus, when Kissinger becomes secretary of state, he asks him whether he wishes to be called Mr. Secretary or Dr. Secretary.

The serious comment in these early pages is also less than wholly original. The author notes, for example, that "when it came to press and congressional relations, Kissinger was his own best agent; he had a flair for self-promotion. As a former high-ranking State Department official described it, 'Henry was able to project his personality in a favorable light to a wide spectrum of observers.' " I do concede that this official's spectrography has a ring of authenticity — more, perhaps, than Adenauer's statement. But does it add relentlessly to human knowledge?

All of this, to repeat, is in the first few pages, and one hopes for improvement. Alas, the latter part of the book, since it is more of the same, seems worse. One learns that we once had a "classic . . . World Series"; that Canada is one of our two closest neighbors; that on the way to China the author "had a touch of sinusitis (to go with [his] touch of Sinology)"; that at about the same time "visions of Henry's Delhi belly in Pakistan danced in our typewriters"; that Angola once "seethed with civil war"; that "at the policy level, Kissinger was decidedly Big-Power-oriented"; that he once wrote that "the art of statesmanship is to understand the nature of the world and the trend of history"; that sometimes Mr. Valeriani and other reporters "sat for an hour or more" listening to Kissinger "pour out profundities and analyses," presumably of similar truths; and that "one of the least-known coincidences of all time" occurred on the night Mao Tse-tung died, when the author,

having investigated the matter, learned that all three network correspondents covering the State Department had that evening dined at
Chinese restaurants. Some coincidences scream to remain unknown.

Going on in a different vein, the author tells that Ken Freed of the
Associated Press, in describing a caviar feast, said that "two Caspian
Sea sturgeon died today for Henry Kissinger"; and that Tom Braden,
the distinguished columnist, "who socialized with Kissinger off duty" —
socializing being here, I judge, a rather innocent thing unrelated to
property confiscation — thought the secretary successful because of his
"boyishness," all the while wondering if "boyishness is not a necessary
ingredient in the personalities of really first-rate men." And Valeriani
states flatly that "as head of the KGB, [General Yuri] Andropov was a
powerful man."

Washington correspondents who must live, travel and drink together
almost always write well of each other's books — a kindly and harmless
practice. They may have trouble with this work, although on balance
it is probably better than the recent memoirs of Margaret Trudeau.

It is also a heavy blow at Henry Kissinger, and conspiracy theories
what they are these days, some will think that all this is a cover for
some deeper political aggression. I don't agree. One should not attribute to bad or devious motives what can readily be explained by terminal
superficiality. Richard Valeriani, to repeat, seems a very nice man. His
concluding sentence, "Actually, I liked Henry Kissinger," is to be believed.

15

MOHANDAS (MAHATMA) GANDHI*

(1983)

When asked by Film Comment *to review Sir Richard Attenborough's film, and particularly when I heard that for this purpose an advance copy would be sent especially to Boston, I accepted with enthusiasm. The best-regarded comment on what I wrote came from Arthur Schlesinger, an ardent film-goer and long-time film critic. He thought I had not done badly, since, as he suggested, it was my first serious exposure to this art form since* Birth of a Nation.

Mohandas Gandhi is first seen in this film as a young and very bright Inns of Court attorney encountering vociferously proclaimed and violently imposed segregation in South Africa: he is kicked, quite literally, out of the first-class railway compartment in which, with a wholly proper ticket, he is riding, and off the train. This moves him to lead the resistance movement against the pass laws and the mass fingerprinting of the Indian minority; eventually he is confronted by Jan Smuts and the continuing ambiguity of British colonial justice. The latter, in South Africa as in India, sought to combine effective systemic repression with an underlying commitment to the rule of law. It was a conflict that, over a lifetime, Gandhi was to become a genius at exploiting. Under more modern arrangements and rulers, an enduring solution to his opposition would have been found: he would have been dispatched into permanent exile or summarily shot. He himself believed and said that his methods would have been successful — or as successful — only against the dedicatedly civilized British.

The story moves from South Africa to India, to the rise of the Congress Party and Gandhi's growing and eventually enormous influence on the people, to noncooperation, to violence countered by Gandhi's commitment to nonviolence whatever the provocation, to the fasts, the

*Review of the film *Gandhi*.

Great War, jail, the Round Table Conference in London, prison again, another war and then partition and independence and the horrible resulting slaughter in the Punjab and Bengal. It ends on the evening of January 30, 1948, in the garden of G. D. Birla's house in New Delhi, where Gandhi is shot and killed by a Hindu fanatic. He had just announced his intention of going to Pakistan to try by his presence to ease the continuing communal anger in the wake of the partition that he had so devoutly opposed.

The film is wonderfully valid on the Indian scene and sounds; never, watching it, are you away from the cities, villages and countryside. It is even more compelling on the great episodes of the Gandhi era. The Amritsar Massacre, on April 13, 1919, is, perhaps, the high point. This is superbly reproduced, with a special eye on the Gurkha troops, who, in a disciplined way, fired all their available cartridges into the helpless and entrapped crowd. (By modestly more precise calculation than that in the film, 379 people were killed that day and 1200 left wounded.) There are many who think that after Amritsar the eventual British departure from India was inevitable.

The long lines of Hindus filing into India from Pakistan after partition and the reverse flow of Muslims into the Pakistan Punjab are also memorable. So is the riot that breaks out as the two columns clash. The great march to the sea for salt is admirably organized, although I have always imagined that the Indians proceeded at a slightly more leisurely pace than here depicted. Equally impressive is the response of the police. It cannot be doubted that the director, Sir Richard Attenborough, is a master of the riot as an art form.

Where India is concerned, there is always a terrible tendency for the scene and the throngs to dominate. Here the cows and water buffalo as well as the crowds are entirely under control, and the trains, another Indian cliché, are only slightly overused; these are all very much the servant of the story. The temptation, in turn, to skimp on the history, especially to evade the puzzles and seeming contradictions in the Gandhi mystique, is also resisted; the Gandhi story is told, if not in all its length and complexity, at least with an honest commitment to important detail, subtlety and contradiction. I don't suppose that films are ever perfect history by the more somber academic standards; as I've often noted, books can be of any length, lectures can extend to a term, but films cannot go much beyond three hours. However, the effort here to tell all of the story is wholly serious.

There is yet further achievement, and that is in the handling of time. It was, I have heard, Richard Attenborough's belief, prevailing against some skepticism, that Gandhi could be portrayed from youth to death in strict chronological sequence. He was right, but partly because he has kept the audience brilliantly aware of the moment. Something, but not much, is accomplished by artifacts: along with costumes and press headlines, automobiles of appropriate vintage keep showing up on the screen. Mostly the effect is achieved by the portrayal of Gandhi himself; he ages in harmony with the history, and with manifest skill and conviction.

There are, I must now say, some grounds for complaint, one at the very beginning. Gandhi is brought on stage too suddenly in South Africa; one knows nothing and is told nothing about this mannered young man in his exceptionally precise English attire. It is hard to argue that a three-hour film should be even longer, but some later episodes could perhaps have been sacrificed to make room for Gandhi's youth as the son of a sometime Indian official, a member of a culturally rigorous family in one of the lesser princely states. On the lasting effect of this background — including an adolescent marriage and children — Gandhi was eloquent in his autobiography. There was something, many will think much, from this period that would help explain the young man on the South African train and that, if included, would have added to the understanding of the later years.

At some juncture someone also decided that the film should make a gesture to the American audience for which its producers naturally hoped. In consequence, Margaret Bourke-White, the noted *Life* photographer (here played by Candice Bergen), is brought onto the scene to take pictures of Gandhi and engage him in sprightly conversation. It is an embarrassing intrusion. A couple of Americans on the salt march have the same irrelevance. Were something needed to capture American interest, there could have been a reference to Franklin D. Roosevelt and his great-hearted commitment to Gandhi's campaign for Indian independence. It was one matter on which he was wholly willing to challenge Winston Churchill, who had strongly opposed earlier concessions to Indian self-rule and in the war years was proud to say that he had not become the King's first minister to preside over the liquidation of the British Empire.

However, it is on the relationship between the British rulers and the Indian leaders that the film most seriously fails, most of the failure being in its treatment of the British side. The Indians, it has tediously been noted, had a love-hate relationship with the British — there was much about the rulers and their civilization that Gandhi and Nehru admired and even loved. This, on the whole, is evident in the film. But the attitude of the British toward India was also complex. They had come, in some sense, as liberators to a land of petty, exploitative, incompetent and sometimes incoherent despots; they were far better than what had gone before; Marx in the last century, as has often been remarked, thought the British Empire in India a strongly progressive force. Thousands of Englishmen devoted their lives (and frequently gave them) to India and were justly proud of what they did. All things, including imperialism, are in their own time.

Little of this emerges, however, from the film. As portrayed, the rulers range from the disciplined, certain, self-assured awfulness of General Reginald Dyer to run-of-the-mill military idiots to confused and frustrated British civilians in New Delhi, along with an occasional man of intelligence appearing oddly on the scene. Only Louis Mountbatten, coming to proclaim the independence of India, redeems the Raj. The truth on the relationship of rulers to ruled was, to repeat, more kindly as well as more complex. Notice might also have been taken of the fact that by the end of the British era, India was extensively ruled by Indians. These British-trained officials were to continue to govern India (and Pakistan) in the years to come.

Finally, I was troubled, as audiences in general will be, by the handling of Gandhi's death. The face of the murderer appears in the crowd, appears again, and then he raises his gun and shoots. There is no explanation, and even though there *is* no very good explanation of the motive of this Hindu assassin and those who supported him — even though it was a wholly mindless action, in the manner of Sirhan Sirhan's assassination of Robert Kennedy — this needs to be told. Many who see these scenes will ask, "Why don't we learn why he did it?"

As to character authenticity and acting, no one should doubt that my view has all the value of any average member of the audience. I thought the characterization of Gandhi true to the original and Ben Kingsley gifted in making it so. Notably present was Gandhi's recurrent touch of sardonic humor, something that might easily have been overlooked or lost. It was too bad that the script missed his deathless observation on Lord Irwin, later Lord Halifax, and here John Gielgud. Irwin was a churchly man, and one of Gandhi's followers once defended him to the Mahatma, saying that Lord Irwin never took a decision without praying over it first. Gandhi reflected on this information for some moments and finally asked, "Then why do you suppose the Lord so consistently gives him the wrong advice?"

I was much less impressed by Roshan Seth as Jawaharlal Nehru. Throughout the film I felt I was in the presence of Gandhi, both old and, as one could imagine him, relatively young. I never quite thought that Seth was Nehru, and this was also my wife's response. Partly this was because we knew Nehru well, loved him much and hadn't known Gandhi at all. If one has known the original, he adheres in the eye and mind even through the best acting. But partly the film does not do full justice to Nehru. Here he is a slight, slightly diffident figure, standing only a bit above the other members of Gandhi's entourage. In fact, by the time of Gandhi's death, Nehru was a major figure in his own right — with Vallabhbhai Patel, one of the two men who would guide India through the infinitely complex tasks of the early years of independence. He had qualities for this job — the patience, temperament and administrative commitment for heading a government — that Gandhi never possessed. (Patel, who achieved the incorporation of the princely states and who was also an exceedingly effective political operator, died in 1950.) If Nehru isn't quite right in the film, it is because in the scenes dealing with Gandhi's last years he isn't accorded nearly the emphasis he deserves.

The temptation when reviewing any theatrical form is to dwell on the flaws. How else can one establish one's superior knowledge as compared with that of the director, playwright or producer? But let me plead now with the reader: Do not be restrained by this criticism. If the film weren't so good, I wouldn't be commenting on it at such length.

Mohandas Karamchand Gandhi was one of the supreme figures of the century. He was also one of the great political innovators of all time. In the usual dialectic of power, one I have celebrated in a book on the subject, force is countered by force, money by money, propaganda by propaganda. There is a basic symmetry between action and response: men always fight fire with fire. It was Gandhi's genius that he saw the strength that lay in asymmetry. Had he fought the armed power of the Raj with armed force, his movement would not have survived a week. Meeting violence with committed nonviolence, repression with carefully conditioned disobedience, he was invulnerable. It was a lesson later to be used with similar effect by Martin Luther King, Jr. This design is brilliantly here portrayed — the asymmetrical response to violence is the central theme from which the film never deviates. Everyone will understand Gandhi (and India) better for seeing it.

MUHAMMAD ALI JINNAH*

(1984)

Over the last forty years Mohandas Gandhi has had an extensive, admiring and generally approving press, but, as I say here, his great antagonist, Muhammad Ali Jinnah, has faded largely from sight. No one can doubt that this was a fate Jinnah did much to invite. Still, Professor Stanley Wolpert's book is a most welcome effort to retrieve him and restore balance.

History has been less than kind to Muhammad Ali Jinnah, the principal parent of modern Pakistan, much less kind than to his Indian counterparts, Mohandas Gandhi and the two Nehrus, Motilal and Jawaharlal, his son. This is partly, no doubt, because, by all democratic standards, India has thus far been a success while Pakistan has had to suffer a far from attractive succession of military dictators. And India, despite some effort to the contrary, has remained a solid entity, while Pakistan eventually broke apart, something that, at the time of independence, quite a few thought inevitable. But quite aside from the later history, Gandhi and Nehru are generally viewed as greatly intelligent, highly resourceful, personally disinterested statesmen; Jinnah, by comparison, when not forgotten, is remembered by many as a difficult, petulant, self-centered figure, who, out of pride, arrogance and ambition, ruthlessly exploited the Islamic grievances and obsessions of his followers and destroyed the dream of one great unitary commonwealth on the subcontinent.

This highly competent book by a major historian of modern India does something to alter the foregoing impression, especially as regards Jinnah's early career. Though it is billed as a biography of Jinnah, it is actually a detailed, almost year-by-year account of the half century

---

*This was a review, originally published in *Book World* of *The Washington Post*, of *Jinnah of Pakistan* by Stanley Wolpert (New York: Oxford University Press, 1984).

of struggle for Indian self-government and independence and of the long and intensely frustrating effort to find a formula that would be acceptable to the two great religious and cultural communities, the Hindus and the Muslims, as extremist agitation carried them farther and farther apart. That formula had also to be one that accommodated the less vocal concerns of the Sikhs, Untouchables and Christians and of the Indian princes. Eventually the problem for Britain became not whether to grant India independence but how indeed, if at all, to accomplish it.

In all this effort Jinnah, to an extent now largely unacknowledged, was a figure in transition. In the beginning, as a brilliant, socially elegant lawyer back from London with a highly lucrative practice in Bombay, he was a prime apostle of Hindu-Muslim unity, a strong voice against intransigence and resulting communal conflict. Then over the years, and especially in the last decades of his life, he became one of the most intransigent of all, moving to an ever increasing commitment to a separate political existence for the two communities, which was derived from the strongly expressed fear that the British Raj would give way to the Hindu Raj. Eventually, but by no means abruptly, he came to the concept of Pakistan, an idea that, when first mooted by a group of young radicals in Cambridge, England, had been all but universally dismissed as visionary and even eccentric or bizarre. That Jinnah was led to this change by personal pride, prickliness and ambition, Professor Wolpert by no means denies. But he also shows that in the seemingly endless attempts to find a formula for government of, and peaceful coexistence between, the two communities, Jinnah was not the only one at fault. Gandhi's recurring shifts and vagaries and the occasional tactlessness of Jawaharlal Nehru contributed to Jinnah's frustration and alienation. One cannot read this book without wishing that there could have been more patience, tolerance and willingness to yield points on both sides. And one learns how both sides became captive to their own public agitation and oratory. But this being said, it remains that Jinnah was an exceptionally hard man with whom to do business.

In the end, the partition that Jinnah had come to demand had to be accepted — very reluctantly, it must be said, by the Indians and the government of Clement Attlee in London. It had become, or anyhow seemed to be, the least bad — the least conducive to communal violence and death — of the available alternatives. So, in the space of a few weeks in 1947, lines were drawn, slicing the country apart. Jinnah, to the fierce anger of some of his followers, accepted the division of the Punjab and Bengal into their predominantly Hindu and Muslim parts. (Once it had been supposed by many that all of both might go to Pakistan.) Then followed the panic-stricken flight from both sides and the terrible accompanying bloodshed.

Jinnah moved in those summer days from Bombay to Karachi, a city he had left in his boyhood. Professor Wolpert believes he went with no slight sense of his responsibility for the awful events then occurring in the north and distant east. But by this time he was a dying man; indeed, for some years he had been under sentence of death from a devastating combination of tuberculosis and lung cancer aggravated by extreme cigarette addiction. He had refused to surrender to ill health as stubbornly as he had refused to surrender to the numerous proposals for an Indian federation with varied safeguards for the Islamic minority. Still resisting, he died a few days after the first anniversary of independence.

No one will doubt the care with which Professor Wolpert has addressed his present task or the excellent use he has made of British, Pakistani and Indian materials now available. No one certainly will think him negligent as to detail; he could, however, have given more thought to what is really needed. Good history is not every conversation that was held, every trip that was taken, every meeting that was attended. And the author has also a disturbing tendency to interrupt his solid, decent prose with an occasional thrust into grandiose expression and metaphor. "Mountbatten with his brilliant staff of experts was soon to be launched on the fastest mission of major political surgery ever performed by one nation on the pregnant body politic of another." Operation on a body politic perhaps; a pregnant one, please no. But these are faults to be forgiven. I read this book with gratitude and the wish, as regards my own education, that it had been written much earlier.

LORD LOUIS MOUNTBATTEN*

(1985)

I was reared in Canada amidst the suspicion of royalty that the Canadian clansmen retained from ancient times in the Highlands and continued lovingly to preserve and cultivate. At school, under the Canadian establishment influence, we read and heard of the superior intellectual and moral attributes of George V and the wholly unbelievable qualities of his oldest son, the good, young, peripatetic Prince of Wales. At home and by our Scottish neighbors we were told that what was unbelievable was not, indeed, to be believed. The effect of this early conditioning remained with me, and in later years I have read without either surprise or any grave regret of the marital misfortunes of Princess Margaret or of the travels and other presumed exploits of Prince Andrew, Randy Andy.

The only corrective tendency to which I've been subject was from encounters with Louis Mountbatten — first in India and then on one or two lesser social occasions. As the book here reviewed makes clear, he was not a man under whom you would wish to serve on a destroyer. Safer by far to be on that huge staff at Kandy in what is now Sri Lanka. But as someone to encounter on diplomatic business or for no business at all, no one could have been nicer. I've never been certain as to what is charm, and I've no great desire to be told. It was attributed compulsively, even tediously, to Mountbatten, and I'm prepared to believe that those who did so were not wrong.

He was also an accomplished raconteur, and I allow myself an example. Once, many years ago in New York, Mountbatten told me that he had heard I was editing Randolph Churchill's collections of his father's papers. I told him I was not; I was merely reading the first two volumes for possible correction of Churchillian economics.†

*This was a review, originally published in *Book World* of *The Washington Post*, of *Mountbatten* by Philip Ziegler (New York: Knopf, 1985).
†See "Further on Churchill and the Churchill Style," page 306.

"You will find Randolph a difficult chap," Mountbatten said. *"He was with me at the North African landings in 1942. A very difficult chap."*

According to the ensuing story, Churchill transferred himself from Mountbatten's commandos to a guards regiment ashore, and the officer in command, on discovering that he had this new subordinate, was far from pleased. This was the conversation as Mountbatten told of it:

"Major Churchill," said the OC, *"I must tell you that you are most unwelcome!"*

"Why, sir?" Randolph asked, holding himself very erect.

"Your habit of criticizing your superior officers. It is most prejudicial to discipline."

"I've never criticized my superior officers, sir."

The OC now gulped once or twice. *"Why, Major Churchill, you're notorious for your criticism of General Anderson."* (Anderson was the general commanding the British component in Torch, the North African operation, and a not universally approved figure.)

"I'm sorry, sir," said Churchill. *"I'm practically the only man in the whole British army who ever said anything good about him, sir."*

In the early paragraphs of this excellent, even fascinating, but not flawless biography, Philip Ziegler tells of the favorite leisure-time occupation of Lord Louis Mountbatten, Earl Mountbatten of Burma. It was tracing out his genealogy, no slight task, involving, as it did, family connections extending through an intricate German maze back to Charlemagne or perhaps beyond and, in more recent times, establishing him as a great-grandson of Queen Victoria, a nephew of the last Czar and Czarina of Russia and, of course, the uncle of the husband of the current Queen of England. He greatly preferred this genealogical research to reading or other more tedious pursuits. It also reflected sound judgment; no one was ever better served by the accident of birth or put royal connection to greater use.

Family background led, first, to his choice of a naval career. Here he followed his father, Prince Louis of Battenberg, who at the beginning of World War I was the First Sea Lord, effectively the uniformed head of the British Royal Navy, but who in the violent chauvinism of the day was presently expelled from office for having such an unwholesome German name. (This last misfortune was repaired in the course of time by his becoming Lord Milford Haven and the family not Battenberg but Mountbatten. The British do these things well — or used to.)

Louis Mountbatten's early naval service was less than routine: it involved such tasks as accompanying the Prince of Wales, later and with rewarding brevity Edward VIII, on journeys of state to Australia and India. However, he became fully involved with ships at the outbreak of World War II, when, as a destroyer commander, he began to compile one of the war's most remarkable records of disaster. This stemmed from his tendency to proceed at high speed and without evident prior thought as to what, in the way of other ships, mines or enemies, he might encounter. During the tense days of 1940, when England awaited the threatened invasion, he was almost always in dock while his ship was being fixed up following various largely preventable mishaps.

In ensuing months, Mountbatten was promoted to the command of a destroyer division and promptly lost his own ship at Crete, though here perhaps through no grave personal fault. This led, inevitably, to a promise of further promotion to the command of an aircraft carrier, from which, mercifully for the crew, he was diverted to head Combined Operations. Here he planned and directed the raid on Dieppe, which is widely believed to have been the single most ill-advised, costly and generally disastrous operation of the war. Accordingly, or at least predictably, in the months following, he was promoted to the post of Supreme Commander, South-East Asia Command, with headquarters first in New Delhi and then in Kandy in Ceylon, as it then was.

From Asia, Mountbatten lobbied London for permission to conduct amphibious operations against Burma, Malaya and Indonesia, as well as on behalf of his land operations in eastern India and Burma. On the amphibious operations he was not successful until after the Japanese surrender, when there was a landing on some Malayan beaches. Intelligence being poor, it was not known that the sand was exceedingly soft, and so the transport and armored equipment got hopelessly bogged down. However, hostilities having ended, Mountbatten did not immediately get another naval promotion in consequence. The intelligence failure, it should be noted, could not be blamed on a shortage of personnel at his headquarters; by the end of the war Mountbatten had a staff at Kandy of nearly ten thousand, which, it being a time of considerable manpower shortage, even the tolerant authorities back in London thought rather large. Mr. Ziegler, who had access to the Mountbatten papers, cannot conceal his feeling that in the Royal Navy Mountbatten was an outstanding example of upward failure.

There is little doubt that, throughout, Lord Louis was saved and helped by his royal connections — his attention to genealogy continued to show a sound sense of what was important. But he also had three other qualities: great personal charm, as all who knew him can attest; unflagging self-confidence; and an overwhelming desire to get things done. This last, in a military establishment in which caution and respect for tradition verged on inertia, attracted attention, not the least from Winston Churchill. All his life Mountbatten was repeatedly sought out by people who wanted less thought and more action, both of which he could provide.

At the end of the war yet another personal quality became evident:

his ability to see, with the guidance and encouragement of his diversely concerned, rich, talented and unquestionably very difficult wife, that the age of imperialism was over. He made this apparent in both word and action, which extended to associating himself with those seeking independence in Burma, Indonesia and India and not rejecting, as most were inclined to do, those in Burma and Indonesia who had aligned themselves in the war with the Japanese and against their old imperial masters. Most of all, he showed his friendship and sympathy for Gandhi and Nehru, becoming, as even more did Edwina Mountbatten, a devoted friend of Nehru's. This led to the next, and by a wide margin the greatest, of his assignments — to preside as viceroy over the partition of India and the proclamation of Indian and Pakistani independence and to serve, eventually, as governor general of the new Indian state. Then, still a relatively young man, he went back to a naval command, rose to be First Sea Lord, the post from which his father had been sacked, and eventually head of all the more or less unified armed services. As First Sea Lord he strongly resisted the Suez misadventure of Anthony Eden, coming close to taking the unprecedented step of submitting his resignation. In those years he also became deeply aware of the way nuclear arms were robbing war of its old relevance and enjoyments. He was now clearly a force for the good — judgment was for him increasingly an attribute of age.

Leaving office in 1965, Mountbatten passed into a notably reluctant and peripatetic retirement. He was killed in 1979 at the age of seventy-nine by IRA terrorists while sailing near his Irish estate.

Mr. Ziegler has told this quite remarkable story in lucid detail, sometimes — as in the case of the struggles over authority, command, weaponry and especially over rank and personal privilege in the Royal Navy, the British defense establishment and the royal family — in greatly excessive detail, at least for an American reader. He has also spent too much time deciding whether on this action or decision or that Mountbatten was right or wrong. (Especially when Mountbatten was wrong, Ziegler is tedious in his effort to find, however improbably, some trace of redeeming wisdom.) I've never been persuaded that facts speak for themselves; in my observation they can be very reticent as to the real truth. But it is not necessary to pass judgment, as Mr. Ziegler does, on everything.

On Mountbatten's most portentous decision, that taken as viceroy in March 1947 to abandon caution and press forward to Indian and Pakistani independence by mid-August, Mr. Ziegler could not, of course, avoid judgment. That and whether the vicious slaughter, especially in the newly divided Punjab, could have been avoided have been endlessly debated and are still a contentious subject. With others, I've wondered if a more gradual approach, with more appeals for calm and reason, more time for adjustment, might have served better. But Mountbatten, as ever, was impatient for action. The larger truth is that no one knows. By the time the Mountbattens arrived in India, there had ceased to be any alternative to partition. Positions, especially that of Muhammad Ali Jinnah, the head of the Muslim League, were fixed, irrevocable. Perhaps delay would only have meant months of mounting anger and more deaths when partition and independence finally came.

To return to Mountbatten's career as a whole, it was certainly one of the most varied and interesting of the time. If Mr. Ziegler, as I've said, does it slightly more than justice, that is distinctly better than doing it less. No reviewer will risk rebuke for recommending the result.

· IX ·

PORTRAITS AND
REMEMBRANCES

ONE OF THE PENALTIES of longevity is recurring sorrow for
the friends who have not survived or whom geographical
distance has removed from the daily scene. (One can even
mourn the human fallibility and error that have forced a
familiar political figure from office.) But in writing of them,
one is able to bring them back to mind, and with more than
a little joy.

JOHN F. KENNEDY

(1963)

Right after the President's murder, The Washington Post *asked me to write a piece to be published on the morning of his funeral. I was in Washington helping with the terrible minutiae of the time, including the manifold details of the funeral arrangements. I had also had a request from Lyndon Johnson for help on the speech he was presently to give to the Congress. But somehow I found time for this, and I remember being grateful to* The Post; *intense occupation, as has often and tediously been observed, was, indeed, a solvent for sorrow, an escape from reflection on the meaning of this appalling act.*

In these last few hours since the President's death, hundreds, perhaps thousands, have tried to write about John F. Kennedy. This is not wholly a ritual of the modern newspaper, one of the final rites for the great. Millions of people on this dark and somber weekend want to read about and then to reflect on this man who was so profoundly a part of their lives, and this wish the papers are seeking to serve. My justification for my own brief word is that I knew the President a trifle better than most of those who must tell of him in these awful days.

No one knew the President well. In a sense no one could, for it is part of the character of a leader that he cannot be known. The rest of us can indulge our moments when we open the shutters to our soul. We are granted our times of despair — the despair, indeed, that we felt last Friday when that incredible flash came in from Dallas. But a Kennedy or a Roosevelt can never turn the palms of his hands outward to the world and say, "Oh, God. What do we do now?" The armor that ensures confidence in power and certainty in command may never be removed even for a moment. No one ever knew John F. Kennedy as other men are known.

But he carried his armor lightly and with grace and with, one sometimes thought, the knowledge that though he had it without escape, at least it need not be a barrier between him and his associates. He surprised even friends with the easy candor with which he spoke of touchy problems, half-formed plans or personal political dangers. Without malice or pettiness, he reflected aloud on the strengths and weaknesses of high officials and influential politicians. He was constantly and richly amused by the vanity of men in high places. He freely discussed ideas the mention of which would make most men shudder. Last summer during the visit of President Sarvepalli Radhakrishnan of India, allusion was made in a social moment before a formal dinner to some woman politician, and Kennedy turned and asked me why there had been so few women politicians of importance — whether women were poorly adapted to the political art. Here surely was a ticklish subject; women are half the voting population and may not react well to wonder at their political shortcomings. I struggled to come up with examples — the first Elizabeth, Eleanor Roosevelt, one or two others. The President admitted of the exceptions but good-humoredly returned to the rule. He knew he could discuss an interesting point without anyone's supposing that he was against the Nineteenth Amendment.

"The political campaign won't tire me," he said in the spring of 1960, "for I have an advantage. I can be myself." He had learned one of life's hardest lessons, which is that we all have far more liberty than we use. And he knew beyond this that others, because they admired it, would respect the informality with which he passed through life. No President ever said so much to so many friends and acquaintances and so rarely had to disavow or explain.

John F. Kennedy was much interested in writing. This, I think, provides one small clue to understanding him. Good writing requires a sense of economy and of style and the absence of vanity that allows a man to divorce his writing at least a little from himself. A writer can be interesting when he is speaking to others; he is rarely if ever interesting when he is speaking only to himself, except to himself.

Kennedy hated verbosity. Though he rejoiced in politics, he hated the wordiness of the political craft. He never, at least in his adult life, opened his mouth without having something to say. Never, even in conversation, did he speak for the pleasure of hearing his own words and phrases. Many of us have a diminished interest in the words of others, and Kennedy, also, was impatient with garrulous men. But he was the rare case of the man who applied the rules with equal rigor to himself.

The Kennedy style, though it involved detachment from self, involved no self-deprecation. In the early years when he was enlisting followers, he didn't offer a program for universal salvation. He was suspicious of resonant formulae from whatever source — he rightly regarded some of the liturgy of American liberalism as corrupt. It is trundled out at election time as once were the candidate's trains, urged in a torrent of words and then put away for another four years. His case, again, had the merit of candor. He said, essentially, I am a man worth following; you can count on me to be honestly better at the art of government than any other possible contender; and, an important detail, I know how to get elected.

That he was qualified in the art of government there will never be any question. His style called for unremitting good taste and good manners. It called also for a profound commitment to information and reason. He didn't think that man had been civilized as an afterthought; he believed it was for a purpose. Perhaps there are natural men, those who have a native gift for art and insight, but Kennedy, without being so rude as to say so, believed such pretension an excuse for laziness. His reliance was on what men had learned and had come to know.

What he had come to know about the art and substance of American government was prodigious. I first knew Jack Kennedy twenty-five years ago when I was a comparatively young tutor and he was an undergraduate in Winthrop House at Harvard. He was charming, ir-reverent, good-looking and far from diligent. What no one knew at the time was that he also had the priceless notion that education never stops. Some of us who later worked with him on economic issues — farm policy, Federal Reserve policy, the control of inflation, other ar-cane or technical matters — used to say that we had observed three stages in his career in the House of Representatives and more partic-ularly in the Senate: the first was when he called up to ask how we thought he should vote; the second was when he called to ask fifteen or twenty quick questions as to what lay behind the particular action or measure; the third was when he didn't call at all or, if he did, he inquired as to why, as he had gleaned from an article or a letter to *The New York Times*, we seemed to be acting on some misinformation. My Harvard colleague Professor Carl Kaysen, who worked in the White House these last years, has said that when he was asked who was the most knowledgeable of the President's advisers, he always felt obliged to remind his questioner that none was half so well informed as the President himself.

Departments and individuals, in approaching a President, invariably emphasize the matters that impress them most. Kennedy knew how to make the appropriate discounts without anyone's quite realizing they were being made. He had a natural sense for all of the variables in a problem; he could not be carried away by any one.

Like all men of deep intelligence, he respected the intelligence of others. That was why he didn't talk down to the American people; it was why he was contemptuous of the arm-waving circus posturing of the American politician, which so many newspapermen so much admire up to the moment of final defeat. The President faced a speaker with his wide gray-blue eyes and total concentration. And thus he addressed a paper or an article. As far as one could tell, once it was his it was his forever.

This, of course, was not all. Knowledge is power. But knowledge without character and wisdom is nothing, or worse. The last two qualities the President also had in rich measure. But I come back to his grasp of issues, his breadth of information, his power of concentration. Perhaps these came naturally. I suspect, however, that few men in history ever combined such natural ability with such powers of mental self-discipline.

ELEANOR ROOSEVELT

(1983)

This was written for a special issue of Esquire *devoted to the fifty people who "had made a difference" over its fifty-year history. Quite a few of those selected had; but certainly less had to be invented to justify Eleanor Roosevelt than in the case of most.*

I came to know her quite well only after her husband's death. One of our last encounters, perhaps the last, was during the election campaign of 1960, when she sent me to Bernard Baruch to get a contribution and endorsement for Kennedy. (After much early hesitation, she was by then solidly and even ardently on the side of JFK.) I was able when next I saw her to report success, but I had to admit that it had required several hours of ostentatiously careful listening to Baruch's praise of Baruch.

"That's Bernie, all right," she said. "By the time my husband died, he had become rather tired of Bernie and of his using the White House as his personal sounding board. They were not on good terms. But when news came of the President's stroke, Bernie came right over to Warm Springs and stayed with us there. And he came on the train with us to Washington and was with us through the state funeral. Then on to Hyde Park, and he was there for the family funeral. Several times I thought he was going to get into the coffin with Franklin."

This was the whiplash effect we all came to respect — and slightly to fear.

A meticulous assistant of mine, Catherine Aman, advises me, after checking with the Roosevelt Library in Hyde Park, that the opprobrious term "First Lady" was in use, at least colloquially, as early as 1934.

One day in the autumn of 1940, with American entry into World War II in the middle distance, I was giving thought to a task with which I had recently been charged. It was to guide a substantial number of the ordnance and munitions plants then being planned — some sixty in all — into the Southern and South-Central states. White and maybe black workers lost in those days to rural poverty would thus be employed, and a yet greater industrial concentration in the East and Northeast would be avoided. I was chairman of a civilian committee dedicated to this end, and we were making no progress in persuading the War Department, as it then was, to our design.

I turned for help to people knowledgeable in the folkways of the Roosevelt administration, and in particular to Donald Comer, a Birmingham textile manufacturer, the liberal son of an Alabama governor, a power in Southern politics and a man with much experience in making his way around Washington. Could he get me to the President on the issue? Comer said it was far more important to get to Mrs. Roosevelt. And so we did. We made an appointment, boarded the train to New York and went to her Washington Square apartment, where she was staying at the moment. The rooms were of modest size; my memory is of beige slipcovers and upholstery, all on the rusty side. There were three of us in the delegation; our third man was a government functionary who had joined us only to share in the Roosevelt *darshan*. He said not a word, and after the meeting we never saw him again. Comer and I, in contrast, were eloquent, even impassioned. After assuring herself as to our motives, Mrs. Roosevelt promised to help, and in subsequent weeks we found we had the support of the President. A fair number of plants went south; in ensuing years they almost certainly had an effect on the economic development of the region. Eventually one heard of the Sun Belt. It was the kind of difference that all who were around at the time will tell you Eleanor Roosevelt made.

I assume that she did, indeed, speak to the President; in any case, her effect on his policies is not in doubt. But Eleanor Roosevelt's true influence was not by way of her husband; it was directly on the people of the United States and the world at large. There is proof in the fact that it continued undiminished for nearly two decades after the death of Franklin Roosevelt. Had she been confined to the role of a wife, however brilliant and effective, she would have been forgotten long since. Wives of Presidents, with a few notable exceptions, are highly forgettable. I speak, incidentally but very deliberately, of them as *wives*. Eleanor Roosevelt would surely have abhorred the title of First Lady, as it later came into general use. Like others, she would have wondered if the husband of the first woman President would be called the First Gent.

The difference Eleanor Roosevelt made in her own right was threefold. There was, first, her advocacy of civil equality in the Republic. Franklin D. Roosevelt had many things on his side, but a commitment to black and minority rights was not one of them. His coalition — white, mainly rural Southerners by whom white supremacy was assumed and Northern urban political machines and proletarians — would not have

survived an affirmative stand on civil rights for more than a week. But
Eleanor was not deterred; she dared the awful scorn reserved for those
who associated politically with Southern blacks; in those perilous days
she even had her picture taken shaking hands with them. Being willing
to risk that, she both paved the way for others and showed that some,
perhaps much, of the resulting reaction was highly motivated but quite
harmless hot air. She was equally interested in the old, the jobless, the
young and the poor, and these concerns continued and expanded after
the President's death.

Her second achievement was in showing, more than any of her contemporaries, that an American could truly be a world citizen. This was
manifest in her incessant and concerned travels and in her early and
enduring commitment to the United Nations; it was deeply evident in
her speeches and writing and in her innovative support for worldwide
human rights. In this day and age it is pleasant, if somewhat surprising,
to recall that there was a time when American leaders were loved
abroad. So it was with Eleanor Roosevelt. I was ambassador in India
on November 7, 1962, when word came of her death. I had the flag
at the Embassy lowered to half staff, not as the kind of self-gratifying
gesture in which I am deeply experienced; it was what the Indians
expected. Our loss was also theirs.

Finally, more than anyone else in her time, Eleanor Roosevelt proved
that a woman could have an independent — and powerful — position
in political life. This, in turn, is her claim to being one of the pioneer
figures in the modern women's movement. The notion that politics was
in some way a male monopoly never crossed her mind. Nor that she
was entitled to any deference because she was a woman. The thought
that she might somehow resort to feminine wiles or designs to get what
she wanted would surely have struck her as bizarre, and it would certainly have been out of character. She assumed a position of full equality
with men as a matter of course; more than that, she never hesitated to
show the superiority associated with an incisive mind, wide-ranging
information, a superbly accurate assessment of political motives and a
devastating response to political idiocy and pretense.

This last brings me to a most important point. In the past, women
didn't get anywhere in political or other public life because they were
admired or loved. Nor do they now. They began to make progress only
when they were feared. And so it remains. This was the lesson of
Eleanor Roosevelt. I saw her on various occasions, once or twice on
matters to do with the Stevenson campaigns and more specifically when
I was working on behalf of John F. Kennedy. I never came into her
presence without a certain sense of trepidation. When she gave you
her views, including what she thought of your ideas or plans, you were
not left in any doubt — certainly not if you were inadequate or foolish

and she thought so. That sense of anxiety, of tension, is the feeling anyone exercising power must induce, and this she did. The women who led the feminist movement in the years following her death had a similar capacity to command respect, which is another way of saying that men were a little afraid of them. Eleanor Roosevelt, in major measure, was their model.

RICHARD NIXON

(1974)

In 1941 and after, I was in charge of wartime price-control operations in Washington and also, for a time, rationing and rent control. To my staff, more accurately to that of our lawyers, came a young recruit from California. This allows me to say with fair accuracy that I brought Richard Milhous Nixon into public life, launched him on his public career. Of this neither of us has ever made much mention. For a long while in his official biography he said only that he had worked for the Office of Emergency Management; this was the administrative holding company of the wartime agencies. It was as though a former Marine said he had served in the Department of Defense.

In the autumn of 1984, my wife and I attended the funeral in Brattleboro, Vermont, of Ellsworth Bunker, our lifelong friend and Vermont neighbor. So did Mr. Nixon. After the service was over, Norman Runyon, the admirably alert editor of The Brattleboro Reformer, *captured the former President to ask him about Ambassador Bunker. Mr. Nixon praised him warmly, a man of real integrity. In response to a further question, he praised Senator George Aiken, then very ill in the hospital. He affirmed that he, too, was a man of real integrity. When finally asked about me, he replied only that he was aware of my books. Telling me of it afterward, Runyon hazarded the guess that the former President would go only so far in attributing integrity. I prefer to think that he may have seen this piece in* The Boston Globe.

I return here to the vacuous banality of our election reporting. In some future campaign some innovative candidate will advocate all-out nuclear war, and the ensuing learned political comment will be largely, even exclusively, centered on the probable effect of the statement on his standing in the polls.

Richard Nixon has gone, and that is a good thing. To the end he pictured himself as a man of impeccable virtue, but he was always given to overstatement. Still, we've had honest men in our public life and some truly inspired thieves. Mr. Nixon may have been the intermediate case, who didn't know the difference. It will be said by historians that he lacked personal magnetism; in fact, he had a great ability to attract men like himself, although perhaps more those with a talent for public predation as opposed to purely private greed. Mr. Nixon, of course, inclined to both.

While his going is good, we will suffer for it in the days and weeks ahead, because his departure will bring out all that is most loathsome in our literary tradition. There will now be drawing of morals until healthy stomachs retch. Soul searching will be on a production-line basis, soul searching being the metaphor for what columnists and editorial writers of the most soulless sort do when they have a deadline, an inescapable topic and a blank mind.

Someone, I promise you, will say that the fault lies deeply within all of us. Well, the hell it does. It lies with Richard Nixon and the people who voted him into office.

The only lesson to be drawn from the Nixon debacle is that, even after due notice, the wrong man can get elected in this country by a landslide, for Mr. Nixon has been tediously around and visible for close on to thirty-five years. For those who missed his indecent actions against Jerry Voorhis and Helen Gahagan Douglas, there was the awful public charlatanism of the Checkers speech. And after his California gubernatorial defeat there was his even more obscene farewell to the press. And he was President for four years. If the American people didn't know Richard Nixon by 1972, the French didn't know Louis XIV by 1715. Mr. Nixon was a premeditated assault on the public decency and interest committed in broad daylight. Why, how, did it happen?

Four things, I judge, got Mr. Nixon elected and re-elected, of which the first and most important was the Vietnam war. Americans have a reliable tendency to turn on Presidents and parties that get them into war, and it is a sound habit, the resulting Mr. Harding and Mr. Nixon notwithstanding. If any future President involves us in anything as foolish as the Vietnam war, we will have earned another Nixon and maybe an Agnew, too.

The second factor in Mr. Nixon's survival was the decay of the language. He was a pious fraud in the deepest meaning of that phrase, which is to say that whenever he was caught in public falsehood, or other dereliction, he assumed a mood of righteousness and complained that his enemies were having at him again. Yet he was rarely so described in print or on the air. During his campaigns there was scarcely a newspaperman who didn't know that he was a fraud; in private conversation they said so. Among ourselves we still use the language to convey meaning. But such is modern English usage, as accommodated to the cautions, habits and fears, both bureaucratic and commercial, of the newspapers, wire services and networks, that no one can use such a word in public. We praise the increased civility of our public life, which keeps us from saying men are liars or thieves. But this is good only if there are no liars or thieves.

The third thing that helped Richard Nixon is the nature of the modern political campaign. It has in the United States a public fascination as a game that is not present in any other known jurisdiction. In consequence, attention comes to focus on the spectacle, including the spectacle that the participants are making of themselves, rather than on the possible effects of the election. Reporting, television coverage in particular, is of the crowds and their reaction and only secondarily of what was said. And it is deeply concerned with the strategy and tactics of the campaign, which are reported in the same manner as those of a game. There is great discussion as to whether a candidate is gaining or losing ground (note the football metaphor); there is talk of who is up and who is down, who is in and who is out, on the candidate's team (again the echo of athletics); and there is lengthy attention, as though to the coach, to the particular political, intellectual and administrative vacuum who functions as campaign manager and whose notoriety and genius will almost certainly expire forever on Election Day. Above all, there is intense concentration on which candidate will win and which will lose as revealed by the polls.

When thus viewed as a game, politics has no purpose beyond the election; what the winning player does after the crowd goes home is unimportant. Because issues, intelligence and character are an increasingly insignificant part of our concern, it was possible in the 1972 campaign for Mr. Nixon to lurk in the White House or various of the other real estate he had converted to his own use and know that his evasion and reticence would be discussed only as a tactic. He was right; commentators said over and over again that Mr. Nixon was very shrewd not to remind people what he was like. It was decisive against George McGovern, in turn, that he ran a bad campaign. As a measure of what a man would do as President, nothing could be more useless.

Finally, there is the solid preference of many Americans of the highest respectability and the saintliest character for any politician, however depraved, if he seems not to be a threat to their personal wealth and well-being. This is coupled with the remarkable capacity of the American establishment to make ridiculous what seems to threaten its privileges. In the election of 1972, Mr. Nixon was perceived as no threat to the affluent. Senator McGovern inspired no such confidence, to say the least. He advanced a rather sensible program for cutting the indulgence out of the military budget, rearranging public priorities, closing out tax graft, putting a floor under the incomes of the poor while keeping an incentive to work and otherwise improving the civilian functions of the government. None of this got discussed on its merits.

Those adversely affected responded not with a well-reasoned defense of their wealth, inheritance, exemptions, contracts or graft or even with a proper disquisition on the inherent unworthiness of the poor. Instead they resorted to the far more effective device of picturing the man who took these positions as inherently ludicrous.

There is one final lesson from this sordid experience: in appreciable measure Richard Nixon was helped by the ancient belief in the capacity of man for redemption. There was, almost everyone agreed, an old Nixon who was bad. But Christian charity required people to believe that he might have changed — that there was a new Nixon or even, when the new Nixon seemed flawed, a new, new Nixon. It would have been better and safer if we had indulged the same gnawing doubts with which so many agnostics view the presumptively transformed and the born again.

4

SEYMOUR EDWIN HARRIS

(1975)

More than is so with most scholars, judgment being subjective and hostage to fashion, there are some economists who are, in reality, well below their public reputation and others who are well above. Seymour Harris was the latter case — a long-time professor at Harvard, chairman of its department of economics and a very diligent and efficient worker and adviser on community, state and national affairs. He was also one of the genuinely progressive and innovative figures of modern economics, constantly concerned to bring economic knowledge to bear on pressing practical problems. Yet he was only beginning to achieve the esteem he deserved in his last years. This piece, too late alas, was meant to reinforce this salutary gain.

In commenting soon after his death on the qualities of Seymour Harris, my much loved colleague at Harvard, I said that he was the kind of man that the academic community often regards with doubt. Professed scholars do not always set high store by kindness and generosity. A reserved, somewhat calculating approach to life is taken to suggest a better mind; a touch of malice is presumed to indicate a greater depth of personality. Since we are judged by our peers, we are required to have a good opinion of ourselves; no one will improve on our own assessment. And in all universities there are doubts about the man who works too hard; there are implicit trade union rules that all sensitive scholars respect. The good mind cannot be hurried; to do too much is to invite the suspicion of inferior scholarship.

Seymour Harris violated all of these injunctions. He was unfailingly kind. He was also unfailingly generous. In thirty and more years of close friendship I never heard him say a malicious, even a seriously unkind, word about any colleague, perhaps not about any person. He was beset by doubts about himself. He wanted people to think well of him and of his work, but he was not at all sure that they should.

And Seymour Harris was a prodigious worker. By way of preface,

I mention first his nonacademic services. These began during World War II, when he was a senior member of the staff of the Office of Price Administration, the head of the division that administered the prices of exported and imported products. A subtle and intricate task. He also handled relations between the OPA and the Board of Economic Warfare and the Department of State. While doing this, he found time to conduct a school on price control for new staff members, and, inevitably, he wrote a book on the subject. Characteristically, he noted that women were as competent at price administration as men and were not subject to the draft, so his two top deputies in those years were highly professional women economists. Later, in the 1950s, Harris became a close friend of Adlai Stevenson, and in 1956 he was the author of a position paper on virtually every domestic issue of the presidential campaign. He also became a leading participant in the work of the Democratic Advisory Council.

Seymour Harris was also a guiding spirit in the development of the Massachusetts community college system. He was the principal counselor to New England governors on the economic problems of the Northeast and was used and trusted equally by leaders of both political parties. Members of Congress and congressional committees called on him times without number; I doubt that he ever refused. Under Presidents Kennedy and Johnson he was the major liaison between the United States Treasury and the academic community.

Except for a tragic accident of history, Seymour would have ended his career as a member of the Board of Governors of the Federal Reserve System. In the late summer of 1963, there were two vacancies to be filled, one of which was to go to an orthodox practitioner. Those who were present remember President Kennedy's delight in announcing that the other place on the board was to go to Seymour Harris; the expected tremors in the financial community were pleasantly on the President's mind. Politics dictated that the more conservative appointment be made first; President Kennedy was killed in Dallas before he could make the second, and Lyndon Johnson had another candidate in mind. Seymour's appointment would surely have been fitting, for his first major published work was a two-volume history of the System and its policies.

At Harvard, Seymour had nearly unlimited time for both the routine and the special tasks of the university. These extended from delighted service on the committee on athletics to attendance at every meeting of the Faculty of Arts and Sciences; he always familiarized himself in advance with the agenda; it was known and expected that he would have something useful to say on any significant item of business. He was, with all else, a faithful, careful, affectionate, though none would say inspired, teacher.

He was also, as all in the academic world know, the editor of *The*

Review of Economics and Statistics. He searched constantly for articles; he was a resourceful organizer of symposia; and he had an unfailing sense of what is now called relevance and what he considered the ordinary obligation of the economist to be useful. The considerable standing of *The Review* is attributable in very large measure to Seymour Harris's efforts.

With all of this, he found time for a truly formidable number of books. Not a few, not a dozen, but some forty in all. These were not works of finished craftsmanship; as he readily conceded, he was an indifferent writer. Some were entrepreneurial efforts in which he enlisted the assistance of his colleagues in opening up a new subject. But everything he wrote also reflected a high sense of responsibility for some problem of immediate and important public concern. On the economics of health care, education, Social Security, international monetary policy, central-bank policy, monetary history and literally a dozen other topics, he provided the basic source material from which scholars, public officials and legislators learned what could be done, what should be done and how it might be done.

His greatest accomplishment, however, was in bringing the ideas of John Maynard Keynes to the United States. With Alvin Hansen and Paul Samuelson, he was one of the three American economists who translated the Keynesian ideas into American terms and made them available to their American colleagues and the larger public.

Could anyone so kind, so generous, so filled with doubts and so phenomenally hard-working be really first rate? One tendency in the professional response to that question is understandable: surely anyone so motivated must lack the hard cutting edge, the capacity to concentrate many hours on small details, that is the mark of the true scholar. For a time, Seymour Harris did suffer for his virtues — was, indeed, regarded with doubt. And not being indifferent to the opinions of his peers, he was, I believe, a little hurt. Fortunately, this is a story with a happy ending.

For, as the years passed, it came to be known and accepted, not only at Harvard but among economists in general, that Seymour Edwin Harris was one of the remarkable men of our time. This was evident in the growing affection and esteem in which he was held by his colleagues. It was clear in the reliance that public officials and legislators placed on his guidance and advice. It was recognized in his selection and service as chairman of the department of economics at Harvard during one of its normally troubled passages. It was apparent also in his long and distinguished connection with the American Economic Association and his offices therein. And it was manifest in the grief with which the news of his death was received. There is satisfaction that a man who was so good and so much loved, who was so responsible, so concerned and so diligent, was, in the end, so rightly honored.

5

GEORGE KISTIAKOWSKY

(1983)

George Kistiakowsky, a Harvard professor of chemistry for many years, friend and science adviser of President Dwight D. Eisenhower, was one of the most noted and certainly one of the most respected scientists of his time. He was present in those fateful months at Los Alamos and designed the detonating device of the first atomic bomb. He led in warnings of the threat of nuclear war, in urging the need for an effective end to the arms race. "I will doubtless die in bed," he told his younger colleagues; "you will die of heat, radiation and blast." Others spoke of these matters at the Harvard memorial service following his death; I, of a more personal and affectionate association.

It is my purpose to speak of George Kistiakowsky not as a scientist, a scholar, a uniquely influential public official, a presidential adviser, but as a friend and a keeper of the public conscience. George Kistiakowsky had a deep and enduring sense of responsibility for his community and all who made it up. And this being sensed, it was reciprocated. We cared for him because he cared so deeply for all of us.

George's concern was no casual thing. When he saw something he didn't like, he didn't repine; his instinct was immediately to ask what should and could be done to correct it. And, it is fair to add, after a few minutes' thought he was never in any great doubt as to a course of action. The Pentagon archons were contemplating something foolish; they and the country must be so advised. *The New York Times* or *The Boston Globe* or someone therein had taken a wrong or damaging or inane view; he or she must promptly be set straight. The university was doing something not quite right. This required action, and George assumed responsibility as a matter of course. There was a memorable occasion some years back when Harvard seemed not to be stressing its excellence in the sciences in its appeal for funds and for the best students and in its claim to general public regard. No one who attended the ensuing faculty meeting has forgotten the eloquence and vigor with which George made that error known.

Above all, there was the arms race. Here, indeed, he was our conscience. Nearly all of us reflect in these days on the consequences of this competition; many express their concern and join with others in doing so. It was deeply characteristic of George Kistiakowsky that he did more, proceeding to put together, lead and even dominate one of the most effective national organizations seeking an end to this insanity — the Council for a Livable World. George didn't believe one changed much by meetings and discussions or by speeches, however impassioned. One accomplished things in a democracy when one elected legislators committed to one's purpose and defeated those who were opposed. Few things are so important in modern life as the distinction between action and the self-gratifying illusion of action. Few men have been so learned in this distinction as George. And none, I may add, was ever so contemptuous of those who failed to see it.

I've said that George Kistiakowsky was the conscience of his friends and his community. He was certainly mine. In the last ten years scarcely a week went by when we didn't speak; it was normal when I returned to my house or office to learn that he was to be called. George never had good news to convey; that didn't interest him; it was a waste of time. (He was annoyed in the last three and a half years of his struggle with cancer if one asked about his health. That, too, was idle comment. He gave a brief clinical account and changed the subject.) George was pre-eminently the purveyor of bad tidings, and he offered them relentlessly and in succinct and compelling detail. Yet one discovered that he was not a pessimist. On the contrary, he was the greatest of optimists, for it was always his belief that something, indeed much, could be done. One had only to go to work on the problem as George himself was already doing. His efforts continued until mere days, one could almost say hours, before the death that he had come quite calmly to accept.

A few days ago I spoke to his wife Elaine to tell her I was writing this appreciation and that I would speak not only of my own love but of that of George's friends. She said, "Ah, but you must also mention his enemies." This I gladly do. George knew that to serve those — and that — which he loved, he had, indeed, to make enemies. Surely no one gave that consequence so little cautious calculation. Or, I sometimes suspected, found more quiet satisfaction in the prospect. Above all, no one had a more enduring history in the effort. George Kistiakowsky began his life in Russia in conflict with Lenin and Leon Trotsky; he ended it in the United States in opposition to Ronald Reagan and Caspar Weinberger. As enemies go, one could hardly ask for greater distinction over a wider ideological span over a longer period of time than that.

I worry that I may be giving too stern a picture of my friend; I could be making George seem to be a solemn, dour, righteous exponent of the public and community good. Nothing could be more remote from the fact. We responded to George's concerns and accepted his leadership in university and public matters, but we also cherished his presence. With all else he was a wonderful companion with a rich vein of humor. This was not anecdotal humor, although George could, on occasion, derive and extend enjoyment from his own experience. It was not the humor of one who sought laughter. Rather, it was the humor that flowed from an acute appreciation of the absurd, a true sense of the fallacies and banalities of our time. Enlargement on these was partly George's way of enhancing reality or advancing his purpose of the moment, and it could be greatly entertaining. Many must have noticed it: when George talked, we all stopped to listen.

A truly great man has gone from among us. There are those who pretend on these occasions to a sense of celebration, who offer thanks for their good fortune in the person they have known. I wish I could share this elation. I feel, rather, that life will never be so full again; as a community we will never quite repair or replace our loss. When sadness is called for, let us not hesitate to be sad.

GUNNAR AND ALVA MYRDAL

(1975)

This paper was prepared for a gathering at the City University of New York to celebrate Alva and Gunnar Myrdal, both Nobel Prize–winners to whom the claim of Sweden is clearly subordinate to that of the world.

There is one error here and one superior prediction. I remembered the film that inspired the Myrdals' sojourn in the United States as being about Yellowstone Park. In reality, Gunnar advised me that night in New York, it was about the rescue of human beings from yellow fever. Why shouldn't the Myrdals do something similar about the blight of racial discrimination? No slight mistake.

I say here that even Ronald Reagan may one day discover John Maynard Keynes. As I've elsewhere stated, that discovery, so far as it concerns deficit financing, has since been made on a scale that Keynes himself could never have imagined.

I first met Gunnar Myrdal in the late autumn of 1937 — nearly forty years ago — and we have been friends ever since. I was in Sweden as a Social Science Research Council Fellow; Gunnar had previously been financed from similar Rockefeller sources, and he was obliged, accordingly, to look after me. When we met for lunch, he told me he had just received a most extraordinary invitation from the United States. The Carnegie Corporation had asked him to come over and, from a fresh, Swedish point of view, study the American race problem. Although he had written a letter of regret, he had not yet recovered from his astonishment; Americans were endlessly peculiar. I expressed amazement that anyone, especially in those meager years, should turn down a free, unsolicited grant of funds from a foundation; I had never heard of its being done; I took his action as reflecting a very odd quirk in the Swedish character. I am not sure at this late date how much of this I told Gunnar, but I do remember the depth of my surprise.

A few days later we met again. He told me that in the interim he and his wife, Alva, had been to the movies, where they had seen a film about Yellowstone Park, and it occurred to them that if they accepted the Carnegie invitation, they could see the American national parks in addition to studying the race problem in the Southern states, all at no cost. He had written to withdraw his earlier letter of refusal, or perhaps it hadn't yet been mailed. The result was *An American Dilemma*. The transformaton in race relations that still proceeds perhaps began and certainly was furthered by this great book. I like to think that some very small part of this achievement was the result of my instruction on the proper response of a scholar to philanthropy.

With Alva Myrdal my association has, of course, been both closer and more professional, for we each served as ambassador to India from our respective countries. While by the time of my arrival in New Delhi in 1961, Alva had gone back to Stockholm, we had opportunity to discuss our similar experiences and roles. From India she proceeded to her superb services to peace, disarmament, the United Nations and the Swedish government. Perhaps it was instruction by Ambassador Myrdal that accounted for my highly unnatural survival, as many saw it, as a diplomat.

This manifestation of modesty and reticence brings me back to Gunnar, for these are qualities we both share. When word came last autumn that he had received the Nobel Prize for economics, I called up his daughter Sissela Bok, a prominent citizen of Cambridge, Massachusetts, married to another prominent citizen, the president of Harvard, to ask for his New York address and to read the telegram of congratulations I had devised. It said that one could tolerate the award being divided, as it was, with our old friend Friedrich von Hayek, one of the finest and most untouched of late-eighteenth-century minds, as long as the other half went to Myrdal. I said to Sissela, "I hope this will not unduly aggravate your father's vanity." She said, "You must not have heard his comment on receiving the award." I asked her what it was. He had said, " 'I can't say I'm pleased, but it does remove a minor source of irritation.' "

Gunnar Myrdal is worth celebrating for his contribution to civil rights and civil decency in the United States. And for his role as an international civil servant — as the executive secretary of the United Nations Economic Commission for Europe. And for his acute and perceptive comments on the problems of the developing countries and the unwisdom of asking too much from governments that are already overburdened — governments in which administrative capacity and political will are scarce resources. But I have long been impressed by how few people are aware of another of his achievements. The name of John Maynard Keynes is greatly and properly celebrated in economics. It is associated with the idea of active intervention by the state to sustain employment — a principle that the most retarded Republican now accepts and that a few years hence may even be avowed by Ronald Reagan. When Keynes's *General Theory of Employment Interest and Money* was published in 1936, the notion of a budget balanced only at full employment — of the purposeful use of the deficit at other times to sustain employment — was already a commonplace in Stockholm. It had been developed by men for whom ideas were not important until they were made operative. And you will not be in doubt as to who was their leader; it was Gunnar Myrdal. What is today called the Keynesian Revolution might, justly, have been called the Myrdal Revolution.

During my stay in Stockholm in 1937, Gunnar directed me to make a pilgrimage to a suburb of the city to see the great Gustav Cassel. By then retired, Cassel was an economist of the old school — the very old school. Some of his views would have been regarded as a trifle inflexible by John Knox and slightly archaic by Gustavus Adolphus. Cassel came down the stairs to greet me with that peculiar majesty and presence that characterizes all men of great height. His opening sentence I remember to this day: "I suppose you have been visiting Myrdal and the rest of my Red students in Stockholm." Cassel regarded Myrdal as worthy of mention separate from his fellow Bolshevists.

It is regularly and compulsively said that in honoring someone, we honor ourselves. This evening we are assembled in New York, a long way from Stockholm but very much in the fraternity of scholars. Our purpose is to do homage to two of the most original, intelligent and civilized people of our time, who happen, by one of the happiest accidents of scholarship, to be married, one to the other. Their light shines on us all.

7

DAVID NIVEN

(1983)

The Boston Globe asked for this reminiscence after David Niven's death, and it was later reprinted in other newspapers. To it let me now add only another tear to the one here shed.

To all who knew and loved David Niven — I try to use the word *love* with reserve — there was never a doubt as to why he was one of the truly great theatrical personalities of his time. He did not need to act, certainly not to contrive. He was the same person off the screen as on — informed, amusing, a source of endless instruction and, there is no other word for it, enchanting. Perhaps he was even better off the screen, for then, free from script, he had full range for his diverse recollections, his frequent invention and his accomplished delight in the ludicrous and the pompously insane.

With all this, I could be giving a false impression, for David was intensely interested in the world. He pressed conversation on politics, current events and, with less visible reluctance than most, on economics, and I never saw him that he did not add something to my always meager knowledge of the theater, the arts and artists.

The Nivens were our friends for nearly twenty years — in Switzerland we were near neighbors, as distance is now regarded. I went to Gstaad each winter to write and, in past times, to ski. In later years while between films at his chalet in Château d'Oex, David was also much involved with his memoirs, his wonderful account of Hollywood in its lunar prime, and latterly with his novels, the most recent of which, I judge, he could not have finished. For part of the time we were helped by the same secretary, the talented Cathy Ratzburg.

When our writing for the day deteriorated into mere typing, we both went out to ski. This, though, we did only rarely together, for David was required by contract to ski under the protection of a guide and instructor. No one, I regret to say, had a similar investment in me. And it was generally known that the sport was safer if I kept at a distance.

As have many others, I rejoiced in Niven's consistently engaging account of adventures large and, more often, small. He was especially a connoisseur of memorable comment. There was, for example, the day he returned from Les Avants above Lake Geneva and a visit to Noël Coward. Coward was leaving in a day or two for Jamaica for another assault on his own memoirs. David asked him if he had kept lots of notes, diaries, letters and the like.

"No," said Noël, "I have a memory like an elephant. In point of fact, elephants often consult me."

On another day I asked David to tell me, out of his long association with Samuel Goldwyn, about the latter's malapropisms, the best known of which was "If Franklin D. Roosevelt were alive today, he would be turning over in his grave." David thought most of them had been invented, but to one he could personally attest. After World War II, British Field Marshal Bernard Montgomery came to Hollywood while on an American tour, and David was a guest at the luncheon given for him by Goldwyn. As in Washington and Cambridge, people assemble in Hollywood to talk; no one is expected to listen. In consequence, as the meal ended and the time came for the toasts, Goldwyn had great difficulty in getting the attention of the audience. He tapped on his glass, tapped again, tapped a third time and eventually got a semblance of silence. By then he was gravely disoriented and introduced, with some solemnity, "Marshall Field Montgomery."

There was also the luminous evening when David brought Marc Chagall to the château in Switzerland that William F. Buckley, Jr., inhabits in the winter months. Buckley, as fortunately is little known, is an enthusiastic painter, but his respect for his own talent is not widely shared. David had warned Bill that he should not show his work to his guest. Buckley, nonetheless, was determined and, after dinner, took Chagall and Niven to his ground-floor studio and office. Chagall, to David's all but explosive joy, looked sadly at the paintings, then at the palette, and said, "Poor paint."

Almost the last time I saw David, he told me of a phone conversation he had just had with Ronald Reagan. The President had asked him in a warm and compelling way, "How is that lady of yours?" It was, David thought, an extraordinarily nice gesture to his wife, until it became clear that the President was referring to Mrs. Margaret Thatcher.

David Niven's last two years were terrible — the ghastly inevitability of Lou Gehrig's disease — and there will be some who will tell of the courage, even insouciance, with which he faced his ordeal. Of the outer appearance of courage I have no doubt; of the inner suffering I would be even more certain. David Niven enjoyed life richly, lived it every hour and very much wanted to go on living. Once, a year ago last winter, he let his guard down for just a moment and said to us one evening, "Why me?" Last winter we talked only on the telephone; he didn't want even his friends to see his problems in nervous and muscular control.

There is more than a note of deeper anguish beneath the Niven humor in his last letter to my wife — its date is June 3, a slim two months before his death. After explaining that he had to dictate it and that he was shortly going back to Switzerland from Cap Ferrat, he added, "I am pressing on but I'm up against a dirty fighter. If you hear of any miracle cure by any of the geniuses around Cambridge, be sure to tape a message to the leg of the nearest pigeon."

We regularly take the outward aspect of courage on the part of our friends as evidence that they haven't suffered. By attributing heroism, we relegate the despair and in such fashion relieve our own feelings. Better, or anyhow more nearly honest, that we shed a tear for what they have really endured.

8

HENRY ROBINSON LUCE
— AND *FORTUNE* MAGAZINE

(1980)

In New York two or three years ago, I called up Time Inc. to get the current
address of Gilbert Burck, a brilliant and amusing former editor of Fortune
(whose son has now replaced him on the masthead), for he had sometime earlier
moved from his house in Rockland County. I was passed on to Information and
after a pause was told that there was "nothing on him." I was inspired to ask,
"What do you have on Henry Robinson Luce?"

There was an even longer pause. I thought I could hear the click of the
computer keys. The voice returned: "I'm afraid, sir, that we have nothing on
him either."

Sic transit. *This piece, written initially for an anniversary volume on* Fortune *and its writers, will perhaps delay slightly the passage. Maybe extracts*
could go on the Time Inc. computer.

My association with Harry Luce and *Fortune* began at an improbable
time — the autumn of 1943 in the middle of the war. Until earlier that
summer I had enjoyed a position of power in the wartime government — that of price czar, or what was somewhat imaginatively so called,
of the Office of Price Administration. Then Franklin D. Roosevelt, in
one of his few actions ever to win the devout applause of the business
community, had indicated that all would be better, happier and certainly more peaceful in Washington if I were to move from price control
to a job as administrator of Lend-Lease in South Africa. On examination, the South African post turned out, in the manner of most such
official promotions, to be fraudulent, and my next assignment was with
Herbert Lehman, developing plans for postwar relief. This, too, was
unduly theoretical, so I went to see my draft board to tell them I was
available for the American infantry. It was not the greatest disappointment of my life to be advised, I've always thought somewhat informally,
that I was some two or two and a half inches taller than the Army

thought acceptable. So, in the autumn of 1943, I went to work for *Fortune*.

As the years went on, I turned out to be not the most reliable of staff members: when an opportunity opened to assess the effects of our air operations in Europe and Japan, I went to the War Department as a director of the United States Strategic Bombing Survey; then after the war ended, I was away for most of a year in the Department of State. But, off and on, I was at *Fortune* from the autumn of 1943 to the autumn of 1948, and I look back upon it as one of the most instructive periods of my life. No small part of that instruction came from working for and with Harry Luce.

One of the two founding fathers of *Time, Fortune, Life* and various lesser enterprises, Luce was forty-five years old when I joined the magazine, a handsome, rather slender man with heavy eyebrows, restless, searching, somewhat nervous eyes and, in speech, an unparalleled talent for parentheses. As he talked to a company audience, which occasionally he did, there would be bets as to whether he could unravel a sentence and come back to his original subject and verb; often he could.

Such was the complexity of Harry's speech and the generating thought that he rarely, if ever, noticed what he was eating, drinking or smoking. He met for lunch in those days with his senior editors and writers in a dining room on top of the RCA Building in Rockefeller Center. Present always were one or two well-paid sycophants, confident in manner, who tried, with little success, to anticipate his line of thought and guide him to his food. He paid no attention to them. These men, I may say, were regarded with a combination of envy and suitably cautious disdain by their more functional colleagues; the one closest to Luce at the moment was always referred to as "the current Jesus." None ever lasted very long.

To get back to Harry Luce — he would look distractedly at the menu, be diverted and diverted again and eventually point helplessly to whatever was the first item. He would then listen to others only as some seemingly new idea might be voiced. This would rivet his attention, and it didn't matter greatly (China apart) if it was wholly contrary to his generously professed beliefs. Luce was conservative, Republican, Establishmentarian, romantically chauvinist and given strongly to the notion that making (as distinct from having) money was a firm measure of worth. But all this was secondary to his curiosity, a subject to which I will return.

Harry Luce believed that liberals, even socialists, if they could write, were better for reporting on business and economic affairs than conservatives, who were tedious or semiliterate or both. By any political test I was well to the left of Luce, but I didn't feel especially confined.

And once I had become aware of the Luce curiosity, I learned that it could be exploited for yet more degrees of freedom. One might have to go to Harry's office to justify something one had written or had passed as an editor. But, once one was there, it was almost always possible to engage his interest and get his approval by urging the novelty of the case. He would ask innumerable questions, but, in the end, sometimes with a slightly despairing affirmation of disbelief, he would let the article go.

Luce was himself an exceptionally informed and competent business-man. Around him were men who spoke learnedly of circulation and its promotion; advertising and its sales; advertising agencies and their quirks; new magazine ventures and their prospects; competitors and *their* prospects. One soon came to realize that Harry Luce knew more than they and was far less inclined to make wordy optimism and profes-sional cliché a substitute for facts and common sense.

He was also a superb editor. Once or twice a year he would come down to *Fortune* from the managerial heights of the enterprise to take personal charge of an issue; these appearances we called "The Com-ings." His passion was for articles conveying information as opposed to those filled with interpretation or theory. The latter in those days — essays on the unappreciated achievements of the capitalist system or its inevitable collapse under the oppressive impact of the New Deal — carried the derogatory designation of "think pieces." First-rate writing to Harry Luce meant facts, however they might be arranged or mis-arranged for effect.

His further and yet greater editorial passion was for economy; noth-ing so depressed him as wasted words. Sometime in 1944, talent being then scarce, I was put in charge of what was called "the middle of the book" — the principal stories, many of them in that period voyages of discovery into one or another of the large corporations. By then I had learned to drain out excess verbiage. But, as I have often told, it was a marvel to see how much more Harry, with a few sweeps of a soft black pencil, could remove and how little in consequence was lost. Once a wordy draft on the West Coast clothing industry came to him by accident and, a few hours later, my greatly abbreviated version. He remarked with warm approval on the way I had mastered the requisite surgery. I still recall my pleasure. Not since working for Harry Luce have I read through a manuscript, my own or that of someone else, without feeling that he was looking over my shoulder and that his pencil would presently pass through large chunks of prized but redundant prose with the words "This can go."

Harry did not, incidentally, doubt the effect of his editorial instruc-tion. Years later at a luncheon at *Time,* either just before or just after the 1960 election, he said to John F. Kennedy, to the latter's great delight, which was never concealed in frequent retelling, "I taught Kenneth Galbraith how to write. And, I tell you, I've certainly regretted it."

Let me return to the Luce curiosity, for it, too, made him a notable
editor. He asked the question to which you had given, at most, only a
passing thought. And when he asked, you realized that *you* also wanted
to know. On a summer evening I walked with him from Rockefeller
Center to the Waldorf Towers, where he lived when in Manhattan. On
the way he saw the sign of a private detective agency in a second-floor
window. He asked me how detectives worked, if they were licensed,
what kinds of services they performed, what they got paid. I didn't
know, and by the time we reached the Waldorf, I very much wanted
to know. A couple of decades later when I was ambassador in New
Delhi, Harry came to India to attend a great conclave of the Christian
churches. His father had, of course, been a missionary, but discussion
and reciprocal education and admiration, not the rescue of Indian
souls, were the purposes of the convocation. We went together on a
trip to Rajasthan, and in Jaipur I became ill and had to be flown back
to Delhi. Harry returned by car with my wife. It was for her the experience of a lifetime. There was no feature of Indian life — social,
cultural, religious, marital, hygienic or agricultural — on which he didn't
wish information. There were constant detours to villages, temples,
wells, that caught his eye. My wife arrived back at the Embassy in a
state of advanced exhaustion. I could have warned her. In the outlying
bureaus and branches of the Luce empire in those days, thoughtful
and aspiring resident representatives always prepared for a Luce visitation by reading up conscientiously on everything that might be seen
on the route to be traversed.

Harry was a pervading, but by no means an exclusive, presence in my
days at *Fortune*. Two relaxed and civilized gentlemen, Ralph D. Paine,
Jr., the managing editor, and the late Albert Furth, the executive editor,
provided overall direction to the magazine. Both were also open to
amusement and fantasy, a reaction, perhaps, to the terrible solemnity
of the Luce housecarls and in lesser measure of Luce himself. I was
allowed to explore the advantages for New Englanders of forming a
separate sovereignty, complete with its own money, tariffs, foreign
borrowing and balance-of-payments deficit. Wilder Hobson, one of the
most amusing and talented staff members, and I worked on a classification of American businessmen by their dress. We called it "How to
Tell the Birds by Their Feathers." Our categories — Investment Vestments, Anglo–Park Avenue Dash, Southern Comfort — did not, to our
sorrow, ever take hold.

For much of my time at *Fortune* my office adjoined that of Eric

Hodgins, and we shared the same aggressively indifferent and, we believed, unwillingly virginal secretary. Only the fact that he spent most of his life in the relative institutional anonymity of Time Inc. kept Eric Hodgins from being remembered as a major connoisseur of the absurdities of the American business scene. Hodgins had graduated from MIT with a degree conditional, it was said, on a promise never actively to practice any form of engineering. After lesser editorial and writing tasks, including a stint as editor of the MIT alumni magazine, he became successively a writer at *Fortune,* the managing editor, a corporate vice president without perceptible function and then, by his own choice, a much valued writer again. Along the way he won a hard battle with alcohol and in the days of our friendship was a dedicated communicant of Alcoholics Anonymous.

A big man, in clothes that seemed rarely to be changed, with a deeply marked face and an explosive laugh, he suffered from a chronic oversupply of information. All Hodgins's stories, though tightly written, came in at twice or three times the publishable length. We always got the originals from the typing room to read, for editing took out not only valuable material (as distinct from the usual dross) but also sharp changes of pace and recurrent descents into hilarious vulgarity, the latter exquisitely designed to stir the reader out of his normal somnambulance.

> If Mr. Dascomb [he said of an advertising man he celebrated in a venture into near fiction], had chosen the Church for a career, he would have been a bishop, and a bishop among bishops. . . . He had a bishop's overwhelming advantage that although his human frailties might be intermittently evident, it was obvious that he was, nevertheless, in constant two-way communication with the Holy Ghost. . . . Where others had to rely on feeling, or, at best, on facts, Mr. Dascomb had the higher advantage of Revelation. . . . There was, however, a widespread opinion throughout advertising circles in the United States that Mr. Dascomb was a bastard.

As was true of Thorstein Veblen, Eric surveyed and occasionally destroyed without being subject to the greatest source of banality in business writing, which is the obligation, however minimal the writer's qualifications, to be constructive. He also knew, as do depressingly few business writers and editors, what a businessman likes to read. That is not of the high intelligence and brilliant achievements of other business executives and firms; he wishes, far more, to read of their errors and, as occasion offers, of their disasters. These are much more varied and interesting than the success stories and give the reader a rewarding sense of his own superiority.

Hodgins had a high view of Time Inc. as a source of imaginative corporate aberration, and, under his instruction, I came partly to share it. One glowing example remains in my mind. During the war years and again during the Eisenhower interlude, the principal emissary of Time Inc. in Washington was the late C. D. Jackson. A large, effluent man, C.D. exuded a confidence in his own abilities that, manifestly, he thought justified. A couple of years after the war Harry Luce put him in charge of one of his rare mistakes — Time-Life International. With World War II, we had, in Luce's own phrase, entered upon the American Century, and he was fatally susceptible to the view that the principal, indeed inevitable, manifestation of this epoch would be round-the-world coverage by *Time* and *Life* in a large convoy of local English and foreign-language editions. The more accomplished sycophants were predictably enthusiastic. The initial consequence, at a time when few currencies could be converted into dollars and no one needed to advertise goods since they were everywhere in appallingly short supply, was losses that were an impressive subtraction even from Time Inc.'s current earnings. Luce didn't like these losses at all, and C. D. Jackson was given the job of retrieving them. They continued. C.D.'s eventual explanation brought Eric roaring into my office, for it was a truly magnificent example of the triple reverse conditional construction, turning a damaging loss into a major accomplishment. It appeared in a circular to members of the "senior group" at Time Inc., a privileged community of old hands who participated in profits. In it C. D. Jackson advised that "if business conditions in the second half of the year had been as favorable as in the first half, Time-Life International would have been within shooting distance of the break-even point."

All will understand why I found my years at Time Inc. so instructive. Never thereafter did I find anything I couldn't explain. But, as I've indicated, Harry Luce's instruction in writing I also valued, however (as he thought) it was misused. And there was a more important professional dividend. The early *Fortune,* more than any other journal anywhere in the industrial world, saw the modern large corporation as a primary economic and social force. My years there as both writer and editor provided a diversity and intimacy of exposure to its structure, operating goals and economic, social and political influence that could not have been had in any other way. From those years came a lasting immunity to the banalities of the neoclassical textbook economics. And to them I owe the notion of the technostructure as the decisive managerial and innovative instrument in the modern large enterprise, and much else that became part of my Harvard teaching and of *The New Industrial State.* This last, I'm not quite alone in thinking, is my most useful book. My debt to Harry Luce and *Fortune* — or, as some would prefer, their responsibility — is very great.

HAMISH HAMILTON:
AN APPRECIATION
ON HIS EIGHTIETH BIRTHDAY

(1980)

I say here that Hamish Hamilton Ltd. had ceased to be my British publisher. In 1983, on the initiative of Christopher Sinclair-Stevenson, now the distinguished head of that distinguished firm, it became so again. Money and bidding dictated the shifts; this is a tendency among publishers that I nowise regret.

The comments of authors about publishers are suspect, particularly if the publishers are their own. There is always a question, even in the most trusting minds, as to whether fulsome praise may not be related to pecuniary expectation. Happily I am exempt from such justifiable suspicion. Jamie Hamilton has been my friend for a quarter of a century. He was my publisher for a great deal of that time, and it was Jamie who gave to the discriminating British and Commonwealth audience he serves so well the books that I count my most important, *The Affluent Society* and *The New Industrial State*. In time, my possibly excessive output was shifted to another distinguished British house, which, in turn, shared part of it with the BBC. Jamie was nice enough to tell me that he regretted the move. Now he can be content; I am able to talk of him with complete objectivity.

He is, needless to say, a good publisher. I judge that he must like books, partly because he has lived so closely with them but mostly because Hamish Hamilton volumes are the best printed and best produced in the English-speaking world. Jamie is also a close student of their contents. I have always felt, as have other authors, that publishers were as much, perhaps more, in need of education as any other group or profession in modern society. It was thus a great pleasure to have a publisher who read appreciatively what one had written.

But our professional relationship was far from being my only association with Jamie Hamilton. We shared an interest in India, and the Hamiltons were among our most cherished guests when I was representing the American Republic there. In those days I kept a journal with the intention of publishing it at some suitable time in the future, and this I did. Since I didn't rush into print and since I was writing for American, British and Indian audiences, I felt it necessary to identify rather carefully the people who appeared in its pages. In describing Jamie, who arrived in the middle of a large formal dinner for a visiting American Cabinet officer, I said in a footnote, "He is a wealthy London publisher, legendary in his generosity in royalties and advances to authors." Few things ever gave me more pleasure than the knowledge that he would have to choose between censorship and the publication of those memorable words. He remarked on them but never hesitated. Perhaps he simply accepted that they were true.

However, this I doubt. For, among other things, Hamilton is a Scot — not quite a professional Scot, to be sure, but with all the ethnic sensitivities of our race. This last, I may say, resulted in my only major disagreement with him. In Canada, as I have often told, we always called ourselves the Scotch, not the Scots; we followed Dr. Johnson in the older and impeccable usage. While in India I had amused myself by writing a book on the history, polity, agriculture, social life and personal hygiene of the clansmen among whom I grew up, and it appeared in the United States and Canada as *The Scotch*. Jamie rejected the title, arguing that north of the Tweed, the Scotch being now Scots, it would be taken to mean whisky. Instead he called the book *Made to Last,* a phrase I had used to describe the excellent protective skin on the face and hands of my neighbors in Ontario. It was a rare case of misjudgment on his part; an abstract title, one that conveys no sense of the contents to the bookstore shopper, should never be used except for promiscuously highbrow fiction. When, accordingly, the book passed to Penguin, it was given its third title and the worst of all: *The Non-Potable Scotch*. I shudder when I recall that I endorsed this ghastly designation.

My friendship with Jamie Hamilton gives me great joy. As others doubtless have, I have always thought it nice that he lived on Hamilton Terrace; not many people get their streets named after them. There can be few places in London where there is a more civilized dismissal of national identity than one encounters at his house. This is because Jamie's knowledge of British and American writing is equally intimate and extensive. So to this day when I go into a bookstore, if I see the tree-shaded H's on the back of a book, I know that while the book may not be to my particular interest or taste, it will always be good.

ARCHIBALD MACLEISH

(1982)

In the lovely spring of 1982, my wife and I went to Greenfield, Massachusetts, to a gathering of the friends and admirers of Archibald MacLeish. It was at the excellent Greenfield Community College and had been planned as a celebration of Archie's ninetieth birthday, which he had failed to make by just a few weeks. This is what I said on that occasion.

My few words followed a long message read for then Massachusetts Governor King, a right-wing aberration in our otherwise well-governed commonwealth. While I was on the platform, I rewrote my introduction to say: "We have just heard a long encomium by Governor Edward J. King on the departure from the scene of Archibald MacLeish. The thought passes through my mind that it might have been better were it MacLeish on King." But I had been taught never to wish anyone ill, not even Ed King, and so self-censorship being a far more pervasive intrusion on speech than any censorship, I struck it out. Or rather saved it for later reading to Ada MacLeish, who approved.

The previous essay but one has already told much about Harry Luce; I could have added that he so admired MacLeish in spite of his socialist leanings that he arranged to have him work six months on and six months off so that he wouldn't lack time for his poetry.

One day last September we drove down from Vermont on a golden day in late summer to visit Archie and Ada MacLeish. It was one of many such excursions over the many years. He and I walked around the garden, saw the flowers, came in for a drink and for lunch, and, most of all, as so often before, we talked. This time it was of our years at *Fortune,* his before the war, mine a little later. Could there have been a more improbable business journalist than Archibald MacLeish? Yet when I joined the staff, he was a legend. People got his articles out of the files to read. There was half a whole issue he wrote on Japan in the 1930s, which brought him admiration not only from American readers but durably from the Japanese; visiting Tokyo in later years, I was regularly asked if I knew him. Archie was especially known for the way he could give the sweep of his subject in a few opening sentences. It was a faith of the magazine at the time that it was a far, far better thing to have a poet of qualified free-enterprise faith who could write than a specialist in business affairs who was illiterate — or boring. Thus MacLeish the business journalist.

There is other biographical history — some of it equally improbable. There was MacLeish the parent of the first embryonic intelligence service; it was called in those innocent days the Office of Facts and Figures; later it was the OSS, then the CIA. Maybe it was the MacLeish genius to know a bad business when he encountered it and get out in good season. There was MacLeish the librarian, the presiding officer of the Library of Congress, the largest bureaucracy in the world of books. And MacLeish the friend and confidant of Franklin D. Roosevelt. There was MacLeish the assistant secretary of state; that was when assistant secretaries were meant to be visible and known and were safely so. And there was MacLeish the father figure and father confessor of journalists; with the late well-loved Louis Lyons he made the Nieman program at Harvard the most noted experience of its kind. Last week, while I was meeting with a colleague of senior years at the university, our talk turned, as so often in these days, to our friend. "Ah, yes," he said, "it was Archie who taught me my first course in constitutional law." That was MacLeish the law professor. He was also a Harvard House master and a most successful playwright.

But this is not the whole nor is it even the most. There was MacLeish the man of love and eloquence. His poetry and his love were for all who shared his life and deserved his affection but most of all for his companion for all the years.

> *This poem is for my wife.*
> *I have made it plainly and honestly:*
> *The mark is on it*
> *Like the burl on the knife.*
>
> *I have not made it for praise.*
> *She has no more need for praise*
> *Than summer has*
> *Or the bright days.*
>
> *In all that becomes a woman*
> *Her words and her ways are beautiful:*
> *Love's lovely duty,*
> *The well-swept room.*

Wherever she is there is sun
And time and a sweet air;
Peace is there,
Work done. . . .

ACKNOWLEDGMENTS

INDEX

⸬ ACKNOWLEDGMENTS ⸲

WHEN TOLD by the author that it was the editor's pleasant task to acknowledge and thank gratefully all those who helped bring this book to the printer and ultimately to the reading public, I was struck by how many people do, in fact, contribute to such enterprises. For *A View from the Stands* there was, first, Janey Siepmann, whose all-seeing eye and devoted perseverance in retrieving these pieces have already been noted in the Introduction but who also brought to her job a light heart and an unfailing charm which brightened our days.

Next came the movement of all these words from original copy to completed manuscript, a task complicated by the decidedly difficult handwriting of both author and editor. To accomplish this, Edith Tucker seemed sent to us by a gracious providence; she truly reads what she types — a happy but rare habit — and is fearless and infallible in her criticism, adept at finding overlooked repetition and, like Noël Coward (mentioned herein), blessed with a memory that is both accurate and sure.

Protecting us on those infrequent occasions when a mistyping or a misreading crept in unawares, we had as proofreaders Sarah Lodge and Tilia Klebenov, two informed, skillful and enthusiastic young women released for the summer from nursing school and college.

To do research and checking on a book of this size and diversity requires imagination, diligence and conscientious attention to detail. All these Catherine Aman most certainly has; she is, not less, a great pleasure to work with as well.

While all these jobs were being done, real life did go on, and Professor Galbraith's appointments, travel, phone calls, errands, weekly schedules and all else were handled with grace, good humor and much intelligence by Therese Horsey.

Finally, a word should be said about the author himself and the considerable debt we all owe him. The felicity of his prose, the clarity of his thought, the consistency and humanity of his views, make working with his words especially easy, while his good humor, his tolerance and his wit make working with him a special joy. Having so written — and knowing that this, inevitably, will be seen by him before publication — I would refer JKG and also the reader to what he says in this book about Hamish Hamilton under similar circumstances, the only difference being that my words are all true.

ANDREA D. WILLIAMS

· INDEX ·

Abortion, and *An American Tragedy*,
    69
Absurdity
  in foreign and military policy, 46
  in scholarly teachings, 119–21
  See also Convenient Reverse Logic;
    Reasoning, ways of
Academic freedom
  and *The Double Helix*, 117
  and laziness, 57
Academic life
  in Britain, 106
  commencement address in, 34–35
  and Harvard governing system,
    110–13, 114–16, 118
  judgment of personal virtues in,
    397, 399
  self-scrutiny needed in, 134
  solemnity in, 119–21
  and standards, 132
  tenure, 45, 127–28
Acheson, Dean
  and Kennan, 358, 359
  Muggeridge on, 85
Action, vs. illusion of action, 401
Activities (Keynes), 316, 317
Adams, John, and Agnew, 120
Adenauer, Konrad, and Kissinger,
    366, 367
Aesthetics. *See* Art; Environment
Affirmative action
  and logical thinking, 35
  MAP as, 26, 27, 28–33
Affluent (rich) individuals
  in American novel, 68–71, 72
  of Argentina, 255
  concealment of policies favoring,
    181
  and economic recommendations,
    231
  government aid to, 171, 221
  incomes as incentive for, 19, 36,
    50, 175
  and Nixon-McGovern contest,
    395–96

and noneconomic achievements,
    41
  nuclear annihilation loss for, 18
  and public services, 4–5, 21, 218
  and Reagan administration, 179–
    81
  Reagan's friends as, 73
  revolt of against poor, 95
  and social tranquillity, 239
  and taxation, 36
  Veblen on, 292
  Weeks's efforts for, 121
Affluent Society, The (Galbraith), 134,
    167, 211, 415
Afghanistan, Soviet invasion of, 14
African culture, in Brazil, 245
Aga Khan, Prince Sadruddin, 8
Agee, William, 73
Age of Uncertainty, The, 285–87,
    290–91, 293, 294–95
Aging
  and Harvard professors, 129–30
  and lovely women, 129
  and retirement policy, 45
  and U.S. Congress, 224
Agnew, Spiro, 81, 90, 120, 394
Agriculture
  Green Revolution in, 262, 337
  in India, 260, 262
  Khrushchev's interest in corn,
    363, 365
  Marx contemptuous of, 290
Aiken, George, 393
Air power
  effectiveness of, 37
  Strategic Bombing Survey on,
    299, 355, 356, 410
  "surgical strikes" by, 327
Alcohol, as Brazilian fuel, 236,
    244
Alcohol consumption
  and Harvard alumni, 131, 134
  at Harvard football game, 182
  and Harvard status, 131
  in Kremlin, 364

Alcohol consumption, contd.
  and U.S. business transactions,
    216–17
Alefounder, John, 160
Alfonsín, Raúl, 251, 255, 256, 257
Alsop brothers, 330
Alumni, Harvard
  and alcohol, 131, 134
  vs. Auchincloss characters, 72
  power of criticism by, 133–34
Aman, Catherine, 389, 423
American Academy and Institute of
    Arts and Letters, 98
American Century, in Luce's view,
    414
American Committee on East-West
    Accord, 13, 267, 358
American Dilemma, An (Myrdal), 404
American Enterprise Institute, 173
American Establishment. *See* Estab-
    lishment, American
American Institute of Arts and Let-
    ters, 358
American Revolution
  Scotch in, 278
  Adam Smith on, 287
Americans for Democratic Action,
    220
American Tragedy, An (Dreiser), 68–69
American University, commence-
    ment address at, 34
Amory, Mark, 77, 79
Amritsar Massacre, 370
Amtrak, 215, 217
Andropov, Yuri, 368
Angola, concern about, 47
Annenberg, Walter, 222–23
Anniversaries, as ambiguous, 34
Anti-Communism
  in Congress, 360
  of Paul Douglas, 346
  of John Foster Dulles, 349
  as foreign policy expertise, 342–43
    in LBJ's viewpoint, 337–38
  and nuclear confrontation, 6
  and U.S. Latin American policy,
    242
  See also Cold War; Vietnam war
Anti-Semitism, in 1930s Harvard,
    130
Appointment in Samarra (O'Hara), 71
Arbatov, Georgy, 8, 267, 286–87

Arbatov Institute, 267, 268
Archer, Mildred (Mrs. W. G.), 160–61
Archer, W. G., 156–58, 160
Architecture
  of Boston Government Center,
    229
  of Brasília, 240, 242
  and economics, 150
Argentina, 247–57
  Austral Plan in, 254–55
  external debt of, 247–48, 253,
    256–57
  and Friedman, 239
  inflation in, 247, 250, 252–54,
    255, 256
  military on trial in, 255–56
Aristotle, slavery approved by, 145
Arms control, 1
  and Brazilian fears, 237
  Convenient Reverse Logic on, 38
  and Harriman's achievment of test
    ban treaty, 342
  and intelligence operations, 53
  lectures on in Argentina, 251
  and military establishment power,
    14–17
  public's vs. specialists' role in, 9,
    11–13
  requirements for attaining, 9–10,
    17–18, 275
  and US-USSR relations, 9, 11–12,
    13–14, 17, 38, 265
Arms race
  and Convenient Reverse Logic,
    37–38
  See also Nuclear war
Arnold, Henry ("Hap"), 353
Art
  Brazilian Indian featherwork, 240
  and economics, 144–51
  and industry, 140–41, 148–50
  LBJ's history as, 336
  public appreciation of, 141–42
  Reagan performance as, 49–50
  vs. science and engineering, 139–
    40
  and state, 142–43, 148
  support for, 145
  writing about, 163–64
Art of India, 152–53, 154, 156,
    157–58, 163, 259
  and Archer, 156–58

Art of India, contd.
  and Coomaraswamy, 152–54, 156
  by Englishmen, 159–60
  from Himalayan valleys, 152,
    155–56, 157–58
  of Husain, 162–64
Arthur, Chester A., 281
Art of sitting, 206
Arturo Illia Foundation, 249
Arvey, Jake, 347
Ascent of Man, The, 285
Askew, Reubin, 177
Asymmetry
  Gandhi's use of, 373
  of Keynesian corrections, 253
Athletics
  basketball, 182
  football games, 131, 182–83
  golf, 284
  and Harvard status, 131
  and reporting of political cam-
    paigns, 395
  Scottish contribution to, 284
  skiing, 90, 406–7
Attenborough, Sir Richard, 369,
  370
Attlee, Clement, 81, 375
Attwood, William, 267
Auchincloss, Louis, 70, 71–72
Austral Plan, 254–55
Autobiography, 80, 104
  of R. A. Butler, 207–9
  of Paul Douglas, 345
  of Gandhi, 371
  of Mencken, 59–60
  of Malcolm Muggeridge, 81–83
  of A. J. P. Taylor, 105–6
  of Trollope, 199

Babbitt (Lewis), 59, 70
Bailey, John, 331, 332
Bailey, Pearl, 269
Bailout
  corporate, 170–72
  of Wall Street, 221
Baker, James, 225
Ball, George, 75, 267, 327, 339
Banality. *See* Dullness
Baran, Paul, 210
Barchester Towers (Trollope), 199–
  203
Baroody, Jamil, 92, 93

Baruch, Bernard, 275, 389
Basketball, and Galbraith, 182
Battenburg, Prince Louis of, 378
Bayh, Birch, 225
Bay of Pigs invasion
  and Bowles, 331
  and Dulles, 350
BBC, 105, 415
Beach Book, The (Steinem), 204
Beaches, attraction of, 204–6
Beatty, Warren, as Scotch, 282
Beautification, roadside, 167
Beauty, *See* Art
Beecher, Henry Ward, 294
Bell, Alexander Graham, 283
Bell, Vanessa, 316
Belmont Syndrome, 135
Belo Horizonte, Brazil, 243, 244
Bendre, N. S., 163
Bennett, James Gordon, 282
Bentham, Jeremy, 190, 289–90
Benton, Thomas, 282
Bergen, Candice, 371
Berkeley, University of California
  at. *See* University of California
  at Berkeley
Berlin, Isaiah, 317
Bernstein, Leonard, 219
Billboards, 167
  in Argentina, 250
Biography, authorized, 80–81
Birla, G. D., 84, 370
Birth control, and India, 262
Bissell, Richard, Jr., 354
Black Mischief (Waugh), 77, 79
Blacks
  employment discrimination
    against, 27–28
  and MAP, 28–33
Blashfield Lecture, 98
Bloomsbury group, 316
Bok, Sissela, 404
Book Class, The (Auchincloss), 71
Book reviews
  and truthfulness, 329
  and Washington correspondents,
    368
Borges, Jorge Luis, 251
Boston, Massachusetts, 229
  Coomaraswamy collection in, 152,
    154, 156
Boswell, James, Scotland trip of, 276

Bourke-White, Margaret, 371
Bowles, Chester, 184, 222, 329–33
Braden, Tom, 368
Bradley, Bill, 50
Brasília, 240–42
Braun, Wernher von, 353
Brazil, 234–46
    development of, 245–46
    energy conservation in, 236, 244
    external debt of, 235, 237, 246,
        247
    inflation in, 238, 242
    living-standard descrepancies in,
        239
    and U.S. politics, 237, 242
    workers' influx to cities in, 240,
        243, 245, 246
Bretton Woods system, 320–21
Brevity
    and television, 293, 295
    in writing, 276
Bridges, Styles, 349
Bright-Holmes, John, 84
Bronowski, Jacob, 285
Brooks, C. Wayland, 346
Brown, George, 364
Brown, Harold, 12
Bruccoli, Matthew J., 65
Bryan, William Jennings, Mencken
    obituary on, 58–59
Buchanan, James, 281
Buckley, James, 219
Buckley, William F., Jr., 87–93
    and Muggeridge, 81
    as painter, 407
Budget deficits, federal, 102, 173,
    174–75, 320
Bullock, C. J., 345
Bundy, McGeorge, 222
Bunker, Ellsworth, 114, 393
Burck, Gilbert, 409
Bureaucracy
    Buckley garbage plan circum-
        vents, 87
    Buckley and liberals tamed by,
        92–93
    and consistency vs. change, 365
    disciplined obedience in, 15
    discriminatory comments on, 53
    Library of Congress as, 418
Burke, Arleigh, 354

Burns, Arthur F., 13
Bush, George, 8, 10
Business confidence, and govern-
    ment policy, 231–32
Business Executives for National
    Security, 10
Businessmen
    reading preference of, 413
    Adam Smith on, 291
    in U.S., 230–33
    See also Corporate man or person-
        ality
Butler, Nicholas Murray, 221
Butler, R. A. (Rab), 81, 207–9
Butz, Earl, 90

Caesar, Julius, 310
Cairns, Huntington, 58
Calhoun, John C., 282
California, 5, 228
Cambodia, concern over, 47
Cambridge, Massachusetts, and civil
    defense, 10–11
Campaigns, political
    media coverage of, 176–78, 393,
        395
    See also Politics
Canadian identity, 98–99
Canadian Scotch (Scots), 83, 279,
    377, 416. See also Scotch, the
Canal Zone. See Panama Canal de-
    bate
Capital (Marx), 290
Capitalism
    and colonialism, 290
    excesses of, 266
    and individualism vs. community, 5
    Marx on, 252, 288, 291
    as nuclear war victim, 9
    as organization, 264–65
    as prior to socialism, 14, 46
    and workers from countrysides,
        246, 274
Capitalism, Socialism and Democracy
    (Schumpeter), 288
Carnegie, Andrew, 280
Carnegie-Mellon University, 280
Carter, Jimmy
    Brazilian view of, 237
    and MX, 12
    and racial politics, 227

Carver, T. N., 345
Cassell, Gustav, 405
Castro, Fidel
  and international Communism,
    338
  and sugar cane, 245
Catholic Bishops, nuclear-war letter
  of, 13
Catholicism, and Waugh, 79
Caviar
  Kissinger's feast of, 368
  Niven story on, 282
Central American policy
  Convenient Reverse Logic on, 36–
    37
  See also Latin America
Central Intelligence Agency. *See*
  CIA
Cerf, Bennett, 62
Chagall, Marc, 407
Charter Day, University of Califor-
  nia, 3
Chavez, Cesar, 68
Chayes, Abram, 332
Chazov, Yevgeny, 269
Cheyenne Mountain, NORAD
  headquarters in, 285
Chiang Kai-shek, 303, 349
Chicago, Illinois, 229
  and Paul Douglas, 347
Chile, and Friedman, 239
China, and social cohesiveness,
  95
China, Communist
  India invaded by, 326–27
  U.S. view toward, 14
Christian charity, toward Nixon,
  396
Chrysler Corporation bailout, 171–
  72
Chuikov, Vasily, 356
Church, Frank (Senator), 361
Churchill, Randolph
  as editor of father's papers, 307
  Mountbatten on, 377–78
  Muggeridge on, 85
  and Waugh, 77, 78
Churchill, Winston
  certainty of, 307
  on criticizing government, 8
  on democracy, 128

funeral of, 311
and gold standard, 307–8
and Indian independence, 307,
  308, 371
Keynes on, 318
and language, 299, 308–9, 311
and Mountbatten, 379
Muggeridge on, 81, 85
papers of, 306–9
Churchill-Roosevelt correspondence, 300–304
CIA (Central Intelligence Agency)
  and Convenient Reverse Logic, 37
  Allen Dulles as head of, 350, 354–
    55
  Khrushchev book attributed to,
    363
  location of, 223
  and MacLeish, 418
  and Middle East conference, 53
  officers of in India, 51–52
Cities
  of Brazil, 235–45
  environmental planning for, 23–
    25
  and welfare burden, 22
  See also specific cities
Civility
  of public life, 395
  in US-USSR relations, 9, 13, 265
Class system
  American consciousness of, 216
  in New York City, 219
  O'Hara vs. good Americans on,
    64–65
Clay, Henry, 282
Clifford, Clark, 335
Clive, Robert, 192
Coffin, William Sloane, 81
Cohen, Wilbur, 337
Cold War
  and Cuban missile crisis, 327–28
  distrust of Soviets from, 365
  and Kennan, 358–60
  and Kennedy, 324
  Khrushchev's impact on, 365
  and LBJ's viewpoint, 337–38, 340
  St. Pierre syndrome in, 47–48
  Washington bureaucracy stance
    on, 93
  See also Arms race; Soviet Union

Colonialism
  of British rule in India, 82–83, 85,
    192–93, 196, 293, 370, 371–72
  Buckley allied with, 91
  Marx vs. Lenin on, 290
  modern view of, 191, 293–94
Colson, Charles, 81
Colt, Samuel, 283
Columbia University, student explo-
  sion at, 110–11, 113
Colville, John, 299
Comer, Donald, 390
Commencement addresses, 34–35
Committee rule, lowest common de-
  nominator from, 40
Communism
  difficulties of, 46
  LBJ stance on, 336, 338
  as nuclear war victim, 9
  and St. Pierre/Miquelon threat,
    47–48
  social unrest blamed on, 338, 349,
    360
  Washington bureaucracy vigilance
    toward, 93
  See also Soviet Union
Communist Manifesto, The (Marx and
  Engels), 291
Community, 3–4, 5
  attack on, 5–6
  and economic development, 95
  vs. economics, 24
Company School (of art), 159
Conant, James B., 133, 134
Confidentiality. See Privacy, invasion
  of
Confi-Guide (to Harvard courses),
  129, 133
Connally, John B., 120, 227
Connecticut Yankee in King Arthur's
  Court, A (Twain), 42
Conservatives
  and attack on community, 5
  concerns of, 20
  and fiscal austerity, 173
  and government aid to rich, 221
  and Luce, 410
  and nuclear danger, 18
  and social cost, 87
  in Texas, 227
  See also Capitalism

Conspicuous consumption, 292
Consumer culture, and Soviet econ-
  omy, 270–72
Consumption taxes, 174, 239
Convenient Reverse Logic, 35–38
Cooke, Alistair, 58
Coolidge, Calvin
  as economic observer, 223
  on unemployment, 180
  on war loan repayment, 249
Coomaraswamy, Ananda K., 152–
    54, 155, 156
Coomaraswamy, Doña Luisa (wife
  of Ananda), 154
Coomaraswamy, Rama P. (son of
  Ananda), 154
Cooper, Alexander, 113–14
Cooper, John Sherman, 361
Corporate man or personality, 39–
    41
  and American novel, 73–74
  and Hemingway, 61
  and myth of classical capitalism,
    233
  and personal fulfilment, 43
  and tax reductions, 175
  See also Businessmen
Corporations
  discrimination in, 28
  as force for change, 293
  government bailouts sought by,
    170–72
  investment by, 175
  Luce's view of, 414
  and military-industrial complex,
    17, 38, 180
  planning by, 23, 73
  reasoning capacity of, 168–69
  as science/technology framework,
    140
  technostructure of, 414
Council for a Livable World, 10,
    401
Courage
  and Cuban missile crisis, 327–28
  of Niven, 407–8
  vs. personal interest in Washing-
    ton, 333
Cousins, Norman, 266
Coward, Noël, 407, 423
Crankshaw, Edward, 364

Critics. *See* Literary critics
Crossman, Richard, 85
Cuba, concern over, 47
Cuban missile crisis, 326–28
Cunningham, Mary, 73
Customs or immigration officers,
 215, 218, 267

Dahrendorf, Ralf, 287
Daley, Richard, 229, 347
D'Amato, Alfonse, 50
Danish Society of Industrial Design,
 lecture to, 139
Darwinism, in economic life, 292
Davies, Robertson, 55, 98–103
Davis, John W., Mencken on, 58
Davis, Sammy, Jr., 310
Decentralization, Soviet debate on,
 272
Decline and Fall (Waugh), 75, 76, 77
de Gaulle, Charles. *See* Gaulle,
 Charles de
Democracy, American, and geron-
 tocracy, 224
Democratic National Convention
 (1980, 1984), nuclear issues in,
 12
Democratic Party
 and Deep South, 227
 and New York, 218–19
 position of, 215, 225
 presidential aspirants in (1972),
 225
Depew, Chauncey, 282
Design
 and industrial corporation, 140
 Italian excellence in, 149
 public appreciation of, 141–42
Despair
 and heroism, 408
 and power, 385
Development. *See* Economic growth
DeVoto, Bernard, 121
Dewey, Thomas E., 232
Diaries, of Malcolm Muggeridge,
 83–86
Dickens, Charles, 67, 198, 199
Dieppe raid, 379
Dillon, Douglas, 222
Dirksen, Everett McKinley, 346

Discrimination, in employment, 27–
 28. *See also* Equality
Dobbs, Kitty, 82
Dodd, Thomas J., 331
Dominican Republic, and LBJ, 336,
 338
Dos Passos, John, 69
Double Helix, The (Watson), 109,
 117–18
Douglas, Donald, 283
Douglas, Helen Gahagan, 394
Douglas, Paul, 344–47
Douglas, Stephen, 282
Douglas-Home, Alec, 81
Draper, Theodore, 10
Dreiser, Theodore, 68–69
Drew, Daniel, 292
Drinking. *See* Alcohol consumption
Dulles, Allen, 82, 222, 348–50,
 351–52, 355, 356
Dulles, Eleanor (sister of Allen and
 John Foster), 349, 351, 354, 356
Dulles, John Foster, 342–43, 348–
 50, 352
 as Establishment member, 222,
 324
 and India–Middle East area, 332
 Kennan on, 358, 359, 360
 liberal doubts about, 93
Dulles group, 337–38
Dullness
 of corporate executive, 40–41
 of football game, 182–83
 of Nixon White House, 226
 of O'Hara prototypes, 66
Dunlop, John, 106
Dyer, Reginald, 372

*Economic Consequences of the Peace,
 The* (Keynes), 318
Economic growth
 of Brazil, 245–46
 excesses in, 266
 limitations of, 20
 social cohesiveness required for,
 95
Economics
 abundance of current literature
 in, 71
 and *Age of Uncertainty*, 286–95
 and arts, 144–51

Economics, contd.
and Churchill, 307, 308
Darwinism in, 292
funny teachings of, 119–20
of gold standard vs. Keynesian
management, 252–53
micro- vs. macro-, 320
of Soviet Union, 266, 268, 270–74
specialization in, 315
textbook banalities vs. close view
of corporation in, 414
and urban crisis, 22–24
in U.S., 230–33
wishful thinking in, 102
Economists
American, 231
and Argentine and Israeli economies, 251
and Belmont Syndrome, 135
and crisis of cities, 19
and historical digressions, 286
leading figures among, 287–92
obscurity in writings of, 94, 319
rationalization vs. activism of, 288
Scotch and Jewish, 283
Soviet, 266
Eden, Anthony, 208, 302, 380
Editing, of diaries, 84
Edmonds, Richard R., 113, 114,
115
Education
of artists, 142
of Chicago children, 229
vs. Convenient Reverse Logic, 35, 38
of John Kennedy, 387
as poverty cure, 21
Scotch concern for, 280
See also Universities
Erlichman, John, 81
Eisenhower, Dwight D.
and business, 232
and de Gaulle, 312
good will accumulated by, 348
Khrushchev's exchange with, 364
and Kistiakowsky, 400
memoirs of, 364
and military establishment, 16, 17,
180
Election campaigns
of Buckley, 87–89
media coverage of, 176–78, 393,
395

See also Politics
Electronic environment, 206
Elites, privilege presupposed by, 28
Elizabeth I (queen of England), 386
Elizabeth II (queen of England), Ricardo's estate purchased by, 289
El Salvador, concern with, 47
Employment. *See* Retirement; Work
Employment equality, 26–33
Energy, Brazil's conservation of,
236, 244
Engels, Friedrich, 290, 291
Engineering
vs. arts, 139–40
in industrial development, 148
Environment
and economic growth, 20
electronic, 206
roadside, 167
urban, 20, 23–24
Equality
affirmative action for, 26, 27, 28–
33, 35
and employment practices, 27–28
and European-origin groups, 32
policy requirements for, 26–27
Establishment, American, 221–23,
324–25, 346
and budget deficit, 174
and McCarthyism, 360
McGovern as threat to, 395–96
Ethiopia
Marxism in, 14
U.S. concern with, 47
Waugh novels in, 77
Ethnic identity. *See* Identity, ethnic
Ethnicity, and excessive study, 131
Ethnic politics, and New England,
229
"Excursion in Reality" (Waugh), 140
External (overseas) debt
of Argentina, 247–48, 253, 256–
57
of Brazil, 235, 237, 246, 247
nonrepayment of, 235, 248–49

Falklands war, 255
Farley, James A., 177
Faulkner, William, fictional world
of, 101
Favelas (slums), of Brazil, 237, 243
Fecher, Charles A., 58

Federal government. *See* Government, U.S.
Feeney, Father, and Waugh letters, 79
Feldstein, Martin, 283
Field, Noel, 351, 354
Fifth Business (Davies), 99, 100
"First Lady," 389, 390
Fish, Mrs. Stuyvesant, 292
Fisher, Irving, 295
Fisk, Jim, 292
Fitzgerald, F. Scott, 69–70, 101
Fleming, Ann (Mrs. Ian), 78
Fleming, Ian, 208
Flynn, Errol, 310
Football, dreariness of, 131, 182–83
Ford, Gerald
  and business, 232, 233
  and Butz, 90
Foreign debt. *See* External debt
Foreign policy
  Convenient Reverse Logic on, 36–37
  Kennan on, 360
  small country concern in, 46–48
  See also Anti-Communism; Arms control; Cold War
Foreign policy authority
  anti-Communism as, 342–43
  Dulles brothers' claim to, 349
Foreign Service
  in Brazil, 239, 241
  Dulles's sacrifice of members of, 349
Forster, E. M., 85, 196, 197
Forsythe, John, 282
Fortune magazine, 410, 411, 412–13, 414, 417
France, Anatole, 281
Franco, Francisco, as seemingly immortal, 130, 224, 341
Frank, Harry B., 62–63
Franklin, Benjamin, and Pennsylvania Scotch-Irish, 277
Fraud, societal forms of, 42
Freed, Ken, 368
Freedom, as first-person, 4
Free enterprise
  business warnings on, 233
  chaos as serving, 17
  and corporate bailouts, 170, 171, 172

Dulles for, 360
and MAP, 33
and Adam Smith, 291
and U.S. rail passenger transport, 217
of Wall Street, 220–21
Free Speech Movement, 228
Freeze, nuclear, 11–13, 17, 38. *See also* Arms control
French, Sir John, 312
Friedman, Milton, 5, 89, 95, 236, 239, 283
Friedrich Naumann Foundation, 249
Fritchey, Clayton, 364
Fulbright, J. William, 90–91, 267, 335, 338, 361
Fuller, Buckminster, 266
Fulton, Robert, 282–83
Furth, Albert, 412

Gaitskell, Hugh, 208
Galbraith, John Kenneth
  and Bowles, 332
  candidates supported by, 237
  LBJ speech help requested of, 385
  and OPA, 329, 330
Galbraith, Thomas, 277
Galbraith, William Archibald (father of John Kenneth), 334
Galbraith's First Law of Intelligence, 52
Gandhi, Mohandas (Mahatma), 297, 369–73
  and Mountbatten, 380
  and Muggeridge, 81
  press on, 374
Gardner, John, 337
Garst, Roswell, 362–63
Gary, Elbert, 292
Gaulle, Charles de, 310–13
  and Roosevelt/Churchill, 302–3
  and St. Pierre and Miquelon, 48
Gayler, Noel, 38
Geese, at New Delhi embassy, 186
General Theory of Employment Interest and Money (Keynes), 252, 316, 317, 319, 405
George, Henry, 291
Germany
  Dulles for dismemberment of, 350
  reparations by, 318–19

Gerontocracy, and U.S. Congress, 224

Ghana, intelligence operations in, 52–53

Gielgud, John, 372

Gilbert, Martin S., 307

God
and "immortality" of Hoover/Franco/Harriman, 130, 224, 341
laughter through public figures from, 346

Gold mining, in Brazil, 243–44

Gold standard, 252, 307–8, 318

Goldwater, Barry, 20

Goldwyn, Samuel, 407

Golf, 284

Goodwin, Richard, 338

Gorbachev, Mikhail, 14

Gould, Jay, 292

Government
and arts, 142–43, 148
attack on, 4–5
city, 25
community expressed through, 5–6
by and for the rich, 19
Ward on role of, 94–95
See also Public services

Government, U.S.
bailouts sought from, 170–72
budget deficit of, 173, 174–75
bureaucracy in, 226
Congress, 224–25
courage vs. personal interest in, 333
and Establishment, 221–23, 324–25 (see also Establishment, American)
and MAP, 27–33
minimum income from, 22
policy making in, 223–24
professors in, 106, 110

Graham, Katharine, 287

Grant, Duncan, 316

Grant, Ulysses S., 281

Grapes of Wrath, The (Steinbeck), 68, 69

Great Gatsby, The (Fitzgerald), 69–70

Greeley, Horace, 282

Greene, Graham, 78, 85

Greenfield Community College, MacLeish celebration at, 417

Green Revolution, in India, 262, 337

Gromyko, Andrei, 14, 264

Groupe de Bellerive, 8

Gruening, Ernest, 338, 361

Guffey, J. M., 283

Guggenheim family, 293

Gunther, John, 310

Haar, Charles, 337

Haig, Alexander, 348

Halifax, Lord, 354, 372

Hamilton, Alexander, and Connally, 120

Hamilton, Hamish, 415–16, 423

Hanna, Mark, as Scotch, 282

Hansen, Alvin, 135, 399

Harding, Warren Gamaliel, 225, 394

Harriman, Averell, 332–33, 341–43
and American Committee on East-West Accord, 267
and anti-Communist doctrine, 338
in Dulles, 354
good will accumulated by, 348
Khrushchev met at house of, 362
and nuclear predicament, 13

Harriman, Pamela (Mrs. Averell), 299

Harris, Seymour Edwin, 397–99

Hart, Gary, 176, 275

Hartman, Arthur, 269

Harvard Business School
graduates of, 41
Willis Wayde from, 73

Harvard Crimson, The, 131

Harvard Lampoon, The, speech to, 119–21

Harvard University
academic style at, 119–21
alumni of, 71, 131, 133–34
and Berkeley, 228
constitutional obsolescence at, 110–13, 114–16, 118
and Double Helix publication, 109, 112, 117–18
Paul Douglas at, 345
economics department of, 133, 135

Harvard University, contd.
and Father Feeney, 79
Seymour Harris on, 398
improvements noted in, 130–34
insiders and outsiders in, 134–35
Jack Kennedy at, 387
MacLeish at, 418
Middle East conference at, 53
nuclear war study at, 13
parietal rules of, 122–23, 132
and sexual harassment, 124–26
Shah of Iran degree from, 97
special divinity of, 135–36
student revolt of 1969 in, 109
tenure review process in, 128
and Tsuru, 210
Hastings, Warren, portraits of, 160
Hatfield, Mark, 361
Hauge, Gabriel, 232–33
Hawaii
highway advertising abolished in,
229
sugar cultivation in, 245
Hayek, Friedrich von, 404
Hayes, Helen, 282
Hayes, Rutherford B., 281
Heads of state, little problems as
fatal for, 365
Heath, Edward, 286–87
Hegel, G. W. F., 289
Height, bodily
majesty in, 405
military exemption in, 409–10
Heller, Joseph, 73
Helms, Jesse, 81, 92
Hemingway, Ernest, 61–63
and class distinctions, 69
fictional world of, 101
Hemingway, Mary (Mrs. Ernest),
61, 62
Henderson, Leon, 330
Henry, Patrick, 282
Herbert, Laura (wife of Evelyn
Waugh), 78
Hermitage Museum, 264, 270
Herter, Christian, 222
Heston, Charlton, as Scotch, 282
Hickey, Thomas, 160
Highland Clearances, 278
Highlands of Scotland, 278
Hill, Fanny, 310

Hispanics
employment discrimination
against, 27–28
and MAP, 28–33
Historical figures, responsibility for
evils perpetrated in name of,
291
History, LBJ's approach to, 336
History of British India, The (Mill),
190–97
Hitler, Adolf
decisions of, 303
in *Dulles,* 351
Mencken on, 58
Speer on, 364
Taylor on, 105
Hobson, Wilder, 412
Hodgins, Eric, 412–13, 414
Hoff, Philip, 167
Hoffman, Paul, 348
Home, Robert, 160
Hoopes, Townsend, 335
Hoover, Herbert
and Bullock, 345
and businessmen, 232
on war loan repayment, 249
Hoover, J. Edgar
and crime, 224
as seemingly immortal, 130, 224,
341
and student unrest, 113
Hopkins, Harry, 302
Hotchner, A. E., 61–63
House of Commons, and Trollope's
writing, 199
Howe, Edward, 258
How to Control the Military (Gal-
braith), 241
Hughes, Harold, 225
Hughes, Tom, 332
Hull, Cordell, 302
Human rights, Buckley appoint-
ment on, 90–91, 92
Hume, Joseph, 190
Humor
academic style as suppression of,
119–21
God as expressing through public
figures, 346
of Husain, 163
by Khrushchev, 362

Humor, contd.
  of Kissinger, 367
  of Kistiakowsky, 402
  of Niven, 407, 408
Humphrey, Hubert, 229, 237
Hunt, E. Howard, 82
Husain, Maqbool Fida, 162–64

Identity, ethnic
  Canadian, 98–99
  and Scotch, 276–77, 279
  for WASPs vs. other groups,
    71–72
Identity, personal, of corporate ex-
    ecutives, 41
Iguazú Falls, 250
Immigration or customs officers,
    215, 218, 267
Imperialism. *See* Colonialism
Incentives (motivation)
  for the affluent, 19, 36, 50, 175
  Convenient Reverse Logic on, 36
  for the poor, 36, 50
  and tax reduction, 175, 180
  and welfare system, 22
Incomes policy
  and forecasting difficulty, 231
  minimum income, 21–22
Indexing of payments, in Brazil,
    238
India, 258–63
  art of, 152–53, 154, 156, 157–58,
    163, 259 (*see also* Art of India)
  associations from living in, 80
  Bowles as ambassador to, 329, 330
  British rule over, 82–83, 85, 192–
    93, 196, 260, 293, 370, 371–72
  and Butler, 208
  Chinese invasion of, 326–27
  and Churchill, 307, 308, 371
  and CIA Nepal operation, 350
  CIA "spies" in, 51–52, 53
  and Coomaraswamy, 152–54, 156
  diversity in, 258–61
  English painters in, 159–60
  and Gandhi, 369–73
  and Jamie Hamilton, 415–16
  Himalayan valleys in, 155
  and Husain, 162–64
  Keynes's study on banking in, 315

Luce visit to, 412
Mill's history of, 190–92, 193–97
modernization and tradition in,
    196–97, 260, 261–63
Muggeridge in, 82, 84, 85
Alva Myrdal as ambassador to, 404
and Pakistan, 374
partition of, 374–75, 380–81
and Eleanor Roosevelt's death, 391
snake removal in, 184–85
U.S. Embassy Chancery in, 150–
    51, 186
U.S. grain supply to, 151, 337
Indians, American
  employment discrimination
    against, 27–28
  and MAP, 28–33
Individualism
  as attack on community, 5–6
  rise of, 95
Indochina
  Nixon urges intervention in, 347
  See also Laos; Vietnam war
Inertia, as beach attraction, 205–6
Inflation
  in Argentina, 247, 250, 252–54,
    255, 256
  in Brazil, 238, 242
  and budget deficits, 173
  economists' acceptance of, 288
  and foreign exchange rates, 321
  Friedman's remedy for, 239
  Mobil Oil advertisement on, 168–
    69
  Soviet version of, 273–74
Information, military management
    of, 16
*Inquiry into the Nature and Causes of
    the Wealth of Nations* (Smith),
    287–88
Institute for World Economy and
    International Relations, 268
Intellectuals, American, pessimism
    of, 224
Intelligence operatives, 52–53
International Monetary Fund, 254,
    256, 320
International trade, and Bretton
    Woods system, 320–21
In the Fullness of Time (Douglas),
    345–46

Invasion of privacy. *See* Privacy, invasion of
Inverchapel, Lord, 354
Ireland, potato famine in, 279
Iron law of wages, 289
Irving, Washington, 282
Irwin, Lord (later Lord Halifax), 372
"Isms," as symbols of evil, 14
Israel
  economic management in, 251
  and inflation management, 253
Italy, design supremacy in, 149

Jackson, Andrew, 281
Jackson, Barbara Ward, 94–97
Jackson, C. D., 414
Jahan, Shah, 150, 194
James, Daniel (Danny Santiago), 71
Japan
  and *The Age of Uncertainty*, 285
  and Brazil, 245–46
  MacLeish article on, 417–18
  and Tsuru, 210–12
Jarvis, Howard, 5, 95
Jay, John, and John Mitchell, 120
Jenner, William, 360
Jinnah, Muhammad Ali, 297, 374–76, 381
Joffre, Joseph-Jacques-Césaire (Marshal), 312
John F. Kennedy Airport, 217–18, 229, 249
Johnson, Andrew, 281
Johnson, Lady Bird (Mrs. Lyndon B.), 220, 335–36
Johnson, Lyndon B., 334–40
  and business, 232
  and Daley, 229
  and Paul Douglas, 346
  on education, 21
  and Seymour Harris, 398
  and imaginative writing, 364
  retirement of, 220, 228
  speech at JFK's death by, 385
  and Vietnam war, 334, 336, 338–40, 360, 365
  and Barbara Ward, 96
Johnson, Samuel (Dr.)
  and pursuit of wealth, 181
  and the Scotch, 276, 278, 416

Johnson, Samuel Ealy (father of Lyndon), 334
Johnson, U. Alexis, 332
Jones, David, 38
Jones, Jack, 287
Jungle, The (Sinclair), 68

Kashmir, Vale of, 155
Kaysen, Carl, 338, 387
Kelly, Ed, 347
Kendall, Donald, 267, 358
Kennan, George, 13, 267, 358–61
Kennedy, Edward, 225, 237, 361
Kennedy, John F., 322–25, 385–88
  and Bowles, 331–32
  and business, 232
  and Cuban missile crisis, 326–28
  and Allen Dulles, 222, 355
  and Seymour Harris, 398
  and Laos, 47
  and LBJ, 336, 338–39
  Luce remark to, 411–12
  Muggeridge on, 81
  on reform, 133
  and Eleanor Roosevelt, 389
  on secrets, 52
  and Barbara Ward, 96
Kennedy, Robert F.
  assassination of, 372
  and Cuban missile crisis, 327, 328
  and LBJ, 335, 336
Kennedy administration
  and Bowles, 329
  liberals processed by, 93
Kennedy Airport, 217–18, 229, 249
Kettle, Tilly, 160
Keynes, John Maynard, 252–53, 288, 314–21
  and arts, 145
  and Butler, 208
  and conservatives, 173
  on corporate investment, 175
  and Seymour Harris, 399
  and Myrdal, 404–5
  and Reagan, 320, 403, 405
  on rule of ideas, 286
Khandalawala, Karl, 156
Khrushchev, Nikita, 266, 362–65
Kimball, Warren F., 300
King, Edward J., 417

King, Martin Luther, Jr., 373
Kingsley, Ben, 372
Kipling, Rudyard, 294
Kissinger, Henry, 366–68
    on *Age of Uncertainty* panel, 286–
        87
    as exception to dull White House,
        226
    as Harvard faculty, 106
    and telephone transcripts, 309
Kistiakowsky, George, 17, 400–402
Kleindienst, Richard, 81, 120
Knopf, Alfred A., 58
Knox, John, 280
Knox College, 280
Korean War, 359–60
Kuh, Edwin, 26
Kuznets, Simon, 283

Labor theory of value, 289
Laffer, Arthur, 95
La Follette, Robert M. (Jr. and Sr.),
    344
Lange, Oskar, 67
Langmuir, Irving, 283
Language
    of Churchill, 299, 308–9, 311
    Luce's complexity of, 410
    and Nixon, 394
    See also Writing
Laos, 47, 93, 342
Lardner, Ring, 70
La Rocque, Gene, 38
Latin America
    loans to, 248–49
    U.S. policy on, 237, 242
Laughter. *See* Humor
Law, John, 283
Leahy, William, 302
Lee, Ivy, 293
Lee, John Marshall, 38
Lee, Robert E., and Muggeridge
    diary, 84
Lehman, Herbert, 218, 409
LeMay, Curtis, 61, 359
Lend-Lease Administration, 299
Lenin (Vladimir Ilyich Ulyanov),
    290
    and consumer economics, 271
    and Kistiakowsky, 401
Levi, Edward, 120

Levin, Harry, 205, 292
Lewis, Sinclair, 70, 72
Liberalism, Kennedy on, 386–87
Liberals
    and Bowles's career, 331–32
    Bowles and Harriman as, 332–33
    economic goals of, 20
    and Luce, 410
    and McCarthyism, 360
    and military establishment, 16
    and Mobil Oil advertisement,
        168–69
    among New York Democrats, 219
    in Texas, 227
Library of Congress, 418
Liddy, G. Gordon, 82, 120
Lindbergh, Charles, and committee
    rule, 40
Lindsay, John, 88
Linkletter, Art, 310
Lipsey, Roger, 154
Literary critics
    specialization by, 57
    vs. writers, 65
Literature. *See* Autobiography;
    Novelists; Writing; *specific writers
    and books*
Lloyd George, David, 307
Lockhart, Bruce, 85
Lockheed bailout, 170, 172
Logan, Douglas, 76
Logic, Convenient Reverse, 35–38.
    See also Reasoning, ways of
London, Jack, 68
London
    airport(s) of, 217, 218
    and arts, 149
Lopokova, Lydia, 288, 316
Lothian, Lord, 351, 354, 356
Love Nest, The (Lardner), 70
Low, David, 17
Low income. *See* Poverty
Lowlands of Scotland, 278
Luce, Henry Robinson, 409–12,
    414
    Randolph Churchill on, 78
    and Mary Hemingway, 61
    and Archibald MacLeish, 417
Lukas, J. Anthony, 186
Lygon, Lady Dorothy, 78
Lygon, Lady Mary, 78

Lynch, Valeria, 250
Lyons, Louis, 418

Macalaster College, 280
MacArthur, Douglas, 281, 346
McCarran, Patrick, 360
McCarthy, Eugene
  Galbraith support for, 237
  on level of Presidents and Vice
    Presidents, 120
  student support for, 132
  Wall Street support for, 220
McCarthy, Joseph R., 89–90, 349,
    358, 360
McCarthy, Mary, 205
McClellan, George B., 281
McClellan, John, 282
McCloy, John J., 221
McCone, John A., 355
McCormick, Cyrus, 283
McCormick, Senator Robert, 346
McCormick, Robert Rutherford,
    282
Macdonald, Dwight, 205, 282
MacDonald, Ramsay, 81
McEnroe, John, 283
McGovern, George
  and foreign policy, 361
  Galbraith support for, 237
  as liberal from conservative state,
    225
  media view of, 395
McKinley, William, 281
MacLaine, Shirley, 282
MacLeish, Ada (Mrs. Archibald),
    417, 418–19
MacLeish, Archibald, 417–19
  on O'Hara characters' sexual en-
    counters, 65
  and Luce, 417
  as Scotch, 282
McMillan, Edwin, 283
Macmillan, Harold
  memoirs of, 364
  Muggeridge on, 81
McNamara, Robert, 222, 267, 323,
    327, 336
Macroeconomics, 320
Made to Last (Galbraith), 416
Madras, India, CIA "spies" in, 51–
    52, 53

Magruder, Jeb Stuart, 81
Malapropisms, of Samuel Goldwyn,
    407
Malone, Adrian, 8, 285
Malthus, Thomas, 190, 289
Malvinas war, 255
Manchester, William, 58
Man in the Gray Flannel Suit, The
    (Wilson), 73
Manticore, The (Davies), 99, 102
Mantoux, Étienne, 318
Mantoux, Paul, 318
Manual work. *See* Physical work
MAP (Minorities Advancement
    Plan), 26, 27, 28–33
Marble quarry, as Air Force target,
    37
Marine Corps, Paul Douglas in,
    344–45, 345–46
Market, free
  economists' assumption of, 120
  reliance on, 19, 49
  and urban environment, 23
  See also Capitalism; Free enterprise
Marquand, John, 73
Marriage
  and British libel laws, 106
  in Trollope's novels, 202
Marshall, Alfred, 290
Marshall, George, 61, 302, 348
Marshall, Mary Paley (Mrs. Alfred),
    316–17
Marx, Karl, 288, 291, 294, 315
  on capitalism, 252, 288, 291
  and capitalist community, 5
  and consumer economics, 271
  on economic development as edu-
    cation, 95
  and Engels and Lenin, 290
  reinterpretation of, 291
  and socialism before capitalism,
    14
  as theorist of past, 236
Masculine decisiveness, in Cuban
    missile crisis, 327
Mason, Edward, 96
Massachusetts, 229
Massive retaliation, 349
Matheson, Scott, 282
Maugham, W. Somerset, 72
Maxwell, William, 64

Media
  Buckley complaints against, 89
  and military news management, 16
  political coverage by, 59, 77, 176–
    78, 199, 393, 395
  Waugh's account of, 77
  See also Newspapers; Television
Melia, Daniel F., 127, 128
Mellon family, 283, 292, 293
Melville, Herman, 282
Mencken, H. L., 57–60, 80
Metaphysics, 154
Mexico, overseas debt of, 247
Meyer, Edward C., 37
Michener, James, 266
Microeconomics, 320
Middle East conference, CIA sup-
    port of, 53
Mikoyan, Anastas I., 365
Military establishment (Pentagon)
  power of, 15–17, 223, 225
  simulated effort in, 121
Military-industrial complex, 17, 38, 180
Mill, James, 189–97, 198, 283, 289
Mill, John Stuart, 189, 190, 191,
    198, 283, 289
Millikan, Robert A., 283
Minimum income, 21–22
Minorities
  and Buckley campaign, 89
  European-origin groups as, 32
  in New York, 219–20
  See also Discrimination; specific
    groups
Minorities Advancement Plan
    (MAP), 26, 27, 28–33
Miquelon, 47–48
Missile crisis, Cuban, 326–28
Mississippi Company, 283
Mitchell, John, 120
Mitford, Nancy, 78
Mobil Oil Corporation, advertise-
    ment of, 168–69
Modigliani, Franco, 254
Mondale, Walter, and military
    budget, 15
Monetary policy
  class bias of, 180
  of repressive governments, 239
Monopolies, 292
Monroe, James, 281

Montgomery, Bernard, and Gold-
    wyn, 407
Montias, Michael, 265
Moore, William H., 170
Moos, Malcolm, 58, 59
Moraes, Frank, 258
Moral courage
  and Cuban missile crisis, 327–28
  See also Courage
Morgan, J. P., 292
Morgenthau plan, 320
Morse, Samuel F. B., 283
Morse, Wayne, 338, 361
Mosley, Leonard, 350–56
Motivation. See Incentives
Mountbatten, Edwina (wife of
    Louis), 380
Mountbatten, Lord Louis, 372, 376,
    377–80
Moynihan, Daniel Patrick, 50, 106
Mozambique, Marxism in, 14
Muggeridge, Malcolm, 80–86, 104
Mughal dynasty, 158, 192, 194,
    259
Multinational corporations
  in The Age of Uncertainty, 293
  in Brazil, 242, 246
Munich agreement, Butler on, 208
Murdoch, Rupert, 282
Museum of Fine Arts, Boston,
    Coomaraswamy collection in,
    152, 154, 156
Muskie, Edmund, 225
MX missile, 12, 17
Myrdal, Gunnar and Alva, 403–5

Nasser, Gamal Abdel, 349–50
National Assembly of State Art
    Agencies, lecture at, 144
National Conference of Catholic
    Bishops, on nuclear war preven-
    tion, 13
National Defense Advisory Com-
    mission, 299
Nationalism, and Vietnam war, 339
Needs
  economic vs. environmental, 23
  quantitative vs. qualitative, 139,
    147
Negotiation. See Persuasion and ne-
    gotiation

Nehru, Jawaharlal
  and British, 371
  and Cuban missile crisis, 326
  in *Gandhi*, 372–73
  history's treatment of, 374
  and Jinnah, 375
  and Mountbatten, 380
  Muggeridge on, 81
Nehru, Motilal, 374
New Delhi
  sand cooling of, 259
  snake removal in, 184–85
  U.S. Embassy Chancery in, 150–51, 186
New Economic Policy (Soviet), 270, 341
New England, 229
New Industrial State, The (Galbraith), 265, 414, 415
Newspapers
  Soviet reading of, 266–67
  See also Media
New York City
  and arts, 149
  Buckley's campaign in, 87–90
  as Democratic stronghold, 218–19
  public austerity in, 218
  social structure of, 219–20
  UN in, 220
  Wall Street in, 220–21
New York Tribune, and Marx, 291
Nicaragua, shifting concern with, 47
Nieman program, Harvard, 418
Nitze, Paul, 354
Niven, David, 282, 295, 406–8
Nixon, Richard Milhous, 393–96
  Buckley nominated by, 90
  and business, 232
  and Cambodia/Laos, 365
  and Dulles brothers, 352
  Indochina intervention (1950s) urged by, 347
  Moscow and Peking pilgrimmages of, 361
  as non-Establishment, 222
  Southern Strategy of, 227
  as temporary intruder, 225
  and Trollope's Slope, 201
  George Washington compared with, 120
  White House under, 226
Nkrumah, Kwame, 362, 363

Non-Potable Scotch, The (Galbraith), 416
NORAD, headquarters of, 285
Norris, Frank, 67, 68
Norris, George, 344, 347
Novelists, American
  and corporate executive, 73–74
  modern, 71–74
  social critics, 68–69
  sympathizers toward wealthy, 69–71
Nuclear war
  consequences of, 8–9
  Cuban missile crisis as threat of, 328
  and Dulles doctrines, 349–50
  and John Kennedy, 324
  prevention of, 6–7
  psychological denial toward, 9
  public attitude toward, 10–11
  Soviet fear of, 275
  See also Arms control
Nuclear winter, 10, 251
Nutting, Wallace H., 37

Office of Emergency Management, and Nixon, 393
Office of Price Administration, 316, 329–30, 398, 409
Office of Strategic Services, 51
O'Hara, John, 64–66, 70–71
Old age. *See* Aging
Ontario Agricultural College, 281, 334–35
Organization
  age of, 265
  and corporate man, 39–41, 73
  of military, 15
  present-day commitment to, 264
Ortiz, Frank, 250–51
Ouro Preto, Brazil, 243–44
Overlord, and Churchill, 302, 305
Overseas debt. *See* External debt

Paine, Ralph D., Jr., 412
Painting. *See* Art
Pakistan, 374, 375
Palmer, Arnold, 284
Panama, and LBJ, 336, 338
Panama Canal debate, and Brazilian fears, 237

Parietal rules, at Harvard, 122–23, 132
Paris, and arts, 149
Paris Commune of *1871*, 291
Parsons, Talcott, 117
Passage to India, A (Forster), 196, 197
Patel, Vallabhbhai, 372–73
Paternalism, toward Latin America, 242–43
Paterson, William, 283
Patterson, Joseph M., 282
Paxton Boys, 277
Peenemunde raid, 351, 353, 356
Pentagon. *See* Military establishment
Pentagon Papers, 222, 339
Percy, Charles H., 344
Peretz, Martin, 97
Perle, Richard, 8
Persuasion and negotiation
  of Bowles, 330, 331
  in Churchill-Roosevelt relation, 301, 302, 304
  and corporate man, 40
Pessimism
  of American intellectuals, 224
  of public persons, 257
Philanthropy
  and reputation of predatory rich, 293
  and steel mills, 280
Physical work
  as applauded for others, 274
  vs. satisfying "work," 43
Physicians for Social Responsibility, 10
Picasso, Pablo, 163
Plagiarism
  scholarship as, 129
  as unwitting, 42
Planning
  of Brasília, 240, 241
  cities' need for, 23–24
  corporate, 23, 73
  vs. Soviet consumer economy, 270–71
Poe, Edgar Allan, 282
Poland, Churchill-Roosevelt correspondence on, 303
Political conventions, and Mencken, 59

Political conventions (1980, 1984), nuclear issues in, 12
Political memoir, 207
Politicians, natural goodness of, 347
Politics
  and Buckley campaign, 88–89
  and Cuban missile crisis, 328
  of economic curtailment, 253
  ethnic, 229
  Kistiakowsky's belief in, 401
  media coverage of, 59, 77, 176–78, 199, 393, 395
  as theater (Reagan), 49–50
  "what is truth in?," 241
  and women, 386, 391
Polk, James K., 281
Polls
  media devotion to, 177–78
  Reagan's high standing in, 50
Poore, Charles, 64
Population explosion in India, 262
Potato blight, in Scottish Highlands, 279
Poverty
  and art, 145, 146
  in Chicago, 229
  Convenient Reverse Logic on, 35–36
  LBJ's efforts against, 334, 365
  McGovern program against, 395–96
  and minimum income, 21–22
  and politics of economic curtailment, 253
  and preoccupation with production, 19
  and public services, 21
  Reagan circle on, 73
  war on, 21, 336
Power
  academic teaching on, 120
  despair incompatible with, 385
  dialectic of, 373
  expectation of, 227
  keeping company with, 364
  of military establishment, 15–17, 223, 225
  money as, 16
  in U.S. government, 222
Pramoj, Kukrit, 287
Prebisch, Raúl, 251

Press
  Buckley complaints against, 89
  Waugh's account of, 77
  See also Media
Princeton University, 280
Privacy, invasion of
  and Hemingway conversations,
    62–63
  and Taylor autobiography, 106
Private enterprise. *See* Free enter-
    prise
Production of goods, preoccupation
  with, 19–20, 23
Progress for a Small Planet (Ward),
  94, 96
Public figures
  God-given laughter through, 346
  pessimism of, 257
Public Law *480,* 337
Public office, perilousness of, 365
Public-private sector balance, 20–21
Public services
  Brazilian slums' lack of, 237, 243
  as denied to cities, 24
  as progressive, 4–5, 21
  as restraining freedom, 4
  Soviet areas of superiority in,
    274–75
  See also Government
Pusey, Nathan (Harvard president),
    113, 114, 115, 134

Rabbit Is Rich (Updike), 72–73
Radcliffe College, 131–32
Radford, Arthur, 359
Radhakrishnan, Sarvepalli, 386
Radical Chic, 219
Radioactive fallout, and Harriman,
    342
Rail passenger transport, 217
Rancho Seco power plant, 6
Randhawa, Mohinder Singh, 156
Ratzburg, Cathy, 406
Reader's Digest, 276
Reagan, Ronald, 228
  and affluent, 179–81
  and American novels, 73
  Brazilian view of, 237
  on Communist China, 14
  and Gorbachev, 14
  and Keynes, 320, 403, 405

and Kistiakowsky, 401
and military establishment, 15, 16
and Muggeridge, 81
Nixon conversation with, 407
problem of reporting on, 177
on Soviet Union, 37, 265
theatrical performance by, 49–50
and University of California, 228
Reagan administration
  and affirmative action, 26
  anti-Soviet rhetoric of, 13
  and Chester Bowles, 329
  and deficit, 102, 173, 174–75, 320
  on nuclear war, 10
  warlike talk from, 275
Reasoning, ways of
  Convenient Reverse Logic in, 35–
    38
  by Establishment, 223, 395–96
  in Mobil Oil advertisement, 168–
    69
  in Reagan's theatrical script, 49–50
  in social thought, 145
Rebel Angels, The (Davies), 100,
    101–2
Recycling of oil revenues, 248
Reformation, in Scotland, 280
Reich, Robert, 73
Reith Lectures, 358
Reparations
  post-WWI, 318–19
  post-WWII, 319
Republican National Convention,
    nuclear issues in, 12
Republican Party
  in Great Plains, 228
  platform of (1980), 242
Restaurants, in U.S., 216–17
Retirement
  and corporate man, 40, 73–74
  and work vs. real work, 43, 44–45
Reviews, and truthfulness, 329
Reynolds, Lloyd, 265
Ricardo, David, 289, 315
Rich persons. *See* Affluent individu-
  als
Rio de Janeiro, 235–38
Roadside beautification, 167
Robb, Charles, 282
Rockefeller, David, 221, 266
Rockefeller, John D., 41, 292

Rockefeller, Nelson, 293
Rockefeller family, 293
Rooney, John J., 362, 363
Roosevelt, Eleanor, 389–92
  as exemplar, 386
  Muggeridge on, 81
Roosevelt, Franklin D.
  businessmen against, 232
  and Eleanor, 390
  and Farley, 177
  Galbraith transferred by, 409
  and Gandhi, 371
  issues made understandable by,
    330
  and Lyndon Johnson, 334, 336
  and MacLeish, 418
  Mencken on, 58, 59
  and minority rights, 390–91
  Muggeridge on, 81
  as New York governor, 218
Roosevelt, Theodore, 292
Roosevelt-Churchill correspon-
    dence, 300–304
Rositzke, Harry, 356
Rosovsky, Henry, 124–26
Royal Institute of British Architects,
    lecture at, 144
Runyon, Norman, 393
Rusk, Dean
  and anti-Communism doctrine,
    338
  in books on JFK, 323
  and Bowles, 331–32
  in Dulles, 351, 352, 355
  as Establishment figure, 221, 222
  and persuasive talk, 330
  picture of in RFK book, 328
Russell, Bertrand, on Keynes, 316
Russia. See Soviet Union
Rust, Bernhard, 96

Sagan, Carl, 10
St. Pierre, 47–48
Saint-Simon, Duc de, 310
Salant, Walter, 317
Saltonstall, Leverett, 229
Salvador, Brazil, 244–45
Samuelson, Paul, 283, 399
SANE, 10
San Francisco, 229

São Paulo, 238–40, 245
Sarnoff, David, 362
Saudi Arabia, and Buckley-Baroody
    clash, 92
Scali, John, 92, 93
Schell, Jonathan, 10
Schlesinger, Arthur, Jr.
  and beach inertia, 205
  and Bowles, 332
  foreign policy skepticism of, 47,
    338
  on Galbraith's film-going, 369
  and John Kennedy, 322, 323–25
Schlesinger, James, 106
Schmidt, Robert, 267
Schoenbrun, David, 310–13, 366
Scholarship, as plagiarism, 129
Schulberg, Budd, 140
Schumacher, Fritz, 149–50
Schumpeter, Joseph, 147, 150, 288,
    344
Science
  vs. arts, 139–40
  in industrial development, 148
Scoop (Waugh), 75, 77
Scotch, the, 276–84
  Canadian, 83, 377, 416
  and ethnic self-identification, 276–
    77, 279
  famous persons among, 281–84
  Hamish Hamilton from, 416
  personal characteristics of, 279–80
Scotch, The (Galbraith), 416
Scotch-Irish, 277–78
Scotland, Lowland beauty of, 278
Scott, C. P., 82
Scott, Paul, 85
Scoville, Herbert, 12
Secrets
  John Kennedy on, 52
  about public officials, 324
Securities Investors Protection Cor-
    poration, 221
Segretti, Donald, 348, 350
Self-censorship, 417
Self-concern, celebration of, 4–5
Senility
  among professors, 45
  and U.S. Congress, 224
  See also Aging
Seth, Roshan, 372

Sex
and need for academic solemnity,
121
in O'Hara's novels, 65
and parietal rules, 122–23, 132
among rural Canadians, 99
among rural Scotch, 280–81
and Taylor autobiography, 106
Sexual escapades, FBI dossiers on,
224
Sexual harassment, 124–26
Seychelles, concern with, 47
Shah of Iran, Harvard honorary
degree to, 97
Shah Jahan, 150, 194
Sheean, Vincent, 310
Shore, Sir John, 195
Simon, Norton, 266
Simons, Thomas W., 51
Sincerely Willis Wayde (Marquand),
73
Sinclair, Upton, 68
Sinclair-Stevenson, Christopher, 415
Sirhan, Sirhan, 372
Sitting, art of, 206
Skiing, 90, 406–7
Sloan, Alfred P., Jr., 41
Slums (*favelas*), of Brazil, 237, 243
"Small is beautiful," 149–50
Smith, Adam, 287–88, 315
and Bullock, 345
on businessmen, 291
and Friedman, 236
on ruin in nation, 233
Smith, Alfred E., 218
Smuts, Jan, 369
Snake removal, in New Delhi, 184–
85
Social awareness, in student body,
132
Social Darwinism, 145, 292
Social ethic, 3–4
See also Community; Public ser-
vices
Social ills
Convenient Reverse Logic on, 35
Reagan's script on, 49–50
See also Discrimination; Poverty
Socialism
from advanced industrial prob-
lems, 237

Amtrak as, 217
and capitalist excesses, 266
and consumer orientation, 270–72
through corporate bailouts, 170,
172
difficulties of, 46, 266
as organization, 264–65
as publicly owned deficit operations, 256
for the rich, 221
and St. Pierre/Miquelon threat,
47–48
social cohesiveness required for,
95
Social programs
and IMF-induced austerity, 256
See also Public services
Social thought
convenience of conclusions in, 145
Convenient Reverse Logic in, 35–
38
Social unrest
Communism blamed for, 338,
349, 360
Convenient Reverse Logic on, 36–
37
Sociology, and scholastic delin-
quents, 131
Solar energy, 95
Solemnity
in academic life, 119–21
in grant application, 75
in politics, 209
Solzhenitsyn, Alexander, 92, 365
Somalia, concern with, 47
Something Happened (Heller), 73
Somoza Debayle, Anastasio, 237,
242
Sorensen, Theodore, 322–24
Sourrouille, Juan, 250
South Africa
and Buckley, 91
Galbraith assignment in, 409
Gandhi in, 369
Reagan characterization of, 49
South Vietnam
and anti-Communist view, 339
strategic concern with, 47
See also Vietnam war
Soviet Union, 264–75
and arms control/arms race, 6–7,

Soviet Union, contd.
   9, 11–12, 13–14, 17, 38, 265
   (*see also* Arms control)
   and Central American unrest, 37
   and Cuban missile crisis, 327–28
   economy of, 266, 268, 270–74
   as grain customer, 257, 272–73
   and Harriman, 341–42
   and Kennan, 358–59
   military establishment in, 17, 38
   and Muggeridge, 82
   need for information on, 53
   reform possibilities in, 272–74
   as war victim, 6, 18
   See also Cold War; Communism
Speakes, Larry, 49, 50
Specialization, 314–15
   in economics, 315
   and Keynes, 319–20
   in literary criticism, 57
Specter, Arlen, 50
Speeches, as vacuum that fills a vacuum, 35
Speer, Albert
   on life with Hitler, 364
   and V-2 firing, 353, 356
Spencer, Herbert, 145, 292
Spies
   and friendly governments, 53
   usefulness of, 51–53
Spooner, Paul, Jr., 167
Sports. *See* Athletics
Stalin, Joseph
   and Churchill/Roosevelt, 303
   and Khrushchev, 364, 365
   Muggeridge on, 81
Star Wars (Strategic Defense Initia-
   tive), 10, 17, 38, 50
State. *See* Government
Steffens, Lincoln, 275, 280
Stein, Herbert, 173
Steinbeck, John, 68
Steinem, Gloria, 204
Stephenson, Jan, 284
Stern, Philip, 345
Stettinius, Edward, 302, 317–18
Stevens, Ted, 8
Stevenson, Adlai
   and Cuban missile crisis, 326,
   327–28
   and Paul Douglas, 347

Galbraith support for, 237
   and Seymour Harris, 398
   and Barbara Ward, 96
Stimson, Henry, 221
Stockman, David, 180
Stone, Edward Durell, 150, 186
Strachey, Lytton, 316
Strategic Bombing Survey, 299,
   355, 356, 410
Strategic Defense Initiative (Star
   Wars), 10, 17, 38, 50
Strategic planning, in *Sincerely Willis
   Wayde*, 73
Stratford Shakespeare Festival, lec-
   ture at, 144
Stuart, Sir John and Lady Jane, 189
Students
   at commencement addresses, 34–
   35
   and educational policy, 132
   and Harvard constitutional obso-
   lescence, 111–12
   Harvard parietal rules for, 122–
   23, 132
   as judges of teaching, 114, 132–
   33, 210
   revolts by, 109, 110–11, 113, 228
   and social issues, 3, 132
   and sexual harassment, 124–26
Subversive Activities Control Board,
   91
Suez crisis, and Dulles, 349–50
Suffering, and heroism, 408
Sugar cultivation, social consequences of, 245
Suharto, 339
Summit meetings, 304
Sun Belt, 390
Supply-side economics, tax reduc-
   tions in, 49, 180
"Surgical strike," and Cuban missile
   crisis, 327
"Survival of the fittest," 292
Sutherland, Duchess of, 278
Sycophants, of Luce, 410, 414

Taft, Charles, 91
Taft, Robert A., 91, 330
Talbot, Phillips, 332
Taxation
   and budget deficit, 174–75

Taxation, contd.
and business confidence vs. economic performance, 231–32
Convenient Reverse Logic on, 36
price gradation of, 239
and Reagan, 180, 131
Taylor, A. J. P. (Alan), 104–6
Taylor, Elizabeth, 282
Taylor, Maxwell, 327
Technostructure, 414
and art, 140–41
Television
condensation in, 293, 295
and political conventions, 59
See also Age of Uncertainty, The;
Media
Tender Is the Night (Fitzgerald), 69–70
Tenure, academic, 45, 127–28
Test, George, 42
Test ban treaty, and Harriman, 342
Texas, 227
Texas Observer, The, 227
Thatcher, Margaret, Reagan inquiry on, 407
Theater
Reagan performance as, 49–50
and social issues, 294
See also Art
Theory of the Leisure Class, The (Veblen), 292
Thinking, *See* Reasoning, way of
Third World, Malthusian anxiety of, 289
Thomas, Dylan, and Taylor, 106
Thrift, of Scotch, 279
Thurmond, Strom, 92
Thurow, Lester, 26
Time-Life International, 414
Timmons, Benson E. L., III, 184–85
Travelogues, 213
Trier, Roman ruins in, 294
Triumph, The (Galbraith), 234
Trollope, Anthony, 94, 198–203
Trollope, Frances Milton (mother of Anthony), 198
Trotsky, Leon, 401
Trudeau, Margaret, 368
Truman, Harry S.
and business, 232

good will accumulated by, 348
and MacArthur, 281
Muggeridge on, 85
Truth, and book reviews, 329
Tsuru, Shigeto, 210–12
Tuchman, Barbara, 13
Tufts University, commencement address at, 34
Turkey, obsolete nuclear weapons in, 327–28
Twain, Mark
on Congress, 225
on work, 42

Ulam, Adam, 290
Ulyanov, Vladimir Ilyich. *See* Lenin
Unemployment
disguised, 52
economists' acceptance of, 288
and logical thinking, 35
as restraint policy, 35
and Soviet system, 271
summit meetings as, 304
Union of Concerned Scientists, 10
United Nations, 220
Buckley in, 90–93
Myrdals in, 404
Eleanor Roosevelt's commitment to, 391
United States, 215–29
class-consciousness of, 216, 219
commentaries on, 198
Congress of, 224–25
economics/business rules on, 230–33
Establishment in, 221–23 (*see also* Establishment, American)
Latin American policy of, 237, 242
misinformation on, 215–16
public decision-making in, 223–24
and rail passenger transport, 217
United States, regions of
California, 228
Chicago, 229
Great Plains, 228
New England, 229
New York City, 218–21 (*see also* New York City)
South, 227
Texas, 227

Universities
  commencement addresses at, 34–
    35
  governing structure of, 109–110
  and Vietnam war, 228
  See also Harvard University
University of California at Berkeley,
  228
  and age of atom, 7
  Charter Day at, 3
University of California at Davis,
  commencement address at, 34
University of Chicago, Paul Douglas
  at, 345
Unrest. *See* Social unrest
Updike, John, 72–73
Upward failure, of Mountbatten,
  379
Urban environment, 20, 23–24. *See
  also* Architecture; Cities
USSR. *See* Soviet Union
Utilitarianism
  and Mill's *History*, 194
  See also Bentham, Jeremy
U-2 flight, 350

Vale of Kashmir, 155
Valeriani, Richard, 366–68
Value, labor theory of, 289
Vanderbilt family, 292
van Voorst, Bruce, 366
Veblen, Thorstein, 280, 291–92,
  413
Vermont
  highway advertising abolished in,
    167, 229
  Kipling as resident of, 294
  television reception in, 285
Victoria and Albert Museum, London, Archer collection in, 155,
  157
Vietnam war
  and academic community, 112, 115
  and air power, 37
  and anti-Communism, 343
  and Paul Douglas, 344, 346–47
  and Establishment, 222, 223
  and Harriman, 342, 343
  and LBJ, 334, 336, 338–40, 360,
    365
  and Eugene McCarthy, 220

  and Nixon election, 394
  and policymakers' certainty, 307
  student involvement in, 132
  and Maxwell Taylor, 327
  universities against, 228
  and war on poverty, 21, 22
Volcker, Paul, 273–74
Voorhis, Jerry, 394

Wade, James O'Shea, 352–57
Wade, Richard, 344
Wages, iron law of, 289
Wagner, Robert F., 344
Wallace, George, 227
Wall Street, 220–21
  Dulles brothers of, 349
Wants. *See* Needs
War
  Convenient Reverse Logic in, 37
  leaders' psychological denial in,
    305
  See also Air power; World War II
War, nuclear. *See* Nuclear war
Warburg, Joan, 267
Ward, Barbara, 94–97
War on poverty, 21, 336
Washington, George, and Nixon,
  120
Washington, D.C., as seat of gov-
  ernment, 223
Washington bar, 225–26
WASPs
  fictional difficulties of, 71–72
  of New York, 219–20
  and social position, 133
Watergate, and legal ethics, 120
Watson, James, 109, 112, 117–18
Watson, Thomas J. (of IBM), 41
Watson, Tom (golfer), 284
Waugh, Evelyn, 57, 75–79
  and American food, 217
  and artist vs. bureaucracy, 140
  Muggeridge on, 85, 86
  politics and social outlook of, 77,
    78, 80
Wealth
  and American novelists, 68–71
  as highest duty, 4
  See also Affluent individuals
Wealth of Nations (Smith), 287–88
Weaver, Robert, 337

Webster, Daniel, 282
Weeks, Sinclair, 121, 134
Weidling, Helmuth, 356
Weinberger, Caspar, 401
Welfare system, and incentive, 22
West at Bay, The (Ward), 96
Westmoreland, William C., 15
What Makes Sammy Run? (Schulberg), 140
Wheeler-Bennett, John, 208
White, James, 113–14
White, Theodore, 130–31
White House, 226
Wiesner, Jerome, 14–15, 17
Willens, Harold, 10
Williams, Shirley, 287
Williams Memorial Lecture, 144
Wilson, Edmund, 65
Wilson, Horace Hayman, 191, 195–96
Wilson, Sloan, 73
Wilson, Woodrow, 281
Winter Palace Museum, 264, 270
Winthrop House, 122, 130, 387
Wodehouse, P. G., 83
Wolpert, Stanley, 374–76
Women
  and aging men's advances, 129
  employment discrimination against, 27–28
  as executives, 39
  as heads of poor families, 22
  Kennedy remark on, 386
  and MAP, 28–33
  at 1930s Harvard, 131–32
  in OPA, 398
  and Eleanor Roosevelt, 391–92
Wood, Robert, 337
Woolf, Leonard, 316
Woolf, Virginia, 316

Work
  fraudulent reference to, 42–45
  payment of authors for, 67
  physical, 43, 274
  simulated, 121
World Bank, 320
World of Wonders (Davies), 99, 101, 102
World War I
  German reparations after, 318–19
  as turning point, 294–95
World War II
  and Churchill-Roosevelt correspondence, 300–304
  Dulles statements on, 351, 353–54
  Galbraith in, 299–300, 316, 329, 330
  German reparations after, 319
  in Luce's view, 414
  marble quarry bombing in, 37
  Mountbatten's career in, 378–79
Writer(s)
  Buckley as, 90, 91
  vs. critics, 65
  John Kennedy as, 386
  Robert Kennedy as, 328
  Khrushchev as, 363–64
  Mencken as, 58
  See also Autobiography; *specific writers and books*
Writing
  brevity in, 276
  devious motives vs. superficiality in, 368
  economists' obscurity in, 319
  and Luce, 411–12
  See also Language

Yemen, concern with, 47

Zaire, concern with, 47
Ziegler, Philip, 378–81